Archive Stories

Edited by Antoinette Burton

Archive Stories

FACTS, FICTIONS, AND THE WRITING OF HISTORY

Duke University Press Durham & London

2005

© 2005 Duke University Press

All rights reserved

Printed in the United States of America on acid-free paper ∞

Designed by C. H. Westmoreland

Typeset in Dante by Keystone Typesetting, Inc.

Library of Congress Cataloging-in-Publication Data appear on

the last printed page of this book.

for D. H. B.

dedicated historian

fabulous storyteller

beloved father

Contents

Acknowledgments

THIS BOOK IS THE RESULT of many people's willingness—their eagerness, even—to tell me their archive stories. I wish to thank not only all the contributors, but also everyone who shared their accounts of what it is like to encounter an archive, struggle in and with and against it, and even abandon it altogether. Several colleagues have been especially patient with the particular strain of "archive fever" that has beset me while working on this project: Jean Allman, Tony Ballantyne, Marilyn Booth, Clare Crowston, Ania Loomba, Kathy Oberdeck, Adele Perry, Srirupa Prasad, Dana Rabin, and all those who took Gender and Colonialism at the University of Illinois in the spring of 2003—especially Lauren Heckler, Danielle Kinsey, Karen Rodriguez'G, Rachel Schulman, Jamie Warren, and Karen Yuen. My thanks to them, and especially to Tony Ballantyne, whose enthusiasm for the ideas I have tried to develop here has been boundless. As did Tony, Anjali Arondekar, Ann Curthoys, Ian Fletcher, Durba Ghosh, Laura Mayhall, Horacio N. Roque Ramírez, John Randolph, Anu Rao, and Renée Sentilles all offered insightful and eminently useful feedback to me on the Introduction to the book. I appreciate their critical engagement, which is born at least in part out of their own struggles with and against archives of all kinds. Parts of my introductory essay have been given as talks at the Canadian Historical Association and the University of Otago, where audiences helped me to refine my arguments, for which I am very grateful. The two readers for Duke University Press also deserve special thanks for their comments and suggestions, which have made the collection more tightly woven than it was. Miriam Angress is, as ever, the perfect editor. Without her guidance and enthusiasm and wisdom—on matters large and small—this book would not be what it is. Without the love, support—and of course, the technical and pop culture assistance—of Paul Arroyo, none of this would have been possible. I remain as amazed by as I am indebted to him for his generosity and his belief in me. Nick and Olivia did what they could to cure my archive fever, and but for them I would have succumbed long ago. Thanks to them for helping me daily to appreciate which are the most important stories to tell.

A version of Laura Mayhall's essay, "Creating the 'Suffragette Spirit': British Feminism and the Historical Imagination," was published in *Women's History Review* 4, 3 (1996): 319–44 and is reprinted with permission from Triangle Journals.

A version of Craig Robertson's essay, "Mechanisms of Exclusion: Historicizing the Archive and the Passport," was published as "The Archive, Disciplinarity and Governing: Cultural Studies and the Writing of History," in *Cultural Studies / Critical Methodologies* 4, 4 (2004): 450–71 and is reprinted with permission from Sage.

Antoinette Burton

Introduction

ARCHIVE FEVER, ARCHIVE STORIES

[L'archive] est difficile dans sa materialité.

—Arlette Farge, *Le goût de 1'archive* (1989)

[The archivist] is the keeper of countless objects of desire.

—Martha Cooley, *The Archivist* (1998)

IN AN ERA WHEN THE ECHO chambers of cyberspace have given a whole new dimension to the concept of the archive, questions about the relationship between evidence and history are at the forefront not just of academic discourse but of public debate across the world. From undergraduate classrooms to the trials of Holocaust deniers to the tribunals of the Truth and Reconciliation Commission in South Africa to the very public revelations of plagiarism among prominent popular historians in the United States, the relationship between fact and fiction, truth and lies, is a matter of heated discussion. While charges of inaccurate footnoting may have done little to damage the reputation of a public historian like the late Stephen Ambrose (whose book *The Wild Blue* drew fire for borrowing sentences and phrases from another historian without proper attribution), it remains to be seen what impact the public inquiry into Michael Bellesiles (who resigned his position at Emory University over charges of fraud in connection with his 2000 book *Arming America: The Origins of a National Gun Culture*) will do to his scholarly career—and to the reputation of historians as archival truth-tellers—in the long term.[1] Elsewhere in the world, debates that engage the challenges of "telling the truth about history" have had very real political and material consequences.[2] In South Africa, for example, the Truth and Reconciliation Commission actively engaged with the question of archival evidence, deliberately choosing to "wrestle with . . . notions of truth in relation to factual or forensic truth"— and producing in the process a nationwide public debate about the nature of citizenship after apartheid.[3] Such a project was and is tied to "making public memory, publicly," and as such it often pits conventional forms of knowledge about the past (History) against the claims of groups who have typically been disenfranchised by dominant regimes of truth but who are also seeking political rights—in ways that endanger the status and liveli-hoods of some, traumatize others, and make visible the extent to which national identities are founded on archival elisions, distortions, and se-crets.[4] The public contretemps in South Africa has been echoed in trials over tribal rights and indigenous sovereignty from Canada to New Zea-land, in debates over memory and forgetting in postwar contexts from Germany to Korea, and, increasingly, in human rights claims from Bosnia to Bhopal—raising provocative questions about the nature and use of archives and the stories they have to tell, not just about the past, but in and for the present as well.[5]

Equally striking is the extent to which in the new millennium "archive stories" are to be found in domains outside the academy and the law. For although historians arguably have the most at stake in these debates— given their historical attachment to archival evidence for their professional self-definition and legitimacy—neither professional practitioners of the discipline nor the political elites who often rely on them are the only ones engaging with the limits and possibilities of the archive as a site of knowl-edge production, an arbiter of truth, and a mechanism for shaping the narratives of history. Take the case of the Lower East Side Squatters and Homesteaders Archive Project, which recently received a grant from the state of New York to create and maintain an archival collection document-ing the culture of squatters as well as their battles with developers and city officials. As one of the group's founders told the *New York Times*, "we want this archive to be a collection that anyone, friend or foe, can access to write our history."[6] The squatters' project is one of hundreds, perhaps thousands of similar archive enterprises taken up by groups who believe that their histories have not been written because they have not been considered legitimate subjects of history—and hence of archivization per se. The fact that many of these archive entrepreneurs rely on the Internet as their storage space represents a tremendous challenge to the basic assumptions of archival fixity and materiality, as well as to the historian's craft itself. At the same time, recourse to the virtual archive does not mean that their posterity is any more secure. As Roy Rosenzweig reminds us, while the digital age may make for "a world of unheard-of historical abundance" and hence perhaps less elitist histories, the archives which cyberspace houses are no less fragile or vulnerable to disappearance, for a variety of technological, economic, and political reasons.[7]

Of course, archives—that is, traces of the past collected either intentionally or haphazardly as "evidence"—are by no means limited to official spaces or state repositories. They have been housed in a variety of unofficial sites since time immemorial. From the Rosetta stone to medieval tapestry to Victorian house museums to African body tattoos, scholars have been "reading" historical evidence off of any number of different archival incarnations for centuries, though the extent to which a still quite positivist contemporary historical profession (both in the West and outside it) recognizes all such traces as legitimate archival sources is a matter of some debate. The respectability which oral history has gradually gained in the past twenty five years, together with the emergent phenomenon of the Internet-as-archive, has helped to prize open canonical notions of what counts as an archive and what role the provenance of historical artifacts of all kinds should play in History as a disciplinary project. Nor is what Jacques Derrida has famously called "archive fever"—that passion for origins and genealogies which, he suggests, is an inheritance from the ancient world—limited to denizens of the street or the Internet.[8] The following is an excerpt from the script of *Star Wars II: Attack of the Clones*, in which the young Jedi knight Obi-Wan Kenobi goes to the Archives Library at the Jedi Temple to consult with Madame Jocasta Nu, the resident archivist:

JOCASTA NU: Are you having a problem, Master Kenobi?

OBI-WAN: Yes, I'm trying to find a planet system called Kamino. It doesn't seem to show upon any of the archive charts.

JOCASTA NU: Kamino? It's not a system I'm familiar with . . . Let me see . . . Are you sure you have the right co-ordinates?

OBI-WAN (nodding): According to my information, it should be in this quadrant somewhere . . . just south of the Rishi Maze.

JOCASTA NU: No co-ordinates? It sounds like the kind of directions you'd get from a street tout . . . some old miner or Furbog trader . . . Are you sure it exists?

OBI-WAN: Absolutely.

JOCASTA NU: Let me do a gravitational scan. . . . There are some inconsisten-
cies here. Maybe the planet you're looking for was destroyed.

OBI-WAN: Wouldn't that be on record?

JOCASTA NU: It ought to be. Unless it was very recent. (shakes her head) I hate
to say it, but it looks like the system you're searching for doesn't exist.

OBI-WAN: That's impossible . . . perhaps the archives are incomplete.

JOCASTA NU: The archives are comprehensive and totally secure, my young
Jedi. One thing you may be absolutely sure of—if an item does not appear in
our records, it does not exist![9]

Not only is Obi-Wan Kenobi schooled in archival logic as part of his
training in the arts of war, he comes to the archive with "common" knowledge (of the kind he might get "from a street tout")—only to be reassured
of the total knowledge which the official archive guarantees. An equally
revealing example of the popularity of the archive idiom is the fall 2003
Marshall Field's Direct catalog, where shoppers are encouraged to buy
vintage clothing and other items from "The Archive" collection with the
following copy: "Step into the Marshall Field's Direct archive, a stylish
collection inspired by the landmark Marshall Field's Store at Chicago's
State Street. On these pages you'll find faithful replications from the store's
architecture, history, and traditions, reinvented for today's eye."[10] The
availability of archival sources of all kinds online arguably makes us all
archivists now. And, given the convergence of virtual archives and cor-
porate commodity culture, it would seem that we are all archive consumers—at least potentially—as well.

What *Wired* magazine has called "Googlemania" is thus at least partially
akin to Derrida's archive fever, with everyone acting as his or her own
arkheion.[11] The short-term and long-term political ramifications of that
convergence have yet to be fully historicized in this, the information age,
even as the connections between archiving information, accessing knowledge, and working the public sphere are proving crucial to political movements of all kinds. As Wes Boyd of MoveOn.org put it: "Google rocks. It
raises my perceived IQ by at least 20 points. I can pull a reference or quote
in seconds, and I can figure out who I'm talking to and what they are
known for—a key feature for those of us who are name-memory challenged."[12] But the playfulness with which so many different kinds of popular media are representing the archive should not prevent us from appreciating the ways in which contemporary archive fever is bound up with

convictions about the power of science to get at truth. Indeed, the most popular archive stories of the new millennium are shaped by a belief in the capacity of material evidence to create and sustain tests of verifiability. From the consistently high ratings of the various *csi* television shows in America to the BBC's *Waking the Dead* to mass popular fiction like Patricia Cornwell's Kay Scarpetta novels to "high" literature like Michael Ondaatje's *Anil's Ghost*—all of these point to an investment in forensics and a deep-seated faith in the capacity of science to read certain types of archives (corpses, crime scenes, DNA samples) that are highly material and embodied, in contrast to or perhaps in tension with the ascendancy of the kind of virtual space that Internet access has accelerated at a dizzying pace in the last decade.[13] The resurgence of this positivism in popular generic forms, together with the heightened authority of archival cultures of law in the global arena since 1945,[14] means that the archive (as a trope, but also as a ideological and material resource) has acquired a new kind of sacral character in a variety of contemporary domains. This sacralization occurs as more and more people seek and help to create access to a more democratic vision of the archive: that is, as different kinds of archival subjects and archive users proliferate, with their own archive stories to tell.

As the cultural theorists Larry Grossberg and Meaghan Morris have so trenchantly noted, this fear of the disappearance of "everything" into daily life—of which the democratization of the archive is just one instantiation—is not new to the twenty-first century, though it is perhaps especially threatening to contemporary historians at accelerating moments of interdisciplinarity because of the ways it strikes at the heart of the evidentiary elitism of the discipline.[15] This is a fear which scholars engaged in oral histories have had especially to confront. In her study of memory and the Third Reich, Tina Campt addresses the anxieties which some academics feel at the possibility that "everything" might be an archive—including the comparatively slight oral histories of two Afro-Germans she uses. Campt insists that "the minute" and the "monumental" must be in constant dialogue, arguing that such anxieties say more about canonical disciplinary notions than about the legitimacy of memory work as an archive (especially if we understand that evidence is not facticity per se).[16] Unease about the possibility that the archive is everywhere and hence nowhere is strikingly at odds, then, with the consumerist exuberance of the Marshall Field's catalog—even as some of the most democratic of archives still arrive at our sightlines as if they were shrink-wrapped, that is, with very little trace of how they were compiled, massaged, and otherwise packaged for mass consumption (Campt's excepted).

This liberal triumphalist (and one must add, mass market–capitalist) incarnation of the archive at the height of globalization rhetorics and practices makes it all the more imperative that we talk frankly and openly about the archives and the encounters that we as scholars and especially as historians have with them. For archives do not simply arrive or emerge fully formed; nor are they innocent of struggles for power in either their creation or their interpretive applications. Though their own origins are often occluded and the exclusions on which they are premised often dimly understood, all archives come into being in and as history as a result of specific political, cultural, and socioeconomic pressures—pressures which leave traces and which render archives themselves artifacts of history. By foregrounding a variety of archive stories, this collection aims to unpack some of those histories and to begin to diffuse the aura which now more than ever surrounds the notion of "real" archives, especially those with which historians have dealt. The essays that follow try to denaturalize the presumptive boundaries of official archive space, historicize the production of some well-known and not-so-well-known archival collections, and point to some contemporary political consequences of archive fever. Taken as a whole, *Archive Stories* contends that the claims to objectivity associated with the traditional archive pose a challenge which must be met in part by telling stories about its provenance, its histories, its effect on its users, and above all, its power to shape all the narratives which are to be "found" there. What follows, in other words, are not merely histories or genealogies of archives or "the archive" but, rather, self-conscious ethnographies of one of the chief investigative foundations of History as a discipline.

Our emphasis on the need for archive stories—narratives about how archives are created, drawn upon, and experienced by those who use them to write history—follows in the first instance from a move in the Western academy (and also beyond it) to recognize that all archives are "figured." That is, they all have dynamic relationships, not just to the past and the present, but to the fate of regimes, the physical environment, the serendipity of bureaucrats, and the care and neglect of archivists as well.[17] To some extent the work of Michel Foucault, with its focus on archives as "documents of exclusion" and "monuments to particular configurations of power," is responsible for the shifting fortunes of archival discourse in the academy.[18] According to Carolyn Steedman, the appeal of archives is also inspired by the modern romance of dust: that "immutable, obdurate set of beliefs about the material world, past and present"—whether emanating from the state or from a rag rug—which has its own passions, its own dramas, its own dreams.[19] Postcolonial studies and theory have provided another important fillip to the notion that archives are not just sources or repositories as such, but constitute full-fledged historical actors as well. This is in part because of the ways in which the colonial archives served as technologies of imperial power, conquest, and hegemony. In the context of Spanish-speaking empires, both Jorge Cañizares-Esguerra and Diana Taylor have demonstrated how histories of writing have helped to establish scales of credibility and legitimacy against which societies with either oral or expressive traditions (or both) were deemed inferior. These maneuvers effectively consolidated performance and embodiment as "native" and the text and especially the alphabet as European—and, by extension, civilized.[20] The regimes of credibility and truth secured by later European imperial dominion were different in degree rather than kind, as the work of Ann Stoler and Nicholas Dirks has shown for the Dutch East Indies and British India respectively.[21] Renewed attention to the question of the archive has also been motivated by postcolonial history itself, whether in South Africa where "many established ideas about the nature and location of the archive are under challenge" or in a less well-known but equally compelling context like the Virgin Islands, where *sankofa* (reclamation) sentiments inspired by the disappearance of historical records and hence of community histories have prompted provocative debates about the very possibility of memory without official archives.[22]

But our insistence on the necessity of talking about the backstage of archives—how they are constructed, policed, experienced, and manipulated—stems equally from our sense that even the most sophisticated work on archives has not gone far enough in addressing head-on the lingering presumptions about, and attachments to, the claims to objectivity with which archives have historically been synonymous, at least since the extended moment of positivistic science on the German model in the nineteenth century.[23] *Archive Stories* is motivated, in other words, by our conviction that history is not merely a project of fact-retrieval (the kind of empiricism reflected in the csi paradigm as well as in public debates about plagiarism or the Truth and Reconciliation Commission) but also a set of complex processes of selection, interpretation, and even creative invention—processes set in motion by, among other things, one's personal encounter with the archive, the history of the archive itself, and the pressure of the contemporary moment on one's reading of what is to be found there. This may seem a self-evident, even a pedestrian claim; and indeed, many if not most historians operate under the assumption that history is a highly interpretive act—even as critics equate such views with the death of history or worse, "the killing of history" per se.[24] This is no mere rhetorical flourish, of course, since what archives hold and what they do not has implications not just for the writing of history but for the political fortunes of both minority and dominant communities the world over, with public contests over Maori history in New Zealand and the rewriting of textbooks shorn of anything but Hindutva politics in India standing as just two of many "global" examples.[25] But whether historians concede or fully countenance the impact of such contingencies on their work is another question. They certainly rarely speak of them, and even more rarely do they do so in print—though they are quite ready and even eager to tell their archive stories when asked, as I discovered in the course of work on this book.

Many of the tales I have heard—prompted by the remark "I'm working on a book about people's archive stories"—have been structured around the "boot-camp" narrative and involve the drama of getting to archives, living in terrible digs while working there, and enduring dilapidated work conditions and capricious archivists.[26] Most have been framed by confessions of archive pleasure—what one historian called the "the thrill of the archival 'pay dirt' moment"—or, alternatively, confessions of archive aversion.[27] For some scholars, it is memories of the labor of research that are evoked by the subject of archive stories, whether they think of such labor as trawling, reading card catalogs against the grain, or engaging in a dreaded solitary existence. Others wax rapturous about the capacity of archival discoveries to bring one into contact with the past. In the context of a public discussion of archive stories, for example, a historian of early modern France I know recounted coming upon the collar of a priest in a Jansenist archive, folded and secreted inside layers of powder. She surmised that the authorities had arrested him and seized his collar, the material presence of which she found "a breathtaking and amazing thing."[28] And she added that its power had everything to do with finding it there, in the archive, an observation which echoes Achille Mbembe's conviction that "the archive has neither status nor power without an architectural dimension"—that is, a material presence which structures access, imposes its own meanings on the evidence contained therein, and watches over users both literally and figuratively.[29] For if the official archive is a workplace, it is also a panopticon whose claim to total knowledge is matched by its capacity for total surveillance. This makes archive users into stealth strategists and even, if only figuratively, into thieves as well. More than one scholar has confessed to me a desire to take objects from the archive—a photo of Tito signed by Churchill, a nineteenth-century pencil dangling from a hand-written diary—and who knows how many others have actually done so.

Given these conditions of archive creation, surveillance, and use, what is at risk in the variety of archive stories we have collected here is not merely the claims to objectivity which continue to underwrite the production of history and especially to endow it with its virtually unparalleled legitimacy as an arbiter of truth in a variety of public arenas, but also historians' comparative silence about the personal, structural, and political pressures which the archive places on the histories they end up writing—as well as those they do not. Crucial to the task of re-materializing the multiple contingencies of history writing is the project of historicizing the emergence of state and local archives; interrogating how archive logics work, what subjects they produce, and which they silence in specific historical and cultural contexts; enumerating the ways in which archival work is an embodied experience, one shaped as much by national identity, gender, race, and class as by professional training or credentials; pressing the limits of disciplinary boundaries to consider what kind of archive work different genres, material artifacts, and aesthetic forms do, for what audiences and to what ends; recognizing, and accounting for, the relative evidentiary weight given to sources of various types and what Suvir Kaul calls "the play of rhetorical difference in each archive"; and not least, imagining counter-histories of the archive and its regimes of truth in a variety of times and places.[30]

We open in Part I with an emphasis on "Close Encounters: The Archive as Contact Zone" by foregrounding a variety of personal archive stories: testimonies about the embodied experiences of the physical, emotional, intellectual, and political encounters between the scholar and the archive itself. We do so because of our belief that the material spaces of archives exert tremendous and largely unspoken influences on their users, producing knowledges and insights which in turn impact the narratives they craft and the histories they write. We do so too because as I have suggested above, there is a marked contrast between the silences in print about these experiences and the volubility of historians about their archive stories when asked. Durba Ghosh's account of her research in Britain and India, for example, dramatizes the ways in which gender and race as forms of embodiment can mark the experience of the historian, subjecting her to certain kinds of surveillance and even limiting her access to documents. As an "Indian" woman seeking evidence of Indian women either silenced or marginalized by the colonial state and its archives, she was not only reading the archives, the archives were also reading her. As important, her determination to find traces of interracial sex in the archives called into question the legitimacy of the topic and her very respectability in the confines of a variety of archival spaces—spaces in which archivists she encountered were reacting as much to the imprint of contemporary anxieties about race and sexuality as they were to the pressure which unspoken colonial histories continue to exert on the present.

In his stories about research in Uzbekistan Jeff Sahadeo explicitly identifies the archive as a contact zone—in this context, as a site where past and present converge in the architecture of the space itself, whose very materiality is linked to regime changes past, present, and future. Sahadeo's account of the creation of the Central State Archive (which sports a sign over the door that reads "without the past there is no future") focuses on its Soviet and post-Soviet histories by way of setting the stage for a larger discussion of contemporary conditions of work in and on Central Asia. Here again, access and its denial rest on, among other things, one's capacity to navigate highly charged relationships between local archivists and scholars. In terms of embodiment, this involves countenancing the starkly privileged lives which even Western graduate students lead compared with archivists who might be willing to receive chocolate or magazines from researchers—if not in direct exchange for services, then at least in recognition of the asymmetries of power and material opportunities between them, at both micro and macro levels (as reflected in requests for help with obtaining prescription drugs and emigration). Taken together, Ghosh and Sahadeo remind us of the varied economies of desire—those systems of material and symbolic power which structure experiences of yearning for and seduction by "the past"—at the heart of archival encounters.

If desire is in fact a crucial constituent of the archive experience, discourses of rationalization—of archive logics—have helped to obscure this dynamic at least since the nineteenth century, the heyday of objectivist claims about evidence and identity. Craig Robertson's piece on the passport and its archives makes clear the role of archive rationalization in establishing the very grounds of modern identity, both individual and national. He does so in part by parodying the surveillance regime of the U.S. National Archives and Records Administration where, post-9/11, even an official NARA card does not prevent the guards from screening his newspaper (though not his umbrella). But Robertson also links his archive story to the history of exclusion as embodied by the passport, the would-be panoptical technology for archiving personal identification via a catalog of bodily characteristics. He does so, significantly, not through an exercise in empirical research, but through a discursive reading of the fictions of access and transparency that modern bureaucracies perform. If the archive is a contact zone between past and present as well as between researchers and structures of local, national, and global power, the logistical difficulties Robertson faces as he tries to gain access to the materials he needs return us time and again to the bureaucratic nature of archival encounters—and to the ways in which the administrative apparatus of archives can limit the stories that are told. Indeed, the story of how archives come to be rationalized can and should be part of the histories we write, precisely because the literal, physical encounter with them can have such a profound effect on how one comes to understand and appreciate the histories they throw into bold relief.

This is the thrust of Tony Ballantyne's essay, which describes his experience of reading the archives of "Mr. Peal" in New Zealand as a graduate student trained at Cambridge trying to come to terms with the limits of national boundaries for understanding the circulation of colonial and imperial knowledge. Ballantyne reconstructs not only the multi-sited provenance of Peal's papers but also the impact which his own intellectual biography had on how he saw what he found as a way of re-materializing Peal and the circuits of production which undergirded Ballantyne's dissertation and later monograph, *Orientalism and Race*. Though not as graphic as, say, Ghosh, about the bodily experience of his encounter, Ballantyne provides an instructive example of how the face-to-face encounter with archival collections can raise the intellectual stakes of a project, particularly when that encounter is embedded in larger debates about postcolonial identity, indigenous sovereignty, and bi-culturalism of the kind which have shaped the National Library in which the Peal collection is housed.

The two essays which bring Part I to a close reflect rather differently on the question of how contact with "the archive" and what is found there shape the stories which historians can tell. Horacio N. Roque Ramírez's piece on Teresita la Campesina—the Latina transgender artist who was fifty-five years old and living with AIDS when he first met her—underscores the power of oral history to queer conventional notions of what counts as an archive. Her testimonials constitute "living evidence," not just of her personal historical experiences, but also of how imperfectly either Latino historiography or even lesbian and gay histories have been able to capture stories like hers. In part because he resists reducing Teresita simply to "an archive," Roque Ramírez deftly captures her lived experiences *and* the way she works actively to frame them into a historical narrative of her own making. No doubt it would have pleased Teresita to know that her autobiography stands as a challenge to the presumption that archives must be disinterested and disembodied, as well as testimony to the fact that archives of ordinary people are, if not ubiquitous, then at least eminently "creatable" out of personal memories and reflections. Her "back talk" underscores the elasticity of the concept of the archive, and not just as a domain open to subjects beyond the privileged—though this kind of democratizing practice is clearly entailed by the claims which oral history makes on traditional assumptions about what kind of speech, what kind of talk, can count as archival. It is also, of course, evidence of what Thomas Osborne calls the "ordinariness of the archive" as well.[31] Teresita's "archive talk" is, in short, lively evidence indeed of the ways in which all archival sources are at once primary and secondary sources: neither raw nor fully cooked, to borrow an ethnographic metaphor, but richly textured as both narrative and meta-narrative, as both archive and history-in-the-making.

The case of Adah Isaacs Menken which Renée Sentilles offers us in her essay "Toiling in the Archives of Cyberspace" functions, at least at first glance, as a pointed contrast to the living embodiment of history which Teresita strategically articulates. Sentilles's account of her use of the Internet to research Menken, a Civil War actress and poet, moves from shock at the number of hits that typing her subject's name into Google produces, to intrigue about what a virtual, disembodied research experience will be like, to skepticism about the ultimate utility of the Web as a tool of archival research. In one sense, Sentilles produces a story of encounter that is less transformative for her sense of identity as an archive user or the history she will ultimately write than do Ghosh, Sahadeo, Robertson, Ballantyne, and Ramírez. At the same time, as she wrestles aloud with the challenges which virtual archives pose to historians' professional training—their sense of what "mastery" is, of what archives count, of the durability or impermanence of the past as secured by archives, not to mention the romance of toiling in the "real thing" as opposed to surfing the Net—the same questions of identity and experience, access and denial, power and desire emerge as structuring features of her narrative. Not unlike Teresita, Sentilles is herself living evidence of how historians in the first generation of cyber-research are experiencing and above all historicizing the ever-shifting figure of the archive, even as they leave evidence of (and simultaneously historicize) their own encounters for future scholars of the discipline and its cultures to analyze and interpret.

Part II, "States of the Art: 'Official' Archives and Counter-Histories," features genealogies of five specific institutional archival sites and the story of one "fictional" one in order to address the putatively transhistorical status of the official archive and its opposites, as well as the alternative histories they both have the capacity to yield. The first four pieces in this section historicize the origins and development of a particular institutional site with an eye to challenging the Olympian stature of "the archive" in its official incarnations, particularizing what have come to be seen (again, often implicitly) as universal sites of departure for historical narrative, and above all demystifying the processes through which documents and other forms of evidence are consolidated as the basis of History. Jennifer Milligan's essay excavates the history of one of the most influential archival institutions in the modern West, the Archives nationales in Paris. Not surprisingly, the foundation of this archive is coterminous with the Revolutionary state; its symbolic and material fate in the nineteenth century is linked to regime change and to the various forms of state power those changes inaugurated, policed, and memorialized. Even more telling is the way that putatively private events could shape the direction and organization of this ostensibly public institution, as Milligan's account of the Praslin affair (1847) demonstrates. The scandal surrounding the Duc du Praslin (who murdered his wife and later committed suicide) raised questions about the boundaries between state interests and private honor—giving rise to discourses about "public interest" (in the form of state prerogative and broadsheet gossip) through which the Archives nationales secured its own legitimacy on the eve of the Revolution of 1848. As Milligan illustrates, not only did the archives actively articulate the relationship between the nation and the state, they participated as actively in the fate of the political regimes that sought to control them.

The ineluctable, even agonistic, vulnerability of archives to political whim and social upheaval is a theme that Peter Fritzsche pursues in his essay, "The Archive and the Case of the German Nation." Acknowledging that "wars trigger archives" and that the state in Germany was as invested as any other modern nation form in utilizing the official archive as a mechanism for memorializing the logics of military and political power, he also argues for the traces of ordinary lives (what he calls the vernacular and racial archives) and intimate violences which are to be found there. He does so, not to recuperate or rehabilitate the German state archives for history, but rather to suggest their capacity for making visible (however imperfectly and distortedly) some of the most fragmented and fugitive traces of historical subjectivity. The nation and, by extension, its archives, are rarely if ever, in other words, the juggernaut the state may have intended them to be; Fritzsche's account of the possibilities of accessing domestic time and the storied character of public and private histories is a salutary reminder of the limits, if not the aspirations, of hegemony. John Randolph takes yet another approach to the problem of the nation and the archive by drawing our attention to a particular archival collection with enormous influence in the story of modern Russia: that of the Bakunin family. Arguing for the value of appreciating archives as objects about which we can produce biographical accounts, Randolph emphasizes the ways in which the rhythms of daily life and especially of domesticity helped to consolidate (through "selecting, stitching, and guarding" its ephemeral pieces) the family archive. That this collection was fashioned primarily by a Bakunin sister-in-law, Natalia Semenovna Bakunina, is especially significant given the traditionally gendered equations of archive as public and male and domesticity as private and female. Although its survival was literally out of her hands, she effectively saved the collection from politically motivated arson by sending it away from its (and her) original home, after which it eventually found its way into a Soviet institution and to Randolph's own sightline in the context of "the new Russia" at the end of the twentieth century. Randolph ends his meditation with a short but compelling analysis of one letter in the archive, written by

Mikhail Bakunin about his sister Varvara, which appears to be marked in Bakunin's hand with the words "TO BE BURNT"—more evidence of the precariousness of archival evidence in the face not just of the state or the archivist, but of the very historical subjects who author them.

Laura Mayhall's piece, "Creating the 'Suffragette Spirit,' " shows with particular vividness how influential the creation, maintenance, and regulation of a specific archival collection has been in shaping specific narrative outcomes. The Suffragette Fellowship Collection, begun to preserve and memorialize the British women's suffrage movement in the wake of women's formal emancipation after World War I, was spearheaded by those who had been active in or sympathetic to The Cause. To be sure, most if not all institutionalized archival collections bear the traces of such ideological investment and self-interest. But as Mayhall demonstrates, these foremothers instantiated a very particular strain of suffrage history at the heart of their archival project. Deeply influenced by one dimension of suffrage agitation and protest—one which equated militancy with window-smashing and especially hunger-striking and subsequent imprisonment— the creators of what was to become the Suffragette Fellowship Collection reproduced this aspect of the movement to the occlusion, if not the exclusion, of all others. As Mayhall relates it, the construction of the archive tended to follow the interpretive commitments of the militants, shaped as it was by ex-suffragettes with a definition of militancy that was not just narrow, but actively circumscribed the terms and hence the evidentiary and documentary basis upon which the Fellowship Collection was built. By enshrining this narrative not just *in* but *as* the archive, its founders promoted a historical account of British women's emancipation in which only some suffrage women were legitimate and visible—in ways with enduring (if fundamentally inaccurate) popular appeal, as the figure of Mrs. Banks in Disney's *Mary Poppins* testifies.[32]

Kathryn J. Oberdeck takes up the relationship between archives and historical narrative from a different perspective in her essay on the company town of Kohler, Wisconsin. Reading the documents of and plans for the "unbuilt environment" in and around the village community—that is, those streets and buildings which were never built—Oberdeck argues for the importance of understanding spaces which were never materialized in or as history. Such a project takes aim at the telos that undergirds even some of the most nuanced disciplinary work, bound as it still is to using sources to explain "what happened" or to evaluate those policies, movements, and subjects which managed to leave their mark on the historical landscape, as opposed to tracking those phenomena which have disappeared from view. Oberdeck reads the Kohler archives in the first instance to recapture its founder's vision of American civic identity, but also to examine the conflicts between Walter Kohler and his landscape architect, Henry V. Hubbard, thereby uncovering what never happened and also revealing competing agendas for an industrial village-cum-community over the course of its history. If Hubbard's dreams were unrealized, they were kept alive in the archives and hence in the minds of later Kohler workers and village residents into the 1930s, 1940s, and 1950s—historical moments when UAW strikes materialized in spatial terms what was at stake in control over the layout and organization of a "model" town. Oberdeck, for her part, makes clear the role that "cast-off plans" in the "dusty drawers" of the archives can play in illuminating the dreamscapes of what might have been but never was.

In the last essay in Part II, Marilyn Booth strikes a contrapuntal note for this section on "official" archives large and small by drawing out the story of Zaynab Fawwaz, a late-nineteenth-century Egyptian biographer, novelist, and journalist who strove to register nationalist and Islamicist female subjectivity in and for the modern historical record. Fawwaz did so not in state or local archives but in fiction, specifically in her 1899 novel *Good Consequences, or the Lovely Maid of al-Zahira* and in her writings for the fin-de-siècle Egyptian press. Booth's lively and rigorous reading, not just of Fawwaz's texts, but also of her canniness about the political stakes of representing multidimensional women characters in the public sphere, complicates our notions of what an archive is, whom it houses, and how dynamically it responds to and is shaped by local pressures, in both a temporal and geographical sense. Straining against all manner of contemporary conventions—nationalist, Islamicist, and even feminist—Fawwaz emerges as a historical subject keenly aware of the power of the word to shape contemporary political events and with them, the contours of History itself. Her determination to interpolate the reader of the time as an active participant in and maker of that History, both locally and internationally, articulates an archival imaginary that is coterminous with the nation but also exceeds it. Not least, Booth's insistence on the press and especially on the novel as legitimate archives (that is to say, as makers of History) forces us to confront the limits of the official archive by acknowledging the power of literature to materialize those countless historical subjects who may never have come under the archival gaze. Like Roque Ramírez's Teresita, Booth's Fawaaz requires us to expand the definition of archival material—to see oral and print cultures as legitimate and powerfully articulate archival locations. While claims to total knowledge implicit in the official archive are indeed fictions, thanks to the interventions of a figure like Fawwaz we are privy to a whole different order of archival imaginary. Especially when ranged against the evocatively materialized architectural spaces of the Archives nationales, the Bakunin estate, and the Kohler leisure-scapes that precede Booth's essay, Fawaaz's discursive archive is powerful testimony to the alternative historical narratives available to us when we wander outside the conventional "houses of history."

Part III, "Archive Matters: The Past in the Present," closes the volume with a turn toward the contemporary through an examination of the imprint of history on recent events and archival configurations. Each of the three essays in this section makes indubitably clear the pressures which present-day politics place on the past: they illustrate, with three fascinating and timely examples, the stakes of archive stories for contemporary history-writing, politics, and culture. "In Good Hands," Helena Pohlandt-McCormick's account of the 1976 Soweto uprising and her experience researching it in the 1990s in the context of South Africa during and after apartheid, raises crucial questions about how, why, and to what extent the methods of the historian both in and out of the archive are shaped both by immediate political events *and* by the knowledge that her archival work will participate in narratives of historical change themselves in South Africa and beyond. Her evocations hark back to Sahadeo's essay in Part I, reminding us of the high-stakes political game in which many scholars endeavor to create new histories, especially outside the West. Her stories of petitioning for access to archives of the uprising never before seen and of sitting in the reading room knowing that the Vierkleur South African flag had been recently replaced by one resonant with African National Congress colors; her reading of the politically charged student documents; her use of photographs and autopsy documents to historicize the violence which the rising engendered; and not least, the humility of her recognition of herself as an agent of history and history-making—all this makes for breathtaking reading as well as a powerful commentary on the porousness of "official" memories and, ultimately, the flexibility and malleability of even the most disciplining of archives. Pohlandt-McCormick's effort to make some of that evidence available to the Hector Pieterson Memorial

Museum Project—arguably an "Other" of the national archive—speaks as well to the emancipatory (if not exactly utopian) possibilities of archive stories, even as it represents the transfer of custodial power from one political enterprise to another.

Adele Perry's analysis of the *Delgamuukw* case (like *Mabo* in Australia, the case about aboriginal land rights discussed by Ann Curthoys) addresses the work of archives, documents, and historical records in shaping current debates about dispossession, the colonial past, and the postcolonial future in British Columbia. As Perry so skillfully argues, Chief Justice Allan McEachern's 1991 decision put the limits of the official archive on trial by revealing the incommensurability of Anglo and white settler legal codes, procedures, and evidence with the kinds of oral testimonies so crucial to aboriginal identities and histories across the world. If McEachern's observations about the relationship between orality (understood here to be an incapacity for the textual) and primitiveness are staggering, they testify to lingering presumptions about the epistemological stakes of subaltern political and cultural forms, not to mention the risk to modern Western geopolitical imaginaries from non-European "historical" traditions. MacEachern may be read as a caricature of certain nineteenth-century modes of discourse and practice, but late-twentieth-century scholarly response to his judgment and the ways in which that response reflect more widely held (if liberal) convictions about white settler community and history is equally instructive. Perry's essay offers a multi-storied account of the contretemps set in motion by the trial, critiques the commonly held belief in the power of a "total archive," and suggests that the enduring legacy of the *Delgamuukw* case is as an object lesson about the presence—and I would argue, the persistence—of history in the present and the ongoing revisionism which that dynamic and fraught relationship requires of us.

Thanks at least in part to the dizzying possibilities of archives old and new, history is never over but renews itself through a variety of new interpretive frameworks. Ann Curthoys's elaborate genealogy of the Windschuttle controversy underlines the ferocity of scholarly and to some extent public reaction to History and its engagement with the problem of "facts," specifically with respect to the numbers of dead in an infamous massacre of aborigines in Tasmania. In a widely read and much publicized 2002 book, Keith Windschuttle argued that historians had fabricated evidence involved in arriving at the number of people killed—a claim which, as Curthoys amply demonstrates, resonated in both Australia and the United States, where calls to "tell the truth about history" dominated the history wars from the last decade of the twentieth century into the first years of the twenty-first. Curthoys turns her critical eye not just on the massacre in question but on the historical figure of James Bonwick—so crucial to Windschuttle's claims about fabrication—and in turn back to the vexed and ultimately political question of archival reliability itself. Keen to remind us that the Windschuttle debate was and is as much about fin-de-siècle local politics (in the wake of the *Mabo* decision and in the context of a conservative government avowedly opposed to aboriginal rights), Curthoys uses this particular "antipodean" archive story to raise questions about the politics and ethics of historical practice and perhaps most significantly, about the question of audience.

This is an appropriate note upon which to end the collection, since there would appear to be an ever-growing divide between the multiplicity of interpretive possibilities many historians hope to see the archive yield and the expectations of absolute truth which a variety of more general publics, undergraduate and graduate students included, not only desire but demand. The relationship of archival presences and absences to biographical "truths" about the U.S. presidential candidates in the spring and summer of 2004, and the flurry of debate about archives which it engendered, is only one of the more high-profile examples of the market demand for a certain kind of archival logic—one that is tied to the kind of "sequential" view of history that many archive makers and users are interested in challenging, if not refuting.[33] What's more, the fetish of the archive as a surveillance apparatus has been matched in recent years by the fantasy that history is or can be a delivery system for absolute truth. Such a fantasy is not, of course, historically new; it is one of many Enlightenment legacies to modern Western historical thought. But the appeal of that fantasy has intensified and has perhaps even been democratized in an extended moment of political crisis in the West, where the "end of history" as we have apparently all known it has been prophesied with a combination of apprehension, moral certitude, and ideological triumph—and all this well before the catastrophic events of September 11, 2001.[34] Particularly in the current conjuncture, when the evidence of daily lives, community identities, and confessional practices is increasingly archived because it is perceived to be nothing less than a matter of national and international "security," the task of understanding the role of archives and of critically examining the kinds of stories which emanate from them has, perhaps, never been more urgent.

At the same time, we would not like to end on yet another triumphalist note, because we recognize that the telling of stories, like the production of history itself, has no intrinsically redemptive power, whether revolutionary or conformist. Stories—in whatever narrative form—embed as many secrets and distortions as archives themselves; their telling encodes selective disclosures, half truths, and partial pasts no more or less than do histories "proper." If this means that archive stories, including those on offer here, are eminently open to critique and interpretive contest, it also means that they participate in and help to fuel what Gayatri Spivak calls "the fear of undecidability in the subject of humanism."[35] Nor would we like to stage yet another (ultimately unproductive and anti-interdisciplinary) contest between the unverifiability of "literary" narratives (of the kind which feature here as subjective personal accounts) versus the apparently self-evidentiary nature of "historical" documents. We resist this as much because such rehearsals beg the question of the historicity of disciplinary formations like Literature and History as because the very empirical status of "archival" materials is so repeatedly open to question when one ceases to take evidence (whether documents or testimony) at face value.[36] In the end, the burden of this collection is not to show that archives tell stories but rather to illustrate that archives are always already stories: they produce speech and especially speech effects, of which history is but one. Talking about that speech and its effects—and arguing over its meanings—is vitally important for history as a practice, especially at a moment when many other disciplines invoke history as a self-evident methodological procedure and the archive as its instrument. Rather than promising a cure-all for archive fever, the species of archive talk made available in *Archive Stories* provides the possibility of a genealogical engagement with one of the chief modalities of History itself. Not incidentally, this comes at a time when academic history does so little to capture the popular imagination and even less to make people outside the university care about it. In offering a more transparent and ultimately, we believe, a more accountable basis for the production of knowledge about the past, *Archive Stories* aspires to illustrate the possibilities of an ethnographic approach to those traces which remain legible to us as history—a turn which astute observers like Anjali Arondekar have noted even the best and especially the most agonistic work on archives has failed to take.[37] In pursuing this ethnographic re-orientation, we move resolutely if experimentally beyond naïve positivism and utopian deconstructionism, beyond secrecy and revelation, toward a robust, imaginative, and interpretively responsible method of critical engagement with the past. If in the process archives as such are rendered less Olympian, more pedestrian, this does not mean either the end of the archive as an analytically vigorous category or the death of the discipline.[38] Hopefully, the kind of interrogations on offer here forms one of the bases from which histories in the twentieth century, with all their passion for and humility about what can and cannot be known, will come to be written.

Notes

1 For the beginning of this debate, see Fred Barnes, "Now Stephen Ambrose," *The Weekly Standard*, January 9, 2002; http://historynewsnetwork.org/articles/article.html?id=499. For Bellesiles, see Michael de la Meced, "Bellesiles resigns as fraud investigation ends," *The Emory Wheel*, October 25, 2002; http://www.emorywheel.com/vnews/display.v/ART/2002/10/25/3db9bc0a08df2.

2 Wilmot James and Linda Van de Vijver, eds., *After the TRC: Reflections on Truth and Reconciliation in South Africa* (Cape Town: David Philip Publishers, 2000; Athens: Ohio University Press, 2001).

3 Charles Villa-Vicencio, "On the Limitations of Academic History: The Quest for Truth Demands Both More and Less," in James and Van de Vijver, eds., *After the TRC*, 21–31.

4 See Mark J. Osiel, "Making Public Memory, Publicly," in Carla Hesse and Robert Post, eds., *Human Rights in Political Transitions: Gettysburg to Bosnia* (New York: Zone Books, 1999), 217–62.

5 Mark Philip Bradley and Patrice Petro, eds., *Truth Claims: Representation and Human Rights* (New Brunswick, N.J.: Rutgers University Press, 2002).

6 Colin Moynihan, "Homesteading a Little Place in History," *New York Times*, December 8, 2003. I am grateful to John Randolph for bringing this story to my attention.

7 Roy Rosenzweig, "Scarcity or Abundance? Preserving the Past in a Digital Era," *American Historical Review* 108, 3 (June 2003): 735–62. Jonathan Spence's recent interview with Judith Schiff, chief research archivist at Yale University Library, is a reminder that this is not the only revolutionary age of information for scholars: she cites 1962, when the first volume of the National Union Catalog was published. See Spence, "A Life in the Archives," *Perspectives* 42, 3 (March 2004): 6.

8 Jacques Derrida, *Archive Fever: A Freudian Impression*, trans. E. Prenowitz (Chicago: University of Chicago Press, 1995).

9 *Star Wars II: Attack of the Clones* script; http://www.geocities.com/jedi_vega/ep2_script.html

10 Marshall Field's Direct catalog (code MBL01095), October 8–13, 2003.

11 See the special issue of *Wired* called "Googlemania," 12, 3 (March 2004).

12 Ibid., 122.

13 I am grateful to Tony Ballantyne for impressing this point upon me, as well as for suggesting a myriad of pop culture examples.

14 I am thinking here of how the Tokyo Judgment and the Nuremberg Trials ushered in such a culture, particularly with respect to "fact" and "truth" about criminal guilt and national responsibility on the world-juridical stage. See Timothy Brooks, "The Tokyo Judgment and the Rape of Nanking," *Journal of Asian Studies* 60, 3 (2001): 673–700.

15 See Grossberg's essay "The Formations of Cultural Studies: An American Birmingham," *Strategies* 2 (198): 144, and Morris's discussion of it in her *Too Soon Too Late: History in Popular Culture* (Bloomington: Indiana University Press, 1998), 1–4. For current anxieties about the dilution of the term *archive*, see Lesley Hall's contribution to the Victoria H-Net Listserv: "As an archivist I'm rather concerned about the erosion of the term 'archive' as I was taught to understand it when doing my Diploma in Archive Administration, i.e., as the traces on paper, parchment, etc. left behind of the activities of a government body or organisation (and by extension, of an individual). People seem increasingly to be using 'archive' to mean any research resource, sometimes not even with the meaning of primary materials, when these are not, by this definition, 'archival'. (Not to mention the people who think that 'old' = 'archival' and therefore consider non-current issues of journals to be 'archives')" (Lesley Hall on VICTORIA@LIST SERV.INDIANA.EDU, September 9, 2004). Hall is, in addition to being an archivist, also an active and well-respected historian of gender and medicine. Thanks to Melissa Free for bringing this discussion on Victoria to my attention.

16 Tina M. Campt, *Other Germans: Black Germans and the Politics of Race, Gender and Memory in the Third Reich* (Ann Arbor: University of Michigan Press, 2004), 88 and ff.

17 See the introduction to Carolyn Hamilton, Verne Harris, Jane Taylor, Michele Pickover, Graeme Reid, and Razia Saleh, eds., *Refiguring the Archive* (Cape Town: David Philip, 2002), 7.

18 Ibid., p. 8.

19 Carolyn Steedman, *Dust: The Archive and Cultural History* (Manchester: Manchester University Press, 2001).

20 Jorge Cañizares-Esguerra, *How to Write the History of the New World: Histories, Epistemologies, and Identities in the Eighteenth-Century Atlantic World* (Stanford, Calif.: Stanford University Press, 2001); and Diana Taylor, *The Archive and the Repertoire: Performing Cultural Meaning in the Americas* (Durham: Duke University Press, 2003).

21 Ann Laura Stoler, *Carnal Knowledge and Imperial Power* (Berkeley: University of California Press, 2002) and her "Colonial Archives and the Arts of Governance: On the Content in the Form," in Hamilton et al., eds., *Refiguring the Archive*, 83–100; Nicholas B. Dirks, "Colonial Histories and Native Informants:

Biography of an Archive," in Carol Breckenridge and Peter van der Veer, eds., *Orientalism and the Postcolonial Predicament: Perspectives on South Asia* (University of Pennsylvania Press, 1993), 279–313, and his "Annals of the Archive," in Brian Keith Axel, ed., *From the Margins: Historical Anthropology and its Futures* (Durham: Duke University Press, 2002), 47–65.

22 Jeannette Allis Bastion, *Owning Memory: How a Caribbean Community Lost Its Archives and Found Its History* (Westport, Conn.: Libraries Unlimited, 2003).

23 See, for example, Dipesh Chakrabarty, *Provincializing Europe: Postcolonial Thought and Historical Difference* (Princeton: Princeton University Press, 2000); Bonnie Smith, *The Gender of History: Men, Women and Historical Practice* (Cambridge, Mass.: Harvard University Press, 2000); and Rolf Torstendahl, "Fact, Truth and Text: The Quest for a Firm Basis for Historical Knowledge around 1900," *History and Theory* 42 (October 2003): 305–31.

24 See Keith Windschuttle, *The Killing of History: How a Discipline Is Being Murdered by Literary Critics and Some Theorists* (Sydney: Macleay Press, 1994), as well as Ann Curthoys's essay on his work, below. Clearly this critique is entailed by the larger "turn toward history," and hence the (re)turn to the archive, since the 1970s. For quite divergent readings of this phenomenon, see Terrence MacDonald, ed., *The Historic Turn in the Human Sciences* (Ann Arbor: University of Michigan Press, 1996) and Amy J. Elias, "Hip Librarians, Dweeb Chic: Romances of the Archive," *Postmodern Culture* 13, 1 (2002). Thanks to Tony Ballantyne for the latter reference.

25 For two examples, see Neeladri Bhattacharya, "The Problem," *Seminar* 522 (special issue, "Rewriting History: A Symposium on Ways of Representing Our Shared Past"): 12–18; and Jeannette Wikkaira, "Kaitiakitanga: The Role of the Maori Archivist," *Archifacts* (April 2004): 46–50. I am grateful to Ania Loomba and Tony Ballantyne respectively for these references.

26 For an account of the lodgings problem, see Carolyn Steedman, "Something She Called a Fever: Michelet, Derrida, and Dust," *American Historical Review* 106, 4 (2001): 1164–65.

27 For some of these narratives in the context of archive usage in the British empire, see Antoinette Burton, "Archive Stories: Gender and the Making of Imperial and Colonial Histories," in Philippa Levine, ed., *Gender and the British Empire* (Oxford: Oxford University Press, 2004), 281–93.

28 Graduate Proseminar, University of Illinois, fall 2003.

29 Achille Mbembe, "The Power of the Archive and Its Limits," in Hamilton et al., eds., *Refiguring the Archive*, 19.

30 See Suvir Kaul, review of Gyanendra Pandey, *Remembering Partition: Violence, Nationalism and History* in India, *Journal of Colonialism and Colonial History* 3, 3 (winter 2002). http://muse.jhu.edu/journals/journal_of_colonialism_and_colonial_history/toc/cch3.3.html.

31 Thomas Osborne, "The Ordinariness of the Archive," *History of Human Sciences* 12, 2 (1999): 516–64.

32 For a wide-ranging discussion of suffrage representation, see Laura May-

hall, "Domesticating Emmeline: Representing the Suffragette, 1930–1993," *National Women's Studies Association Journal* 11, 2 (1999): 1–24.

33 See Caroline Alexander, "Foolscap and Favored Sons," *New York Times* Op-ed Page, Friday, July 23, 2004 ("one man's military records reveal more than just his story," referring to George W. Bush's National Guard service), and Eric Lichtblau, "Archives Installed Cameras after Berger Took Papers," *New York Times*, also July 23, 2004. For one popular take on the narrative sequence at the heart of History, I cannot resist quoting an Old Navy advertisement (for teen clothing) which ran on NBC during the Summer 2004 Olympic Games, in which a young woman bursts forth in the middle of a big lecture class with the exclamation: "History! I love History! First one thing happens, then another thing happens. So sequential! Thank you, first guy, for writing history down!"

34 Francis Fukuyama, *The End of History and the Last Man* (New York: Avon Books, 1992).

35 Gayatri Spivak, *Death of a Discipline* (New York: Columbia University Press, 2003), 25.

36 See especially Anjali Arondekar, "Without a Trace: Sexuality and the Colonial Archive," *Journal of the History of Sexuality* 14, 1–2 (winter–spring 2005) (a prepublication copy was provided by the author) and Betty Joseph, *Reading the East India Company: Colonial Currencies of Gender* (Chicago: University of Chicago Press, 2004).

37 Arondekar, "Without a Trace."

38 I use the term as an ironic point of departure, *pace* Spivak, *Death of a Discipline*.

PART I

Close Encounters

Durba Ghosh

National Narratives

and the Politics of Miscegenation

BRITAIN AND INDIA

HISTORIANS LONG TO TELL their archive stories, but unlike anthropologists, sociologists, and even political scientists, our narratives of field-work have little purchase within the professional standards of our discipline, which demand a certain level of professional distance that makes history "objective," rendering the archive as a finite site of knowledge about the past.[1] And yet historians' archive stories often reflect the process by which historical knowledge is gathered, narrated, and represented. Archival research is an important credential in the career of a historian, often making or breaking our claims to "truth" and positivism. In processing the so-called primary sources of the archives into the secondary sources used by other scholars and students of history, it is a largely inadmissible secret that our work is often shaped by archival conditions beyond our control, conditions such as whether the archivist or librarian is sympathetic or drawn to the project, whether the proposed topic or research is congenial to particular types of national narratives, and whether the nation-state in which we do our research is invested in preserving and protecting the records we need.

My archive stories are drawn from the radically different responses in the two nations in which I did research, showing the ways in which what seemed like a great project in Britain was a terrible, even unspeakable one in India. If there is a lesson in these anecdotes, it is that national narratives and identities remain strong features in the production of histories, particularly in the ways that histories are fashioned from the spaces and conventions of national archives and libraries. In spite of recent efforts to downplay the importance of the nation and look at our historical projects transnationally, the ways in which archives are national institutions that regulate access by scholars, both formally and informally, often structure the information historians are able to retrieve. In presenting a personal "ethnography of the archive," this essay examines the stories and advice that were offered to me in encounters that I had with people who inhabit the archive—archivists, librarians, and other scholars—as a way of exploring the national and political investments that many archives and archive dwellers maintain in spite of a quickly globalizing and transnational world.[2]

This essay seeks to expand our definitions of the kinds of knowledges that archives produce by destabilizing the notion that archives are only places of impersonal encounters with printed documents. As Nicholas Dirks and Ann Stoler have argued, a complete ethnography of the archive examines the logic of the archive, its forms of classification, ordering, and exclusions.[3] As well, however, I would argue that an ethnography of the archive should include accounts of our exchanges with the people we meet and dialogue with in the process of our research. Doing research in archives in which we are "foreign" (in one way or another) is particularly fraught. As Jeff Sahadeo shows in his essay in this volume, the archive is an important "contact zone" that brings foreign scholars together with indigenous scholars and archivists, often producing a confrontation over what counts as history. When historians research colonial histories drawing largely from documents that are housed within the archives of colonizing and colonized nations, safeguarded by civil servants whose own relationship to the archive is a central part of the historian's archival encounter, the histories we write are inextricably bound up with archive stories. By telling these stories explicitly, we can remain mindful of the very powerful political and nationalist investments that continue to gird historical narratives, particularly when our projects challenge the history that those committed to maintaining the archive would like us to write and record.

My research topic was on local women who cohabited with or married European men in the long eighteenth century, circa 1760 to 1840, that coincided with roughly the first century of British rule in India. Represented in many historical accounts as a golden age in which racial hierarchies were nonexistent, the coupling of white men and brown women represented the tolerance observed between Britons and Indians in the late eighteenth century and the early nineteenth.[4] Sometimes partnered with a lowercase orientalism, in which East India Company men studied Asian languages and cultures for pleasure and curiosity, living conjugally with a native woman was often read as a sign of living like a native, participating in local culture to its fullest, and reflecting the most productive (and reproductive) aspects of early Anglo-Indian "friendship."[5] For my own part, I have always been suspicious that these relationships were as carefree and consensual for the native women as they were for the men, so I started the project hoping to find out more about how women became involved in these relationships, what sorts of cultural and ethnic borders they crossed, and what kinds of racial, class, and gender dynamics structured their experiences.

Although my project was an investigation into the intimate domestic lives of British men living in India some two hundred years ago, it impinged greatly on the public perceptions that Indians and Britons today have of their past. My experience of doing research demonstrated that this shared history between Britain and India was hotly contested, given their respective nationalist narratives. In India, both in Calcutta and in New Delhi where I did my research, many archivists and librarians denied that native women became sexually involved with European men. In the process of delegitimizing the topic as an appropriate one for writing a dissertation, they marginalized the practice of interracial cohabitation as something that was "not respectable" or, alternately, "something Muslim women did." Distaste for the notion of interracial sex involving Indian (read: Hindu) women was expressed to me many times over by historians, archivists, librarians, and various library hangers-on, even security guards with time to waste, as they examined the contents of my purse. Much as in Craig Robertson's account of his encounter with the archives of the United States in this volume, these men and women acted as gatekeepers to the archive, controlling and mediating my entry into Indian archives by stressing what they thought was "important" to archive and catalogue. Their antipathy, by no means uncommon in my travels through the archives of northern India, reflects the ways in which contemporary anxieties about the sexual purity of Hindu Indian women are folded into a historical imagination in which "good" Indian women were necessarily Hindu and only ever slept with men of their own race, religion, and caste.

Perhaps because I am female, and was then young and unmarried, and so perceived as naïve about the workings of interracial sex, my presence invited advice of many sorts. My own status as a high-caste Hindu woman was often referred to; one gentleman in the Calcutta High Court library, upon noting that I seemed like a girl of a good family, asked if my parents knew what type of research I was doing. Another gentleman, while delivering my documents to me, noted that what I was working on was not particularly savory or respectable. The equivalent of "what is a nice girl like you doing working on something like this?," these questions highlight how closely our topics for study make us the objects of everyday surveillance within the archive. One archivist, upon hearing that my topic was on something that was, in his mind, mundane and everyday could not believe that I was doing a Ph.D. at Berkeley, an American institution that he held in high esteem; after some convincing that I was a "real" historian, he shook his head and concluded that Berkeley had once been a fine institution—implying that Berkeley's perceived downfall in academic circles was directly related to my outré topic. While I was busy reading the archives, I found the archives were reading me.

In London, on the other hand, from the white-haired old ladies doing genealogical research to the young Cambridge-educated journalists and the many librarians and archivists who staff the reference desk at the India Office Library, it seemed that everyone I talked to about my topic was keen to tell me about their familial connection to a native woman. Among those doing family history in the rooms of the old India Office Library on Blackfriars Road, I became a type of resident expert, helping them to decode the archival proof of native women, particularly since the colonial archives had been especially effective at restricting the ways in which the names of native women were registered in colonial records.[6] For some Britons, admitting that one is mixed-race, even a little, has recently become a sign of a cosmopolitan identity, making light brown into the new black in cool Britannia, at least in some circles. Despite the longstanding ambivalence Britain has had in its dealings with black Britons, library goers and archive hangers-on in Britain seemed especially drawn to accounts of cross-cultural sex.[7] Indeed, the recent bestseller by William Dalrymple, *White Mughals*, about a British political agent in the court at Hyderabad and his love affair with a young native noblewoman, has sold over sixty thousand copies in the British Isles, showing the extent of the mainstream appeal for colonial histories of interracial sex.[8] Dalrymple's book, a true story skillfully dramatized by his narrative style, has proved so enticing that it has been optioned for a Hollywood film treatment and a play at the National Theater.

These differing claims about the relative acceptability of histories of interracial conjugality suggest that miscegenation and racial hybridity have an appeal in Britain that they certainly do not in India. As noted, to be mostly white, with a tinge of brown, is to be cosmopolitan for some in an increasingly multicultural Britain. Having a native woman as ancestor perhaps gives people license to claim they are not racist or intolerant of racial and ethnic difference. While this is an admirable sign of cross-cultural and interracial appreciation, a celebration of miscegenation serves a particular type of postcolonial agenda in Britain: it diminishes the overall violence of colonial activity and promotes a vision (not always accurate) of a culturally and racially tolerant postimperial twenty-first-century Britain in which Indians are putatively claimed as biologically and culturally part of the colonial family. The problems of racial tension are overwritten by narratives of familial sentiment, conjugal and companionate love, and more important, by narratives of romantic intimacy that suggest that both sides were somehow uplifted by the multilayered experience of the colonial encounter.

For many Indians, to have the slightest tinge of white is to be racially contaminated, socially suspect, and more important, insufficiently Indian. To the many Indian archivists, librarians, and scholars that I spoke with, the idea that "Indian" women slept with Europeans was only acceptable if they were marked as Muslim—or Portuguese; this type of marking implicitly supported the common belief that only women of marginal groups were likely to be sexually promiscuous with foreigners and other outsiders. This sanitized history of interracial sex rewrites India's colonial centuries as ones in which Hindus remained racially pure by observing endogamy, Hindu women remained sexually faithful to their tribes and castes, and Europeans slept only with women who were marginal to Indian society. The impression many had that only non-Hindu women slept with foreigners and that this was not an appropriate history to write is consonant with a longstanding and enduring vision of history that dates to the colonial era in which non-Hindu, low-caste women are not seen as Indian or as rightful subjects of India's pasts and history.[9] Moreover, relying on what has become a hegemonic female ideal in Hindutva ideology, these often expressed views positing Hindu female virtue and purity versus Muslim promiscuity show the ways in which communal categories remain very prominent in mainstream and common cultural perceptions within India about what kinds of topics are worthy for history dissertations on colonial South Asia.

In both nations, these competing visions of history intersect with politi-

cal and cultural agendas that reflect how contemporary Britons and Indians identify and affiliate with their respective postcolonial nations. As in
Sahadeo's account of the Central State Archive in Uzbekistan below, there
might as well have been a sign over the door of the archives I visited that
read "Without the past there is no future." By consolidating and defending
national identifications with particular pasts, the archive dwellers and
hangers-on I encountered showed me that researching, sharing, and writing histories are necessarily shaped by highly politicized visions of India's
and Britain's future. In India, colonialism, in spite of all its cataclysmic
effects, becomes a historical development that left (and continues to leave)
the contemporary middle-class Indian (again, read: Hindu) family untouched and "pure." Enacting a version of Partha Chatterjee's model
middle-class Bengali household, narratives that deny the existence of interracial sex protect the putative Indian family's women from the "material"
and penetrative forces of colonialism, particularly European men.[10] In
Britain, common references to an Indian granny or half-sister or niece
seemed to bring empire into biological if not psychological proximity at a
time when the British empire itself is territorially small and ebbing away
from mainstream awareness.

If the goal of transnational histories is to unsettle national narratives,
what is clear is that people who identify as "British" or "Indian" are deeply
invested in maintaining certain forms of national belonging, providing
historians of empire with an important challenge to the project of breaking down the boundaries between metropole and colony, between colonizers and those who were formerly colonized.[11] While I am largely sympathetic with Tony Ballantyne's ground-breaking strategies for examining
archives transnationally and undercutting national histories, we can make
more of the confrontations between different national histories and the
ways in which they produce competing fictions to which men and women
become attached as a part of forming national affiliations.[12] My use of
"fiction" here is not meant to pit literature against history but to examine
the productive tensions between the two. Following Doris Sommer, who
argues that national literatures act as allegories for the nation because they
enable communities to imagine and discipline themselves as a collective,[13]
my goal is to examine the ways in which the types of stories people told
me in relation to my project indicated their investments in their respective
nations and the ways in which they felt I should conduct my research.
Many Indians were reluctant to admit that their history was shared in such

an intimate way with Britons and discouraged such a topic, while some Britons were keen to acknowledge a certain level of familial and conjugal attachment and applauded my project. This disjuncture often affected the documents that became available to me in the archives in which I did research.

While I am describing archival encounters at a particular postcolonial moment, 1997, the year that India celebrated fifty years of independence from Britain, the moment is marked by the reestablishment of some recognizably colonial dynamics. The newfound British predilection for claiming native women as part of one's ancestry might be seen by some as an extension of an old role of colonizer, recolonizing the Indian family yet again and adopting native women to the British fold. Indian distaste for the notion of colonial concubinage might be seen as reinstating Indians into the role of the colonized, shoring up the borders and keeping those who are threatening to a putatively national culture outside the family and the nation. What these split histories do is to remind us that a shared colonial past continues to influence how Britons and Indians define themselves against each other, with Britons desiring histories that remind them of their ability to be intimate with members of other groups, be sympathetic and accepting of others, cosmopolitan and open-minded, and Indians wanting to forget that colonialism touched all members of Indian society, even the most marginal, outcast women who took up with European men. The futures that are being imagined by these nations require an acceptable past, one in which archival proof of interracial sex becomes a highly contested set of events.

Although this is a diagnosis of a particular moment in Britain's and India's postcolonial present, the relative acceptability of histories or accounts of interracial conjugality has had mixed fortunes in the course of colonial history on both sides of the colonial divide. Until recently, British documents represented a distinct reluctance to record the interracial dalliances of its officials. Elsewhere, I have discussed the obstacles of finding proof of native women in eighteenth-century British documents, which were strongly invested in registering subaltern female subjects in particular ways, often renaming women with nicknames or European names or leaving them unnamed in baptismal records. Reading "along the grain," I argued that early colonial archives erased or partially registered native women's names in order to suppress their existence in colonial households and families.[14] This process of erasure and selective recording continued well into the twentieth century, when *Bengal Past and Present*, the journal of the Calcutta Historical Society, published the baptism and marriage registers of St. John's Church in Calcutta, but did not print the names of "natural" or illegitimate and mixed-race children who were born to European men and native women. As the compiler, Walter K. Firminger, noted, "The names of natural children when that circumstance is stated have for obvious reasons been omitted."[15] While excluding the proper and complete personal names of native women in wills and church records was a way in which early colonial record keepers kept native women out of the historical records, excising mixed-race children in records reprinted in the early twentieth century was a continuation of strategies to mask the level of interracial sex that British men were engaged in during the eighteenth century. That such an "obvious" exclusion in printed records made sense to the imagined reader suggests the ways in which the imagined community of the English-reading audience of *Bengal Past and Present* constituted itself.

While English-language records kept by colonial officials were largely silent about the lives and experiences of native women, vernacular records from the turn of the eighteenth to the nineteenth century are even less forthcoming of evidence on subaltern women. Persian-language histories, often the dominant local source until the 1830s, appear completely uninterested in recording the lives of poorer, lower-caste, and working women who indeed formed the bulk of the populations that became involved with European men.[16] When I raised the question of vernacular sources in informal discussions with archivists, academics, and family members, what came up repeatedly were novels written and published in Bengali in the early twentieth century. While I suspect that most of my informants suggested I read these as texts that represented history from a Bengali point of view, the novels—and their widespread popularity as part of the canon of Bengal literature—demonstrate the level of awareness that many Bengali readers have of interracial relationships in the colonial era, in spite of the constant disavowals that only marginal subjects, like Muslims and mixed-race Portuguese, engaged in sexual activities with Europeans. Nonetheless, these novels show how such sexual transgressions might be resolved or incorporated into a particular type of nationalist history. Paradoxically, much like British colonial records in which the names of native women were erased or carefully suppressed, in many Bengali novels, the figure of the native woman or mother remains on the margins, thereby containing the figure of disrespectability so she does not contaminate the moral and social order of the larger body politic.

Two novels were most often mentioned to me when I did research in India. Written in Bengali, they are set in the shadow of interracial sexual contact that lurks throughout the narrative but is never explicitly ad dressed. *Gora*, by Rabindranath Tagore (1924), profiles the story of Gourmohun Mukherjee, a Brahmin living in Calcutta who becomes increasingly convinced that the way to reform Hindu society is to preserve orthodox caste-based practices. Nicknamed Gora, which colloquially means the equivalent of "Whitey," a surprise ending—albeit foreshadowed by the title of the book—revealed that Gourmohun was fathered by an Irishman. The explicitly ecumenical and nationalist tone of the book, marked by various references to religious and ethnic tolerance, disavowing caste prejudices, and securing a spiritual high ground, is balanced against Gora's simple-minded intolerance for lower-caste members of society, for the uneducated, the poor. When it is revealed that Gora had an Irish father (his mother is assumed to be a native, but she is never named), his worldview comes crashing down, and he realizes how the nationalist vision of tolerance and open-mindedness is better for India's identity than his own vision of orthodox Brahmin superiority. Tagore's fable played out through Gora suggests that European white racial prejudices fractured India by creating intolerance between whites and others, between high-castes and low-caste and between Hindu and Muslim. By bringing Gora into the Rabindrik nationalist vision, rather than excluding him because he was not completely Indian, tolerance becomes the hallmark of modern Indianness and serves as Gora's final redemption.[17]

Another novel, *Saptapadi* by Tarashankar Bandhopadhyay (1943), is the story of a local doctor, a converted Christian.[18] Through flashbacks, we find out that the doctor had a friendship in college with a young British girl named Rina Brown which turned romantic. They were prevented from marrying because she was British and he was Indian, yet he converted to Christianity to prove his devotion to her. She renounced him, noting that only a Hindu could change his religion at an instant, and he turned to helping the rural poor during World War II. As the story moves between the doctor's life as a general do-gooder, living among poor villagers, and his past living in the city, the juxtaposition between the insularity of village life and the cosmopolitanism of urban life is put into stark relief. This rural-urban split is breached one day when an American soldier appears in the village with a drunken woman, who is understood to be his sexual companion, and the doctor is asked to take care of her. In the process, the villagers observe the loud, uncouth behavior of the American, who verbally abuses the woman, calling her a bitch and a whore, and implying that her drunkenness is endemic to her character. The doctor rescues her from the abusive man and discovers that she is his old friend, Rina Brown. By reversing the British narrative of rescue, the Indian doctor becomes the savior of this young woman who is presumed British, an alleged prostitute, drunken and destitute.

In the final pages of the story, we find out that Rina Brown was the mixed-race daughter of her British father and her Indian ayah. The ayah, who remained in the background throughout the story, was deeply attached to Rina and was also the target of the Brown household's jokes. Mr. Brown and his new wife derided her for being slow; she was accused of being superstitious; worst of all, Rina treated her as an embarrassment to her British friends. After Rina discovered her ancestry, she became indelibly depressed and ended up as a camp follower to an American regiment. In the end, Rina marries Charles Clayton, the doctor's old school friend and the son of a British officer; by moving Rina into a more British social milieu, the narrative removes her from her Indian roots and suggests she will only gain respectability when she returns to England with her British husband. This book was made into a film that is periodically shown on Bengali Doordarshan (Indian state television).

As snapshots of society in Bengal, which was the capital of British operations on the subcontinent from the middle of the eighteenth century until 1911, these novels evoke the ways that Bengalis felt and feel about a history of having white colonizers in their midst. Reversing British stereotypes of Bengalis as effeminate and physically slight, Bengalis sketched Europeans as lumbering, clumsy, and not especially bright.[19] In *Gora*, the protagonist is described as "incredibly white, his complexion untouched by any pigment." He was tall, big-boned, "with fists like the paws of a tiger." Compared to his friend, Binoy-bhusan Chatterji, who is described as a well-educated refined Bengali gentleman, Gora was unable to keep up in school and relied on his friend to shepherd him through his exams.[20] More significant, these novels remain important parts of Bengal's postcolonial imaginary, frequently invoked in discussions about the practice of interracial conjugality and making sense of a past that few think of as respectable. If "making empire respectable" was a key concern of colonizers, these novels and the object lessons embedded within them suggest that respectability was a similarly central anxiety for those who were colonized.[21]

These literary accounts of colonial India remind us that India and Indian national identity were inextricably but uneasily linked with British colonialism. As the "intimate enemy" within the realm of nationalist consciousness,[22] Britain's metaphorical intimacy with India was replayed through literary subjects who were the biological products of British-Indian sexual intimacy; while some of these subjects, like Gora or Rina Brown, are undone by their parentage, others triumphed over this disability by adhering to the norms and behavior of the Bengali middle-classes.

Common to literary discourses in Bengali and to colonial archives of British rule in India is a shared understanding that native mothers of Anglo-Indian offspring remain on the margins of the story. British archives were especially effective at containing the effects of sex between colonizers and colonized by recording only the names of those who were legitimately considered parts of the European community. Similarly, Bengali literary archives selectively recorded characters with whom the reader could identify, which often did not include the figure of the native women who crossed racial, religious, and ethnic boundaries to form conjugal units with Europeans. Gora is found abandoned by his unnamed mother who states that his father was an Irishman; Rina is cared for by a woman who she never realizes is her mother. By removing the indigenous woman from direct involvement in the narrative and keeping her sexual transgressions out of the historical and literary record, the imagined domestic spaces of British India exist as pure, contained scenes in which British middle-class domesticity is staged as simultaneous to—but alternate from—Bengali middle-class domesticity.[23] In these parallel British and Bengali family imaginaries, the marginal body of the indigenous mother is made invisible in order to sustain British and Indian fictions that the national family remained unsullied under colonial contact. As Ann Stoler has noted, "If this [the family] was one of the principal discursive sites where bourgeois culture defined and defended its interests, in colonial perspective, it was also one of the key sites in which racial transgressions were evident and national identities formed."[24]

The divergent attitudes that archive dwellers in India and Britain expressed about my topic in 1997 are diagnostic, as I have noted, of the ways that histories serve particular political and national aims. More important, perhaps, were the ways in which these competing attitudes led me to very different types of sources. No one I met in Britain suggested I read vernacular historical novels of the early twentieth century, while few in India recommended that I spend months (as I ultimately did) reading East India Company proceedings volumes of wills, church records, and court cases and combing them for fragments of evidence about native women's lives. Without my archival informants, it is clear that my road to finding archival material for my project would have been very different. As Tony Ballantyne notes of his own work in his essay in this volume, the intellectual labor behind retrieving archival documents was just as crucial as the history I eventually wrote.

Although archivists at the India Office Library were unfailingly enthusiastic, documents that spoke directly to my topic were difficult to find, highlighting how marginal the question of native women, however beloved they might have been to their European masters, keepers, and descendants, were to the politics of colonial governance at the turn of the nineteenth century. In Britain, ways of cataloging and listing the archive's contents made it extremely unlikely that I would easily find proof of native women's lives since most of the documents are ordered by and collected under categories like revenue, judicial, foreign, political—all matters that likely barely touched these women's lives. Ironically, in addition to the novels, the most useful and productive colonial-era documents that I found in Calcutta were largely uncatalogued and out of chronological order, tied up in bundles with bits of twine, putting documents from 1765 with documents from 1896 next to each other, lumping civil suits with criminal cases, cases of petty theft, vagrancy, and domestic violence. Many of the materials I found there were about matters which were deemed unworthy of transport to London, perhaps because they were seen as inconsequential to the order and profitability of the colonial government, and so remained in the dusty rooms of the High Court, St. John's Church, and the national archives and library. While the haphazard nature of these piles of unkempt documents—unbound, wormy, dusty, dog-eared—indicated the lack of concern the present government of India has for colonial-era documents, the disorder contravened the aims and logics of colonial governance. The chaotic way in which these documents were kept forced me to look through all the documents and not just those in particular categories or bound volumes that I was directed to by archivists, librarians, and card catalogues.

Looking through unsorted and uncatalogued material is perhaps not the most efficient way to do historical research, nor does it guarantee a productive outcome. But the comparison between how colonial documents are stored in Britain and in India shows that the guardians of these respective national archives and libraries guard and protect the national past in different ways, yet to comparable ends. In Britain, where many were sure that I would find what I needed, archivists and librarians pointed me to various indexes and reference aids; what neither I nor they recognized was the degree to which colonial Britons were determined to keep evidence of sexual activity across racial lines from being recorded as a part of Britain's colonial legacy. In India, although the archive and records were rich and dense because they were disordered and comprised accounts and events that colonial officials felt were better left in India, archivists and other inhabitants of the archive warned me that my topic was unsavory and unsuitable as a subject of "proper" history, discouraging me from my pursuit of such a topic because this past has no value in the present. In Britain, then, recorders of the past—from the middle of the eighteenth century to Firminger in the early twentieth—have already sanitized Britain's colonial history of its sexual transgressions, while in India, modern-day gatekeepers keep histories of India clean of interracial conjugality in myriad ways. In their own ways, Britain's and India's archives produce silences that reinforce each other on a topic that is, if nothing else, a history of transgressive behavior that threatens the respectability and racial purity of the family and of the nation. The project I chose was a history of "private" behaviors in the late eighteenth century and the early nineteenth, yet its impact was central to how the "public" of both these nations have seen and continue to see themselves throughout the twentieth century.

History is a discipline with its own rules and standards. Historical research as it is commonly carried out in government archives disciplines historians toward particular national narratives that are appealing or acceptable to those who are the archive's gatekeepers. My archive stories were informative to the project because they demonstrated the ways in which the people I encountered attempted to discipline me into writing a history that resonated for them. Challenging my efforts to put Britain and India into a single frame by constructing such a topic, my archival encounters with Indian and British archivists, librarians, and other archive inhabitants showed that they had radically differing visions of this shared past and even diverged as to what might be suitable material for a historical research project. Nonetheless, it is crucial to put British and Indian national narratives and archival agendas into tension with one another, precisely because such a framing destabilizes the conceit that one's own national archive is the only site from which histories can be written. This kind of strategy undermines the archive's nationalist aims. By incorporating our archival confrontations and encounters in our writing and research practices, we continue to interrogate and unsettle the ways in which history writing remains an important component of forming national affiliations.

As Carolyn Steedman has suggested, inhaling dust is a critical part of doing historical work: the constant circulation of dust and historical narratives is why historians keep returning to the archives.[25]

In the summer of 2000, I returned to the Oriental and India Office Collections in London to do some more research on my project. Having filed the dissertation, I finally knew what I was looking for, and I continued my quest. I also found out at that time that I was newly pregnant, blessed with a very keen sense of smell that was meant to warn me away from smelly soft cheeses and other types of bacteria-laden goods. This new sense of smell also made me easily nauseated when I was in the proximity of the orange-red leather (and its fragments) of the East India Company's records.[26] In what was a case of real *mal d'archives*, I found myself rushing out to the bathroom upon receiving my documents for the day.

Thus I started on a new project: one that is based in the twentieth century (making it not quite so smelly or worm-ridden). My new project is about two terrorist parties that were founded by Hindu *bhadralok* (middle class) in Bengal in the early part of the twentieth century and were galvanized in resistance to the first partition of Bengal in 1905. Organized in cells by students, young professionals, and religious leaders, the movement had a strong ideological component that was expressed by acts of political violence, such as blowing up buildings, trains, and homes, assassinating colonial officials, and robbing banks and post offices. One of the most interesting elements of this movement was that it originated from the bhadralok classes, those who were most likely to have benefited from British education and paradoxically felt resentful of the limits imposed by the colonial state. Many of these men and women had traveled to Britain and had been radicalized upon their return. Stunned at the revolt of its

most loyal cadres, British officials called these men "gentlemanly terrorists" and grappled for over a generation over how to deal with insurgents
from the elite classes of Bengal who had previously been subservient.

When I returned to India in the winter of 2002–3, I found myself facing
some of the same archivists, librarians, and scholars I had met on previous
trips. Upon explaining what I was doing, they full-heartedly embraced this
new project, telling me that the subject had long been ignored by "professional" historians and felt that a fresh look at a part of Bengal's tradition of
political violence was one that was a much-needed corrective to the narrative of Gandhian nonviolent resistance. By "professional," many meant
that the project needed to be taken up by a foreign historian who could
bring international attention to the topic. For many, a history on Bengali
terrorism would restore Bengal, which has long been marginalized in
histories of the independence movement by Gandhi and the rise of the
Congress party, to its rightful place in the struggle to rid India of British
rule. Many admitted that their ancestors had been political militants who
had spent time in jail for committing violence against the colonial state
and hoped that my project would restore glory to a band of gentlemanly
assassins, robbers, and bandits. My local beadle, the archivist who had
initially been suspicious that I was at Berkeley, concluded knowingly that
he knew I would never get a Ph.D. working on that other, less respectable
project and that he felt sure that if I kept my nose to the grindstone in
researching this worthy historical topic, I would eventually be granted a
degree. Dependent on the beadle for access to the archives, I was too timid
to say that I already had a Ph.D. and a tenure-track job.

While I suppose I should be grateful for the unmitigated support for my
new project on revolutionary terrorists, I find the applause for this topic a
telling sign of what kinds of historical research are considered legitimate
or commendable because they conform to and consolidate nationalist
agendas of the past and of the present. In addition to wondering whether
we need another history of a privileged elite—Bengali bhadralok are no-
ticeably overrepresented in South Asian histories—I wonder why a project
involving political violence and terrorism seems more appropriate and
respectable for a woman of a good family to do research on than one on
interracial sex. As of yet, no one in India has asked what a nice girl like me
is doing studying a group of men and women the British would call
terrorists.

Notes

1   On scholars' accounts of research, see Paul Rabinow, *Reflections on Fieldwork in Morocco* (Berkeley: University of California Press, 1977); Kamala Visweswaran, *Fictions of Feminist Ethnography* (Minneapolis: University of Minnesota, 1994). On objectivity and history, see Peter Novick, *That Noble Dream: The "Objectivity Question" and the American Historical Profession* (Cambridge: Cambridge University Press, 1988).

2   On the transnational perspective, see Bernard S. Cohn, *Colonialism and Its Forms of Knowledge: The British in India* (Princeton: Princeton University Press, 1996), 3–4; Frederick Cooper and Ann Stoler, "Between Metropole and Colony: Rethinking a Research Agenda," in Frederick Cooper and Ann Laura Stoler, eds., *Tensions of Empire: Colonial Cultures in a Bourgeois World* (Berkeley: University of California Press, 1997), 18; Sudipta Sen, *Distant Sovereignty: National Imperialism and the Origins of British India* (New York: Routledge, 2003), xxiv–xxviii; and Kathleen Wilson, *The Island Empire: Englishness, Empire and Gender in the Eighteenth Century* (New York: Routledge, 2003), 16–18. On the ethnology of archives, see Nicholas Dirks, "Annals of the Archive: Ethnographic Notes on the Sources of History," in Brian Axel, ed., *From the Margins: Historical Anthropology and Its Futures* (Durham: Duke University Press, 2002); Ann Laura Stoler, "Colonial Archives and the Arts of Governance: On the Content in the Form," in Carolyn Hamilton, Verne Harris, Jane Taylor, Michele Pickover, Graeme Reid, and Razia Saleh, eds, *Refiguring the Archive* (Cape Town: David Philip, 2002).

3   Dirks, "Annals of the Archive"; Stoler, "Colonial Archives"; see also Nicholas Dirks, "The Crimes of Colonialism: Anthropology and the Textualization of India," in Peter Pels and Oscar Salemink, eds., *Colonial Subjects: Essays on the Practical History of Anthropology* (Ann Arbor: University of Michigan Press, 1999).

4   The classic statement of this position is T. C. P. Spear, *The Nabobs: English Social Life in 18th-Century India* (New York: Penguin, 1963); see also Ronald Hyam, *Empire and Sexuality: The British Experience* (Manchester: Manchester University Press, 1991).

5   The term friendship is taken from Thomas R. Trautmann, *Aryans and British India* (Berkeley: University of California Press, 1997), 15–16. See also Rosanne Rocher, "British Orientalism in the Eighteenth Century: The Dialectics of Knowledge and Government," in Carol A. Breckinridge and Peter van der Veer, eds., *Orientalism and the Postcolonial Predicament* (Philadelphia: University of Pennsylvania Press, 1993).

6   For more on this, see Durba Ghosh, "Decoding the Nameless: Gender, Subjectivity, and Historical Methodologies in Reading the Archives of Colonial India," in Kathleen Wilson, ed., *A New Imperial History: Culture, Identity, Modernity, 1660–1840* (Cambridge: Cambridge University Press, 2004).

7   For manifestations of anti-black prejudice in Britain, see, for instance, Paul Gilroy, *"There Ain't No Black in the Union Jack": The Cultural Politics of Race and*

Nation (Chicago: University of Chicago Press, 1991); Bikhu Pareth et al., *The Future of Multi-Ethnic Britain: Report of the Commission on the Future of Multi-Ethnic Britain*, commissioned by the Runnymede Commission (London: Profile Books, 2000); Paul Rich, *Race and Empire in British Politics* (Cambridge: Cambridge University Press, 1986); Laura Tabili, *We Ask for British Justice: Workers and Racial Difference in Late Imperial Britain* (Ithaca: Cornell University Press, 1994).

8 E-mail communication with William Dalrymple, August 11, 2003. And see Dalrymple, *The White Mughals: Love and Betrayal in Eighteenth-Century India* (London: HarperCollins, 2002).

9 Uma Chakravarti, "What Happened to the Vedic Dasi? Orientalism, Nationalism, and a Script for the Past," in Kumkum Sangari and Sudesh Vaid, eds., *Recasting Women: Essays in Indian Colonial History* (New Brunswick, N.J.: Rutgers University Press, 1989).

10 Partha Chatterjee, "The Nationalist Resolution of the Women's Question," in Sangari and Vaid, eds., *Recasting Women*.

11 For Britain, current attachments to the nation as such have been well examined by Antoinette Burton, "Who Needs the Nation? Interrogating 'British History,'" *Journal of Historical Sociology* 10 (1997): 227–48; and "When Was Britain? Nostalgia for the Nation at the End of the 'American Century,'" *Journal of Modern History* 75 (2003): 359–74.

12 Tony Ballantyne, "Rereading the Archive and Opening Up the Nation-State: Colonial Knowledge in South Asia (and Beyond)," in Antoinette Burton, ed., *After the Imperial Turn: Thinking with and through the Nation* (Durham: Duke University Press, 2003).

13 Doris Sommer, *Foundational Fictions: The National Romances of Latin America* (Berkeley: University of California Press, 1991), 30–51.

14 Ghosh, "Decoding the Nameless."

15 "Baptisms at Calcutta, 1759–1766," compiled and annotated by W. K. Firminger, *Bengal Past and Present* 5 (1910): 325–32.

16 Indrani Chatterjee, "Testing the Local against the Colonial Archive," *History Workshop Journal* 44 (1997): 215–24.

17 Notably, Gora is born of an Irish father, not a Scot or an Englishman; this detail brought the contemporary Irish struggle for independence into India's nationalist imaginary. Gora joining Rabindranath's nationalist community symbolically joined the two anticolonial resistance movements.

18 Tarashankar Bandhopadhyay, *Saptapadi*, in *Tin Kahini* (Calcutta: Bengal Publishing Ltd., 1994; original printing, 1943). Saptapadi, which translates to "seven steps," signifies the seven steps of the Hindu marriage ceremony; after seven steps together, a couple is said to be wedded through eternity.

19 See Indira Chowdhury, *The Frail Hero and Virile History: Gender and the Politics of Culture in Colonial Bengal* (Delhi: Oxford University Press, 1998), especially chaps. 2 and 6. See also Mrinalini Sinha, *Colonial Masculinity: The "Manly Englishman" and the "Effeminate Bengali" in the Late Nineteenth Century* (Manchester: Manchester University Press, 1995).

20 Rabindranath Tagore, *Gora*, (Calcutta: Subarnalekha, 1978; 1st ed., 1924), 6–7.

21 Ann Laura Stoler, "Making Empire Respectable: The Politics of Race and Sexual Morality in 20th-Century Colonial Cultures," *American Ethnologist* 16 (1989): 634–60.

22 See Ashis Nandy, *The Intimate Enemy: Loss and Recovery under Colonialism* (Delhi: Oxford University Press, 1983); see also Sudipta Kaviraj, *The Unhappy Consciousness: Bankimchandra Chattopadhyay and the Formation of Nationalist Discourse in India* (Delhi: Oxford University Press, 1995).

23 For more on the construction of an alternate modernity among Bengali bourgeois classes in the domestic arena, see Dipesh Chakrabarty, *Provincializing Europe: Postcolonial Thought and Historical Difference* (Princeton: Princeton University Press, 2000), chaps. 5–6; and his "The Difference-Deferral of a Colonial Modernity: Public Debates on Domesticity in British India," *Subaltern Studies* VIII (New Delhi: Oxford University Press, 1994).

24 Ann Laura Stoler, *Race and the Education of Desire* (Durham: Duke University Press, 1995), 137.

25 Carolyn Steedman, *Dust: The Archive and Cultural History* (New Brunswick, N.J.: Rutgers University Press, 2002).

26 This is apparently a common illness striking those who work with leather from East India. See Steedman, *Dust*, p. 26.

Jeff Sahadeo What happens when gov't + history collide

"Without the Past There Is No Future"

ARCHIVES, HISTORY, AND AUTHORITY IN UZBEKISTAN

A NEW SIGN ABOVE THE DOOR of the Central State Archive of the Republic of Uzbekistan greeted the motley collection of researchers arriving one spring morning in 1998. Painted over a whitewashed wooden board, the sign read "Without the past there is no future" (*O'tmishsiz kelajak yoq*). At the time, I took its appearance as a cry for relevance—after all, I had spent many days over the last several months alone in the archive or with a couple of retired Uzbek scholars. Once every few weeks, a collection of bored schoolchildren marched in, glanced at some of the archive guides, and left. My experience seemed to confirm the fears of Uzbek intellectuals I had befriended during my stay in the nation's capital, Tashkent. Tightening state censorship had combined with worsening economic difficulties to drive Uzbek historians from the archive. This benefited the new post-Soviet regime, which has sought to limit the examination of archival documents, to avoid in particular the exposure of links between the former Communist Party and the current government, both led by the same figure, Islam Karimov.

Many of these intellectuals also feared that the government decision to switch alphabets—the sixth such change over the last century—would distance Uzbek youth and future generations from documents and literature produced in previous decades. Although recognizing the symbolism of abandoning Soviet-imposed Cyrillic lettering in favor of the Latin script, these Uzbeks saw their own past being forsaken as the state moved from one foreign superpower's alphabet to another. As Uzbek youth scrambled to learn English, would the past disappear? How would Uzbekistan build a future as an independent state without an understanding of its history? The sign above the archive door, itself penned in the Latin script, symbolized the troubled relationship between past, present, and future in post-Soviet Uzbekistan.

Uzbek leaders, meanwhile, are shaping the past to secure their own political futures. President Karimov has encouraged initiatives publicizing selected aspects of regional history. Beginning in 1999, images of the eras of Russian and Soviet rule joined multiple displays of the fourteenth-century Central Asian leader Timur. Local historians, financed by the state, have excavated documents from archives closed to foreigners and most Uzbeks to expose selected injustices perpetrated by Russian colonial masters. This new turn, coming after years of silence on the recent past, accompanies other projects of President Karimov designed to move Uzbekistan away from a Russian orientation. In such a way history, and archives, serve the future of at least the Uzbek regime.

The Uzbek leadership's relationship with history has at once posed challenges and afforded opportunities for Western scholars. Since 1991–92, when virtually all records were thrown open for inspection, Uzbek authorities have steadily narrowed access to historical documents. Aside from censorship, funding cuts have strangled libraries and archives. Current limits to access nonetheless constitute an improvement over the Soviet era, when all Uzbek libraries and archives were closed to Western researchers. Western prestige and money can now open doors to the regional past that remain closed to scholars from poor neighboring post-Soviet states and elsewhere in the world. Doctoral candidates especially have undertaken intensive fieldwork, using Uzbek history to advance their own futures in academia. Archival documents unearthing Central Asia's significance in European and Russian imperial and modernization drives have raised the region's visibility in the Western scholarly world. Yet the excitement over the archives' richness risks fetishizing them. Given, among other factors, the particularities of still-in-place Soviet organizational schema, as well as mounting limits on access, an overreliance on archives leaves many black holes in the region's history.

Intellectual challenges of working in independent Uzbekistan are accompanied by numerous personal ones. I and my colleagues have witnessed the deteriorating living and working conditions of our Uzbek counterparts. In this era of transformation, as we gain perhaps an inflated sense of our own role as guardians of Uzbek history, Western scholars are developing grant projects to improve the situation of the historical profession in the region. This effort, of course, runs the risk of imposing our own agendas on local academics. Westerners, finally, find themselves playing diverse roles ranging from philanthropists to friends to those who are losing hope in the future of an independent Uzbekistan.

The regime's newfound interest in deploying archival material is on display at the Victims of Repression Memorial Museum, opened on August 31, 2002. President Karimov's official visit opened the museum, the latest addition to the Martyrs' Memorial Complex in central Tashkent. Karimov inspected displays of Russian and Soviet domination since the mid-nineteenth-century conquest. Archival documents and photographs illustrated tsarist repression of multiple Central Asian uprisings. Most prominently, documents exposed the scope of Stalinist campaigns that resulted in hundreds of thousands of Central Asian deaths in the 1930s. Charts from the archives of the State Security Committee (KGB) detailed the numbers of livestock and other items taken from Uzbek peasants considered "kulaks." Copies of arrest warrants, execution orders, signed confessions, and pleas from family members during the purges of the late 1930s constituted another major part of the display. Other efforts to evoke the colonial past included mannequins of a Russian NKVD officer interrogating a haggard Uzbek man in a mock jail.[1] Karimov, after his tour, declared that: "The politics of colonialism always bring suffering and humiliation. Our people suffered terribly during many years. Thousands of innocent, true sons of the people were victims. The people respect their history and ancestors at all times. This is one of the main factors in a people's self- recognition."[2]

Karimov's support for the Martyrs' Memorial Complex, dating back to a presidential decree of March 2, 1999, surprised Western and local observers. In the years surrounding independence, the Uzbek leader had displayed ambivalence toward the Russian legacy. Himself a product of the Soviet system, Karimov ascended Communist Party ranks to the position of First Secretary of the Uzbek Soviet Socialist Republic in 1986. He was one of the last leaders to declare independence from the Soviet Union following the failed August 1991 coup, at which point he renamed the Communist Party the People's Democratic Party of Uzbekistan and continued in power as a "nationalist." Yet now-President Karimov spoke with a degree of nostalgia for the previous regime in a 1993 speech when he declared that "those who think that the seventy-four years of Soviet history have disappeared without a trace are mistaken. Values have been formed during this period."[3] The Uzbek president was leery of provoking instability and driving away ethnic Russians, who occupied leading administrative and economic posts. Uzbek authorities' efforts to control the communist past began in the summer or 1992, when Baymirza Hayit, an émigré Uzbek historian who had arrived for his first visit since leaving his homeland fifty years before, was ordered to depart. Hayit, whose stern condemnations of Soviet rule had begun to be published in the Uzbek press, intended to work with archival evidence on local resistance against the early Bolsheviks. The Communist Party and KGB archives, the sources for the documents displayed at the Victims of Repression museum, were, and remain, closed to foreigners and most Uzbeks.[4] Karimov's efforts culminated in the closure of many independent academic institutes established following the Soviet collapse.

In fall 2002, the sociologist Laura Adams asked Dr. Naim Karimov, the head of the Martyrs' Memorial Fund, the reason for recent initiatives condemning Russian rule. Dr. Karimov responded that "family members of the victims wanted to find out what happened to their relatives. . . . [The initiative] came from the people."[5] Such a claim, however, must be greeted with caution. By 1999, Islam Karimov had expanded security services, installed a powerful censorship regime, and quashed buds of a civil society that had sprouted since the collapse of communism, arresting all accused of even minor dissent.[6] Several purges at post-secondary history departments have produced an intellectual elite closely aligned to the regime.

Karimov's support for the Martyrs' Memorial Complex coincides with recent political undertakings designed to move the country away from a Russian orbit. This separation began in Russia itself; strapped for cash and struggling with its own reforms in the mid-to-late 1990s, the Russian Federation government opted for a policy of nonengagement with Central Asia. At the same time, other major powers, most notably the United States, displayed increased interest in the region. In February 1999, Uzbekistan pulled out of a collective security agreement with Russia and pursued increased cooperation with the United States, contacts that have borne special fruit since September 11, 2001.[7] The opening of the Victims of Repression Memorial Museum comes as well at a time of increased desire among the Uzbek population for links with Russia. The rebounding Russian economy has attracted many Uzbeks. Longing for the "good old days" of the Soviet Union grows as current living standards fall.[8] Such factors may well have contributed to Karimov's ventures into colonial history. He has cast his lot with the United States at a time when President Vladimir V. Putin is reinforcing Russian presence throughout Central Asia.[9] Karimov's turn to the past looms as a warning about the potential of a future once more tied to Russian power.

The Uzbek regime's use of archives to create national myths and legitimize existing power structures finds parallels across the globe, particularly, as this volume demonstrates, in states seeking to come to terms with the legacy of European imperialism. Tony Ballantyne, Ann Curthoys, and Adele Perry argue below that conservative historians in New Zealand and Australia and a judge in Canada have selectively used archival evidence to construct a national past that supports the efforts of descendants of European settlers to deny rights and compensation to indigenous populations. In "postcolonial" states, such as India, Durba Ghosh has also found new national elites seeking to construct selective, purified versions of the past. President Karimov is attempting to exploit, if not construct, a sense of anger over the injustices of colonialism that, in South Africa, in the words of Helena Pohlandt-McCormick (also in this volume) has turned "tragedies of the past into building blocks of the future."

President Karimov's efforts to construct a new national history have also been guided by an immediate local precedent, one created by a state also seeking to come to terms with the legacy of European imperial expansion. Communist administrators and historians probed archives to link past events, present policies, and future designs throughout the Soviet era. Bolshevik leaders, attuned by their Marxist pedigree to the importance of displaying historical progress, quickly seized control of tsarist archives after the 1917 revolutions. Communist historians marshaled material to demonstrate past "progressive" and "reactionary" trends as guides for thought and action. Debates over history textbooks reached the top level of the Communist Party, with Stalin himself editing material in the 1930s.[10] Party concerns focused on how to present the Russian-dominated Soviet Union as a liberator, rather than an oppressor, of the non-Russian peoples and lands that had been conquered by the tsarist empire and were now integral parts of the new state.

Access to archives remained severely circumscribed during the Soviet era, especially in collections outside the "two capitals" of Leningrad and Moscow. Archivists allowed entry only to those approved by the Party and even then limited selection of documents. Patrons presented their notebooks at the end of each day to the staff, who unceremoniously snipped out any passages that appeared to threaten official versions of history. Leading communist historians, in the meantime, extracted selected documents for publication, to highlight a teleological view of history that culminated in the progressive Bolshevik seizure of power across the Soviet Union. Such compilations, in allowing for the publication of "raw" documents, nonetheless afforded historians and readers space to present and consider a more nuanced view of the past. The archive emerged as a site of contestation as well as comfort throughout the Soviet period.

Soviet efforts to publicize archival material began in 1922 with the journal *Red Archive*. Its inaugural issue stated as its mission to show that "there is nothing secret which will not become clear."[11] The journal published tsarist-era documents, accompanied by didactic commentary to underscore the inequities and corruption present under the imperial regime. Some were designed to ridicule. A 1936 article to commemorate the twentieth anniversary of a Central Asian uprising against tsarist rule contained an account of the efforts of the Fergana district military governor, General-Lieutenant Gippius, to quell increasing unrest. Gippius, according to the document credited to a tsarist functionary, donned a Muslim robe and skullcap before an assembled local crowd, and kissed the Koran before reading sections that urged followers to "obey the regime." The story told in the document, however, allows for a variety of interpretations, going far beyond the annotator's suggestion of the simple incompetence of a regime forced to place "a governor in the role of preaching the Koran."[12]

Archival documents emerged as critical tools in the ever-shifting efforts to distinguish past tsarist and contemporary Western imperial systems from the Soviet "brotherhood of peoples." As early as 1917, V. I. Lenin himself strove to realize this distinction, demanding an end to "Great Russian chauvinism" across the lands of the former tsarist empire.[13] Leading Bolshevik internationalists hoped to use Central Asia to showcase the advanced postcolonial nature of Soviet socialism and attract activists from across Asia to spread revolution eastward.[14] These principles emerged in early Soviet histories of Central Asia, culminating in the 1929 work of P. G. Galuzo. Galuzo used archives recently reordered under communist rule to vilify Russian "chauvinists," both in the late imperial and early Soviet years, in his survey *Turkestan as a Colony*.[15] He exposed as sources the words of local Uzbeks, citing numerous petitions complaining of abuses as evidence of the repugnant behaviour of Russian settlers and administrators in Central Asia. Willingness to expose this past, now corrected by Soviet policies promoting equality, demonstrated a desire to uplift these once-repressed peoples.[16]

By this time, however, the regime's characterization of past Russian rule was changing course. V. Zykin's 1931 study of imperial Tashkent, entitled "Between Two Presses," used archival evidence to expose repression of Central Asian masses, not just by Russian colonizers, but by their own elites.[17] Zykin's article coincided with Stalin's efforts to deemphasize the legacy and threat of "Russian chauvinism" and instead to highlight "bourgeois nationalism," the communist term for present non-Russian efforts to gain greater autonomy within the Soviet Union.[18] Stalin's notations in 1934 textbooks demanded that histories of different Soviet peoples needed greater "coordination," with the location of antagonistic classes for each nation in the prerevolutionary period.[19] Historians of the 1930s consequently searched for documents to support the portrayal of the imperial past as riven primarily by social rather than national divisions. By 1937, Stalin had formulated a new interpretation of tsarist imperialism: historians were to characterize it as not an "absolute evil," but a "lesser evil," as the subject peoples had at least fallen to Russians, whose working classes were far more progressive than those of other European empires.

Soviet historians continued this formula in the postwar era. In 1953, A. V. Piaskovskii discussed the "progressive significance" of the "annexation," which replaced the term "conquest" in historical writing. These interpretations wound their way into public discourse: a 1956 speech of the Uzbek Communist Party First Secretary entitled "In the Fraternal Family of Peoples of the Soviet Union" dated an alliance between Russians and Uzbeks to the tsarist conquest. Yet the need for numerous conferences on the subject, whose proceedings were published in the party newspaper *Pravda Vostoka* (Truth of the East), indicated the discomfort felt by some historians over imposed interpretations. Certain Uzbek historians decried the characterization of Russian leadership in "objectively progressive phenomena" such as gender equity and economic growth, supposed benefits of tsarist rule. They spoke out against the marginalization of local resistance that appeared so important to observers whose words were in the archive.[20]

In response, historians in Uzbekistan loyal to the Party line started work on a series of document collections, including *Of the History of the Spread of the Marxist-Leninist Idea in Uzbekistan*, to offer "objective" evidence of the alliance of Russian and Uzbek workers and the progressive nature of Russian control.[21] Such compilations were designed as well to address a small number of Western studies on Russian rule in Central Asia. Western historians, locked out of the archive, based their studies on early Leninist histories and insisted on linkages between tsarist imperial and Soviet policies.[22] Labeling them as "bourgeois falsifiers," Soviet historians accused their counterparts of being slaves to Western cold war ideology.[23] They also vehemently rejected arguments that Russians pursued imperial goals in conscious imitation of, and with similar policies to, nineteenth-century Western powers.

Yet the publication of hundreds of pages of carefully selected but apparently unedited documents from newspapers and archives offered more nuanced glimpses into tsarist and early Soviet rule than those described in official histories.[24] Among the documents included were several that displayed the enmity of Russian workers toward the colonized. One reprinted document from a 1905 socialist newspaper implored Russian workers to "put into the archive" their beliefs in "higher and lower races, by which one is destined to supremacy, and the other—the lower race— is destined gradually to disappear from the arena of human history."[25] Such words contested official interpretations of Russian and Central Asian masses unifying to throw off tsarist and "bourgeois nationalist" elites.

Historians employed other tactics involving the archive to challenge, albeit subtly, the retroactive doctrine of "friendship of peoples." B. V. Lunin focused his studies on realms considered by the regime "cultural," and therefore less subject to official attention. His works, including *Scholarly Societies of Turkestan and Their Progressive Activities*, nonetheless engaged the political. Lunin discovered, as did Tony Ballantyne in the case of Samuel E. Peal, that intellectuals in colonized lands held great authority through their intellectual endeavours and their closeness to agents of colonial power.[26] Society debates exhibited the contempt of "progressive" Russian intellectuals for the local culture they were so intently cataloguing and classifying, though Lunin downplayed the overt sense of "racialism" that Ballantyne found with Mr. Peal. Lunin as well avoided discussing the participation of these intellectuals in the numerous international Orientalist conferences in the late nineteenth century and the early twentieth, neglecting to focus on, in Ballantyne's words, a "connective" history of empire. Yet Lunin's studies included comprehensive bibliographies that guided readers to unedited versions of works written by these intellectuals

or secondary sources published when the Leninist view of Russian imperi
alism predominated.[27]

Lunin's work in the archives motivated his challenge to party orthodoxy
once Mikhail Gorbachev enacted his policy of *glasnost* across the Soviet
Union. In 1987, Lunin joined E. Yu. Yusupov, vice president of the Uzbek
Academy of Sciences, to contest the doctrine of the "progressive significance" of the tsarist era. The historians pointed to archival sources that
contradicted the orthodox interpretation of an 1898 Fergana valley revolt
as driven by "religious fanaticism." Instead, Lunin argued, the actions
of Russian officials and settlers, accused by a contemporary observer of
"bribe-taking, requisitions, and seeing Muslims as a lower race," played
roles in a rebellion that had complex roots and dynamics.[28] Other Uzbek
historians turned simultaneously to the archive and sources of the early
Soviet period to condemn the violence of the tsarist conquest and subsequent repression of the local population.[29]

James Critchlow has argued that Islam Karimov set the tone for new historical interpretations in his own effort to gain greater power from the
center in the late 1980s. Karimov's desire to redefine the Soviet Union as an
"association of independent states" allowed historians to depict favourably
the short-lived Turkestan Autonomous Government, established by a
broad base of Central Asian leaders after the 1917 tsarist collapse, but
quickly crushed by Russians acting through the Tashkent soviet.[30] Yet
neither Karimov nor local historians anticipated the 1991 disintegration of
the Soviet Union and the subsequent popular desire to cast aside Soviet
methods of censorship and control. One major consequence was the opening of manuscript libraries and archives to Uzbeks and foreigners alike. The
new pluralism in Uzbek society permitted the study of documents from
the region's past to those outside the Soviet academic establishment.

Western historians had bridled for decades at the inaccessibility of Soviet
archival documents. Richard Pierce, the author of one of the few outside
studies of Central Asia, had argued that "limited materials at hand" should
not dissuade non-Soviet historians from examining the region's past.[31]
Yet his call went largely unheeded. Westerners focused on Moscow and
St. Petersburg, where they had greater access to archives as well as published documents. The Soviet collapse, however, significantly expanded
the scope for doing work across Central Asia. The opening of archives was
to revolutionize the field; nine years after the collapse, the renowned
historian Sheila Fitzpatrick argued that scholars of the former Soviet

Union "leaped from a something like a seventeenth-century source base to a twentieth-century one almost overnight."[32]

The first outside historians given the opportunity to work in Uzbekistan experienced the immediate post-Soviet euphoria. Shoshana Keller, an Indiana University doctoral candidate, received support from local academics who had broken away from official educational institutions to gain access, albeit limited, to the Communist Party Archive, renamed as the Party Archive of the Central Soviet of the People's Democratic Party of Uzbekistan. At the state archive, where a number of Westerners began to work, access seemed virtually unlimited. As Helena Pohlandt-McCormick describes in the case of South Africa, a sense emerged among both local and Western historians that "the truth" about the nature of previous, repressive regimes could be told. Western historians, armed with new weapons of postcolonial theory, looked to place Central Asia within a global imperial system and reveal the penetration of colonialism into local culture and society. The exhilaration of working in institutions closed for so many decades, to which is now added the fear that these archives may reclose at any moment, continues to make the archive a privileged site among historians who have entered its doors. Researching in archives, however, means more than ever dealing with the confusing present of a country amid a stressful transformation.

The opening of Uzbek archives has transformed them into "contact zones" between Western historiography and former Soviet archival practices on the one hand and Western historians and their Uzbek colleagues on the other.[33] My own experience, combined with the results of surveying nine other scholars, reveals the social and political, as well as intellectual, significance of encounters with the people and procedures which facilitate, or in some cases hinder, archival access. Survey respondents found themselves thrust into roles other than that of researcher and came away with highly personal stories of the conjuncture between past and present in contemporary Uzbekistan.[34] We gained an appreciation for the extent and limits not only of the power of the archive, but of our own power as Westerners as well as the regime's power to shape history.

Western researchers' first, inevitably frustrating contact with the Uzbek present comes with gaining archival access. Entrance to any archive requires an affiliation with a locally based and officially recognized academic institution, which can charge a significant amount for its services. New procedures enacted in March 2002 further complicated access. One respondent heard a story that, earlier that year, a foreign journalist used archival material to write an unflattering article about the regime.[35] The timing also coincided with the regime's campaign to display tsarist and Soviet archival documents. Archives now require a letter of approval from the Ministry of Foreign Affairs. The process, which takes two to four weeks, can only be initiated after arrival in Uzbekistan. Researchers must request an official cable from their embassies to the ministry concerning their background, status, and research topic. This new procedure adds an extra layer of surveillance to a researcher's presence.

Another roadblock confronting Western historians' efforts to tell their stories about the Uzbek past involves the limitation of the archival finding aids. We are quickly made aware of the fact stated most explicitly in this volume by Craig Robertson, that "archives do not neutrally store documents." Soviet-era published guides, still the first documents handed to new patrons, worked, just as did published archival material, to promote a particular vision of politics and society.[36] In guides to both the tsarist and Soviet eras, catalogues of files of central political-administrative and economic institutions dominate. The tsarist-era guide concludes with brief mentions of independent social and cultural organizations, before a final section entitled "religious cults." Last, somewhat ironically, in the final edition of the guide to the Soviet archives are files of labor and social welfare bodies designed to treat the interests of individual workers. Compilers of these guides, who justified their schemas for "ease of use," fail to mention that their guides exclude significant portions of the archive's holdings. The partition of not simply the guides, but the archive itself, into "historical" and "revolutionary" sections divided by 1917 deter any efforts to locate continuities across regimes. These efforts, which display, in the words of Thomas Richards, a "fantasy of organization," have, by their durability, proven his point that "it was much easier to unify an archive composed of texts than to unify an empire composed of territory."[37]

Present priorities also hinder access to archival documents. Survey respondents, already banned from the Party and KGB archives, discovered continued censorship in state and local institutions. One respondent was shown a copy of an early 1990s Uzbek Council of Ministers order to destroy all procuracy records from the 1930s to the late 1950s. In addition, researchers have had requests for documents unfulfilled due, ostensibly, to loss or damage stemming from poor storage conditions in these horribly underfunded institutions.

Western researchers have designed a number of strategies to locate material not privileged by the Soviet and Uzbek regimes. I found an examination of early Soviet histories particularly useful; Zykin's 1931 article, which focused on an 1892 cholera epidemic and subsequent riot, provided references to judicial interview transcripts with Central Asians not mentioned in archive guides.[38] As Pohlandt-McCormick discovered in her work on the Soweto uprising, these incidents of unrest, shaking the foundations of state power, compelled the state to investigate and record the voices of the dispossessed. Gaining access to these subaltern voices, so rare in the published as well as archival literature on Central Asia, provided great excitement for many survey respondents.[39] Discoveries included personal accounts of the impact of the 1930s Soviet closings of mosques. Certainly, this material, told to and recorded by functionaries, needs to be treated carefully. We must read "against the grain" of the documents, conscious of Verne Harris's argument that information can be distorted by, among other factors, the agendas or mentalities of those who recorded and stored information.[40] Almost all survey respondents reported significant voids where they expected to find material, confirming their own suspicions of the limits of the archive. I discovered numerous files stuffed with information on prostitution in imperial Tashkent, documents rife with complaints of miscegenation, but, in a striking parallel with Durba Ghosh, no information on unions or children from relationships between Russian and Central Asians. In the end, however, for better or for worse, I as well as my respondents, and apparently Ghosh, chose not to let these gaps open the door to an explicit self-questioning of the archive's overall value. We complemented our studies with other published and unpublished material to produce as nuanced a study as we considered possible.

Efforts in offering new interpretations of the Uzbek past involved establishing personal connections in the present. Historians of the former Soviet Union have long been aware of the need to couch their topics so as not to appear too controversial, thereby avoiding some of the scorn that greeted Ghosh from Indian archivists. This began for political reasons, to gain access to the limited collections in Soviet Moscow and Leningrad, but continued for personal ones, to have archivists feel comfortable dealing with and retrieving information for a foreign researcher, whose topic may in fact be quite unsettling. One researcher's investigation on homo-sexuality in the Soviet Union was described as a study on "public health." Ghosh herself in the end decided that revealing the "whole truth" to archivists is not worth potential negative consequences.

In the case of Uzbekistan, respondents underlined the goodwill of archi-vists toward them, which I attributed to their happiness to see outsiders, especially privileged Westerners, taking an interest in local history. My discovery of the riot interview transcripts only bore fruit because of the state archivist Sharafat Fazylovna Muminjanova's willingness to track down the material from outdated citations. Virtually all survey respon-dents reported useful material discovered through the eagerness of archi val staff to locate, or even suggest, material not described in the official guides or to ignore Soviet-era censorship labels. A friendly connection with the archive director allowed some past the curious ban on foreigners using the institution's card catalogue, another Soviet-era finding aid, but one that can turn up new sources. Several respondents lauded staff for their willingness to produce even very large numbers of requested files quickly, which, according to one, enabled his research strategy to "cast a wide net and 'read like hell.' "[41]

Establishing personal connections offered different benefits at each in-stitution. After sharing stories and melons with the staff at the rare book room of the Alisher Navoi State Library, I was allowed to wander into the stacks and survey poorly catalogued holdings from the earliest days of the institution, opened in 1871. British and French tales of adventure and con-quest in foreign lands, as well as scholarly works from across Europe, attested to Russian intellectuals' efforts to place themselves in a global imperial system. Staff at smaller regional and local archives traced hard-to-find documents, as well as allowed patrons to work beyond the narrow hours staff preferred to keep the archive open. Respondents also reported that the poorly trained staff's lack of knowledge of censorship dictates combined with trust in the patron allowed access to "sensitive" World War II and postwar documents.[42]

Connections with local historians, however, rarely produced significant results. One respondent summed up the general feeling as "lots of contact, little help."[43] Large gaps divide Western and local scholars. In a culture that pays great respect to age, senior Uzbek historians adopt patronizing atti-tudes toward the doctoral candidates who compose the majority of West-ern historians in Central Asia. Conversely, patronizing attitudes persist among Westerners that Uzbek historians still operate, like the regime, with a Soviet mindset. As the Indiana University graduate student Stephen Hegarty argued in 1995, "[Uzbek] historians have issued oblique condemnations . . . that much of their history has been 'blacked out' and that the Uzbeks have been 'cut off from their heritage,' but with few exceptions they have not confronted the Soviet manipulation and perversion of their history head on."[44] Uzbek historians are seen to accept the categories and discourse of history as presented in the Soviet-era archival guides.

At the same time, Western scholars recognize the difficulties, and dangers, for local historians. Islam Karimov's wide-ranging crackdown following a mysterious 1999 bombing in central Tashkent has left those in the profession fearing, at the very least, losing their jobs if they are seen to be acting against the regime's interests.[45] Unlike their Canadian counterparts, as Adele Perry discusses, Uzbek historians lack the power or authority to question state-sanctioned historical narratives. Nor is there space for the vigorous scholarly debate based on archival evidence that Ann Curthoys portrays in Australia. No Truth and Reconciliation Commission, with its open hearings and widespread dissemination of documents, as Pohlandt-McCormick describes, will be established in Uzbekistan, even as the regime publicizes selected acts of violence by its predecessors. Given Karimov's recent ventures into history, scholars have no idea which figures, events, or interpretations might become lionized or demonized by official campaigns. Sharing knowledge with Westerners is considered a risky act.

Economic considerations also divide Western and Uzbek historians. Respondents unanimously noted the decayed, if not devastated, state of Uzbek academia. Abysmal salaries drive historians away from the archive, as they search for affordable goods or more remunerative employment. Westerners become sources of income rather than colleagues. As a graduate student, I hired a senior philologist from the Academy of Sciences as a research assistant for twenty-five dollars weekly, quadruple his regular salary. Uzbek historians' only opportunities for significant compensation as scholars require links to Western grant organizations or contracts from the Uzbek government to write histories conforming to state dictates.

Archival staff face similar challenges. A 2003 report placed salaries in Samarkand at fourteen dollars monthly. Employees were also expected to perform extra work painting, cleaning, and weeding buildings and grounds.[46] Uzbeks' ability to survive on such meagre income leads Westerners to admit that the economy works in ways not entirely familiar to them. We have nonetheless seen signs of desperation, such as the purchase by local counterparts of the cheapest rice and flour available, which then must be separated from various insects. Yet, even as gifts—chocolate, magazines—offered at the end of a research trip are graciously accepted, I have never heard of any request of payment for services, nor any hints that financial compensation might give patrons preferential treatment, such as seeing censored files. The price of photocopies at the state archive, about ten cents each, is extremely low by the region's standards. I have even seen delicate scrolls unrolled on the copier by the archive director, who makes all copies, perhaps because the machine is the archive's most valuable piece of equipment. Survey respondents felt universally thankful for the services rendered to them by the various archival staffs, all of whom, as lower-level state employees, represent the "new poor" in independent Uzbekistan.[47]

Beyond the intellectual realm as well, respondents appreciated the desire of local archivists to befriend them. The mid-afternoon tea poured by the central archive staff to researchers as they examine their documents is a potent memory. Archivists' interest in foreigners and their cultures mirrors researchers' interest in the Central Asian past, and conversation quickly strays from archival matters to issues of family and home. Western researchers also find themselves the subject of great interest beyond the archive. Few foreigners speak either Russian or Uzbek, the two common street languages, or live outside the narrow expatriate world of embassies and nongovernmental organizations. I quickly discovered that the almost daily occurrence of an Uzbek asking me the time was a pretext for further conversation. Getting to the archive became a task in itself, and I avoided particularly chatty street vendors on heavy work days. Daily conversations with Uzbeks generally took three forms: requests for English language help, a barrage of questions about life abroad, and a desire to complain about the difficulties of everyday life. Complaints, however, were never directed at the upper reaches of the regime. Questioning on this subject generally elicited responses such as "we have no time [*or* we're lucky we don't need] to worry about politics." Men focused complaints on the ubiquitous police forces, particularly traffic cops, notorious for stopping motorists for "infractions," in the expectation of a bribe. Women discussed stresses on family life and the difficulty in finding affordable goods. Younger women sought English-language help or perhaps a job opportunity with a Western firm.

Casual conversation also afforded opportunities to see the way that past and present combine in the outlooks of contemporary Uzbeks. Weeks after my arrival at the archive, one of the militia who ostensibly guarded the institution asked for my documentation. The request caught me by surprise—unlike Craig Robertson's experience at the United States National Archives, I had passed into and out of the reading room unhindered, bringing with me all manner of writing implements and snacks, and could easily have removed all manner of documents past the snoozing guards, whose semi-automatic machine guns lay drooping on the floor. Boredom seemed to his main reason for stopping me, however. He thumbed leisurely through my passport before examining my personal information and asking my "origin." I have spent enough time in Eastern Europe to know that to answer "Canadian" elicits blank stares at best, and usually scowls, followed by the next question, "no, by ethnicity." I responded "Hindustan" and a smile broke across his face. "Ah, Hindustan," he responded, rubbing his fingers together. "Millionaire!" I was too surprised to ask him why a millionaire might be spending time in an Uzbek archive. In the archive, however, I discovered the vital role of Hindu traders and money-lenders in nineteenth-century Central Asia and realized that Uzbeks today applied this category to those who were not white or East Asian "by ethnicity" but appeared "Western." India's past role in the region has given the land a privileged place in the Uzbek imagination.

I, as well as the other respondents, have seen the friendship accorded us as genuine and have been flattered by Uzbeks' attention. Yet, the prestige and privileges of belonging to the Western world undeniably translate into power in the contact zone of the archive and beyond. What we may pass off as relatively inexpensive favors—such as changing money at a slightly less than market rate—provides significant extra benefits to local staff and others. Even graduate students are wealthy beyond the dreams of most Uzbeks, and there is always the hope that contact can entail material gain. Association with Westerners, moreover, is considered a form of cultural capital in Uzbekistan.

Westerners are distinguished as well for their mere ability to do research in the archive for significant periods. Many historians, particularly from elsewhere in the former Soviet Union, cannot afford transport and accommodation, even if they are able to attain a local affiliation. For scholars in Kazakhstan, Kyrgyzstan, Tajikistan, and Turkmenistan, these problems in effect sever them from their own histories, as tsarist and early Soviet records for the Turkestan district, which covered all these states, are centralized in Tashkent.

Westerners maintain an elevated status as the regime showcases the interest of "advanced" countries, particularly the United States, in Uzbekistan. Several survey respondents were interviewed for various media, although television appearances generally consisted of an Uzbek reporter asking "yes" or "no" questions and pulling back the microphone before other comments could be added.[48] One respondent reported that interest in him grew significantly following September 11, 2001, after a state order that all institutions should publicize "longstanding" ties with the United States.

Western privilege complicates as well as enables personal relationships. Uzbeks have their own interests in allowing us to share intimate details of their daily lives. Many locals that Western scholars encounter are isolated from the clan and familial networks that provide lower-income earners with a cushion from the harshness of post-Soviet life. Local friends regularly solicit assistance, which, to their surprise, neither I nor other survey respondents could provide. These included obtaining prescription drugs, seeing a Western dentist or doctor, assistance to emigrate, or the use of diplomatic connections to resolve administrative snafus. Russell Zanca, an anthropologist working on an oral history project of Soviet collectivization, has noted that requests for material assistance come frequently, but uniquely, from young village Uzbeks; the elders, he believes, have too much pride to request help despite their often desperate situation.[49] Respondents were unanimous in noting a sharp decline in optimism and hope for the future since the mid-1990s. A retreat to private life has offered some comfort, but, for many, their hopes rest on their children's potential to take advantage of growing connections with the world to find a better livelihood and life.

In the shadow of deteriorating living conditions for the majority of the Uzbek population, Karimov's efforts to mobilize popular and elite support, domestic and foreign, through history and the archive have intensified. His Martyrs' Memorial Complex is the most recent addition to a strategy that has focused on the elevation of the fourteenth-century ruler of Central Asia, Amir Timur, or Tamerlane. The campaign began with the erection of a large statue of Timur, astride a massive mount, on September 1, 1993. The placement of the statue in Tashkent's central square, now renamed Amir Timur Square, was highly symbolic. The square itself, having hosted an ever-changing series of monuments to imperial Russia and the Soviet Union, honoring successively the first governor-general of Russian Turkestan, Konstantin Petrovich fon-Kaufman, Lenin, Stalin, and Marx, has existed as a public archive of power and ideology. Karimov, in a speech before the unveiling of the monument, heralded its role in freeing Uzbekistan from a "colonial vise."[50]

Reasons behind Karimov's turn to Timur as a figure linking past and present are evident at the Amir Timur Museum, opened in 1996. Quotes and images of the Uzbek president are prominent throughout the museum. Karimov has glorified the Mongol ruler as a synthesis of culture, power, and prestige that he claims to see in the Uzbek nation and that the Uzbek nation should see in both Amir Timur and himself.[51] Beatrice Forbes Manz has argued that Timur rose in the pantheon of national heroes largely because of his international repute, as Uzbek leaders hoped to publicize the simple existence, much less the history and culture, of their new state.[52] Karimov himself has appeared at international conferences honouring Amir Timur's legacy. At the same time, the president employs parallels to justify increasingly authoritarian rule. The inscription on Amir Timur's monument, in English as well as Uzbek, lauds his supposed practice of "justice through strength." Karimov has justified his crackdowns on dissent through his arguments that, like Timur, he has been able to build a stable, powerful, and even cultured state in a dangerous world that includes war-torn neighbors like Tajikistan and Afghanistan. The centuries between the two leaders have been characterized a time of chaos, decline, and subjection for the Uzbek people and lands.

Karimov has tied Amir Timur and his subsequent initiative condemning Russian rule to one of his major political goals: to emerge as a regional power. He has worked hard to maintain an image, fostered even during the Soviet era, of Uzbeks as the most advanced and powerful people in Central Asia.[53] Karimov has intervened militarily in Kazakhstan, Kyrgyzstan, Tajikistan, and Afghanistan in efforts to enforce "regional security." His effort to promote himself as a regional chief, in effect to replace Russia, was recently on display at the Martyrs' Memorial Complex. At a 2002 regional conference, Karimov led the leaders of all Central Asian states to a wreath-laying ceremony at the complex's central square to commemorate the victims of Russian colonialism.

Economic as well as political priorities of the Uzbek regime have played large roles in dictating the present and future of Uzbek historical records. Archives and libraries are falling prey to the post-Soviet market. Shortly after independence, the staff and the archive of the Tashkent city museum were ejected from their downtown offices, which now house local and Western businesses, to the basement of the museum itself. Museum historians deflected my inquiries as to where the archival material had gone, simply stating that nothing in the collections would interest me. In spring 2003, the Uzbek government demolished the state library to make way for government office buildings. Approximately 80 percent of the collection, including tsarist-era books and newspapers, is apparently in storage. Shoshana Keller reported that bound newspapers are on a nearby gymnasium floor; to get at certain volumes one must step over other piles. There is no word on the location of the five-hundred-plus volume *Turkestan Collection*, an assemblage of scholarly works and newspaper and journal articles compiled by bibliographers as a semi-official record of the Russian experience in Turkestan in the tsarist era. Keller heard alarming, but unverified, rumours that librarians are selling valuable books to augment their miserable salaries.[54] Other reports across the region confirm that librarians are purging older material to make way for new Uzbek language publications. The regime's underfunding of archives and libraries combined with tightening censorship has validated local intellectuals' fears that the general population is losing the means to study the Uzbek past, forced instead to rely on state-sponsored historical expeditions designed to enforce the regime's priorities.

The archive constitutes a source of power and authority in Uzbekistan. It is at the nexus of a number of different and overlapping clashes: between the West, Russia and the former Soviet Union, and the local; between state elites and society; between the Uzbek government and its neighbors; and, above all, between past, present, and future. Western researchers no longer face Soviet-era restrictions, but Uzbek leaders have felt free to place limits on archival access, even as they seek to exploit Westerners' presence. Karimov's desire to expose Russian crimes and Uzbek "martyrs" has further constrained the arena for dissemination and debate of archival material. Local historians and archivists are themselves caught in a dual press, with the only sources of significant support coming from Westerners or the central state, each with its own projects and agendas. Completely powerless, meanwhile, are scholars from neighboring states, who lack the economic means or the political clout to examine material of their own

projects &
agendas in
archives

pasts. Even for scholars in outlying parts of Uzbekistan, being able to employ the archive is a distant dream. Trends of destruction and removal of records seem only set to deepen as the Uzbek state feels unconstrained by the limited Western pressure to preserve freedom of information. A number of violent attacks linked to Islamist groups in Tashkent in 2004 has only deepened Karimov's resolve to crack down on opposition, real or imagined, using tactics of arbitrary detention, harassment, and torture.[55] As the Soviet experience showed, use of the archive to produce "official" histories for an authoritarian state can produce counternarratives, albeit subtle, that may provoke eventual challenges to the regime's legitimacy. Yet such long-term hopes are of little comfort to Uzbek historians and archivists, even as Uzbekistan's increased visibility furthers the careers of Western scholars who have benefited from their hospitality.

Notes

1 Laura Adams, "Tashkent Museum Allows for Discussion of Recent Past," Eurasianet.org; www.eurasianet.org / departments / culture / articles / eavii01 02.shtml (07 / 17 / 03).

2 Uzbekistan press service, www.press-service.uz / eng / novosti_ eng / no902 2002.htm.

3 Cassandra Cavanaugh, "Historiography in Independent Uzbekistan: The Search for a National Identity," *Central Asia Monitor* 1994, no. 1: 32.

4 Stephen Hegarty, "The Rehabilitation of Timur: Reconstructing National History in Uzbekistan," *Central Asia Monitor*, 1995, no. 1: 29.

5 Laura Adams, personal communication.

6 Kathleen Collins, "Clans, Pacts, and Politics in Central Asia," *Journal of Democracy* 13, 3 (2002): 150.

7 Martha Brill Olcott, "Taking Stock of Central Asia," *Journal of International Affairs* 56, 2 (spring 2003): 4–8.

8 Zamira Eshanova, "Uzbekistan: Russia's Image on the Rise in Central Asia (Part 1)," *Radio Liberty / Radio Free Europe*; rferl.org / nca / features / 2002 / 11 / 12112002171406.asp.

9 Bruce Pannier, "Russia: With U.S. Attention on Iraq, Moscow Wooing Central Asia," *Radio Liberty / Radio Free Europe*; rferl.org / nca / features / 2003 / 04 / 22042003161714.asp.

10 Lowell Tillett, *The Great Friendship: Soviet Historians on the Non-Russian Nationalities* (Chapel Hill: University of North Carolina Press, 1969), 5.

11 *Krasnyi Arkhiv*, 1922, no. 1: 1.

12 "Gubernator v roli propovednika Korana," *Krasnyi Arkhiv*, 75 (1936): 187–90.

13 Hélène Carrère d'Encausse, *The Great Challenge: Nationalities and the Bolshevik State, 1917–1930*, trans. Nancy Festinger (New York : Holmes & Meier, 1992).

14 "Soviet Central Asia: The Turkestan Commission, 1919–1920," *Central Asian Review* 12, 1 (1964): 6.

15 P. G. Galuzo, *Turkestan—Koloniia* (Moscow: Izdanie Kommunisticheskago Universiteta Trudiashchikhsia Vostoka imena I. V. Stalin, 1929).

16 On these policies, see Terry Martin, *The Affirmative Action Empire: Nations and Nationalism in the Soviet Union, 1923–1939* (Ithaca: Cornell University Press, 2001).

17 V. Zykin, "Pod Dvoinom Pressom: Vosstanie v Tashkent v 1892 t.n. 'Kholernyi Bunt,'" *Uchenye Zapiski Permskogo Gosudarstvennogo Universiteta (otdel Obshchestvennykh Nauk)* Vyp. II (Perm, 1931): 315–52.

18 Alexandre Benningsen and Chantal Quelquejay, *Les mouvements nationaux chez les musulmans de Russie* (Paris: Mouton, 1960).

19 Tillett, *The Great Friendship*, 41–42.

20 Ibid., 180, 252, 255.

21 I. M. Muminov, ed., *Iz istorii rasprostranenie marksist-leninskikh idei v Uzbekistane. Sbornik Materialov* (Tashkent: Izdatel'stvo Akademii Nauk UzSSR, 1962).

22 See for example, Olaf Caroe, *Soviet Empire: The Turks of Central Asia and Stalinism* (London: Macmillan, 1953).

23 R. Tuzmuhamedov, *How the National Question Was Solved in Soviet Central Asia (A Reply to Falsifiers)*, trans. David Fidlon (Moscow: Progress Publishers, 1973).

24 I verified many of the documents I intended to use in my work from the collections with those in the actual archive.

25 From *Russkii Turkestan*, December 6, 1905, republished in Muminov, *Iz istorii rasprostranenie*, 33.

26 B. V. Lunin, *Nauchnye obshchestva Turkestana i ikh progressivnaia deiatel'nost'* (konets XIX–nachalo XX v.) (Tashkent: Izdatel'stvo Akademii Nauk Uzbekskoi SSR, 1967), 21.

27 B. V. Lunin, *Istoriia Obshchestvennykh Nauk v Uzbekistane: Bio-bibliograficheskie ocherk.* (Tashkent: Izdatel'stvo "Fan," 1974).

28 E. Iu. Iusupov and B. V Lunin, "Andizhansoe vosstanie 1898 g. v sovetskoi istoricheskoi literature," *Obshchestvnnye nauki v Uzbekistane* 1987, no. 1.

29 James Critchlow, *Nationalism in Uzbekistan: A Soviet Republic's Road to Sovereignty* (Boulder, Colo.: Westview Press, 1991), 119–34.

30 Ibid., 124–27.

31 Richard A. Pierce, *Soviet Central Asia: A Bibliography*, Part 3: 1917–67 (Berkeley: University of California Press, 1966).

32 Sheila Fitzpatrick, ed., *Stalinism: New Directions* (London: Routledge, 2000), 5.

33 I liberally adapt the term "contact zone" from Mary Louise Pratt, *Imperial Eyes: Travel Writing and Transculturation* (London: Routledge. 1992).

34 I performed this survey in spring and summer 2003, sending questionnaires to Western scholars I was aware of who had worked in the archive. Questionnaires contained five sections: Personal information; Archive support [gaining entrance to the archive]; Work in the archives; Archives and Uzbekistan [interactions with people and politics]; and Miscellaneous. I received nine responses. All scholars agreed to have their names and information used for this article (though in one case asked for some responses to be kept off the record). Subsequent notes will give the scholar's name, institutional affiliation, and years archival research was done.

35 Paul Stronski, Stanford University, 2000–2002.

36 See, for example, Z. I. Agafanov and N. A. Khalfin, *Istoricheskii Arkhiv UzSSR: Putevoditel'* (Tashkent: Istoricheskii Arkhiv UzSSR, 1948) and *Katalog Fondov Sovetskogo Perioda* (Tashkent: Tsentral'nyi Gosudarstvennyi Arkhiv Uzbekskoi SSR, 1975).

37 Thomas Richards, *The Imperial Archive: Knowledge and the Fantasy of Empire* (London: Verso, 1993), 4.

38 Jeff Sahadeo, "Creating a Russian Colonial Community: City, Nation, and Empire in the Tashkent, 1865–1923" (Ph.D. diss., University of Illinois at Urbana-Champaign, 2000).

39 On the difficulty of finding non-elite or non-official written sources in a culture that preferred oral transmission, see Adeeb Khalid, *The Politics of Muslim Cultural Reform: Jadidism in Central Asia* (Berkeley: University of California Press, 1998).

40 On reading "against the archival grain," see Verne Harris, "The Archival Sliver: A Perspective on the Construction of Social Memory in Archives and the Transition from Apartheid to Democracy," in Carolyn Hamilton, Verne Harris, Jane Taylor, Michele Pickover, Graeme Reid and Razia Saleh, eds., *Refiguring the Archive* (Dordrecht: Kluwer Academic Pubilshers, 2002), 135–36; and Ann Laura Stoler, "Colonial Archives and the Arts of Governance: On the Content in the Form," in Hamilton et. al, eds., *Refiguring the Archive*, 91–92.

41 Mike Thurman, Indiana University, 1994–96.

42 Adeeb Khalid, Carleton College, 2000–2001; Stronski, 2000–2002.

43 Thurman 1994–96.

44 Hegarty, "The Rehabilitation of Timur," 30.

45 On these fears, see Gregory Feifer, "Uzbekistan's Eternal Realities: A Report from Tashkent," *World Policy Journal* 19, 1 (spring 2002): 81–89.

46 Christine Evans, "Research Conditions in Uzbekistan: Archival Access and Conditions in Samarkand," *Central Eurasian Studies Review* 2, 3 (fall 2003): 17.

47 Alisher Ilkhamov, "Impoverishment of the Masses in a New Transition Period: Signs of an Emerging 'New Poor' Ideology in Uzbekistan," *Central Asian Survey* 20, 1 (2001): 33–54.

48 Thurman, 1994–96.

49 Personal communication, Russell Zanca, October 5, 2003.

50 Hegarty, "The Rehabilitation of Timur," 29. Images of the various monuments can be viewed at http://tashkent.freenet.uz/e_sk.htm.

51 Hegarty, "The Rehabilitation of Timur," 30.

52 Beatrice Forbes Manz, "Tamerlane's Career and Its Uses," *Journal of World History*, spring 2002, 1–25.

53 On this legacy, and Timur's role in it, see ibid., 15–20.

54 Shoshana Keller, "Library Conditions in Uzbekistan," *Central Eurasian Studies Review* 2, 3 (2003) 17.

55 "Uzbekistan: Torture, Unfair Trials in Wake of Attacks," Human Rights News, Human Rights Watch; http://www.hrw.org/english/docs/2004/09/10/uzbeki9324.htm.

Craig Robertson

Mechanisms of Exclusion

.

HISTORICIZING THE ARCHIVE AND THE PASSPORT

A Visit to the Archive

IT IS SPRING 2002, and I am on a public bus that is approaching the driveway to Archive II, the main branch of the National Archives and Records Administration of the United States (NARA), located in College Park, Maryland. As the bus turns into the half-mile looped driveway, we pass the first of three armed checkpoints—today all three are staffed by older gray-haired men with large aviator-style glasses that make the men comic and their guns more threatening. I get off the bus and approach the glasshouse frontage of Archive II carrying an umbrella I had grabbed in the rush to get to the Metro for my daily thirty-minute train journey, but with the sun having seemingly arrived for good, it now appears redundant. I am also carrying and reading a newspaper bought to fill in the fifty-minute wait when I missed my intended bus by the exact amount of time it took me to locate my umbrella. In addition I have a laptop strung over my shoulder in a case that is doing bad things to my spine. After I enter the building and present my NARA ID card, I dutifully put my laptop on the conveyor belt to be screened. I also go to put my umbrella there, but the guard policing this part of the entrance examination isn't interested in my umbrella. I can carry that through the metal detector. He wants my newspaper scanned. Only later does this surprise me. At the time, two weeks into my second visit to the D.C. area for research, I no longer waste any excess energy on my dealings with the "guardian of heritage." The staff here, like all workers in documentary archives, knows the power of the printed and written word. They recognize the need to police the documents that enter and leave an archive, and to control them once they have been admitted. At this point of entry I guess they just don't know what ideas and opinions might be in those newspaper words. Maybe they are unclassifiable? More than likely they are not worthy of being in this particular archive. The guard was definitely right; my newspaper needed to be scanned, its contents made transparent in order to be assessed by the archive. My umbrella did not set off the metal detector.

The Problems of "the Archive"

I am at NARA to research my doctoral dissertation—a history of the emergence of the passport in the United States. After my morning security check I spend the rest of each day scavenging through the archive's large collection of diplomatic correspondence and its smattering of Passport Office documents for comments and observations on the passport to go with what I have found in books, periodicals, newspapers, magazines, and congressional records. With the passing of each successful or unsuccessful hour at NARA, my thoughts wander to the collection of nineteenth-century and early-twentieth-century Passport Office files boxed up in the Department of State to which I have been denied access; a denial that has caused me to again question what makes it into a state archive. Documents do not simply appear in state archives. Individuals for whom they have been everyday files determine which documents are sent to archives, where they are then selected and classified according to specific criteria. Once anointed with the objectivity of their location in the archive, officials select who can read them and under what conditions.

The bespectacled, armed, older white male employees of the state in the Archive II driveway make explicit the exclusionary practices associated with state archives, and archives in general. The previous essays by Durba Ghosh and Jeff Sahadeo highlight other ways in which researchers can be excluded from archives: censorship, economic conditions, and the markings of gender and race. However, in the archive there is not simply the researcher's problem of exclusion; there is, more significantly, the effective exclusion of the memories and pasts of communities and peoples from official archival collections and institutions; Horacio Roque Ramírez's chapter provides a critical example of the importance of "community archives" to the articulation of collective identities excluded from official archives.

Therefore, my distracted ponderings in the reading rooms of the National Archives led me to consider, in light of the increasingly frequent analysis of the archive within the academy, what it means to "be cognizant of [the archive's] horizons, wary of its distortions, skeptical of its truth claims and critical of its collaboration with state apparatuses."[1] In other words, how does one effectively historicize the archive? One possible approach to this question is to focus on the logics and practices of "the archive": interpretation, classification, identity, evidence, and authenticity. I have found Allan Sekula's "archival rationalization" a useful concept to productively think about the archive in terms of practices not institutions—as Burton has put it, "a process whereby archives became part of the quest for a 'truth apparatus', which undergirded a variety of social practices."[2] Sekula argues that the emergence of photography in criminal identification (his object of analysis) must be located in a broader context that cannot be adequately reduced to the optical model provided by the camera. Instead he insightfully integrates identification photography in a "bureaucratic-clerical-statistical system of intelligence."[3]

A key figure in Sekula's argument is Alphonse Bertillon, the French police official who invented anthropometry, the "scientific" study of the measurements and proportions of the human body. Sekula positions Bertillon as a "prophet of rationalization," akin to Frederick Taylor. He argues that Bertillon enabled photography to deliver on its archival promise through the creation of a system of classification that allowed untrained clerks to identify criminals with the efficiency and speed necessary in a modern world of telegraphs and trains. Bertillon's model, which reduced the multiple signs of the criminal body to a textual shorthand and numerical series, proved prescient for an emergent bibliographic science that "articulated an operationalist model of knowledge based on the 'general equivalence' established by the numerical shorthand code. This was a system for regulating and accelerating the flow of texts, profoundly linked to the logic of Taylorism."[4]

The central artifact of this archival practice is the filing cabinet. In this system of intelligence the act of classifying, of filing, transforms the identity of the referent. This last point is more implicit in Sekula's article, but for my argument it needs to be explicitly stated: to locate archives within a larger process makes apparent that archives do not neutrally store documents; rather, objects captured through archival practices are transformed into knowledge. Recent work in imperial history has provided thoughtful articulations of this argument. Tony Ballantyne, in this volume and elsewhere, has stressed the importance of archives both to colonial governance and to what he argues is the problematic use of the nation-state as the basic unit of analysis in imperial history.[5] Ballantyne draws on Matthew Edney's work and particularly Bernard Cohn's "investigative modalities": "the definition of a body of information that is needed, the procedures by which appropriate knowledge is gathered, its ordering and classification, and then how it is transformed into usable forms." These might include published reports, statistical returns, histories, gazetteers, legal codes, and encyclopedias.[6] I add identification documents, and specifically the passport, to this list.

The U.S. passport illustrates how in a period prior to the establishment of a National Archive, developing archival practices were articulated to a truth apparatus that sought to secure national identity and manage difference through citizenship. The passport and citizenship make explicit the link between nation and archive as mechanisms of exclusion.[7] A state archive works to articulate the nation and the state, to link them as the nation-state, and to offer claims and evidence for their shared story. In their contributions to this volume Ghosh, Sahadeo, and Ballantyne illustrate that the "historicization" of state archives can make explicit how archives create national narratives and, more importantly, national characters, prioritizing and privileging specific stories and peoples. Ballantyne goes further to argue that the nationalization of archives has limited the analytical units historians use. And elsewhere Antoinette Burton has pointed out that "clearly the politics of who or what is the subject of a 'national' history begs the question of how a subject becomes nationalized as well as what kind of disciplinary action such a process requires."[8] In this chapter I offer the passport as an archival technology as one way to answer this question. Using the passport to objectify archival practices as bureaucratic forces a historicization of the archive to engage with the production of particular identities and identity categories, to recognize the role of archival practices in the disciplining and nationalization of a subject.

Although my intention is to historicize the archive through foregrounding its origin in bureaucratic practices of rationalization, my encounters with NARA and the U.S. Department of State also emphasize the often arbitrary ways in which, in the name of "the state" and the objectivity of the archive, specific individuals control access to documents. Bureaucratic logics become bureaucratic practices and policies through bureaucrats, in this case "the people who inhabit the archive" as Ghosh puts it. However, both the analysis of bureaucratic rationalization and the individual application of bureaucratic policies serve as examples for a broader analysis of exclusion, objectivity, and rationalization.

The Archon and "the State"

In the opening pages of *Archive Fever* Jacques Derrida offers an etymology of the word "archive." He leads the reader via the Greek word *arkhe*, where things begin and where power originates, to the *archon*, the magistrate, and his house, his justice room, and his law books. The meaning of archive comes from the Greek *arkheion*, the superior magistrate's residence that also stored official documents. At this location the archon exercised the power of procedure and precedent and enabled laws to operate through his right to interpret documents.[9]

Over the last two years, as I have been denied access to the archive that I understand contains the historical records that discuss the development of the passport as an identification document, my thoughts have often returned to the archon. I now have a name for him, James E. Schwartz. Despite the fact that many of the documents in this particular archive date back to the nineteenth century, they remain in the possession of the Passport Office, an agency located within the Department of State. Or more particularly they are in the care of one long-term official—Mr. Schwartz. I discovered this after a month of phone calls to NARA and the Passport Office. An initial friendly phone call in which Schwartz informed me he had just completed an unofficial history of the United States passport has been followed by no contact except for a meeting that one of his superiors brought about. It seems that the archon does not consider that I have any right to interpret the documents in his archive, an archive that had been the Passport Office Library until officials decided that the precedent—which determined their policy decisions—no longer needed such a detailed (re)collection.

Miss Frances Knight established the Passport Library in the 1950s, early in her reign over the "independent, untouchable empire" that was then the Passport Division. Knight, "the J. Edgar Hoover of the State Department," ruled as chief of the division from 1953 until she was forced into retirement in 1977.[10] She had replaced Mrs. Ruth Shipley, who had been chief of the Passport Division for a quarter of a century, from 1928. In that time, as the only woman to head a division in the State Department, "Ma Shipley" herself became notorious, publicly represented as the individual who decided on all passport applications. Newspaper and magazine articles described Shipley through comparisons to schoolmistresses or chairs of ladies' clubs, in an attempt to make her authority imaginable for their readers.[11] Knight replaced Shipley when her often arbitrary refusals, which had been made orally, without recording reasons in files, became part of the controversy over the denial of passports to suspected communists in the early 1950s. For opponents Shipley's Passport Division was "government by a woman, rather than by law."[12] However, under Knight, "government by a woman" would continue to be daily practice in the issuance of passports, although it would be more carefully underwritten by documents.

It is not surprising that in the 1950s the Passport Division still had a large collection of documents dating back to the nineteenth century which Knight could turn into a library—not surprising if one considers the United States had only instituted a functioning national archive a little over a decade earlier. Although the United States had not followed the majority of European states in establishing centralized archives in the nineteenth century, there had been occasional moments of public concern about the preservation of historic government documents (especially those of the Continental and Confederation congresses). In 1810 Congress created a committee to investigate the state of government records and archives. The committee's suggestion for fireproofing some government rooms became moot when the British burnt entire government buildings during their occupation of Washington in 1814. The subsequent rebuilding of the nation's capital did include designated storage rooms, but not an official archive.[13] However, an archive existed in the form of a separate collection of historical documents, at least according to the 1829 *Encyclopedia Americana*, in which its editor, Francis Lieber, appended the following sentence to the Americanized version of its European-based entry on "archives": "The archives of the U. States are easily accessible, and proper recommendation will open them to anyone who wants to use them for scientific purposes."[14] What one would find within this collection is unclear. In 1825 a State Department clerk complained of the "disorder and confusion" of these records, while in 1827 a researcher found the records "much more full and perfect" than he anticipated.[15]

Throughout the rest of the century public calls for a centralized record hall or archive amplified as fires in federal offices became more frequent (254 between 1833 and 1915),[16] the developing bureaucracy produced more records, and the number of experts outside of the government who needed a national archive increased. Although in the decades prior to the Civil War some departments in the federal government had begun to haphazardly introduce bureaucratic procedures, the introduction of precision, standardization, and impersonal written rules accelerated in the postbellum era as the federal government expanded. In the second half of the nineteenth century each bureau in the State Department became responsible for copying, recording, and filing its own correspondence. These practices of archival rationalization prioritized efficient processes of retrieval and comparison that potentially allowed officials to prioritize and isolate what they considered important. Although not uniformly adopted, when introduced they indicated the gradual formation of a new set of epistemological assumptions and practices through which rationalization "simplified" the objects of government.[17] In the name of bureaucracy, practices of archival rationalization offered the possibility of stable, mobile, comparable, and combinable objects for government; thus through representation and transcription the production of knowledge can be said to have made an intervention in "reality." However, into the 1880s and 1890s many departments and bureaus continued to operate "in ways that were more reminiscent of small, informal, and even family-run businesses."[18] In the State Department long-term officials continued to be the primary source of the department's archival memory. A former assistant secretary of state described one such employee as the "personification of the department's work . . . its memory, its guiding hand."[19]

Within this environment it is perhaps not surprising that the American Historical Association (AHA) had little success in persuading the federal government to establish a national archive. After its formation in 1884 the AHA is credited with leading the campaign to centralize the government's historical records. In 1894 a member complained that the government had not "arranged, classified and calendared" its historical records, and the State Department had "no archivist who understands their management or has time to give to the needs of historical investigation." There were also accusations of unequal access and favoritism being shown to East Coast scholars, particularly those from Boston.[20] It took more than thirty years of false starts within Congress before appropriations for a national archive finally passed. The construction of a building began in 1931, and in 1934, one year before its completion, an act of Congress finally created occupants for the building. Consequently, the newly created "National

Archives Establishment" had no say in the planning of the building it would occupy.[21]

After moving into that building, the National Archives took shape in a tension between an initial perception that its cultural function would be to actively assist in the development of a national history and its subsequent incorporation in 1949 into the newly established General Services Administration, "a mammoth service-oriented bureaucracy" that pushed the National Archives into a records management role.[22] During the National Archives's first two decades, the State Department followed the archival path of most departments. Its officials exhibited an initial reluctance to give up ownership and control of records, but that reluctance then met the reality of an increasing lack of space, especially after document production accelerated in World War II. By 1960 the majority of State Department records more than fifteen years old were in NARA.[23]

Departments are not obliged to send their old documents to NARA. The Passport Office, for example, has regularly sent passport applications to NARA but apparently retained most of its historical records as part of its library. Some correspondence regarding passport refusals, passport fees, and passport fraud from the interwar period appeared in NARA in the 1990s. This, along with the State Department's nineteenth-century diplomatic correspondence, occupied me in my time at NARA. But the internal memos, reports, and correspondence not sent to NARA remain nominally in the possession of the State Department. Therefore, if a member of the public wants access to them, it is necessary to file a request under the Freedom of Information Act (FOIA). The online FOIA guide informs the reader that if you want *a document more than twenty years old,* it will be in NARA. This statement highlights the limitations of FOIA in my situation. I did not know what specific documents I wanted. I needed to access this sizable collection of historic documents as if they were in a publicly accessible archive; by box number or lot number, not as individual documents. Without these I had to submit a very general and broad request. This resulted in what my FOIA case manager described as "a most unusual request."

Three years later this FOIA request still has me at the behest of James E. Schwartz. As part of his work with these records he had prepared an index for at least half the collection. This 230-page index for 110 large archival boxes is crucial if I am to make a manageable FOIA request from what I would conservatively estimate is an archive of ten thousand documents.

This is an index of declassified documents that apparently range from 50 to 150 years old. These are not the documents themselves, and such is the number of documents that their summaries would be very brief and general to amount to only 230 pages. But it is an index Schwartz has spent two and a half years (at the time of writing) working through to remove anything that might be considered a security issue or privacy issue. When I question this delay, State Department officials inform me that issues of privacy have caused it. However, NARA archivists regularly remind me that dead people do not have any privacy, and people in documents who would now be over ninety are considered dead and, therefore, have no privacy. Given that I have narrowed my request to records prior to 1930, I can only assume there must be a lot of teenagers from the 1920s in this archive delaying my access; a delay possibly accentuated by a post-fall 2001 shortage of black ink in D.C. to block out their names.

Having spent more than a year successfully positioning myself as a victim, I have also had to recognize this is not just any index. These documents are no longer the Passport Office Library. They are a collection of boxes stored in an undisclosed location in the nation's capital. But more precisely they are Schwartz's archive; it is *his* archive and *his* index. In sorting through it and (importantly) writing a history of the passport from it, James E. Schwartz, the self-labeled "amateur historian," created his own archive. In a part of the government where neither should "properly" be, the archivist and historian have combined, and it seems there is no one, no body, who can (or cares to) tell him what to do. Is this what happens when you create your own archive in an environment that values precedent but has limited use for a past that apparently offers no guide or example to present events—and specifically for a past now contained in a narrative? There has been a noticeable confusion on the part of some State Department officials as to why I would want to write a history of the passport because Schwartz, in a labor of love, has written *the* history of the passport; an as yet unpublished manuscript that I have also been denied access to. *The* history of the passport is apparently not just *his* story. It came from the documents in front of him, and these officials believe I couldn't read anything different in them. Schwartz it seems has written an *objective* history, letting the documents speak the one story they can in "fact" tell. This form of history does not recognize interpretation. Instead it acknowledges a desire to tell the story of the past and an ability to do it through access to documents; it is a history constructed from facts not arguments. The writer's authority comes from the fact he or she has sat in the archive.

I have gained the impression that the failure to recognize interpretation leaves Schwartz believing that I am seeking access to his archive to replicate *the* history of the passport he has written. However, the Schwartz I have constructed makes explicit that it is his story written from his archive. In writing about the past, we all produce our own archive; we do not merely sit in an archive, nor do we sit in an archive on our own terms. The archive we produce has a politics of classification, of location, and of access. Having built his arkheion, the archon uses the power of the state to deny entry (please no passport to the archive jokes). But then perhaps the sense of victimization I created that produced this caricature of James E. Schwartz is caused by my own archive fever. Not Derrida's archive fever, rather the frustration of being denied access to documents, of spending weeks uncovering dead ends—in short the problems and frustrations archival research always promises and tends to deliver more efficiently than any requested documents. But beyond this "considered outburst," the other archival stories in this volume make very clear that specific interactions—at specific moments in the research process—with archival workers and the logics of the archives articulated in architecture, catalogues, and finding aids are a constitutive part of the histories we write; scholars who use archives need to critically analyze not only documents but also the institutions which house them.

Why Study the Passport?
Archival Rationalization and the Problematic of Identification

In recent years a handful of general passport histories have appeared in the form of articles and one book; however, with only two brief exceptions, the facts of the U.S. passport have remained buried in archives as if they were only of interest to genealogists, those seeking information on long-deceased relatives, not the writings of dead German and French philosophers.[24] The limited interest in the U.S. passport provided its own set of problems in the location and retrieval of its archivally bound history, problems which reveal a particular set of values that has structured a dominant form of historical interpretation. Histories of documents such as passports have remained unwritten because they were perceived as primary sources secondary to the objectives of academics. A passport was not considered a critical document to be interrogated; rather it provided a neutral record of facts. This interpretation of the passport as a document that does not need interpretation is made explicit in the location of passport applications and Passport Office records at the National Archives. (See Ballantyne's essay for a detailed discussion of the importance of the physical layout of an archive, in his case to produce specific discursive fields.) All government records in the National Archives associated specifically with the passport are located in Archive I in Washington, D.C. This is the original National Archive building from the mid-1930s. At the time of my research trips it had been partially closed for redevelopment as a more attractive tourist site. As Sahadeo's essay shows, "destination archives" for citizen-tourists are increasingly common.[25] At NARA this redevelopment was to showcase documents of recognized historical significance, such as the Declaration of Independence, as sites of public spectacle. However, Archive I remained open to allow continued access to the less "significant" documents it houses. These are primarily census records, pension records, immigration records, and passport applications that may be of use to those who wish to trace their family history. The majority of the remaining historic government records (including those of the State Department) are held in Archive II, in College Park, Maryland. Therefore, any general guide to the indexing of State Department records (among them, Passport Office records) or any documents that could be used in conjunction with passport records are located at a different archive, a 30- to 45-minute shuttle or public transport ride away from Archive I. The staff at Archive I do not see any purpose in copying these somewhat substantial indexes or records for use at their archive, and needless to say they cannot be removed from Archive II.

However, as I have already argued, I believe the history of the passport is far from self-evident and is open to numerous interpretations; the passport has multiple histories, which raise many questions and provide the basis for a large array of arguments. One of these histories provides a useful approach to the historicization of the archive in the United States. Using Sekula's concept of archival rationalization, the emergence of the U.S. passport as a modern identification document provides a site from which to trace the development within the state of archival practices outside of a national archive. Equally important, locating the production of the passport within archival logics makes explicit what is at stake in the institutional development of state archives. I have drawn a link between the passport and archives to underline the exclusionary work of more traditionally understood archives (especially state archives) to secure national identities through the articulation of nation and state, and the production of a new, national, identity. The archive works to ensure the existence of national populations by securing the borders of a national history and the actions of its characters.

The consequences of the passport as a document to separate citizens and non-citizens are the focus of published passport histories. In the most insightful discussion of this, Radhika Mongia analyzes debates about the contested definitions of subject and citizen, centered on proposed passport requirements in the British Empire around 1900. She uses the exclusionary potential of the passport to argue for the historically specific articulation of nation and state, initially within the empire and subsequently in the metropole. For Mongia nationality as an alibi for race functioned to explicitly and legally distinguish individuals through cultural competencies best understood as "cultural racism." She argues a cultural racism was "cross hatched" with nationalist movements in the colonial world, and the *congealing* of national boundaries around *territories* as much as *populations*. This is the framework for her argument that "cultural racism succeeds, precisely in securing an identity between people and territory such that they both come to be described as 'national' "; thus her interest in the passport as a "technology that nationalizes bodies along racial lines."[26]

While Mongia's article offers a provocative challenge to histories of the passport outside of the British Empire, in the context of this argument I am more interested in the exclusions that occurred in the archival practices which produced the document and the specific identity the passport provides evidence of. The "simplification" of information in the name of bureaucratization I have previously alluded to is apparent in attempts to standardize passport applicants from the second half of the nineteenth century. The requirement that applications be submitted on standardized forms accompanied by specific documentary evidence of citizenship (affidavits for native-born and court-issued certificates for naturalized citizens) produced citizenship as a usable, administrative fact.[27] The novelty of both dealing with the federal government and using documents as a form of identification frustrated many applicants who in these requirements perceived an official questioning of their honesty and the imposition of a particular identity over their claims to state what they considered to be their personal identity.

Through the introduction of these practices, officials sought to lessen the reliance on local "reputational knowledge" and practices of self-verification to produce an "official identity" which could be used to identify an individual in any future interactions with the federal government.[28] It also occurred during a period in which, as Rogers Smith has thoroughly documented, the federal government actively challenged the claims of individual states to determine which individuals could be declared U.S. citizens.[29] This internal challenge was frequently articulated through a challenge to the racial underpinnings of citizenship, both in the contested extension of citizenship to non-whites and in mid-century immigration, which saw "free white men" arrive in a variety and number beyond what many thought the founding fathers had intended when they used whiteness to determine fitness for citizenship.[30]

I label the passport a "technology of verification" to make explicit this specific relationship between identity and the centralizing practices inherent in the issuance of identification documents.[31] Following Peter Miller's reading of Michel Foucault, I define a "technology" as "a way of representing and *acting upon* processes and activities." A technology consolidates various processes and activities as an object—an object with integrity and coherence. The passport is not a technique; it is not a "neutral means of achieving certain ends without introducing any change of [its] own."[32] The passport is thus a *technology* of verification. A history of the passport as an identification document illustrates the historically specific contexts in which practices of verification emerge. The passport "verifies" the true identity of the individual in part by producing the truth of that identity through the valorization of particular technologies, procedures, and authorities both to establish the bearer as a citizen and to link the bearer to the document. The facts, statements, and citations that "verify" the passport as a legitimate and authoritative identification document are produced as true through claims to bureaucratic objectivity and "mechanical objectivity."[33] This is one approach to a question that initiated my dissertation: How did governments come to believe that a sheet of paper could identify an individual accurately enough to secure the borders of a nation-state?

After the federal government took control of the administration of U.S. borders in the late 1870s, the tentative attempts to use passports and other identification documents show that until the outbreak of World War I such documents were not considered to facilitate an accurate determination of an individual's identity. Immigrants were not required to carry identification documents, and officials generally ignored the documents issued to Chinese exempt from the Exclusion acts. In the latter case immigration officials trusted their own ability to verify the identity of Chinese as merchants and students from physical appearance, not some absent authority of Chinese government officials and U.S. diplomatic agents distilled into what they considered a questionable document.[34] It was only during and after World War I that an increased official perception of the value of identification documents led to sufficient enforcement of documentary evidence in the issuance of passports and visas for U.S. officials then to trust them to provide a useful form of individual verification at the border—that is, to perform the specific role of allowing "the state" to remember people who crossed the border at official points of entry.

I have intentionally anthropomorphized "the state" to emphasize that the archiving of information on individuals was an active process carried out in the name of a coherent unity, albeit by disparate departments and officials. The passport emerged as an important document in the development of what Matt Matsuda labels the "memory of the state." Matsuda uses this phrase to describe the incorporation of technologies such as anthropometry and fingerprinting into late-nineteenth-century French police practice, which allowed state officials to store identities and to then "easily" remember an individual's previous interactions with the state when they reappeared as suspects. In Matsuda's argument, memory is an object that is appropriated and politicized; it is nationalized, medicalized, aestheticized, gendered, bought, and sold. Borrowing from Henri Bergson, Matsuda also positions memory as an activity, an act of coordination.[35] Through documents, practices, and institutions that constitute its memory, "the state" does remember, it does act.

In contrast to Europe, in the United States the limited professionalization and nationalization of policing and a more casual approach to the control of immigration produced a more fragmented state memory of individuals before World War I. However, by the 1920s various state practices made explicit the emergence of a specifically modern problematic of identification: the collection, classification, and coordination of information. In the case of the passport, border security had been redefined; indirect surveillance through the collection of information became as important as the more direct surveillance of immigrants' bodies by officials at the point of entry or departure. The history of the emergence of the modern U.S. passport makes explicit how personal identification becomes thought of in terms of government as an archival problem.

In the 1920s the increased administrative reach of the federal government produced a documentary regime of verification in which documents begat documents to produce official identities verified through the archival memory of the state. By the beginning of the 1930s the United States finally achieved near universal birth registration.[36] Although neither citizens nor aliens were issued national identification cards, it became necessary for aliens to carry a variety of documents, particularly when leaving and entering the United States.[37] Public awareness of—and opposition to—increased federal documentation surfaced in the so-called "passport nuisance" and debates around J. Edgar Hoover's campaign for universal fingerprinting.[38] In part this opposition originated in an increasing awareness that collectively state agencies were treating individuals as objects of inquiry, as they historically had documented criminals and the insane. To counter this, officials explained the need to make identification practices universal through a discourse of safety in which collections of fingerprints would be repositories of protection.[39] The archival logic of identification practices supported this claim for the value of preemptive knowledge. To efficiently govern, the federal government needed to know the population collectively and through abstractions such as citizen or subject, as well as individually.

Archival rationalization is an important way to understand the bureaucratic objectivity that grounds the authority of identification as a record-keeping practice and the anticipatory logic that determined the collection of information on individuals. In Sekula's argument the filing cabinet becomes the site of bureaucratic objectivity. It provided a memory for state officials that did not depend on any specific individual, a memory determined by the organization of files, which accommodated the authorship of reports within the nonsubjective space of the cabinet. Developing Sekula's argument, Suren Lalvani emphasizes the file-cabinet-as-archive is a practical solution to a problem of volume, a solution constituted by both spatial and, more importantly, temporal variables.[40] The file cabinet is a "model of duration" that is constantly updated, premised on an archival logic of anticipation that allows for information to be easily retrieved. (In a very different context, this archival pact with the future is made apparent in the offering and collection of testimonies which Roque Ramírez describes in his contribution to this volume.)

As a modern identification document produced within an archival logic, the passport developed into an archival technology—a technology that classifies and orders evidence in the service of the production of truth to be used to explain who "we" are and where "we" come from. It does this in the anticipation of a future need to know. The archival pact with the future is established through the "rationalization" which Sekula foregrounds to articulate archival practices. The privileging of practices of classification, evidence, and authenticity prioritized documents as the basis of a retrievable state memory. Documents came to offer an objective, mobile memory that reduced dependence on the recall of specific individuals, especially when vertical files began to replace cumbersome and poorly indexed bound volumes. In 1906 Secretary of State Elihu Root, reportedly frustrated at being brought these volumes after requesting specific documents, introduced a vertical filing system in which documents were stored in cabinets not volumes.[41]

The passport as an archival technology makes explicit that the varied and diverse archival practices Sekula groups under archival rationalization are practices which partially (in all senses of the word) structure the evidence used to produce the "truth" of national identity for the individual and the state. The passport also emphasizes that before there was an institutional archive, archival practices were utilized to produce truth through a logic of exclusion. This focus on archival practices clarifies that in the name of "the archive" particular technologies and procedures are valorized and prioritized to arrange documents, to produce knowledge that can be more easily consulted. That is, even before documents have been classified in an archive, they have been constructed as "investigative modalities," their very documentary form effecting what has been recorded.

In taking archival practices outside of their specific institutional location and following their dispersal through other sites, "the archive" can be more effectively historicized. The distortions offered in the claims to "objectivity" and "authenticity" granted an archive become more apparent. A focus on technologies recognizes the archive as a domain which orders and makes relevant specific narratives and identities. For, as Michel Foucault argued, "this question of 'who exercises power?' cannot be resolved unless that other question, 'how does it happen?' is resolved at the same time."[42]

Notes

1   Antoinette Burton, *Dwelling in the Archive: Women Writing House, Home and History in Late Colonial India* (New York: Oxford University Press, 2003), 251. See also Tony Ballantyne, "Archive, Discipline, State: Power and Knowledge in South Asian Historiography," *New Zealand Journal of Asian Studies*, 3, 2 (June 2001): 87–105; Carolyn Steedman, *Dust: The Archive and Cultural History* (New Brunswick, N.J.: Rutgers University Press, 2002). The "archival turn" is not limited to history. See the special issue "The Poetics of the Archive" in *Studies in the Literary Imagination* 32, 1; and the two special issues on the archive in the *History of the Human Sciences* 11, 4 and 12, 1.

2   Burton, *Dwelling in the Archive*, 18; and see Allan Sekula, "The Body and the Archive," *October* 39, 3 (1986): 3–64.

3   Sekula, "Body and Archive," 45.

4   Ibid., 57.

5   Ballantyne, "Archive, Discipline, State"; Ballantyne, *Orientalism and Race: Aryanism in the British Empire* (London: Palgrave MacMillan, 2002).

6   Bernard Cohn, *Colonialism and Its Forms of Knowledge: The British in India* (Princeton: Princeton University Press, 1996), 5. See also Matthew Edney, *Mapping an Empire: The Geographical Construction of British India, 1765–1843* (Chicago: University of Chicago Press, 1997). For a critical review of this literature see Ballantyne, "Archive, Discipline, State."

7   Within the broad Foucauldian framework of this argument, I consider it necessary to recognize the passport and the archive can be sites of "domination" not "power." For an explanation of this difference see Michel Foucault, "The Ethic of Care for the Self as a Practice of Freedom," in *The Final Foucault*, ed. James Bernauer and David Rasmussen (Cambridge: MIT Press, 1988), 11–13.

8   Antoinette Burton, "Who Needs the Nation? Interrogating 'British History,'" *Journal of Historical Sociology* 10, 3 (1997): 238.

9   Jacques Derrida, *Archive Fever: A Freudian Impression*, trans E. Prenowitz (Chicago: University of Chicago Press, 1996), 1–2. Steedman, *Dust*, 1–12.

10   Sanford Unger, "J. Edgar Hoover Leaves the State Department," *Foreign Policy* 28 (1977): 114, 110.

11   Harold Hinton, "Guardian of American Passports," *New York Times*, April 27, 1941, SM21; Andre Visson, "Watchdog of the State Department," *Independent Woman* 30 (August 1951): 225–26, 234; Helen Worden Erskine, "You Don't Go If She Says *No*," *Colliers*, July 1953, 62–65.

12   Erskine, "You Don't Go," 62.

13   Donald R. McCoy, "The Struggle to Establish a National Archives in the

United States," in Timothy Walch, ed., *Guardian of Heritage: Essays on the History of the National Archives* (Washington D.C.: National Archives and Record Administration, 1985), 2.

14 Francis Lieber, ed. *Encyclopedia Americana*, vol. 1 (Philadelphia: Carey, Lea and Carey, 1829), 349. McCoy, "The Struggle to Establish," 5.

15 Milton Gustafson, "State Department Records in the National Archives: A Profile," *Prologue* 2, 3 (1970): 176.

16 McCoy, "The Struggle to Establish," 1.

17 In an argument about modern statecraft James Scott labels practices of rationalization and standardization "state simplifications" and outlines five characteristics of such simplifications: (1) interested, utilitarian facts; (2) written (verbal or numerical) documentary facts; (3) static facts; (4) aggregate facts; (5) standardized facts. Scott, *Seeing Like a State: How Certain Schemes to Improve the Human Condition Have Failed* (New Haven: Yale University Press, 1998), 3, 80.

18 Cindy Aron, *Ladies and Gentleman of the Civil Service: Middle-Class Workers in Victorian America* (New York: Oxford University Press, 1987), 130.

19 Graham Stuart, *The Department of State: A History of Its Organization, Procedure and Personnel* (New York: Macmillan Company, 1949), 130.

20 Gustafson, "State Department Records," 177.

21 Virginia C. Purdy, "A Temple to Clio: The National Archives Building," in Walch, ed., *Guardian of Heritage*, 20.

22 James Gregory Bradsher, "The National Archives: Serving Government, the Public and Scholarship, 1950–1965," in Walch, ed., *Guardian of Heritage*, 52. Also see Donald McCoy, *The National Archives* (Chapel Hill: University of North Carolina Press; 1978); and Nathan Reingold, "Clio's Handmaidens Uncovered?" *Reviews in American History*, Sept. 1979, 418–26.

23 Gustafson, "State Department Records," 183.

24 John Torpey, *The Invention of the Passport* (Cambridge: Cambridge University Press, 2000), 93–103, 117–20; Lesley Higgins and Marie-Christine Lep, " 'Passport Please': Legal, Literary and Cultural Fictions of Identity," *College Literature* 25, 1 (1998): 94–95, 115–17.

25 Here I am echoing Barbara Kirshblatt-Gimblet's argument in *Destination Culture: Tourism, Museums, and Heritage* (Berkeley: University of California Press, 1998).

26 Radhika Mongia, "Race, Nationality, and Migration: A History of the Passport" *Public Culture* 11, 3 (1999): 527–56; see 534–35, 528.

27 Galliard Hunt, *The American Passport: Its History and a Digest of Laws, Rulings, and Regulations Governing Its Issuance by the Department of State* (Washington, D.C.: GPO, 1898), 46–47.

28 For "reputational knowledge," Jennifer Mnookin, "Scripting Expertise: The History of Handwriting Identification Evidence and the Judicial Construction of Reliability," Public Law and Legal Theory Research Papers Series, University of Virginia School of Law, December 2001, 165. For "official identity" Pamela Sanker, "State Power and Record-Keeping: The History of Individualized Sur-

veillance in the United States, 1790–1935" (Ph.D. diss., University of Pennsylvania, 1992), 26, 29–30.

29 Rogers Smith, *Civic Ideals: Conflicting Visions of Citizenship in U.S. History* (New Haven: Yale University Press, 1997).

30 Matthew Frye-Jacobson, *Whiteness of a Different Color: European Immigrants and the Alchemy of Race* (Cambridge, Mass.: Harvard University Press, 1998).

31 I would like to thank Vik Kanwar and Lacey Torge for helping me conceptualize the passport as a technology of verification.

32 Peter Miller, "On the Inter-Relation between Accounting and the State," *Accounting, Organizations and Society* 15 (1990): 333; emphasis added.

33 Lorraine Daston and Peter Galison, "The Image of Objectivity," *Representations* 40 (fall 1992): 81–128.

34 Kitty Calavita, "The Paradoxes of Race: Class, Identity and 'Passing': Enforcing the Chinese Exclusion Acts, 1882–1910," *Law and Social Inquiry* 25, 1 (winter 2000): 1–40; Erika Lee, *At America's Gates: Chinese Immigration during the Exclusion Era, 1882–1943* (Chapel Hill: University of North Carolina, 2003).

35 Matt Matsuda, *The Memory of the Modern* (New York: Oxford University Press, 1996), 121–42, 6–8.

36 U.S. Bureau of the Census, *Historical Statistics of the United States: Colonial Times to 1957* (Washington, D.C.: GPO, 1960), 12–14.

37 As well as a passport and visa, aliens also had at different times in the 1920s to carry proof of the payment of income taxes and a reentry certificate issued before departure.

38 Simon Cole, *Suspect Identities: A History of Fingerprinting and Criminal Identification* (Cambridge, Mass: Harvard University Press, 2001), 197–99, 247–49.

39 Courtney Ryley Cooper, "Hold for Identification: Twenty-Five Hundred Fingerprints a Day," *The Saturday Evening Post* 207 (January 19, 1935): 66; Thorsten Sellin, "Identification," in *Encyclopedia of the Social Sciences*, vol. 7 (1932): 573–74.

40 Suren Lalvani, *Photography, Vision and the Production of Modern Bodies* (Albany: SUNY Press, 1996), 115.

41 Gustafson, "State Department Records," 179.

42 Michel Foucault, "On Power," in Lawrence Kritzman, ed., *Michel Foucault: Politics, Philosophy, Culture* (New York: Routledge, 1988), 103.

Tony Ballantyne

Mr. Peal's Archive

MOBILITY AND EXCHANGE IN HISTORIES OF EMPIRE

ARCHIVAL REPOSITORIES, libraries, museums, and monuments cluster around the heart of New Zealand's capital city, Wellington. Although the city was not planned in such a way as to project power in the coherent and imposing manner of other imperial cities such as Washington, D.C., London, or New Delhi, and lacks the orchestrated modernity of Australia's capital, Canberra, Wellington's center contains a complex of buildings that forcefully embody and enact the power of the state. Nestled around the junction of Lambton Quay and Molesworth Street, the parliamentary precinct contains the Old Government Buildings, the Beehive (which houses the members of Parliament and the prime minister's office), and the Parliament Buildings, while the state's judicial powers are embodied in a nearby network of buildings on Molesworth Street (the High Court), the corner of Bowen and Stout streets (the recently created Supreme Court), and Featherston Street (the Waitangi Tribunal). The state's memory and the nation's identity are preserved and projected at a network of institutions that are located close to these sources of power. While the national museum, Te Papa o Tongarewa, sits on the edge of Lambton harbour, Archives New Zealand (on Mulgrave street) and the National Library (on Molesworth Street) are immediately adjacent to the parliamentary precinct, embodying the New Zealand state's deep investment in archiving the nation's past.

This essay explores one body of materials within this large, multi-institutional archival complex. It focuses on my own encounter with an archive collated by Samuel E. Peal and the ways in which this archive forced me to reconceptualize my own work and to explore a new way of imagining the structure of the British empire. Peal was a leading botanist and ethnographer based on India's northeast frontier who donated his ethnographic archive to the Polynesian Society on his death in 1897. Peal's bequest forms one small part of the substantial collections of manuscripts, books, and other materials that made up the archive of the Polynesian Society, which now forms the Polynesian Society Collection (PSC), housed within the Alexander Turnbull Library (ATL), which in turn is organizationally and physically part of New Zealand's National Library. In discussing this material, the essay tells three archive stories. It begins by reconstructing the story of Peal's collection itself—charting Peal's efforts to develop a substantial archive of materials relating to the "primitive peoples" of Asia and the Pacific, the place of this collection within imperial ethnography, and Peal's involvement with the Polynesian Society. The second archival story narrated here is my own "discovery" of this particular collection a century after Peal's death and the role this engagement played in shaping the transnational vision of the structure and culture of the British empire articulated in my monograph *Orientalism and Race: Aryanism in the British Empire*.[1] The third archival story recounted is that of the increasing marginalization of Peal's work within the Polynesian Society, the history of anthropology, and the intellectual history of British imperialism during the twentieth century, as both anthropology and history became increasingly tied to the nation-state and its narratives. In other words, I narrate the neglect of Peal's papers, which form a largely forgotten archival fragment within the Polynesian Society Collection, a body of material that has stood at the very heart of New Zealand's intellectual history over the last century. The essay concludes by reflecting upon these stories, to ask what collections such as Peal's can tell us about the institutional structures, forms of intellectual sociability, and correspondence networks that conditioned the production of knowledge within imperial systems. By foregrounding complex processes of collection, ordering, and dissemination that were central to the production of colonial archives, this essay marks a further step toward mapping the interregional and transnational structures that enabled the integrative, if highly uneven, work of modern empires.

Mr. Peal's Archive

Samuel E. Peal made his name on India's northeast frontier as a naturalist and a leading expert on the Naga peoples. Peal does not seem to have found much success as a tea-planter, as his correspondence records his strained financial circumstances, and his obituary in the *Calcutta English-man* noted that it was "perhaps a mistake that Peal was a tea-planter at all."[2] He did play a central role in opening up Assam's natural resources to the colonial state and private British interests, identifying materials for paper production and locating rich deposits of petroleum and coal in the vicinity of Margherita, information that enabled the exploitation of Asia's first significant oilfield.[3] As a naturalist, he gained some renown for his discovery in the early 1870s of the "tea-bug" which had until then blighted the tea plantations of Assam, and he also identified several new species of snakes, beetles, and butterflies during his travels in hilly frontier lands of Assam and Burma.[4] In addition to publishing his botanical researches in the Agri-Horticultural Society's *Journal*, Peal established a substantial reputation amongst the many missionaries, social reformers, military officers, and colonial officials who developed interests in ethnography, and as a result emerged as a significant man of science in late-nineteenth-century India.[5] His published anthropological work explored the language, material culture, social organization, and ancient history of the Naga peoples and included essays on issues as diverse as Naga architecture and tree-climbing techniques.[6]

Late in his life, Peal's wide reading on the anthropology of the Pacific stimulated his interest in the question of Polynesian origins, an issue he believed his research in northeast India could shed significant light upon. He became an important member of the Polynesian Society, a scholarly society dedicated to study of the "manners and customs of the Oceanic races" established in New Zealand in 1892.[7] Soon after its establishment, Peal contributed two essays on Māori origins to the society's journal and was invited by one of the society's joint secretaries, S. Percy Smith, to serve as a "Corresponding Member."[8] After establishing good relationships with both Smith and Elsdon Best (a leading expert on Māori), Peal offered to donate his ethnographic materials to the Polynesian Society in 1896, and his papers were deposited with the society following his death on July 29, 1897.[9]

Peal's archive is a small fragment in the very large and rich collection of material that the ATL holds relating to the Polynesian Society. In addition to the 495 files of the main "Polynesian Society Collection" (Ms-Group-0677), the Turnbull holds an additional nineteen boxes, twenty-seven volumes, and one folder of material in the society's "Further Records" (80–115 series), and the society's substantial anthropological library. Given the wide scope of the Polynesian Society's activities and the energy of its editors and chief contributors, substantial amounts of material relating to the intellectual and political context of its operation are in the large collections of individual papers produced by the driving forces behind the early operation of the society: S. Percy Smith, Edward Tregear, and Elsdon Best.[10]

Materials relating to Peal can be found scattered through these different collections. The main body of his own archive is divided into three sets of materials. The bulk of his correspondence (which contains newspaper clippings, word lists, and extensive discussion of Asian and Pacific ethnography), is held within the main Polynesian Society Collection. These papers record his exchanges with some thirty-two correspondents, a veritable who's who of anthropology in Asia-Pacific at that time.[11] A second group of Peal materials is held within the PSC "Further Records" series. This is a variegated body of records, featuring clippings from newspapers and journals, off-prints of Peal's publications, his printed tables of comparative vocabularies (complete with his annotations), diaries, notes and itineraries from his field trips, draft essays, a few items of correspondence, a notebook, and ethnographic sketches.[12] A significant amount of supplementary manuscript material relating to Peal is scattered through the larger PSC collection and in the individual papers of its leading figures: six letters from Peal and the draft of Smith's obituary for him are in a loose collection of correspondence and manuscripts for publication (MS-Papers-1187–270), while he also figures in the society's correspondence (80–115–02/03 and 80–115–02/05), and his work runs through the exchange of letters between Smith and the prominent "committee man" and colonial scientist Dr. A. K. Newman in Newman's papers (Ms-Papers-1187–269). The third main concentration of Peal materials is a sizable collection of thirty-five dictionaries, grammars, and ethnographic works that he donated to the society. Although this may seem a small body of texts, it seems that this collection formed at least 41 percent of the library at the point of Peal's death, and this resource was crucial in providing evidence for the work of anthropologists intent on tracing Māori back to India and interpreting Māori religion as a form of transplanted Hinduism.[13]

Peal's collection was produced through two avenues of research. His initial published work, which focused on Assam, its peoples, plants, and natural resources, was grounded in extensive travel in the region and firsthand description: this material is represented in the field notes, sketches, and journals that are prominent in the Peal collection. In the 1880s, Peal began to supplement this fieldwork with extensive comparative reading, both in his own library and in the libraries of Calcutta. Material relating to this broader research forms the bulk of his archive and is of particular relevance to the history of Polynesian anthropology. In researching the place of the peoples of Assam in the broader pattern of "racial history," Peal believed that he had identified some similarities between Polynesian languages, material culture, and religion, and the customs of the tribal peoples of northeast India. In light of these "racial customs," Peal encouraged Smith and his society to pursue the study of racial affinities. Such research would finally fix the place of Polynesians in the history of civilization, since Peal hoped it would confirm his belief that Polynesians ultimately shared their origins with the "Dravidians, Kols, IndoMongols . . . Malays, Dyads [Dyaks], Papuans, the Massai, Madagascar races, Australians & Formosan savages."[14] Correspondence with Smith and Best convinced him that Māori belonged to a large racial group which spanned east Africa, the mountainous regions and the south of India, most of Southeast Asia and the Pacific. Peal believed that he had identified twenty "singular racial customs" which established the *"former racial unity"* of these peoples.[15] These included the use of "platform dwellings" and other common forms of material culture. Two of Peal's sketches held in the PSC demonstrate this argument and underscore the profoundly comparative sensibility of his work. These documents merge visual representations of the social practices and forms of material culture that Peal identified as establishing the common racial heritage of these apparently diverse peoples with a type of ethnographic shorthand that enabled philological and ethnographic comparison of these decontextualized images.

In an 1897 article in the *Journal of the Polynesian Society* Peal elaborated his theory of "ethnic diffusions," which, he argued, explained the peopling of India *and* the Pacific. According to Peal, in the ancient past various peoples entered north India from central Asia and Tibet. The first of these migrants were the "Nigreto" or "Australo-Dravidian" peoples, who were soon followed by the Tibetan or "Himalic" races. These two waves of migration merged together and intermarried, producing new communities including the Khol, the Bihari, and the Khasia. In India's distant pre-Aryan past these new hybrid racial communities, which Peal termed the "Mon-Anam" or "Gangetic" race, dominated Upper Burma, the Gangetic basin, and much of the north Indian hinterland. A new wave of Tibetan migrants eventually displaced the Mon-Anam, forcing them eastward,

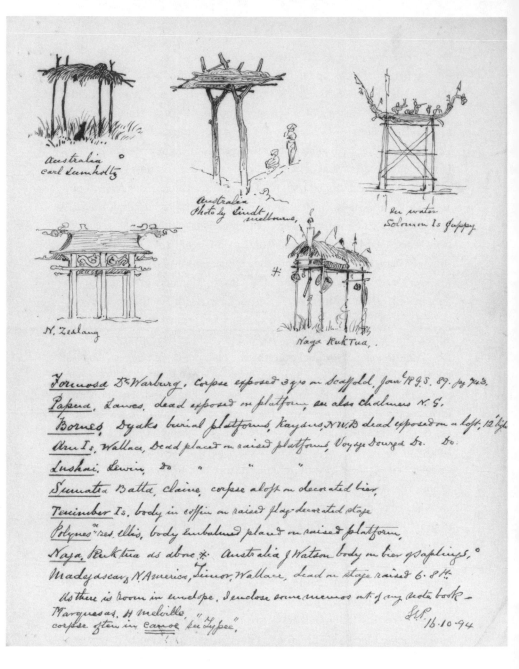

(above) Peal's sketch of "platform dwellings" in Asia and the Pacific. MS-Papers-1187-270, Polynesian Society Collection, Alexander Turnbull Library, Wellington, New Zealand.

(facing page) Peal's sketch of the "racial customs" that supposedly connected the Pacific to Asia. MS-Papers-1187-270, Polynesian Society Collection, Alexander Turnbull Library, Wellington, New Zealand.

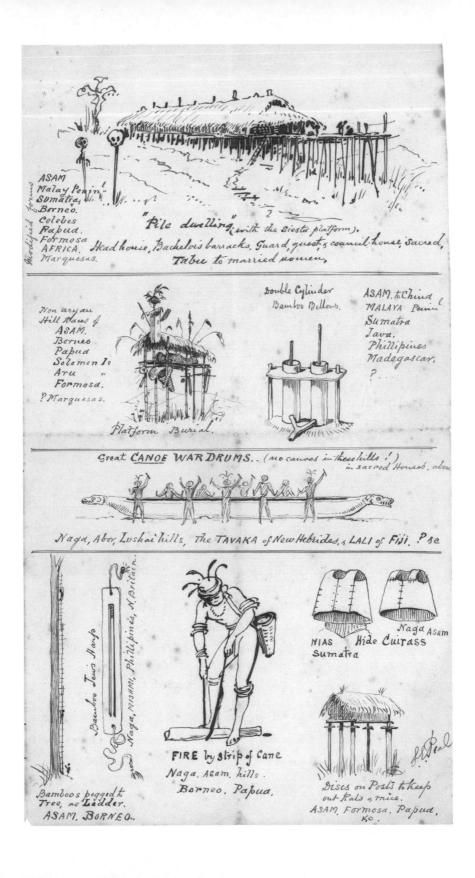

ASAM
Malay Penin?
Sumatra,
Borneo.
Celebes
Papua.
Formosa
AFRICA.
Marquesas.

"Pile dwelling" (with the siesta platform).
Head house, Bachelor's barracks. Guard, guest, & council house, sacred,
Tabu to married women.

Non aryan
Hill Klaus of
ASAM.
Borneo
Papua
Solomon Is
Aru "
Formosa.
? Marquesas.

Platform Burial.

double Cylinder
Bamboo Bellows.

ASAM. to China
MALAYA Penin?
Sumatra
Java.
Phillipines
Madegascar.
? . . . .

Great CANOE WAR DRUMS.. (no canoes in these hills!)
in sacred Houses, above

Naga, Abor, Lushai hills, The TAVAKA of New Hebrides, & LALI of FIJI. ? &c

Bamboo Jews Harp.

Naga, MISHMI, Phillipines, N. Britain.

FIRE by strip of Cane
Naga. Asam. hills.
Borneo. Papua.

NIAS
Sumatra

Hide Cuirass

Naga Asam

Bamboos pegged to
Tree, as Ladder.
ASAM. BORNEO.

Discs on Posts to keep
out Rats & mice.
ASAM. Formosa. Papua.
&c.

where they settled in Southeast Asia and finally in Polynesia. En route to Polynesia the Mon-Anam were exposed to a variety of new cultural forces, most notably Aryan influences resulting from the introduction of Hinduism into Java and the incursion of Muslim traders into Southeast Asia. The resulting veneer of Aryan cultural accretions could not, however, disguise the essentially pre-Aryan nature of Polynesian society.[16] Peal's work here fed into the central debate that energized early anthropological debate in Polynesia: Where was the ancient Polynesian homeland, and, if it was in India, was it to be located in the "Aryan" north, the "Dravidian" south, or amongst the tribal peoples of South Asia's deserts, hills, and frontiers?[17] In asserting that Māori origins were non-Aryan, Peal aligned himself with a tradition of scientific racism that questioned the emphasis placed on Māori capability by many humanitarians, missionaries, and Māori leaders. As the product of pre-Aryan tribal India, Māori were primitive, unassimilable, and likely to die out in the face of New Zealand's "Aryan" European settlers.[18]

The PSC records the influence that Peal's work exercised over Polynesian anthropology, particularly the study of Māori culture, over the three decades after his death. Peal's letters to Smith, Best, and Tregear and his publications in the society's *Journal of the Polynesian Society* (*JPS*) encouraged New Zealand anthropologists' continued engagement with Indian ethnography and Indocentric visions of Māori culture. Alfred K. Newman, for example, attempted to provide the definitive case for Indian origins in his *Who Are the Maoris?* (ca. 1912). During his lengthy research for this volume, Newman used the Peal collection extensively and discussed Peal's work at length in his correspondence with S. Percy Smith. Ultimately, Newman was convinced by Peal's case and concluded that the Nagas of Assam "were the *mothers* of our Maoris."[19] More significantly, correspondence with Peal, who believed that phallus worship was one of the "racial customs" that linked the far-flung members of the Mon-Anam racial family, encouraged Best's work on Māori fertility rites and phallic symbols. In a letter to Peal in 1895, Best reported that he was "much pleased . . . at having discovered the remnants of that most ancient cult—the worship of the phallic symbol, it never having been noted in N.Z. before."[20] Following E. B. Tylor, Best believed that Māori mythology and religion contained important "survivals" from ancient forms of religious practice, especially phallus worship. Best documented these survivals in an important article in *Man* in 1914, which recorded Māori beliefs "concerning the inherent power of the organs of generation in the *genus homo*," and in his massive *Tuhoe* (1925).[21]

But by the 1930s Peal's influence had waned. His correspondents had died (Smith in 1922 and Tregear and Best in 1931), and the work of the pioneering members of the PSC was subjected to critical reassessment. As a result of this process of generational change, the intellectual focus of the Polynesian Society itself was turning to increasingly detailed studies of Māori material culture and the history of Māori culture within New Zealand. While Best's work as an ethnographic collector remained highly respected, the grand diffusionist interpretations formulated by Best, Smith, and Tregear were attacked by David Teviotdale and H. D. Skinner, who jointly served as editor of the journal.[22] A struggle between two generations of scholars and an emergent paradigm shift is recorded in the *JPS*, a reorientation that is powerfully embodied in the work of another Polynesian Society member, Raymond Firth.[23] Bearing the clear imprint of Malinowski's functionalism, Firth's *Primitive Economics of the New Zealand Maori* (1929) set a new agenda for the study of Māori culture. Where Tregear, Smith, and Best constructed a genealogy of Polynesian culture and "excavated" the remnants of Asian influence in modern Māori culture, Firth foregrounded the material frameworks of Māori society and emphasized the importance of internal structures and dynamics.[24] Within a decade of the publication of Firth's landmark study, it was clear that the work of anthropology was unraveling the local development of culture, rather than identifying its distant roots in ancient homelands.

As a result of this paradigm shift, Peal's work was marginalized. The word lists, sketches, and dictionaries which he believed shed light on the ancient origins and history of Māori were of little use to scholars who wanted to understand Māori history within a more narrowly Polynesian or, more commonly still, national framework. When a later generation of scholars, particularly D. R. Simmons, M. P. K. Sorrenson and James Belich, came to identify the Polynesian Society's activities as occupying a central position in settler culture and as providing the central intellectual apparatus of colonization, they exhibited no interest in Peal.[25] Even though he was an influential figure in molding diffusionist interpretations of Māori culture, he was based in India, and his work did not fit easily within the national narratives of identity formation that these historians worked within. Moreover, in the world of modern professional anthropology Peal's racial theories and diffusionist speculation was at best irrelevant and, at worst, an embarrassing reminder of anthropology's amateur and imperial origins. Peal's erasure was reinforced in M. P. K. Sorrenson's *Manifest Duty* (1992), which reconstructed the intellectual and institutional history of the society in considerable detail but paid little attention to the international contexts of the Polynesian anthropology or the imperial networks that energized the field until at least World War II. In narratives that framed the Polynesian Society within the disciplinary history of anthropology or the development of a national identity, Peal had no place.

Encountering Peal

But different historians bring radically different perspectives to bear upon archives and find very different stories in the same repository. For me, encountering the Peal collection was crucial in crystallizing the transnational approach to British imperial history that I elaborated in *Orientalism and Race: Aryanism in the British Empire.* In narrating my own encounter with Peal's papers, I hope to record the context in which I found a body of material that profoundly reoriented my research and my view of empire. The process of working through Peal's papers and reconstructing, however partially, their afterlife in New Zealand, pushed me toward a realization of the complex intellectual traffic that operated over great distances within the empire. The conversations and exchanges recorded in the Peal papers were carried out through a restless and seemingly ceaseless shuttling of paper—letters, postcards, telegrams, the purchase and lending of books and periodicals, and the exchange of field notes, word lists, sketches, and off-prints—between individuals and institutions scattered across the empire and frequently occupying very different subject positions (in terms of wealth, political power, intellectual standing, and cultural capital). Such exchanges moved freely across both modern nation-state boundaries and the analytical units (e.g., settler colonies vs. military-garrison colonies) that historians use to order their work, and played a fundamental role in the history of imperial knowledge production and the cultural lives of many individuals within the empire.

Randoph Starn has recently observed that although "we [historians] routinely sift through and evaluate our documents, we tend to use archives without thinking much about them as institutions."[26] Despite the recent "archival turn" in the humanities (of which this collection is a part),

anthropology vs history

historians in general have been slow to scrutinize their archives, reluctant to explore the institutional history of archives, hesitant to examine the cultural and political work carried out by these institutions, and, most tellingly, loath to chart their individual experience of archives. This is in stark contrast to anthropology, for example, where critical reflections on fieldwork have become commonplace. Indeed, Nicholas Dirks argues that while anthropologists have regularly reflected critically upon their "arrival stories"—which narrate their arrival, especially their "originary arrival," in the field—historians have been slower to record their own archival "arrival stories" and submit them to critical scrutiny.[27]

The significance I have come to attach to the Peal papers was itself the product of the particular moment of my arrival in the archives and the questions I was grappling with at that point in time. Our archival stories should not only recount our work with certain bodies of evidence in particular spaces, but should also record our own political concerns and intellectual preoccupations at the specific moments in which we read, transcribe, paraphrase, and ponder source material. Verne Harris's gloss on Derrida's *Archive Fever* has stressed, "Scholars are not, can never be, exterior to their objects. They are marked before they interrogate the markings, and this pre-impression shapes their interrogation."[28]

My interrogation of the Peal papers was the product of my own research trajectory across the former British empire. In late 1996, the research for my Cambridge Ph.D. brought me home to New Zealand. Initially, at least, my Ph.D. was conceived of as an exercise in comparative history; it would be, I imagined, a project that would explore the development of colonial knowledge in two very different contexts: Punjab and New Zealand. I hoped that by focusing on Punjab, which shared with New Zealand a similar chronology of contact and colonialism,[29] I would be able to explore the divergent place of knowledge production in settler colonies as opposed to India, which by the mid-1990s had assumed a central position in the literature of colonial knowledge as well as in postcolonial thought. This research necessitated work on archival materials held in India, Australasia, and the United Kingdom itself and entailed conscious reflections upon the place of these archives within the project of empire building.

I returned to New Zealand earlier than planned, after my research in India was truncated. Even though I had promptly applied for my research visa for India on arriving in England in the summer of 1995, there was no sign of it a year later when I embarked on the Indian leg of my research. (I did, in fact receive this visa, but only some time after the submission of my Ph.D. thesis.) Once I had arrived in India, it was clear that without the visa I would not be able to work in the National Archives of India and instead focused my efforts in the Nehru Memorial Museum and Library in Teen Murti House, New Delhi, as well as several smaller archives and university libraries. Given the tremendous ability of both the Raj and Indian presses to produce vast bodies of documentation, I quickly assembled a substantial body of material relating to social change in Punjab (and north India more generally) between 1780 and 1914. In terms of my project, it became clear that only the National Archives held a significant collection of resources that I could not access in Britain, so after visiting various historical sites and pilgrimage centers in Himachal Pradesh, Punjab, and Rajasthan, I traveled on to New Zealand.[30]

Early in 1997, I traveled from my hometown of Dunedin to Wellington to carry out research at the ATL, which is one of New Zealand's most important archives, with particularly rich nineteenth-century holdings, and which is now housed within the National Library. I planned to focus my research on the PSC within the ATL, researching the history of this learned society and the work of its linguists, ethnographers, folklorists, historians, and anthropologists on New Zealand's frontiers. In stumbling across the Peal papers on my second day in the archive, I made a "discovery" that radically transformed my research and my vision of history more generally. I spent the best part of a month reading the Peal papers, tracing connections between this collection and other holdings at the ATL, and thinking about how Peal's collection of ethnographic material relating to the "native races" of Asia and the Pacific would sit both within my comparative project and within the historiography of empire.

Unlike other users of the PSC, who typically focus on the relevance of its ethnographic material for understanding the history of Māori or other Pacific peoples or who use the archive as a window into the "intellectual colonization" of New Zealand, I was interested in the way in which the archive sat within a broader imperial context of knowledge production. And slowly I realized that I had identified a body of material that offered a series of compelling insights into the role of archives in the development both of racial thought and of imperial power. Peal's papers were particularly valuable for me because they not only allowed me to connect a host of figures in whom I was already interested (from Best, Smith, and Tregear to the leading North American expert on Polynesia, Horatio Hale;

from E. B. Tylor to the leading evangelical ethnographers, R. N. Cust and William Wyatt Gill) but also revealed the complex operation of a very wide network of ethnographers who were engaged with the same set of questions: What was the relationship between the peoples of Asia and the Pacific? And how was colonialism transforming indigenous peoples? How could these "ancient traditions" be preserved? And how could scholars work together to ensure the efficient recording of information relating to these peoples and how should this information be inserted into the wider story of human development?

In a very stark way Peal's correspondence and networks of exchange forced me to recognize that ethnography and early anthropology were not simply comparative projects, but also connective projects. The store of comparisons between Māori and Indians, especially Punjabis, that I had collected was not born only out of the comparative sensibility of pre-functionalist anthropology, as I had assumed, but rather was fashioned out of the imperial networks that brought missionaries, colonial officials, humanitarians, and pioneering anthropologists together into a shared intellectual space. Although Peal was based in Assam, not Punjab, his papers forced me to entirely rethink my project. They made me grapple with the question of the spatial structure of the empire and, most immediately, forced me to open out my approach to South Asia, moving from a narrow regional focus on Punjab to a more flexible analytical strategy that sought to understand, however imperfectly, both regional variation within British India and British India's place within the larger structures of empire. In materializing the transnational production of imperial knowledge in such a stark way, Peal's work encouraged me to think of my work not as an exercise in *comparative history*, but rather as a *connective history* that would reconstruct the institutions, networks, and discursive fields that provided the fundamental intellectual structure of the empire.

Thus, in effect, Peal forced me to entirely reconceptualize my project. Eight of my nine proposed chapters were scrapped, and my attention now focused firmly on the chapter I had planned on the place of racial thought in colonial knowledge, which was recast as the basis of the entire thesis in an attempt to carefully delineate a set of imperial debates over racial origins and the networks that enabled these debates. Large amounts of the archival research I had conducted in India was now "archived" for future use, while the remainder of my research in New Zealand and an extended period of research on my return to Britain in mid-1997 focused on the

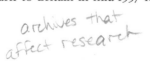

operation of these knowledge networks. Most crucially, the insights I gained from Peal provided a "key" with which I reread the archival evidence I had kept and continued to gather. But in time, Peal himself was overshadowed by the host of other networks I uncovered and by the time the revised version of the Ph.D. was published as *Orientalism and Race* less than five hundred words (of an 85,000-word volume) were devoted to his work. Although Peal and his archive were significant figures in *Orientalism and Race*, the text itself gives no indication of Peal's role in shaping the volume or my vision of the imperial past. In *Orientalism and Race*, like so many other historians before me, I masked my own archival story, an ironic silence in a book that underscored the importance of knowledge-gathering and archival spaces in the dynamics of empire-building.

Disjunctures in the Archive

To this point, it seems that my attachment to the Peal materials remains a particular one, not shared by other historians of the Polynesian Society, colonialism in New Zealand, or the intellectual history of imperialism. In fact, during a recent research trip to the Alexander Turnbull Library in December 2003, one staff member checked the computerized record of usage of the Peal papers and discovered that I have been the only person to the use the papers over the last decade.

How do we explain this recent neglect? I have already suggested the PSC and the JPS allow us to locate the neglect of Peal and the marginalization of his archive within the disciplinary history of anthropology, but this can also be identified as a product of the disjuncture between the actual content of the collection and the broader cultural context of its current archival repository. Just as Durba Ghosh's essay in this collection shows that archivists can play an important role in shaping the research trajectory of historians, the buildings that house archives can suggest certain types of historical vision and legitimate particular historical narratives. Achille Mbembe has suggested that the "status and power of the archive" is produced by the "entanglement of building and documents." The physical space of archives—in their organizational structure, architecture, decoration, signage, and other forms of cultural encoding—provide crucial cues to the kinds of stories that institutions and archivists imagine residing in their collections or want to be produced form their repositories. In other words, as Mbembe has suggested, the "inescapable materiality" of archival spaces provides "an instituting imaginary" that guides those who work with the "fragments of life" recorded and interred therein.[31]

When I was working through the Peal collection in 1997, I was increasingly aware of a profound disjunction between the highly mobile and imperial intellectual visions that were the very stuff of the Peal collection and the "instituting imaginary" of the National Library itself. The addresses, letterheads, postmarks, stamps, postcards, and bookplates found in Peal's collection were testament to the construction of powerful networks that cut across the boundaries of emergent nation-states, but it is housed in an archive that erases such imperial structures as it frames its collections within a postcolonial vision of New Zealand as a nation. In this regard, the National Library plays a key role in projecting national identity and, following Craig Robertson's argument in his essay above, it works to "articulate the nation and the state, to link them as the nation-state, and to offer claims and evidence for their shared story." It is crucial to recognize the particularity of the structure of the state and the specific ideology that underpins debates over national identity in contemporary New Zealand. Since the mid-1970s, New Zealand public institutions have slowly, unevenly, and painfully been reshaped around a particular postcolonial vision: biculturalism. Biculturalism is grounded in the legal power and cultural weight ascribed to the Treaty of Waitangi signed by representatives of the Crown and over five hundred Māori chiefs in 1840. In effect, biculturalism imagines New Zealand as containing two distinct populations—Pakeha settlers of European (but mainly British) descent and the *tangata whenua* (the "people of the land"), Māori. Biculturalism recognizes the authority of traditional Māori leaders, the value of Māori language, culture, and other *taonga* (treasures), and the state's role to protect these rights promised by the treaty.

In keeping with the state's recognition of the Treaty of Waitangi and its cultural implications, the National Library (which houses the Alexander Turnbull Library and the Peal collection) explicitly projects a bicultural image and follows bicultural practice. This commitment to biculturalism is not hidden away in the institution charter or mission statement, but rather shapes the library's public image, its architecture, decoration, and organization. Its bilingual name (the National Library of New Zealand / Te Puna Mātauranga o Aotearoa), the use of both English and Māori signage, the significant space and resources attached to Māori language materials and resources relating to Māori pasts, and the prominence of Māori art within the National Library reflect a concerted attempt to decolonize the archive.³²

These practices, however, not only give Māori materials legitimacy within the archive and respect the particular needs and interests of Māori users, but also place the institution firmly within the apparatus of the state and the bicultural historical vision that the state has projected over the last two decades. Biculturalism has functioned as an increasingly authoritative framework for narrating the nation's past and this narrative is clearly reinforced in the National Library. Library users enter the building by passing under an impressive *pare* "Kūaha: Entranceway" carved by Raymond Smith, John Manukau, and Bernie Rongo, which not only represents Te Wānanga (the source of all knowledge) but also the signatories of the Treaty of Waitangi.³³ The Library's use of the art of Cliff Whiting also forcefully communicates this vision of the library as an embodiment of the nation's bicultural ideology and a repository of its bicultural past. Whiting's *Te Wehenga o Rangi rāua ko Papa*, which represents the separation of the primordial parents Rangi and Paptuanuku, not only dominates the main reading room of the National Library, but it has also been used as a key element within the multimedia presentation that greets users of the National Library's web site. The web site explains this presentation as passing through three stages ("the natural New Zealand landscape and inhabitants in pre-European settlement times"; "the discovery, colonisation and development of early New Zealand society, to illustrate the birth of industry, and the foundations of today's structured society"; and "evolution of the mind and of knowledge, ideas, art, thought and intellectual progress"), replicating a common three-stage model for narrating New Zealand's past: pre-contact Māori history, contact and its outcomes, and the development of modern bicultural New Zealand.³⁴

While it is important to recognize that biculturalism has enabled the slow redress of Māori claims under the treaty and a significant redistribution of resources and authority, it must also be seen as a national imaginary that allows the state to produce a partial and self-legitimating vision of the past. In effect, as a historical vision biculturalism rests upon the prioritization of national identity and the marginalization of histories of ethnic and religious identity, migration, and intellectual connection that transect or transcend the boundaries of the nation-state.³⁵ In this regard, Foucault's formulation in *The Archaeology of Knowledge*, that "the archive is first the law of what can be said," helps us read the cultural work done by the architecture and decoration of the National Library. The archive's physical layout, signage, and artwork help fix the "rules" within "which we speak," enabling particular discursive fields and investing some arguments with particular legitimacy.[36] In the case of the National Library, the archive—both as a physical space and as the product of collation, classification, and cataloguing—does not entirely preclude heterodox readings of the materials it houses, but it does provide a series of powerful ideological statements about the kind of visions of the nation and its past that library users should produce.

Even though the Alexander Turnbull Library was the product of the assiduous efforts of an individual collector rather than the nation-state itself, it has been thoroughly assimilated into the nation-state's archival complex. Although the library's users' guide notes that the ATL is a "storehouse of words, pictures, and sounds that tell us about the activities of people in New Zealand and in the Pacific," it quickly shifts from this broad vision of the ATL's spatial framework to stress that it holds "the *nation's* collection."[37] This slippage between the regional scope of the ATL's collection and its status as a national collection is not entirely out of step with the vision of Alexander Turnbull himself, who identified his library as "the nucleus of a New Zealand National Collection." But he saw his library as fulfilling an important role within broader imperial and narrower local contexts as well as serving the needs of the nation. His will actually bequeathed the library to "His Majesty the King" and stressed the local significance of the collection, specifying that it should "constitute a Reference Library" to be located in "the City of Wellington."[38] This emphasis on both the imperial and the local significance of the library has been erased over time, and since the ATL was absorbed into the National Library in 1966, it has been firmly harnessed to the nation, despite the fact many of its collections (such as the PSC) sit uneasily within a national framework.[39]

Rereading the Archives of Empire

Nicholas Dirks has observed that the "archive is simultaneously the outcome of the historical process and the very condition for the production of historical knowledge."[40] For historians of empire this is a particularly important insight, as it reminds us that the materials that we use to craft historical narratives that scrutinize empire-building are typically products of that process. By their very nature, the constituent components and processes of empire-building (from slavery to colonial administration, from the movement of capital to free migration) operated across significant distances and cut across the boundaries of states. Following Dirks's formulation, this means that the archives produced by empire-building must themselves be imprinted by and record the operation of these "cross-cultural" or "transnational" processes. Yet many historians continue to conceptualize colonial archives as a window on the development of a particular colony. Dirks reminds us that colonial knowledge was "not an archive that was imagined as the basis for a national history, for it was only designed to reap the rewards and to tell tales of imperial interest," but in many colonies, as Durba Ghosh shows in her account of responses to her research in India and Britain or as this exploration of a New Zealand repository demonstrates, this is precisely how colonial archives are frequently used by historians.[41] In other words, New Zealand historians transfigure these collections, which were fundamental in the creation of colonial authority, into repositories where "our" national story might be found. Certainly, treaty breaches, violence, and the alienation of Māori resources figure prominently in these national narratives, but such acts are often assigned to the chaotic early chapters of the nation's past and as such serve to offset the "progress" that began in the 1890s and has accelerated rapidly since the 1960s. Thus, these narratives tend to contain this conflict within an essentially progressive national narrative, rather than reading either cultural conflict or colonial archives themselves as the product of the crucial material and ideological context of New Zealand's development: empire-building.

By locating the work of both Peal and the Polynesian Society within a complex series of imperial networks and a significant tradition of anthropological work that transplanted Indian models to the Pacific, *Orientalism and Race* produced a very different vision of the production of racial thought in colonial New Zealand. Rather than following recent work on the "representation" of Māori or older studies that saw colonial texts as simply the product of nineteenth-century British racism, my work viewed this "Indocentric" tradition of research within the broader dynamics of the textualization of colonized cultures, the creation of learned institutions across the empire, and the comparative sensibility of imperial ethnology and anthropology. This transnational vision of imperial knowledge production did not view colonial anthropology in New Zealand or New Zealand colonial history more generally as a self-sufficient story, but rather interrogated and reframed these "national" stories within an explicitly imperial framework. On reflection, this approach had three advantages. First, it undercut the assumption of some New Zealand historians that Aryanism was a concern unique to the New Zealand frontier, rather revealing the profound entanglement of this vision of racial history with discourses of colonial governance and theories of racial contact throughout the empire. Second, only careful attention to the broader intellectual history of the empire made the allure of Indocentrism in colonial New Zealand explicable. Where earlier New Zealand historians viewed colonial Aryanism as the product of amateur speculation or read it anachronistically through the lens of the Holocaust, the power of this discursive field was less surprising if it was read against the backdrop of the profound intellectual impact of the British "discovery" of Indian languages and Hinduism, by locating it within the institutional development of colonial science in New Zealand or by framing it within the histories of the production, circulation, and consumption of imperial print culture. Third, this approach suggested at the broadest level, that nineteenth-century colonial culture was by its very nature porous, fluid, and energized by the circulation of people, ideas, and ideologies through an almost bewildering array of imperial institutions, networks, and forms of cultural production. In proposing the metaphor of the "web" as a heuristic tool for imperial history, *Orientalism and Race* tried to make sense of these forms of cultural traffic and refocus our historiographical attention on the structures and discourses that integrated the empire (however imperfectly) and underwrote colonial domination. Although not universally applicable to the imperial past, I still find the "web" metaphor a useful heuristic tool for my work as I continue to explore knowledge production and the mobility of culture within the British empire, problematics that necessitate the reconstruction of institutions and media operated over long distances as well as a sensitivity to questions of scale and the layering of social relationships.

Here, I have revisited Peal's archive to foreground the centrality of exchange and mobility in the making of a particular imperial archive. In so doing, this essay questions the overwhelming emphasis on the intimate connection between the archive and the modern nation-state within recent work on the "archive." Although the "new social history" and the "cultural turn" have in some instances produced a less state-focused vision of the archive than that associated with the long-ascendant traditions of economic and political history,[42] much of the recent "archival turn" in the humanities has focused on the relationship between the archive and state, especially the state's legal powers.[43] The sophisticated literature on the development of colonial knowledge in South Asia, for example, has generally focused on the enumerative projects, classificatory regimes, and coercive instruments that enabled the state to levy taxes, wage war, and discipline restive segments of the colonized population. But the unquestioned priority attached to state-produced archives has worked to reinscribe the boundaries of colonial states and, in effect, has tended to remove particular colonial states from the larger imperial systems within which they operated. Although the literature on colonial knowledge production in New Zealand is much smaller and less theoretically engaged, the existing work has also taken the nation-state as its unit of analysis, with little attention devoted to particular locales, broad regional patterns, or structures that transect or transcended the colony's boundaries.

Peal's collection, of course, cannot be easily framed within this national narrative, as both his web of correspondents and his diffusion vision of "racial history" cannot be contained by the nation-state. His archive encourages us to rethink the analytical units that historians use and, more generally still, the very operation of the empire itself. Peal's papers remind us that the individual colonies developed within a larger imperial system and demonstrate the centrality of the creation and dissemination of knowledge in both the intellectual and political life of the empire. Examining the role of archives in the creation of what Mrinalini Sinha has identified as the "imperial social formation," or what C. A. Bayly has termed the empire's "extended political arena," or what I have conceived as the "webs of empire" seems a crucial way ahead for historians of British empire-building.[44] Mapping the reach of colonial archives across space and time, as well as noting their recurrent concerns and highlighting their silences, will not only deepen our understanding of these crucial nodes within the empire but also enrich our reflections on how to make sense of imperialism itself.

Notes

1 Tony Ballantyne, *Orientalism and Race: Aryanism in the British Empire* (Basingstoke: Palgrave-Macmillan, 2001).

2 *Calcutta Englishman*, August 12, 1897.

3 S. E. Peal, "Bamboos for Paper Stock," *Indian Forester* 8 (1882): 50–54; Rajen Saikia, *Social and Economic History of Assam, 1853–1921* (New Delhi: Manohar, 2000), 151; S. N. Visvanath, *A Hundred Years of Oil: A Narrative Account of the Search for Oil in India* (New Delhi: Vikas, 1990), 12–14.

4 These include Peal's Keelback snake (*Amphiesma pealii*) and Peal's palmfly (*Elymnias pealii*.)

5 A good indication of Peal's status as an ethnographic collector are the illustrations and discussions in Gertrude M. Godden, "Naga and Other Frontier Tribes of North-East India (continued)," *The Journal of the Anthropological Institute of Great Britain and Ireland* 27 (1898): 2–51. Also see Verrier Elwin, *The Nagas in the Nineteenth Century* (Oxford: Oxford University Press, 1969), 40, 379.

6 E.g., S. E. Peal, "The Nagas and the Neighbouring Tribes," *Journal of the Anthropological Institute* 3 (1874): 476–81; "Vocabulary of the Banpara Nagas," *Proceedings of the Asiatic Society of Bengal* 42 (1873): appendix I, 30–37; "On the 'Morong,' as Possibly a Relic of Pre-Marriage Communism," *The Journal of the Anthropological Institute of Great Britain and Ireland* 22 (1893): 244–261; "The Communal Barracks of Primitive Races," *Science* 20, 507 (October 1892), 228–29; "Note on the Origin and Orthography of River Names in Further India," *Proceedings of the Royal Geographical Society and Monthly Record of Geography* 11, 2 (1889): 90–95; "Note on Platform-Dwellings in Assam," *The Journal of the Anthropological Institute of Great Britain and Ireland* 11 (1882): 53–56.

7 The circular with this description of the society is held in the archives of the Polynesian Society, Wellington: ms-Papers-1187-125, psc.

8 Peal accepted the offer of the position of corresponding member in a letter to Smith, January 25, 1893, ms-Papers-1187-270, psc.

9 S. Percy Smith to J. Macdonald, undated, 80-115-03/13, psc.

10 S. Percy Smith (e.g., ms-Papers-3527, qms-1833, qms-1837 and ms-1962-2011), Edward Tregear (e.g., ms-Papers-055, ms-Papers-1264, and ms-Papers-1187-185), and Elsdon Best (e.g., ms-Papers-0072, ms-Group-0312, and ms-0173-0176). All of these are held in the atl.

11 This material was originally classified as part of the psc's "Series 10: Ethnological Manuscripts Collection," but during the recent reorganization of the psc it was redesignated ms-Papers-1187-113.

12 In folders 80-115-11/09 and 80-115-11/10, psc; these were recently reclassified from 80-115-11/IA and 80-115-11/IB.

13 This figure is calculated on the basis of my research in the society's library and an inventory of titles I assembled from the library's now defunct card cata-

logue. Some eighty-five volumes in the library were published in or before 1897, but, of course, some of these volumes may have been purchased or donated after 1897, making this a conservative estimate of the significance of the Peal bequest.

14   S. E Peal to Percy Smith, January 17, 1892, MS-Papers-1187-270, PSC.

15   Peal to Smith, undated but marked received April 16, 1892; ibid.

16   S. E. Peal, "The Ancestors of the Maori," *JPS* 6, 24 (1897): 174–76. Most of these terms were originally linguistic designations, but Peal was skeptical of the significance of philology and preferred to read them as racial terms.

17   See my *Orientalism and Race*. The consensus of recent linguistic and anthropological research is that Polynesians are part of the larger Austronesian language family, which is normally divided in four: Atayalic (north Taiwan); Tsoiuc (central Taiwan); Paiwanic (north, central, and eastern Taiwan); and finally the larger Malayo-Polynesian family. Linguistic evidence suggests that the Polynesians migrated into the southern Pacific via Melanesia from their ancient and distant homeland in south China–Taiwan, but many of the distinctive Māori linguistic and cultural forms took shape in the Pacific itself. See Douglas G. Sutton, ed., *The Origins of the First New Zealanders* (Auckland: Auckland University Press, 1994).

18   Ballantyne, *Orientalism and Race*, 70–74, 78–79.

19   Alfred K. Newman to Smith, August 13, 1906, and March 5, 1907; and Smith to Newman March 2, 1907, MS-Papers-1187-268, PSC.

20   Best to Peal, undated, but in response to Peal's letter dated August 31, 1895, MS 80-115-02 / 02, PSC. Peal's letter to Best has not survived, but the phrasing of Best's letter suggests that he was replying to specific questions raised by Peal. Best also sent Peal a newspaper clipping describing a Māori "phallic cult"; Best to Peal May-June 1893, MS-Papers-1187-113, PSC.

21   Elsdon Best, "Maori Beliefs Concerning the Human Organs of Generation," *Man* 14 (1914): 132–34; *Tuhoe: A Sketch of the Origin, History, Myths, and Beliefs of the Tuhoe Tribe of the Maori of New Zealand, With Some Account of Other Early Tribes of the Bay of Plenty District* (New Plymouth: The Polynesian Society, 1925).

22   David Teviotdale, "The Material Culture of the Moa-Hunters in Murihiku," *JPS* 41, 162 (1932): 81–120; H. D. Skinner, "Maori Amulets in Stone, Bone, and Shell," *JPS* 41, 163 (1932): 202–211.

23   M. P. K. Sorrenson, *Manifest Duty: The Polynesian Society over 100 Years* (Auckland: The Polynesian Society, 1992), 75–78; Ballantyne, *Orientalism and Race*.

24   Raymond Firth, *Primitive Economics of the New Zealand Maori* (London: Routledge, 1929). Also see his "Economic Psychology of the Maori," *Journal of the Royal Anthropological Institute of Great Britain and Ireland* 55 (1925): 340–62.

25   D. R. Simmons, *The Great New Zealand Myth: A Study of the Discovery and Origin Traditions of the Maori* (Wellington: A. H. & A. W. Reed, 1976); M. P. K. Sorrenson, *Maori Origins and Migrations: The Genesis of Some Pakeha Myths and Legends* (Auckland: Auckland University Press, 1979); James Belich, "Myth, Race and Identity in New Zealand," *New Zealand Journal of History* 31 (1997): 9–22.

26 Randolph Starn, "Truths in the Archives," *Common Knowledge* 8, 2 (2002), 388.

27 Nicholas B. Dirks, "Annals of the Archive: Ethnographic Notes on the Sources of History," in Brian Axel, ed., *From the Margins: Historical Anthropology and Its Futures* (Durham: Duke University Press, 2002), 48.

28 Verne Harris, "A Shaft of Darkness: Derrida in the Archive," in Carolyn Hamilton, Verne Harris, Jane Taylor, Michele Pickover, Graeme Reid, and Razia Saleh, eds., *Refiguring the Archive* (Cape Town: David Philip, 2002), 65. Derrida made this point with regards to Yoshef Yerushalmi's positioning himself as "exterior to his object" in his *Freud's Moses* (*Archive Fever: A Freudian Impression*, trans E. Prenowitz [Chicago: University of Chicago Press, 1995], 53).

29 For both there was sustained contact with Europeans developing in the 1770s, formal annexation in the 1840s, and sustained armed struggle against the British in the 1840s.

30 During these travels, I became painfully aware of how large my personal colonial archive was, as I heaved my overstuffed bags on and off trains, tuk-tuks, and rickshaws. Eventually, the power of paper won over modern fabric, as my pack split, and archival integrity was only restored when I purchased a massive canvas gear bag from a merchant who sold surplus from the Indian army, an ironic repository given the army's role in "disciplining" Punjab in the wake of Indira Gandhi's assassination.

31 Achille Mbembe, "The Power of the Archive and Its Limits," in Hamilton et al., eds., *Refiguring the Archive*, 19, 22.

32 In this regard, the National Library stands in stark contrast to the India Office Library on Blackfriars Road where I did a great deal of my research (or its current home in the new British Library at St. Pancras), which continues to be dominated by portraits of East India Company officials and an ambiance of imperial authority.

33 The National Library commissioned this work in 1990, the sesquicentennial of the treaty.

34 See the "sitestory" on the library's web site, www.natlib.govt.nz.

35 Tony Ballantyne, "Writing out Asia: Race, Colonialism and Chinese Migration in New Zealand history," in Charles Ferrall and Paul Miller, eds., *East by South* (Wellington: Victoria University Press, 2004).

36 Michel Foucault, *The Archaeology of Knowledge and the Discourse on Language*, trans. A. M Sheridan Smith (New York: Pantheon, 1972), 129, 130.

37 *Alexander Turnbull Library* (guidebook), September 2003, 1.

38 "Notes from the Second Codicil to the Will of Alexander Horsburgh Turnbull," MS-Papers-0006-35, ATL.

39 The relationship between the ATL and the National Library was fiercely debated during the 1960s; see "Some Comments on the Proposed National Library," undated mss, MS-Papers-0006-35, ATL.

40 Dirks, "Annals of the Archive," 48.

41 Nicholas B. Dirks, *Castes of Mind: Colonialism and the Making of Modern India* (Princeton: Princeton University Press, 2001) 108–9.

42 G. Thomas Tanselle has observed that when "when historians speak of 'archives,' they usually mean collections of documents that accumulated as the by-products of the operation of organizations (often governments) and business firms" ("The World as Archive," *Common Knowledge* 8, 2 [2002]: 402).

43 The key locus for this is Derrida's discussion of the Greek derivation of "archive" in *Archive Fever*.

44 Mrinalini Sinha, *Colonial Masculinity: The "Manly Englishman" and the "Effeminate Bengali" in the Late Nineteenth Century* (Manchester: Manchester University Press, 1995); C. A. Bayly, "Informing Empire and Nation: Publicity, Propaganda and the Press 1880–1920," in Hiram Morgan, ed., *Information, Media and Power through the Ages* (Dublin: University College Dublin Press: Dublin, 2001), 179; Ballantyne, *Orientalism and Race*.

Horacio N. Roque Ramírez

A Living Archive of Desire

TERESITA LA CAMPESINA AND THE EMBODIMENT

OF QUEER LATINO COMMUNITY HISTORIES

ON DECEMBER 10, 1999, in a crowd of about fifty Latinos, queer and straight, Teresita la Campesina took to the stage in a well-known community- based arts gallery in San Francisco's Latino Mission District.[1] She prefaced her singing performance that evening with a speech about the importance of voting in the 2000 mayoral election in San Francisco. For the first time in the city's history, one of the two candidates in the runoff election was openly gay.[2] Teresita insisted that all those who cared about gay rights must vote for Tom Ammiano; otherwise the city would see a return to the days of police raids and actions against homosexuals. Even though she had not voted in over thirty years, she admitted, Teresita felt that it was time to stand up and go to the polls to defend her rights as a male-to-female (MTF) transgender, as a queer. Linking the city's mayoral race with the impending California Knight Initiative (Proposition 22), designed to outlaw the recognition of same-sex marriages in California, she called for action against the return to a repressive social climate for queer folk.

Teresita followed her impassioned testimonial at Galería de la Raza with a moving performance. Singing live in Spanish several of the famed Mexican *ranchera* singer Lola Beltrán's classic songs of loss and love, she delivered a strong rendition of Beltran's best-known melodies. That Beltrán had passed away in 1996 made Teresita's songs that much more important to her as the continuation of the Mexican legend, in her own queer way.[3] These were not songs for simple emotional engagement. They were Teresita's tribute to a Mexican singer of great popularity on both sides of the border (national and sexual borders that is), a cultural icon belonging not to the elite but to the masses and their quest for a homeland. Teresita performed the feelings and memories of loss and recapture, a complex structure of historical and cultural relations played out on the battle for land and for bodies. It was, as the playwright Jorge Ignacio Cortiñas commented, loss as strength, with a transgender Latina enacting not just a queer performance, but also a Mexican and Latino national treasure.[4]

Three years before this performance, Teresita had already set the record straight with me. In March 1996, during my first recorded oral history interviews with her, she made it quite clear who it was that I had the privilege of interviewing. "You're talking to me," Teresita said forcefully,

> a pioneer . . . so please wake up and smell the coffee! [followed by thunderous laughter] . . . I made it, and I am here testifying. But, that's why I tell all the people of today: you're so lucky to have these privileges. But then you're not, because in my days they didn't have AIDS. I caught syphilis, gonorrhea—I'm not ashamed to admit it, everything I've done in my life. . . . I was very young and gorgeous. And I'm an old lady now, but looking whory, you know. I refuse to lay down and look like an antique. I like to varnish myself. And so I keep my voice and they say I still look good. . . . They say I've got a young face sometimes. "Oh, she's had facelifts." *So what?!* . . . But I had the money to do it with, and I didn't work *a day for it*. I made it all through prostitution. Because, why lie?[5]

To be "testifying" was no trivial matter for Teresita. A Latina MTF-transgender artist living with AIDS at the age of fifty-five by the time I met her, she found in me a willing and interested listener. Making her musical rounds in Bay Area bars, restaurants, and house parties since the late 1950s, she remained a living legend, not necessarily always or universally well liked, but firmly grounded in what she believed she represented in history. Deeply committed to laying out a living historical record of queer desires, Teresita was not going to be ignored.

In this brief excerpt she explained that she was "testifying": she assumed a responsibility to pass on the stories and histories of the fallen, those who came before the current generations of queer Latino / a community builders. She spoke about her tricks of the trade, how it is that she had survived for more than five decades as a poor, illiterate, transgender Latina, but one with the gift of a powerful voice she always used to her advantage. Talented, proud, outrageous, and big-mouthed, Teresita was an ideal queer narrator if there was ever one. Bridging many periods, peoples, and places, the times and tales of Teresita, famous and infamous, help us understand the contours of queer *and* Latino life in the region.

This essay discusses the life and memory of San Francisco's male-to-female transgender Latina artist, the late Teresita la Campesina (1940–2002). Her life history frames a living archive of evidence that responds to both the whiteness of queer archiving practices and the heteronormativity of Latino historiography. I discuss Teresita's living historiographical intervention in three interrelated areas: the importance of her life as an oppositional history; her life history as an example of what Michel Foucault argued as a "general history" and alternative to a "total history"; and the question of mourning in the time of AIDS and related ongoing creation of community archives for documenting the loss of life.

Teresita's Queer Life: A Memory Narrative of Opposition

As Tina M. Campt notes:

> We think of memory as individual, subjective, and specific. We consider it always partial, inherently flawed, and ultimately intrinsically unreliable in that it can give us only a single individual's perception of the past, colored by that individual's very subjective interpretation of events or experiences. But although memory is in fact all of these things, it is also far more than just an individual's cognitive process. Memory is also a deeply social process through which individuals construct and articulate their relationship to the world and the events transpiring around them, both now and then.[6]

Teresita walked and lived a great deal of her life alone. An outcast transgender Latina, she made a public life in bars and clubs, in homes, and in the street. But after the shows, the parties, and the excitement, home was often a place she occupied alone. The specificity of Teresita's memory captures both of these dimensions: the loneliness that comes from being a "historical pervert" and the complete rejection from blood family, and the collective celebration of life found in the events, venues, and feelings she shared with thousands in public. This "deeply social process" in oral memory that Campt describes as a characteristic of what she in turn refers to as "memory narratives" was part of the archival contribution of Teresita: an individual's perceptive and felt interpretation of social life—subjective, specific, partial—standing against the detached and monumental over-shadowing of national and institutional histories.

Born in Los Angeles on November 29, 1940, to Mexican immigrants, Alberto Nevaerez was the last child of twenty-one. Early on, by the age of five, young Alberto, who eventually changed his name officially to Alberta, began to sing at home. He made his natural gift public in the family by hiding behind their large radio and projecting his voice as if it were actually coming out of the box. Ten years later and in her teens, already pushed out of her home for being *joto*, a "fag" in her Mexican context, Alberta no longer had to pretend. Broadcast live from Hollywood's Club Guatemala under the artistic name of "Margarita," Alberta sang her way across the Los Angeles radio waves via the Spanish-language KW, her renditions of Lola Beltrán making her a very popular artist. Most listeners, of course, likely had no idea who Margarita really was, a fact the club's promoter did not care about as long as club patrons and profits kept coming and, to avoid police surveillances, Alberta did not mess with the men at the club.

Despite her popularity, and the ease of finding sex in the streets of L.A., life for Alberta, like that for most visible "perverts" in the 1950s, was rough. Like many, Alberta was repeatedly arrested for "masquerading," for bending gender identity through dress in public. In postwar Los Angeles, the Hollywood industry manufactured a virulent white heteronormativity that Spanish-speaking brown queers like Alberta found it difficult to navigate. And so in 1958 she set out toward the already presumed Mecca for gays, the famed international city of perverts, San Francisco. The *ranchera* singer and grassroots storyteller was a legend from the moment of her arrival until her death on the 12th of July, 2002.

Teresita was especially known in the city's Latino Mission District. As an artist, she was one of the most important personalities in its queer Latino history, creating through her art a very visible (queer) Latino community. Despite being HIV-positive for more than ten years, she continued to make space for herself, singing to and educating whoever cared to listen to her legendary stories. Peppered with camp, live reenactments of outrageous episodes, and often plain old too-much-information, Teresita made history come alive. Literally walking around with her art form and her history in her mouth, Teresita gave voice to Spanish language, to Latino

Young Alberto Nevaerez in Los Angeles, circa 1941. *Courtesy of Alberta Navaerez / Teresita la Campesina and Sergio Iníguez.*

(below) Alberta Nevaerez / Teresita la Campesina, at a residence in San Francisco's Mission District, circa 1980. *Photo by and courtesy of Daniel Arcos.*

cultural traditions, and to Latino queers in a city with an overwhelmingly white queerness.

Public about her HIV-positive status, Teresita took her singing seriously. She reminded her audiences that she was not only still living despite the toll of AIDS, but that she was an artist—a singer and a good one at that— not simply what she disparagingly referred to as a "lip-sync drag queen." She demanded attention and respect not only for her craft but also for what she felt she represented for queer generations. For Teresita, her living testimony spoke to queer survival despite great odds, a complex narrative of past conditions and struggles and the present need for action—all dramatized through her singing and live narrations. Her narrative served as evidence that in the past things were not that easy for queer Latinos. She enacted a history of queer Latinas and Latinos who did not find accepting communities but who had to fight for them. In her life, in her body, and in her singing, Teresita manifested queer desire as uncompromising and challenging.

For marginalized communities constantly involved in struggles for visibility, political identity, and space—the business of "cultural citizenship"— *testimonios* about their existence are critical acts of documentation.[7] On behalf of her "sisters and brothers"—as she referred to the thousands of other queer Latino community members who made the Bay Area their home for decades, people living with AIDS, those dead and dying from the disease, and her queer family—Teresita took every possible opportunity to narrate her relationship to the city. She connected those who had come with her and were no longer by her side with those from recent generations who she felt must understand what came before them. She also boasted about her own life constantly, flirting, often showing off, on more than one occasion literally raising her blouse and displaying her breasts. To shock and to provide re-gendered historical evidence, Teresita's revelation of her own body was literal queer evidence. Triangulating the lives of those she remembered, her own body, and those she entertained, Teresita was living historical content and interpretation.

Storytelling, autobiography, and the *testimonio* tradition have a central place in history and theory. Situating the power of the story in the formation of theory, Avery Gordon argues that these multiple forms of narration fill a basic epistemological hunger. "We have become adept at discovering the construction of social realities and deconstructing their architecture," Gordon explains, confounding some of the distinctions between culture and science, the factual and the artificial. . . . And we have made considerable representational reparations for past exclusions and silencings, making the previously unknown known, telling new stories, correcting the official records. . . . Yet I have wondered sometimes whether, for example, we have truly taken seriously that the intricate web of connections that characterizes any event or problem *is the story*. Warnings about relativism to the contrary, truth is still what most of us strive for. Partial and insecure surely, and something slightly different from "the facts," but truth nonetheless: the capacity to say "This is so."[8]

This is what Teresita was doing in the recorded conversations with me, telling and arguing with us that "this is so."[9] When she told me to "wake up and smell the coffee," when she asked and declared, "why lie?" she was making claims to important truths about her life, an extensive queer transgender Latina life in the second half of the twentieth century.

That Teresita was a performer herself complicates what Judith Butler offered as a theory of performativity, that gender is not a "natural," self-evident category, but is "performatively produced and compelled by the regulatory practices of gender coherence."[10] In this sense, Teresita indeed performed her gender—the category of "woman" that she claimed and for which she worked. But she also ridiculed it. She became Margarita, Alberta, and Teresita, leaving behind Alberto, and got breast implants and embodied as best as she could a well-known woman singer. She also occupied the categories of "queer" and "pervert" because, in part, society and history would have her do so anyway. As the performer that she was, she also knew the limits of her own performance. While she sang powerfully and many assumed that she was a woman, she also mocked the whole enterprise of wishing to pass as one. She was an example of performative Latina queerness, while still a queer vilified and outcast. While telling the evidence of her gendered desires—the performance and construction of her persona—she also mocked herself and relished on her ability to fool many a man in her sexual exploits.

Speaking differently about "the intricate web of connections" Gordon finds necessary for social analysis, Renato Rosaldo finds the messiness of oral history narratives to be its particular strength. "Does all narrative meander," he asks,

> now bending for another perspective, then for an overview, and again to tell what was happening elsewhere in the meantime? Narrative in fact does not

move in a straight line. And those who restrict narrative to linear chronology (the one-damned-thing-after-another version of history) have both misread history and underestimated the variegated potentialities of story-telling. Indeed, one strength of analytical narratives is that they can do so many jobs at once. Unlike more single-minded hypothetico-deductive propositions, stories can simultaneously encompass a number of distinct plot lines and range yet more widely by describing the lay of the land, taking overviews of the situation, and providing key background information.[11]

In Rosaldo's view, the power of storytelling lies precisely in its open-endedness. Rather than trying to fit it into a neat, linear arrangement of events, the power of the story *is* its messiness, the fact that in both breadth and depth it can take us to places and meanings still undiscovered. Narratives begin to grow precisely at the point where the personal and the historical find common grounds, where biography meets history, as C. Wright Mills told us quite some time back.[12] Because Teresita's life story was one of the few surviving reconstructions of queer Latina and Latino pasts in the 1990s, the historical and evidentiary meanings of her existence prove to be an indispensable archive in the community and beyond. Unlike the inanimate paper archival sources we use (when we are able to locate them), which, as Renée M. Sentilles argues in this volume, are interesting and historical but cannot actually "speak" to us, Teresita did indeed talk back to and with us, ensuring as much as possible that the fluidity and meandering qualities of her existence did not remain in silence.

"To smell the coffee" in Teresita's words was to recognize her pioneering role in singing Mexican songs as a queer subject in history, one admired by queer and straight alike. Pioneering, Teresita argued, in walking the streets in the 1950s and 1960s, before any popularized notion of gay liberation and pride, Latino or not. And not working a day for it? She took pride in the idea of not "working," not because sex work is not "work," but because while it was risky, and stigmatized, and challenging, it was also often pleasurable. All of this insight came in Teresita's meandering memory of less than a minute.

Teresita was an excellent collaborator for the making of public history and public archives. Michael Frisch notes the critical space oral history occupies in its ability to produce at once "a source" for public history and interpretive frames, people's understandings of their own lives. "We need projects," Frisch believes, that will involve people in experiencing what it means to remember, and what to do with memories that make them active and alive, as opposed to mere objects of collection. To the extent this is done, we will be seizing an opportunity not nearly so accessible to conventional academic historical scholarship . . . : the opportunity to help liberate for that active remembering all the intelligence . . . of a people long kept separated from the sense of their own past.[13]

To connect the past to the present, to make of history a collective process of human signification where all of us become agents for its production, is to be "testifying," again in the words of Teresita. For Chicano and Latino history, as Mario T. García has observed, the field is still fresh. As oppositional histories, he explains, testimonios broaden historical authorship and thus the perspectives we bring, can produce political texts able to critique oppressive institutions, and make public records of stories not privileged in dominant narratives.[14] Or, as Yolanda Broyles-González argues in her bilingual testimonio with Mexican American singer Lydia Mendoza, historical narratives like hers interpret history as "past in the present," a necessary collapsing of temporalities to create historical meaning.[15] To try to find the records and memories of people of color like Teresita in institutionalized (queer) archives is simply a leap of faith bound to encounter historical absence. Indeed, meeting Teresita in the Mission District in the 1990s, that is, facing living queer Latina and Latino history extending back to the 1940s as it engaged me directly, forced me to shift my approach and to make research, emotional, and political decisions about the historical work I wanted to conduct: rather than spend valuable research time in that oh-so-revered educational institution of UC Berkeley (where I was earning my Ph.D.) or in queer regional archives that lacked racial ethnic specificity, archival work on both spaces that—I already knew—would prove fruitless in terms of queer Latino anything, I instead spent time walking, talking, waiting, and making and returning calls to the living archives of desire around me. That I was earning my degree in an interdisciplinary field (comparative ethnic studies) that allowed more theoretical and methodological flexibility than an average history department made this shift smoother. As Tony Ballantyne reminds us in this volume, our archive stories should not simply be about the bodies of evidence we use, but must speak to our ongoing concerns and preoccupations on multiple levels. For me, knowing that Teresita was living with AIDS, that no one else before with considerable access to educational resources—grants, time, institutional privilege—had made the effort to record queer Latino community lives, that I as a gay Latino in my twenties did not want to become HIV-positive, and that this historical work had everything to do with my commitment to life and my community's health were all pieces of my appreciation for the living archives I had before me.

Oppositional narratives provide alternative perspectives to the course of history and its archives. Where the course of U.S. history presents mostly a black-and-white racial paradigm, Latinos can speak on behalf of a larger landscape. Where this mainstream historical course marginalizes queer subjectivities, lesbians and gays, transgenders and bisexuals have something to say. And when these narrative exclusions intersect—where queer life is Eurocentric and white, and the Latino body dogmatically heteronormative—someone like Teresita will certainly open her mouth, as she did. Against these intersecting archives of exclusions, Teresita sang, spoke, screamed, posed, and narrated living queer desire.

Long before I arrived in the Bay Area in 1994 and began to listen to Teresita's narratives of opposition, she had already found attentive eyes and ears with others. In all those stories, she uncovered and she recalled with amazing precision just as often as she exaggerated and left glaring holes for her listeners to fill. Teresita's narrative agenda was complicated, not always a noble endeavor, never a tale for passive listening. Because her tales were also musical, to listen to and to enjoy, Teresita was always a multilayered experience of history told and history sung, as pleasurable as it was exhausting. It was not just her testimony but also her actual presence, her living exchange with me, which "proved" for Teresita that she remained a historical participant in queer Latino San Francisco. Well aware of my larger project to produce an archive and a written narrative of the community, Teresita found an ideal situation to lay out a historical framework for her life and those lives around her. In a dialectical relationship between listener and narrator, Teresita and I collaborated to produce this frame as an important piece for queer Latino San Francisco and her role in making it happen. That she trusted me in her final years of life also meant that she set a responsibility for me to do something with the archive she was revealing.[16] The walks and rides we took together in the streets of San Francisco to visit old friends in forgotten old bars to gather old unrecorded memories were the only means and method to her archival practice.

Alberta Nevaerez/Teresita la Campesina performing at the Mexican Museum, San Francisco, at the opening reception for the exhibit of the gay Mexican artist Nahum B. Zenil, March 16, 1996. *Photo by and courtesy of Luis Alberto de la Garza C.*

Teresita was certainly not a passive agent in this telling of her life. She was in a constant battle for memory as AIDS became a final challenge in the last decade of her life. In this battle for life, memory, and historical evidence, she engaged us in different ways and locations: the occasional and irreverent showing off of her breasts in public spaces; her voice and musical demands to interact with her in whatever venue she chose (the street, the bus, the car, the private home, the nonprofit agency); her mocking gestures, often "lovingly" dismissing individuals with "ahh sí, ese jotito"—"ahh yes, that little faggot," that is, certainly not someone with her artistic and historical stature. To Teresita, few others came close to her significance in her community's history or could locate pivotal archival anchors of that history. Her exaggerated irreverence, simultaneously play and challenge, meant that Teresita was pushing me to understand the evidence she laid before me. Similar to Durba Ghosh's detailed discussion of how racially and sexually laden research on colonial relations between India and the British Empire "exposed" her during archival research to gendered and nationally driven expectations, presumptions, and warnings from gatekeepers about what she "should" be doing with particular archives, Teresita "burdened" me with her own demands, expectations, and interpretations of what her living narratives meant and what I could and should do with them.

Advertising her body and talents was not only an individual show but also a means to make space collectively. Teresita's everyday informal performances created a cultural geography of the multilingual intersections of sexuality, race, and desire. The talented and daring transgender artist would take off in Spanish, English, or Spanglish wherever she could get away with it. It was an important accomplishment in queering Latino San Francisco artistically, to create cultural citizenship through music in Spanish. To testify in song and in conversation from the authorial position of "I" spoke to her political truths. Like others located in multiple positions of oppression, Teresita found in oral testimony a practical tool for telling history. Similar to others' testimony involving disempowerment and domination, Teresita's narrative was firsthand knowledge shared for political reasons. That I, as a listener of this history and witness to her reconstruction of its peoples and places, was a community member with an academic connection and professional legitimacy was further evidence for Teresita that she mattered in history. She wanted to talk and to show because she believed she had important lessons to communicate.

A "General" Queer Latino History

Teresita's narrative functioned on many levels, all important for considering queer Latino community formations and destruction in San Francisco. The peoples and places in her memory did not give a "total history," but rather what Michel Foucault referred to as a "general history."[17] "Total histories," Foucault noted, draw all phenomena around a single center, with this single source presumably affecting all levels of society at the same time. In queer total histories, for example, 1969's New York Stonewall Inn Riots mark the "pre" and "post" of gay liberation, a static, simplistically linear progression of history from repression to freedom, with no racial or ethnic specificity. For many of us queers of color, as Martin Manalansan writes about diasporic queer Pacific Islander histories, to be "in the shadows of Stonewall" can be an overwhelming struggle to create identity and community outside the neat contours marketed on behalf of presumed global freedom, what Stonewall is meant to symbolize.[18] In this evolving archive of Stonewall and its worldwide celebrations, the liberated white male gay subject takes center stage as the queer genders and sexualities of color are left scattered in historiographical background.

A "general history," however, speaks to "series, segmentations, limits, differences of level, time lags, anachronistic survivals, possible types of relation."[19] The goal in this general history, Jeffrey Weeks notes further about Foucault's differentiation, is not simply to offer a jumble of different histories, or, to return to Rosaldo, the "one-damn-thing-after-another" model. General histories, Weeks says, help us "determine what forms of relation may legitimately be made between the various forms of social categorization, but to do this without recourse to any master schema, any ultimate theory of causation."[20]

Because Teresita lived on "both sides" of 1969, her own memories of gay liberation and repression provide an excellent *general* historical account of the meanings of freedom and of its presumed "progress." To return to the brief excerpt from Teresita, we see the tensions and unevenness of her general history. As a "pioneer," Teresita dates herself: she came long before most of us queers of the 1980s and 1990s, and at least one generation before the gay liberations of the 1970s. She walked the streets of Los Angeles in the 1950s, often getting arrested but other times surviving well, often even with grace. That she even made local fame as a *cantante mexicana*—Mexican singer—in radio proved to her that her voice was effective for transcending (maybe "masquerading") gender and sexuality, particularly in Spanish and for a large Latino public.

"You're so lucky to have these privileges," Teresita reminded me. Her general queer history also recognized the changes for younger queer Latinas and Latinos. She got to know some of us from university campuses who could organize to get her money to perform; who could invite her to speak and perform her life in our conferences; who in fighting AIDS were able to choose from several health agencies in the city to get services; and who could write, paint, or make videos in community-based projects to explore our gender, sexuality, and race openly, without getting arrested. In all of these instances of public history and memory, we created yet more archives of our lives—flyers, announcements, proposals, video and audio records, photographs, speeches—through the life of this living legend.[21]

Finally, in this general history, Teresita also recognized the limits to this "progress," most clearly in the reality of AIDS as a community challenge. When she spoke at Galería de la Raza calling us to vote, she reminded us that there can indeed be retrenchment in liberation. The lay of the land in Teresita's general history provided many anchors to grasp the queer Latino history—and herstory—some of us are just beginning to document and archive.[22] As a transgender, she spoke about socializing with Latina dykes on the famed 16th Street gay Latino strip, a very important facet of the *multi-gender* queer history of the barrio. She also made sure she named the names of those queer Latinas and Latinos who made space in *straight* bars, again, long before Stonewall. A "general" history, no doubt, but not generic at all, for her testimonies were part of a community's survival strategies in the face of AIDS, gentrification, representational and archival silencings.

For communities excluded, outcast, and marginalized, voice can speak to power: it is literally a weapon of evidence against historical erasure and social analysis that fails to consider the experiences of individuals and communities on their own terms. Teresita had "a big mouth" at times, insensitive and careless in her volunteering information about other people's HIV status, for example. These transgressions were also part of her narrative, problematic of course for those not wishing to be part of her tales. Yet, her insistence on making HIV status part of her storytelling kept this dimension of queer Latino life and death visible. Despite more than two decades of dealing with the disease, there remains much misinformation, silence, stigma, and insensitivity surrounding AIDS and people living with the disease. As a survivor, Teresita exercised her right to speak also to this truth.

The fact that other Latinas and Latinos (queer and not) considered Teresita's testimonio important for their lives adds further meaning to that general history. In my oral history interviews with nearly sixty narrators, she has been by far the most frequent name to emerge as people remembered the local community; she was also one of the ones most often photographed and therefore appearing in the personal archival collections of several narrators. Some narrators found her intriguing and mesmerizing while others found her obnoxious and meddlesome, but nevertheless historical, in the sense that she marked space, time, and place; she was a loaded historical gun. Through her singing and irreverent revelations, her tales of sexual conquest and genital proportions, she earned her place in the collective memory. "Historical and hysterical," as she herself interpreted her life, Teresita's "I" spoke as a queer Latino "we," the shape of a queer Latino testimonio and collective archival body in formation.

Why did Teresita want so much to "testify"? For this generation of queer Latino elders, facing AIDS in their own bodies forced many to come forth. But because many also died in silence—self-imposed, enforced by family or homophobic religious dogma, or a combination of these—Teresita spoke up. Because she had many stages from which to perform this truth about her dying community, she took advantage whenever possible. Teresita was also correcting the queer historical record of the Bay Area. She knew that the more popular histories and narratives of the region make some more visible than others. Her references to José Sarria, for example, the well-known historical figure in San Francisco's gay history, involved commentary about what she argued was his choice to socialize and organize with white queers. Sarria may have a Spanish name, but for Teresita that was not enough for queer Latino significance. She instead remained known in Latino San Francisco, singing in Spanish, finding support and means for survival in Latino nightlife. The Los Angeles sexual outcast of the 1950s wanted to make sure we knew what she had accomplished, because books, films, classes, and archives did not reference her existence or her community's.

The testimonial purpose of oral history is effective for catching experiences where those who lived them are no longer there for their resurrection. Teresita was not alone in doing this. The butch Chicana lesbian Diane Felix, for example, having socialized with many gay Chicano men in the 1970s, most of whom are now dead, had important perspectives to give, not quite on their behalf, but at least in direct relation to their lives.[23] Likewise, as a transgender performer among a dying generation, Teresita was one of the only ones left behind. She was under their shadow, as one of the only ones available to tell "their story," in a way shedding light on the historical debris of her people. Whereas this position can be one of privilege in having the ability to tell what few others can, it can be also one of overwhelming responsibility. Because Teresita had accumulated many losses, to rise to the podium of testimonial history was no easy task. But with no living biological family left and few surviving friends from her generation, Teresita's community testimonio *was* her life at the end. Having lost the majority of photographs of her early life, narrating the fame and the infamy of "Teresita la Campesina" was the only visibility and archive of memory she could use. The seemingly simple and straightforward social act of talking—in video and audio recordings, when singing, or when blurting out the names, dates, and places of queer Latino life in San Francisco—was the living archive Teresita bequeathed to future generations.

Memories like Teresita's are particularly crucial in queer communities where cross-generational dialogue, with the joint participation of younger and older members, is not common. As an elder, Teresita refused "to lay down and look like an antique" among the more visible youth. Through her retelling of stories, she also found a form of companionship, of queer Latino citizenship. Queer companionship as citizenship is not to be taken for granted in an ever smaller queer community of people living with AIDS. This was, of course, citizenship and companionship that I shared as a participant-historian, a community member very much concerned with the business of survival—my own, Teresita's, and our community's—and the recognition of archival significance heretofore ignored.

Community Mourning and the Archives of Desire

As Liz Kennedy and Madeline Davis point out in their study of Buffalo's working class lesbian community, oral history research is necessarily a project of those willing and still able to tell their stories.[24] The stories we queer oral historians process are often those of survivors, of those not having succumbed to social stigma, repression, alcohol and drug abuse, poverty and homelessness, and, from the 1980s onward, the ravages of AIDS. Just as oral history opens up the possibility of documenting the past, creating collective dialogues that are simultaneous acts of living reflection and archive building, highlighting celebration and survival, it also serves as a window into community loss, pain, and death. In this sense, "talking history" is an emotional, mournful enterprise for those of us made invisible and less significant in dominant historical narratives about the Bay Area, about Latinas and Latinos, and about queers.

At the closing of the 1980s, when AIDS deaths were as extensive as the homophobic stigma against the communities it afflicted, the *New York Times* calmed its presumably straight readers by stating that "the disease is still very largely confined to specific risk groups" and that "Once all susceptible members [of these groups] are infected, the numbers of new victims will decline." The critic Douglas Crimp posed two challenging questions facing queer people then in the struggle for survival *and* mourning: "How are we to dissociate our narcissistic satisfactions in being alive from our fight to stay alive? And, insofar as we *identify* with those who have died, how can our satisfactions in being alive escape guilt at having survived?"[25]

The challenges Crimp posed involve several implications for queer sexualities in the times of AIDS. Already marginal on multiple levels, queer *Latino* sexual consciousness confronted a new crisis with AIDS. In the 1960s and 1970s, sexual liberations and struggles for gender, racial, and sexual equalities gave thousands—including Latinas and Latinos—the possibilities to dream about overcoming oppression. For queers, narcissistic satisfaction meant the right to pleasure—to queer pleasures and citizenship long denied. But despite years of denial among Latinos generally and Latino queers specifically that AIDS affected us, AIDS came right in the middle of the sexual consciousness most were just beginning to celebrate. Our own "epidemic of signification," to use Paula A. Treichler's apt phrase, had conveniently but falsely constructed AIDS as only a gay white men's disease.[26] In the meantime, AIDS continued to remove bodies from the community, and, often, all records of these queer lives were literally thrown in the streets.[27]

Thus a new set of sexual, cultural, and political strategies had to be learned to survive the disease, many still unperfected today. Many of us have managed to stay alive, or to remain HIV-negative, often compromising pleasure for safety, even companionship for the promise of life. But many of us have also died, like Teresita, and continue to do so, and those moments of queer pleasures we feel the right to have while staying alive crash against the very success of that survival—because guilt can be overwhelming. The contradictions between queer life and queer death became entangled in a queer Latino triangle: we were trying to celebrate our sexuality, while remaining vigilant about staying alive, and continuously mourning those who died. It is ever so much easier to list these dynamics than to actually live them and survive them. But mourning we had to do, with or without guilt. The living archival record Teresita fought to narrate was itself a mirror of this community dialectic between life and death.

Mourning someone like Teresita, ironically, was actually an anomaly in queer Latino San Francisco. A majority of us knew she had been ill for years (she wouldn't let us forget it, actually), and thus we were more than willing to pay her respect by listening to the very end. But even general histories involve the passage of time and age, and so burying a sixty-one-year-old legend felt different than accepting the death of a thirty-five year old we only knew as a friend for a few years, or finding out at the age of twenty that you're HIV-positive long before any pharmaceutical promises for longevity.

Teresita herself, we can argue, helped us along in our mourning for her years ahead—"I'm an old lady now," she said, six years before her death. She also warned her AIDS social workers months before she died that she did not want to be cremated (as she was not), probably an unthinkable act for a historical pervert who refused to give up on Catholicism (despite the contradictions) and who had her own ideas of what the burning of bodily evidence meant for queer historical memory. Weeks before she died, as she grew sicker, she took the dress she wanted to be buried in to yet another social worker and the few photographs she had of her life. These were the remaining photos she had rescued from her multiple relocations over the decades—from the boy-child she was in 1940s Los Angeles to the regional transgender star she became in the 1960s, 1970s, 1980s, and 1990s—to make sure people knew there was a visual record left of what she had achieved. Teresita did not give us the privilege *not* to identify with her AIDS-related death or to ignore her historical significance, but neither did she burden us more with the guilt for remaining alive after her memory. I want to believe, for I knew Teresita quite well, that she herself knew that all these pieces—the last dress she would wear, the remaining photographs, her own body—surely would be part of the (visual) record of the photographs, the oral histories we would tell, and the feelings we would recall after her death, all of which we have. Perhaps Teresita never had a state-sanctioned passport that would give her a national identity, as a technology of verification that legitimized her in the national imagination, to borrow Craig Robertson's fitting analysis. But she did actively produce the truths of her life and of her multiple identities as she specified in detail how it was that she wanted to be re-membered as a queer citizen of history. As a living archive, Teresita made her self accessible, negotiating her own needs and interests with those like me who valued her experiences and analyses. There were no "restrictions" per se in my research relationship with Teresita, not at all like those described by Jeff Sahadeo in this volume, yet we both knew there was a serious investment we both had to one another for making the archival-like qualities of her oral history matter after her death.

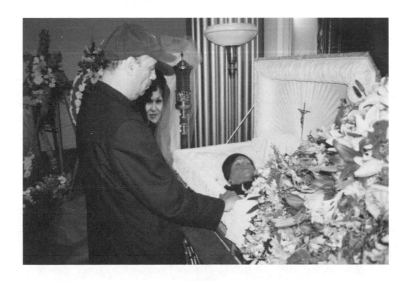

(above) Long-term friend and neighbor Sergio Iníguez looking on at the late Alberta Navaerez / Teresita la Campesina during her wake in San Francisco's Mission District, July 17, 2002. *Photo by and courtesy of Luis Alberto de la Garza C.*

(below) Mariachi Los Cachorros, which accompanied Teresita's live performances for years, playing during her interment, Colma, California, July 18, 2002. *Photo by and courtesy of Luis Alberto de la Garza C.*

To excavate queer lives and queer desires requires careful considerations, beginning with the fact that they are not the priority of mainstream
historicizing and archiving practices. "Where do lesbian and gay lives
appear in the public record," Graeme Reid asks, "and how are these lives
and experiences represented? Of course, how lesbians and gay men appear
in the public record is not unrelated to where they appear."[28] Teresita was
one to straddle multiple sites for her life to be "recorded"—she was arrested several times for sex work, but was also photographed many more
times by folks in her respective communities (Latino, transgender, queer)
and audio and video recorded as well. But, with no automatic repository
for queer Latino archives in the region, most of these artifacts are scattered
and unorganized, often made visible only at the moment when an academic researcher and / or community-based historian makes it a priority
to bring them together for public display, consumption, and interpretation. Teresita's own death created yet more of these archives, with the
many photographs and living narratives during the wake, her interment,
the Catholic mass following, and several fund-raising community activities that brought hundreds of friends and admirers to celebrate collectively
one last time the life of this pioneering queer historical pervert. Where
these photographs and related records eventually find a permanent home
remains one of the critical tasks at hand for the survival of her memory.[29]
These and other records too will attest to her commitment to talking
archives: the process of narrating the lives of those who passed on and
the meanings that archives communicate back to those committed to
listening.

Surviving Archives of Queer Latino Desire

Teresita used her life in critical, meandering ways. Toward the end, enunciating a complex general history of *Latinidad* and queerness in the last six
decades of twentieth-century U.S. history, she allowed us to appreciate her
queer racial desires. This community mourning we did for her as we did
for others in the 1990s has meant the loss of bodies and desires. Narrators
mourned the death of their friends, their lovers, their sisters, and their
brothers, even all those unknown queers. What began to die also as part of
the times of AIDS was a sexual consciousness and politics of liberation.
Latina lesbians mourned too the periodic loss of what they were barely

beginning to achieve, their own social and political spaces of the 1970s and 1980s, reduced to monthly nighttime venues and house gatherings. Queer Latinos, most tired of AIDS, sexual repressions, and ambivalence, had to mourn one another. Bisexuals became an even more embattled identity given the automatic, reductive assumption that they were the bridge of AIDS between straights and queers. The transgender community, MTF Latinas who built public culture through performance, were deeply ravaged by AIDS and often discarded in Latino health agencies and the gay community generally. Female-to-male (FTM) transgenders could hardly mourn as they were only beginning to occupy the space of citizenship and visibility.[30] Caretakers of the dying queer, many of them later dying themselves, knew they were holding on to historical pieces: 1960s gay and lesbian escapades into straight Latino bars; racial escapades into the white gay liberation movements; forging political and social visions in the 1970s and 1980s; surviving the multiple challenges of AIDS to the present.

What we call homophobia is as "American" as racism and patriarchy, and overcoming the intersection of these forms of oppression can be a daunting life-long struggle, one that must include the records of those fights. Teresita made it to the age of sixty-one, a combination of all the lessons learned in the battlefields of her life: against blood family, bashers in the streets, the police state, mental and health agencies, and at least one acquaintance who simply yet viciously mocked her by referring to her as "he," disrespectfully saying "Tereso." Teresita "made it," but not seventeen-year-old MTF transgender Gwen Araujo, who, finding herself at a party on October 3, right across the bay from San Francisco in the city of Newark, became one of thirty transgenders murdered and reported in 2002.[31] That most alluring record of pre-to-post linearity of Stonewall liberation can ring quite hollow even in this queerest of U.S. cities.

The actual benefits of our notions of "progress," "democracy," and "equal citizenship," we queers know, get distributed unevenly. Teresita knew it and complained about it for decades (and sang about it too); Gwen knew it and died very early with her knowledge. Their respective lives, long and short, serve as archival traces of where we have been historically and why we may be where we are at today. Their two lives alone are sufficient to understand the need for historical and political labor that theorizes gender, sexuality, race, and evidence across history with the bodies and the voices of the living and of the dead. The passing of their bodies requires from us the commitment to record and understand the evidentiary qualities of their lives, to be courageous enough to gauge the shapes and voices of the living archives they embodied.

Notes

This essay is dedicated to the memory of the late Alberta Nevaerez, better known as Teresita la Campesina, whose life and work as a "historical pervert" gave much evidence to queer Latino history and culture in the San Francisco Bay Area for four decades. The essay benefits from the discussions with several audiences in 2003 at the University of California, Santa Barbara; Williams College; the University of Illinois, Urbana / Champaign; and Washington State University, Pullman. I thank Antoinette Burton for critical feedback, the anonymous readers for their suggestions, and Luis Alberto de la Garza C. for technical support and for providing several images included here. A University of California MEXUS dissertation completion grant in 1999 and a 2001 UC President's Postdoctoral Fellowship provided financial support to carry out a great deal of the research for this discussion.

1 Conscious of its historical specificity in the late 1980s and 1990s, I nevertheless use the term "queer" as a descriptive shorthand to refer to "lesbian, gay, bisexual, and transgender" ("lgbt") identities and politics. While the term generally conflates multiple non-heterosexual gender and sexualities, it does serve well with its political edge, its perverse and outrageous quality specific to "in your face" political currents of the time, instead of the more (homo)normative "lgbt." In addition, "queer" functions in this discussion about a historical actor and subject, Teresita, who herself used it strategically to narrate her life and to analyze and critique homophobia, stigma, and social exclusion.

2 Although he became the first openly gay president of the city's board of supervisors, Ammiano was, in 1999, not the first openly gay candidate for mayor in the city; he was, however, the first one who appeared to have had a *realistic* chance of winning. In the final count, he captured 40 percent of the votes, compared to the winner and first African American mayor of the city, Willie Brown, who was reelected with 60 percent. The Peruvian lesbian activist Lucrecia Bermúdez also made one unsuccessful run for mayor in 1999 and three additional ones for the board of supervisors in 1996, 1998, and 2000. In none of these occasions was she able to garner sufficient support to make it close to runoff elections. In 1977, Harvey Milk, on his third run for the position, became the first openly gay supervisor during the first citywide district elections. Fellow supervisor Dan White, a former police officer, assassinated both Milk and the then mayor George Moscone on November 27, 1978, in City Hall. See Randy Shilts, *The Mayor of Castro Street: The Life and Times of Harvey Milk* (New York: St. Martin's Press, 1982). As early as 1961, José Sarria, self-described as being of

"Spanish Colombian descent" and famous for his female-impersonating rendition of "Widow Norton" at the Black Cat, captured 5,600 votes in his run for the board of supervisors. See Michael R. Gorman, *The Empress Is a Man: Stories from the Life of José Sarria* (New York: Harrington Park Press, 1998), 24.

3 Lola Beltrán died on March 25, 1996, at the age of sixty-two, after more than forty years of singing in which she recorded nearly eighty albums.

4 Jorge Ignacio Cortiñas, personal communication, March 20, 2001.

5 Teresita la Campesina (nee Alberto Nevaerez), interview by author, tape recording, San Francisco, California, March 3 and April 4, 1996. I discuss at length the significance of Teresita's narratives for capturing queer Latino histories in the Bay Area in chapter 2 of my dissertation, "Communities of Desire: Queer Latina/Latino History and Memory, San Francisco Bay Area, 1960s–1990s" (Ph.D. diss., University of California, Berkeley, 2001), 47–115.

6 Tina M. Campt, *Other Germans: Black Germans and the Politics of Race, Gender, and Memory in the Third Reich* (Ann Arbor: University of Michigan Press, 2004), 86.

7 On the concept of cultural citizenship as a means for Latino enfranchisement in contexts of domination, see William V. Flores and Rina Benmayor, eds., *Latino Cultural Citizenship: Claiming Identity, Space and Rights* (Boston: Beacon Press, 1997). On the creation of cultural texts as historical artifacts for transnational gay Latino cultural citizenship, see Horacio N. Roque Ramírez, "Claiming Queer Cultural Citizenship: Gay Latino (Im)Migrant Acts in San Francisco," in Eithne Luibhéid and Lionel Cantú, Jr., eds., *Queer Migrations: Sexuality, U.S. Citizenship, and Border Crossings* (Minneapolis: University of Minnesota Press, 2005), 161–88.

8 Avery F. Gordon, *Ghostly Matters: Haunting and the Sociological Imagination* (Minneapolis: University of Minnesota Press, 1997), 20; emphasis in original.

9 Another San Francisco gay activist and Chicano cultural worker, Valentín Aguirre, also recorded video interviews with Teresita, as part of his video *Wanted Alive: Teresita la Campesina* (1997). Additionally, weeks before Teresita's death, the lesbian filmmaker Veronica Majano video recorded Teresita at the Mission Cultural Center for Latino Arts, as Teresita, visibly sick, admired black-and-white portraits of her taken in the 1980s by the late gay Chicano activist Rodrigo Reyes.

10 Judith Butler, *Gender Trouble: Feminism and the Subversion of Identity* (New York: Routledge, 1990), 24.

11 Renato Rosaldo, "Doing Oral History," *Social Analysis* 4 (September 1980): 91.

12 C. Wright Mills, *The Sociological Imagination* (London: Oxford University Press, 1959), 5–6.

13 Michael Frisch, *A Shared Authority: Essays on the Craft and Meaning of Oral History* (New York: State University of New York Press, 1990), 27.

14 Mario T. García, *Memories of Chicano History: The Life and Narrative of Bert Corona* (Berkeley: University of California Press, 1994).

15 Yolanda Broyles-González, *Lydia Mendoza's Life in Music / La Historia de Lydia Mendoza: Norteño Tejano Legacies* (New York: Oxford University Press, 2001), 208.

16 I discuss the personal impact Teresita had in my life, and I on hers, through an analysis of blood and queer familial relations in "Teresita's Blood," *CORPUS: An HIV Prevention Publication* 2, 2 (fall 2004): 2–9.

17 Michel Foucault, *The Archeology of Knowledge and the Discourse on Language*, trans. A. M. Sheridan Smith (New York: Harper, 1972), 10.

18 Martin F. Manalansan IV, "In the Shadows of Stonewall: Examining Gay Transnational Politics and the Diasporic Dilemma," in Lisa Lowe and David Lloyd, eds., *The Politics of Culture in the Shadow of Capital* (Durham: Duke University Press, 1997), 485–505.

19 Foucault, *Archeology of Knowledge*, 10.

20 Jeffrey Weeks, "Foucault for Historians," *History Workshop* 14 (autumn 1982): 110.

21 This was the case for the "¡Con la Boca Abierta!" [Mouth Wide Open!] two-day queer Latina and Latino conference at the University of California, Berkeley campus on April 11–12, 1997 (for which I served as principal coordinator), when Teresita performed and narrated part of her life story as part of a panel of queer elders, "Veteranas y Veteranos." About 350 women and men attended this regional gathering, mostly queer but also heterosexual, from high school students to those in their sixties. The audio, video, and print records are in my possession, to be processed and archived in the UCB campus.

22 This multigenerational history of queer Latinas and Latinos has taken form in multiracial, multilingual same-sex and co-gender (women and men) contexts. See María Cora, "Nuestras Auto-Definiciones / Our Self-Definitions: Management of Stigma and Identity by Puerto Rican Lesbians" (master's field study report, San Francisco State University, 2000); Karla Eva Rosales, "Papis, Dykes, Daddies: A Study of Chicana and Latina Self-Identified Butch Lesbians" (master's thesis, San Francisco State University, 2001); and Horacio N. Roque Ramírez, "Praxes of Desire: Remaking Queer Latina and Latino Geographies and Communities through San Francisco's Proyecto ContraSIDA Por Vida," in M. García, M. Leger, and A. N. Valdivia, eds., *Geographies of Latinidad: Latina / o Studies into the Twenty-First Century* (Durham: Duke University Press, forthcoming).

23 I discuss Felix's and other Chicana and Latina lesbians' political and social relations with gay men in " 'That's My Place!': Negotiating Racial, Sexual, and Gender Politics in San Francisco's Gay Latino Alliance, 1975–1983," *Journal of the History of Sexuality* 12, 2 (April 2003): 224–58.

24 Elizabeth Lapovsky Kennedy and Madeline D. Davis, *Boots of Leather, Slippers of Gold: The History of a Lesbian Community* (New York: Routledge, 1993).

25 Douglas Crimp, "The Spectacle of Mourning," in *Melancholia and Moralism: Essays on AIDS and Queer Politics* (Cambridge, Mass.: MIT Press, 2002), 137; *New York Times* quoted on same page.

26   Paula A. Treichler, *How to Have Theory in an Epidemic: Cultural Chronicles of AIDS* (Durham: Duke University Press, 1999), 11.

27   I thank Luis Alberto de la Garza C. for sharing with me several of the stories of blood families and / or landlords discarding the belongings of queer Latino San Francisco residents following their deaths from AIDS-related complications.

28   Graeme Reid, "'The History of the Past Is the Trust of the Present': Preservation and Excavation in the Gay and Lesbian Archives of South Africa," in Carolyn Hamilton, Verne Harris, Jane Taylor, Michele Pickover, Graeme Reid, and Razia Saleh, eds., *Refiguring the Archive* (Dordrecht: Kluwer Academic Publishers), 193–207.

29   Long-term Berkeley resident Luis Alberto de la Garza C. and I helped coordinate fund-raising events following Teresita's death, and Luis took it upon himself to create a collection of hundreds of photographs of these events and the people involved. It has generally been efforts like his, by individuals in the community working independently, that have created any records and archives of their queer lives and those around them. These community members include Danny Arcos, Virginia Benavídez, Ana Berta Campa, María Cora, Diane Felix, Juan Pablo Gutierrez, Silvia Ledesma, Karla Rosales, the late Hank Tavera, and Carlos Díaz Todd. For an analysis of one example of these grassroots archiving efforts, see Luis Alberto de la Garza C. and Horacio N. Roque Ramírez, "Queer Community History and the Evidence of Desire: The Archivo Rodrigo Reyes, a Gay and Lesbian Latino Archive," in Lillian Castillo-Speed and the REFORMA National Conference Publications Committee, eds., *The Power of Language / El Poder de la Palabra* (Englewood, Colo.: Libraries Unlimited, 2001), 181–98.

30   A groundbreaking video documentary using oral history and queer Latina and Latino community archival footage is Karla E. Rosales's "'Mind If I Call You Sir?': Masculinity and Gender Expression in Latina Butches and Latino Female-to-Male (FTM) Transgender Men," conceived and produced by Karla E. Rosales, directed by Mary Guzman, 30 minutes, 2004.

31   See the Web site http: // www.rememberingourdead.org.

Renée M. Sentilles

Toiling in the Archives

of Cyberspace

IF AN ARCHIVE IS A REPOSITORY of documents, the World Wide Web
has the potential to become a collection of those repositories: an archive of
archives, if you will. As a busy teacher and scholar, I embrace the idea of
using my home computer to do primary research. The Internet is a wonderful research tool. But if electronic mediums are touted as having the
potential to *replace* traditional archives, rather than simply to enhance
older methods of research, I would argue that such a thing is simply not
possible. In this essay I investigate the tension between the speed and
quantity of Web sources on the one hand and the comparative slowness
and dearth of resources in traditional archives on the other. The Web can
serve as an archive in a loose sense of the word: a place where scholars can
go to search through collections of information. But, as companion essays
in this text suggest, archives are about much more than a physical gathering of artifacts under one roof, and limitations can be a powerful source of
inspiration. Our relationship with sources changes as they become more
accessible, more abundant, and less tangible.

Let me begin by clarifying what I mean and do not mean by the term
"Internet" and its source material. My understanding is that "World Wide
Web" refers to all web sites accessible by the Internet, which acts as a
highway system. Technically, that would make each web site an archive,
the World Wide Web the archive of those archives, and the Internet a
transportation device. Such rigid boundaries break down quickly, however, because most computer users do not distinguish the Internet from
the World Wide Web. Thus, as is now common in speech, in this essay I
am going to use "World Wide Web," "the Web," and the "Internet" as
synonyms for the archives of cyberspace accessed through computers.
These electronic repositories contain primary and secondary sources, and
both may be digitized (appearing exactly as they appeared on the original

printed page, as if one had taken a picture of that page) or rewritten, so that the wording is the same but the physical structure of the words has changed. Digitized materials are far more useful because (to a limited degree) one can examine the publication in which the artifact appears. They are also more trustworthy since scholars can safely assume that no language has changed in the process of being transformed into an electronic medium. Digitized materials are abundant in subscribed databases, but not so commonly found online. For the purposes of this essay, I am assuming researchers will rely on a mix of material, most of which is not digitized. Because there are many Web archives placed by enthusiasts, I am also writing as if researchers are using sites maintained by individuals as well as by institutions.

My own experience researching and writing a cultural biography on the Civil War actress and poet Adah Isaacs Menken speaks directly to how the development of Internet archives is affecting scholarship. I had been using e-mail since 1996, and regularly relied on research databases like World Cat and American History and Life, but it was 2000 before I actually did any research on the Internet. Up to that point, I had used the Internet to *prepare* to visit traditional archives, but never to retrieve actual material. In my world the idea of reading books and articles online still sounded like scary science fiction (people spoke of *doing away* with books, which I think only people who do not like to read would find the least bit appealing). For me, discovering Google.com changed everything.

I had just mailed my revised manuscript to the publisher when I was introduced to Google, so of course the first words I typed in were "Adah Isaacs Menken." I was truly shocked when 271 web sites featuring Menken popped up on the screen. At that point I knew more about Menken than anyone else living, so I was stunned (and alarmed) to find so much material I had never read. Here I should explain that Menken was a consummate performer who, like Madonna of the 1980s, made a career of shape-shifting. I expected to find web sites discussing Menken as African American, Jewish, and lesbian, but I did not expect to find so many or to see older rumors resurfacing electronically that had disappeared from publications seventy years ago. To give you an idea of the scope, Menken appeared in web sites focusing on the history of sports, magic, theater, Texas, nudity, horse riding, and feminism, among many others. I came across several ambitious conversation threads by playwrights and screenwriters discussing their various prospective projects on Menken. I found notices for conference papers on Menken and prostitution, Menken and Twain, Menken and race, Menken and cross-dressing. I was truly appalled (if not surprised) to see how many web sites perpetuated a multitude of false "facts" about her. By virtue of a slick public medium each claim had a patina of plausibility despite the fact that most web sites had no footnotes, no bibliographies, no corroborating evidence of any kind. Yet no matter how well written or shallow and poorly supported they were, I immediately recognized that I must give them attention in her biography. History is always a relationship between the past and the present, and there was no denying that this explosion of information on Menken (about whom, I hasten to add, most people have never heard) was an expression of present-day understandings of the past.

In later investigations into Menken's presence on the Internet, I discovered another disquieting fact: these web sites were appearing and disappearing at an alarming rate. Five months after the first time I plugged in Menken's name, her name yielded close to 1,400 hits; the number had increased roughly four times in less than half a year. But one year later, only 962 sites answered the search. Perhaps it is this last scenario that I find most peculiar—the question that most makes me most hesitant about using the Internet as an archive: What happened to those more than four hundred web sites between 2002 and 2003? I cannot find them; it is as if they never existed, yet I documented them in an earlier essay. Given traditional reasons for why we note source material (the reader must always be able to go back and review the information source), was my previous Internet research valid? Could I use examples that no longer existed anywhere?

In this essay I pursue particular questions that have arisen in the process of writing a cultural biography of Menken: How does the World Wide Web as an archive of archives change the way we do research, conceive of research and artifacts, and pass that knowledge on to our students? Is it possible to "master" a topic in a world of overly abundant resources? How does immediate access to other scholars reshape our intellectual community? Our scholarship itself? The World Wide Web and its magnificent search engines are an incredible gift in many ways, but they cannot replace traditional archives, because both Internet and traditional archives come with their own limitations. As my research on Menken illustrates, the Internet is mercurial and ephemeral; however well it works, it is always *virtual*. Those of us in the business of research and teaching research are constantly discovering both the limits and possibilities, struggling to see the puzzle whole when we still have only pieces. And I suppose this brings me to the biggest, if unanswerable question: If historical research profoundly changes, does that also signal changes in the historical discipline?

The Profession: Definitions and Resources

There is surprisingly little material written by historians on the subject of the Web as an archive. Ironically, the least helpful resource has been what this essay is about—the Internet. Even when limiting my search to scholarly web sites, I mostly find scholars discussing how to *use* the Web to do research, not how the Internet itself is changing the nature of research. Established historical journals, whether digitized or not, provide the most helpful secondary sources. Yet, with few exceptions, articles about the Internet are quickly outdated because they discuss web sites no longer in existence or speak of advances that now seem primitive.

Roy Rosenzweig is one of few scholars addressing how the expanded capabilities of the Web are changing our methods of historical research. Most recently, he focused on the paradoxical problem of having virtual access to a tremendous amount of material at the same time that digital mediums are constantly threatened with obsolescence. In so doing, he raised one of the main points of concern: "historians need to be thinking simultaneously about how to research, write and teach in a world of unheard of historical abundance and how to avoid a future of record scarcity."[1]

A discussion about the Internet acting as an archive or as a virtual map to a physical archive must begin with some agreement as to what historians do with these sources. History is a discipline tied to repositories. Archives are established and shaped by librarians, curators, financial backers, and current concerns of the society they serve. The histories written from these archives are also created not only by the individual historians and the cultural concerns of their times, but also by the institutions they serve (which give us, for example, hundreds of Civil War historians and extremely few examining American occupation of the Philippines). This does not mean that "writing history merely involves manipulating archives."[2] Archives yield the sources that are used as facts, but interpretation fuels the historical argument. Historians use facts to support their larger argument, and as Lorraine Daston so eloquently puts it, "evidence might be described as facts hammered into signposts, which point beyond themselves and their sheer, brute thingness to states of affairs to which we have no direct access."[3] Archival sources on their own are interesting and historical, but they do not speak.

The "facts" are fixed but the structure of history is fluid. Both professionals and amateurs write and publish history, but they tend to produce significantly different material. Professional historians—historians working in the academy or involved with various historical organizations—write history that contributes to a larger body of knowledge. Each article and monograph must clarify how it adds to the developing narrative patterns. By contrast, amateur historians write about isolated topics; they do not assume that others reading their work will know related texts, have seen a paper presented that challenges their thesis, or care how the biography of a robber baron, for example, elucidates changes in capitalism at the turn of the century. Amateur historians write because they believe the story they tell is inherently interesting, and that is enough. "Mastery" of secondary writing is not critical to amateur historians, but it is part of what defines professional history; every historical work coordinates with other historical work in some way.

Despite the impact of post-structural theory, the guiding force among professional historians remains objective truth.[4] However cynical the scholar, the goal is always to reveal truth, which historians do through their use of "facts," "evidence," and "mastery." Historians meet these criteria primarily through using textual sources, but the Internet has an impact on the way we view these texts by effecting their distribution, their abundance or scarcity, and the intellectual community making use of them.

Limits, Challenges, and Possibilities

Historians are generally more comfortable coping with a scarcity than an abundance of materials. Since the 1960s, the emergence of social history has led to generations of scholars writing history "from the bottom up," which has often meant finding creative ways to scrape that bottom for any smidgen of information. The need for innovative research methods can hardly be overstated when attempting to investigate the history of textually absent or silent groups, like Native American women, colonial-period slaves, or the itinerant poor of the Gilded Age. But now we are living in an age where information is being stored at a furious rate. The *New York Times* recently reported that that in 2002 people stored roughly five billion gigabytes worth of information "on paper, film, optical or magnetic media." That amount of information is double their estimates of information documented in 1999.[5] How can we hope to address or incorporate such a vast quantity of information with research methods created to address the opposite problem?

Abundance, then, causes conceptual problems because it reverses conventional wisdom of most historians and requires of them new skills and methodologies. An enormous amount of information causes a few interrelated conceptual difficulties: when surveying a massive amount of material, the historian must reduce its complexity. Does this compromise the supposed "objectivity" required? If reduction is impossible, then the historian must simply take a smaller slice of the material, rendering a highly specialized monograph that adds to the ongoing historical narrative, but is of little use to any but those writing in the same field. In either case, vast amounts of minutiae make historians more aware, if post structuralism had not already given them a crisis of confidence, that what they are attempting to do is inherently limited. None of this is new, of course. Historians working in fields with an abundance of materials, such as the American Civil War or civil rights, have always had to make these choices. But the Internet greatly exacerbates the situation, bringing the dilemma to a much greater number of fields of study.

One of the requirements of writing serious history is to "master" all extent sources, primary and secondary. To be caught not knowing related texts is intellectually analogous to being caught with one's pants down. But for many scholars "mastery" may be impossible in the age of the Internet. Again, what is "new" about this situation is that it is effecting a far greater proportion of historians than before. From a practical standpoint, the vast quantity of information available "raises the demands on historians to read, analyze, and incorporate vast quantities of documents and information into short articles."[6] Rosenzweig suggests that simply "reading around" is inadequate in the age of abundant information and asserts that we may have to "learn to write complex searches and algorithms that would allow [historians] to sort through this overwhelming record."[7] But even if such methods would work for social and military historians, they would not address the needs of cultural, intellectual, and political ones. My own experiences suggest the futility of trying to meet traditional requirements and keep a conscientious eye on the ever-changing web sites. Even as I was responding to my copy editor's suggestions for the book on Menken, my infrequent Internet searches were yielding new material. Did I need to incorporate information coming out until the galleys were produced? I did set a cut-off date out of practicality, but provocative material kept persuading me to push it back, until I finally received the galleys and addressing new research became prohibitively expensive. Because of the ease of "Googling" Menken, my research never actually reached a point of "rest," let alone completion.

Obviously then, the Internet challenges historians to reconsider the traditional ideal of "mastering" all major material on a subject. Is it necessary to "master" all secondary and primary material on a topic in order to address it? Again, this has never been a practical demand in some fields where there is an abundance of scholarship, but the enormous amount of information available via the Internet is revealing the problem more clearly by spreading it to a greater number of fields. The term "mastery" itself is a strange and problematic one, suggesting a conception of scholarly excellence that, at least on some level, impedes cooperative scholarship. It suggests that we must conquer the material, which makes me think of playing "king" of the hill when I was a child. It was clearly a gendered game that I, as a petite girl, was not expected to win, despite my personal expectation that I *must* win. Perhaps it would be more useful to require that historians simply do what we tell our students to do: to "engage" the work of other historians on the subject. "Engaging" material need not be comprehensive, like mastery, but it must be effective. Many historians already do this out of practicality; I am suggesting that professional historians as a whole change the traditional *concept* of what it means to be a specialist in favor of something more ongoing, interactive, and flexible in its fallibility.

Incorporating a vast, ever-changing array of materials presents yet another problem. We cannot ignore the practical implications of trying to "harness" greater amounts of information, no matter how wedded we are to intellectual goals: one only has so much time to devote to research and writing. Just because we are now using computers for writing and research does not mean we should become one of them. Yet that often becomes the message: now that it is possible to correct every mistake with a minimum of financial expense, scholars are expected to incorporate vast quantities of material into publishable quality manuscripts in a bare minimum of time. But historical work takes time because it usually requires reflection. Using the Internet to follow up on developments on Menken, I often felt like I was in that famous skit from *I Love Lucy*: the one in the candy factory, when the chocolates keep coming faster, and Lucy and Ethel, unable to turn off the machine, cram candy into their mouths and down their bodices in an effort to cope with the overflow. Internet sources can be intellectually exciting, but the speed of materials is increasing and the professional requirements of production are increasing (both in terms of quality and breadth) to the point at which we are reduced to cramming them in without enough reflection.

But there is an odd professional paradox at the heart of all of this electronic archiving: despite worries of having too much material, historians are the ones *most* likely to want to digitize everything. Another rule of the profession is "save everything." One never knows when a piece of information has historic evidence. As much as historians might view the amount of material now available with a certain amount of trepidation, we also have emerged from a culture of scarcity that has preprogrammed us not to discard anything.

And work by other scholars is also increasing the flow of information. The Internet is profoundly changing our intellectual community. Many of the changes are positive and negative at once. A recounting of my experiences with the Menken project helps to illustrate my ambivalence about being part of the Internet community. I mostly consider the ease of communication a good thing, but the negatives are worth discussing because they signal what is lost in the process of all that is gained.

I worked on Menken in isolation until roughly 1998, when I first began to receive e-mails from people who saw my conference papers noted on Internet web sites and discovered my research focus. Our conversations were intellectually enriching and added to the project in the long run, but they also increased the time it took for me to create an overarching narrative able to sustain the increasing variables others added to the story. A rabbi in South Africa, for example, initiated an e-mail exchange that ended with her insisting that my research on Menken's Jewish identity went against her own; she wanted Menken to be Jewish, and demanded that I enlarge my definitions. I stuck with definitions of Jewish identity used in Menken's time, but our exchange did lead me to investigate twentieth-century reflections on Jewish identity and incorporate a more nuanced

discussion on the subject. A magician in Indianapolis electronically introduced me to a retired accountant in upstate New York who admitted,
rather sheepishly, that he believed he might be Menken's descendent. I
decided to include his story for a variety of reasons, but doing so required
significant restructuring. I began to trade e-mails and attached writings
with scholars all over the country—some working on Menken, but many
others focusing on the other figures Menken knew or emulated (Mark
Twain, Lord Byron, Algernon Charles Swinburne), and others who addressed related topics (photography, passing, sporting newspapers).

The Internet community also replaces the isolation traditionally tied to
writing professional history, which makes the discipline far more friendly
to many of us and perhaps less comfortable for many others. Back in 1989,
I remember receiving an application to Tulane's graduate program that
welcomed me and warned me: be prepared that graduate school will be a
lonely experience; you will spend many years researching and writing
alone. The idea horrified me. What was I thinking, going into a profession
that required I give up human contact? Fortunately for me, the Internet
evolved in time to render that prophesy obsolete. I do write in isolation,
but once I put those documents away and click on Internet Explorer, I am
back in a virtual conference that never ends. For me, this is a good thing. I
am a social spirit; I understand my own thoughts better through express-
ing them; I need interaction to be productive. But this is the opposite of
many others who need to be alone with their topic to formulate their own
interpretation. It is true that they could choose to simply stay away, but
what was once a way of life is now a choice that comes with major
limitations.

Because of the Internet, I now know and can converse with all scholars
known to be working on Menken. Again, this is both positive and negative; it creates a rich, creative intellectual community, but it can also make
it difficult to separate oneself to craft one's own approach. In this milieu,
we are no longer isolated scholars meeting up once a year at conferences;
we are in constant conversation. At one point in time, I would have said
that visibility via Internet gave me an advantage; now I would say that
participating in the intellectual community electronically has become so
common that those who do not are at a disadvantage. Many historians
who, partly out of comfort, continue to use only traditional methods and
ignore the electronic medium may find themselves out of touch with
current scholarship. They become the wallflowers in a ballroom filled with

innovative dancers. Much of this breaks down along generational lines, however, causing a paradoxical problem: the ones least invested in the electronic community are often the ones with the most power in academic departments.

Nor can the virtual archive adequately replace the "real" archive in terms of sources, although it can greatly enhance our scholarship. My experiences researching Menken's early life as a celebrity in East Texas illustrate why we need to get our hands dirty. Knowing that Menken had first appeared in newspapers in Liberty and that her first known marriage certificate was signed in Livingston, I drove out to explore the findings of a few regional libraries. In the process of mucking around I not only discovered previously unrecorded evidence of Menken's activities in obscure sources, I also came to understand her ongoing relationship with this part of the country. Because of persistent (and false) stories of her girlhood in Nacogdoches, they still regard her as a treasured legendary figure. Driving through the lush but sparsely populated region, passing cinderblock strip malls now turned over for neighborhood bingo, and looking in vain for a healthy lunch, I realized that she was part of a glorious, mythological past. As a writer, visiting the region helped me both to picture her life there and to understand why legends of her Texas birth persisted despite all evidence. I later found several web sites discussing Menken as a daughter of Texas but, not surprisingly, they were singularly unhelpful. They, too, presented Menken as a legendary figure, but she was now cut free from the gritty, ragged aspects of the region. By virtue of the medium, she was as polished as a debutante from Dallas; the frontier conditions were erased in favor of simplistic frontier mythology. None of the material was new; it had come from hyperbolic texts written in the late nineteenth century. The poetry I had discovered in pages of crumbling newsprint went unmentioned; I would never have found it had I traveled to Texas only by computer.

Durba Ghosh's "National Narratives and the Politics of Miscegenation," in this collection, suggests a similar sense that the location and personnel of the archive may provide critical clues to the project. Ghosh writes, "what seemed like a great project in Britain was a terrible, even unspeakable one in India." It is easy to imagine the absurdity if she had tried to pursue her same methodology relying wholly on the Internet (in the unlikely scenario that both nations had the resources). I picture the British archives posting an exhibit on Colonial alliances between British men and

Indian women, while subject and key word searches on the Indian web sites respond repeatedly with "no such match"—suggesting that the historical subject is a reality in one nation and not another. By Internet alone, Ghosh would have missed the human dimension of the story that explained both the wealth and dearth of sources and the difficulty of finding out the truth of whether or not those relationships "were as carefree and consensual for the native women as for the men."

The experience I had in Texas was repeated over and over again, in California, Ohio, New York, Massachusetts, London, and Paris. The Internet sources corresponding with the places I had explored yielded much of what had appeared in major publications, but little new material. In terms of searching the life of a specific individual—even one with three hundred to fourteen hundred web sites mentioning her name—the Internet was far less helpful than visiting archives for a variety of reasons.

I did have some success when I used the Internet for materials originally produced for national consumption. I was fortunate that Menken was famous during the Civil War years, as there is a slew of web sites giving access to periodicals produced during the war. Through the rather extraordinary Making of America web site, a digital library maintained by the University of Michigan and financially supported by the Andrew W. Mellon Foundation, I was able to find several references to Menken and actually pull up the pages of the materials, visible in their original format. It was not the same as holding *Vanity Fair Magazine* in my hands and seeing where these stories fell within the scope of the magazine, but they were quickly available to me right at my desk, without having to apply for a grant or take a trip.

But had I only relied on digital archives, I would have missed nonverbal clues in my search. What surrounds the material found? How is it placed within the larger document? What does the cover of the item suggest about the target audience and how it was being packaged for sale? Does the quality of paper or print suggest something valuable about its production that changes the way we interpret the words on the page? For scholars of the history of the book and the many historians using material culture, digital reproductions are not adequate substitutions for artifacts.

Because of the nature of my project on Menken, using digital reproductions of most artifacts did not pose a problem for me. But they were not enough; they told tales I had already heard. I needed to see what had been overlooked by curators and archivists posting the materials; I needed to see what had been deemed unimportant. The big difference between trawling the digital archives and visiting physical ones came in the wealth of seemingly useless manuscript material I found tucked in collections around the country. Just as Tony Ballantyne describes the "restless and seemingly ceaseless shuttling of paper" he found and followed in "Mr. Peal's Archive," I found wealth in the sheer volume of supposedly insignificant artifacts. Online catalogs rarely mentioned the details of their collections on Menken or one of her acquaintances, so I was often surprised to find letters, notes, photographs, playbills, and invitations that had managed to survive because some curator at one time made the decision to keep them, despite the fact that few if any had obvious merit. This allowed me to become familiar with Menken's handwriting, stationery, and phrasing at different points in her life—knowledge that became incredibly helpful in determining how to use various other materials. As I have indicated, Menken's bizarre history and circuitous route through popular culture has led to a number of false stories being written about her (which she completely encouraged, I should add). Even those publishing supposedly reliable biographies complete with footnotes have added to the layers of falsehood, for a variety of strange reasons.[8] The bits of flotsam I found collected on archival shores allowed me to make educated decisions about how to use particular material and made it clear where others had embroidered fiction over fact.

Access and Presence: Who's In and Who's Out

I have found the Internet most valuable in clarifying why Menken is compelling in the present day. History is about how the past is alive and active in the present, and never is that more clearly illustrated than on the Web. Because web sites are funded and maintained at a variety of levels by all sorts of entities—corporations, individuals, groups, organizations, enthusiasts working ad hoc—they are completely driven by present-day interests. Only a portion of historical writings on the Internet is "scholarly" in the way that professional historians define the term, that is, an argument written in conversation with previous work on the subject and fully supported by reproducible sources.

Because identity politics are extremely important at the moment to scholars and laypeople alike, Menken is rarely found on the Internet for what she *did* during her lifetime, but rather for what she possibly *was*. Her antics add color and entertainment, so they appear in the articles, but they are not the central reason for featuring her on all of those web sites. What she "was" is further determined by whoever is hosting the web site. If the web site is funded by a Jewish organization, she is Jewish (usually without question). If the web site is one devoted to a conference on race in America, she may show up as African American, but if the conference is about transgender theory, she might appear as an example of nineteenth-century gender transgression. Feminist web sites present Menken as feminist, ignoring the many aspects of her self-performance that would jeopardize that image. Menken may have been all of these things, but each web site features its favored identity over the others.

The variety of Menken images is not unique to the Internet; magazines and books, after all, are also sponsored by organizations with some purpose behind them. A hundred years before the Internet truly blossomed, publications began focusing on Menken because of her identity and highlighting the events of her life that supported whatever claim was in question. What makes the web sites different from the publications on paper is that they disappear from public record when there is no longer interest in the subject on the part of the sponsor. They are thus more closely tied with present-day concerns than conventional publications, because the methods of placing them and then removing them are relatively quick, unmediated, and temporary. With the exception of a few major professionally funded sites, then, using web sites as source material is problematic for two reasons: many disappear without a trace and without warning, and few provide any means for checking their information.

At the same time, this ebb and flow of web sites also suggests the democratic nature of posting material on the Web. In the United States at least, it can be done cheaply and without revealing anything about the person posting the site. This can be a positive good in the case of marginalized historical subjects, such as the Queer Latino community discussed by Horacio N. Roque Ramírez. He rightly points out that "queer lives and queer desires" are not "the priority of mainstream historicizing and archiving practices." The Internet provides a tool for gathering intelligence on topics overlooked by academia and intellectual institutions. In this way, the Internet as archive may be said to go against what Craig Robertson concludes in his essay, "Mechanisms of Exclusion," because the process of placing a web site is not so much determined by power as it is a process of archiving that creates power. As long as the researcher using the site is open to .com or .net information sources, as opposed to .edu, .org, or .gov, the information appears on a level playing field.

One of the central questions about the role the Internet plays in historical research must be one of access, which is directly related to questions of representation. Who does and who does not have access to materials available on the Internet? Certainly some parts of the world are more wired than others, and those are the places most shaping Internet resources. Within those regions, scholarly institutions and the institutions that fund them, such as the Mellon or MacArthur Foundations, are deciding what is of historical importance, and thus, who gets represented.

Internet web sites are publicly available to anyone with access to a computer and the means to get on the Web, and as most public libraries in the United States now have computer, Americans as a whole have access to a wide variety of sources. Databases are the exception. They work much like Internet digital archives, but their use is purchased, usually by an institution. Being a member of a wealthy university, such as Harvard or Princeton, can be a tremendous advantage, because they are able to afford subscriptions to an unbelievable number of databases. I discovered this when I visited the Schlesinger Library this past summer. The library itself has stellar collections and a wonderful staff, but I was equally awed by the number of databases that are accessible through the Harvard computer terminals. I was able to do years worth of research in one month by using keyword searches. For example, using Accessible Archives allowed me to search through fifty-five years of *Godey's Lady's Book* in a fraction of the time it would have taken me to read through all those magazines. Admittedly, key word searches are not exactly subtle; I am sure that I missed a lot of useful material along the way simply because I could not think of the correct terminology. Also, I had no idea how these stories fit into the larger magazine. Were they part of a special series? Were they surrounded with particular advertisements? But for anyone who has spent months searching through newspapers and periodicals the old-fashioned way, it is hard to see the ability to do a keyword search as anything but a godsend.

Perhaps the most obvious problem with electronic archives is that resource-rich cultures and institutions are dominating Internet use and thus determine what is present on the Web. Poorer nations are clearly underrepresented; one is hard pressed to find primary material digitally archived for many countries in Africa, Asia, and South America for exam-

ple. This situation exacerbates, and perhaps surpasses, the existing Western bias found in print culture.⁹ The already problematic situation in
Uzbekistan outlined by Jeff Sahadeo, for example, is compounded. The
complicated history of documentation inside the nation is presented to the
Internet world as simply silence. But we also see this happening within
nations, as groups without consistent access to the technology are absent,
even if they live in wealthy, Internet-oriented cultures, such as the United
States, Canada, and Western Europe. British historian R. J. Morris suggests as much when he comments dryly that "it is easier to communicate
with computer-using colleagues in California, Warsaw and Sydney, than in
those in South London or the West of Scotland who are not (yet) 'on the
network.' "¹⁰ If the scholars of these regions are not using e-mail, then they
are probably not yet funding digital archives either.

Established institutions are determining what gets archived. Do they
leave out traditionally marginalized groups? Does the *way* the material is
archived leave out particular groups? In terms of historical materials, African Americans and women, white and of color, are well represented in
Internet archives because the medium emerged when scholarship in these
fields was at its height. Indeed, African American men and women and
white women are some of the best-documented groups on the Web by
professionals and nonprofessional historical sites alike. For me as a professor, the many reproductions of runaway slave ads, for example, have
added a great deal to my students' ability to work with primary materials
on slavery. Likewise, many web sites devoted to civil rights are meticulous
in scope and often include film footage. That said, there is next to nothing
on other less popular but equally important topics such as African Americans and welfare, grassroots movements, or daily life between Reconstruction and the civil rights era. So, yes, African Americans have a presence,
but that presence is fairly narrow in scope. Sites on women's history are
more comprehensive, in many ways electronically paralleling the sophisticated development of the field. But they, too, are limited by their apparently implicit need to create a history that parallels traditional (read:
white, male, middle-class, Protestant) history. Thus there are several truly
amazing web sites on topics about women in public life: women in politics, medicine, abolitionism, or temperance. Web sites on more domestic
subjects, such as women's dress or food preparation, tend to be posted by
nonprofessional enthusiasts.

And, of course, any material on less studied or less well-documented groups can be much more difficult to find. In my informal rambles through the Web, I have found that groups that are historically textually silent are the most poorly represented, because it takes innovative research methods to write their history. Native American groups, for example, are beginning to use the Web a great deal more, but, like African Americans, a lack of textual materials poses a problem. Individual Native American women who lived before the late twentieth century (with the major exceptions of Pocahontas and Sacagawea) are almost entirely absent. A huge number of immigrant groups of are also left out; if one were to try to track American immigrant history only by Internet, it would appear that most immigration began and ended in the decades around 1900. Poor white Americans outside of the South are also one of the least well-documented groups. Scholarly Latino web sites are beginning to emerge, but material on Latina women before the late twentieth century is still incredibly scarce. Not surprisingly, the same groups that receive little attention within institutions or require greater innovation in order to document their histories are receiving the least attention on the Net.

The irony here is that the Internet has the potential to provide unprecedented access to historical nontextual sources. We can already see some effort to make use of the Internet's ability to convey sound, images, and movement as well as text. There are a few historical archives beginning to address textually silent groups through oral history archives and song archives (where one can hear the person via Internet, as well as read the transcript), film archives, and sites showing material objects that may be viewed from different angles and distances. Most of these sites are rich in primary sources but weak in secondary ones. We need to see a better integration of the two.

Historical work on all groups would be served well by having easy access to digital collections of regional, municipal, and specialized newspapers. Right now the best solution to exhaustive travel is interlibrary loan, if the microfilm is available. Archiving such newspapers would probably best be handled at a state level: the Minnesota state archives, for example, would have a digital collection of all Minnesota newspapers. Doing so, however, would be complicated by the fact that many of Minnesota's historic newspapers cannot be found in Minnesota, but are part of collections in larger archives scattered about the country, such as The American Antiquarian Society or the Library of Congress. Such a site is sorely needed, however, and would go a long way towards providing primary information on groups often left off the radar of national history. Right now the most comprehensive digitally archived newspaper is the *New York Times*.[11] But while it is true that the *New York Times* has been America's national newspaper for the past century, it was not the most influential paper during the nineteenth century and did not even exist in the eighteenth. Nor does a newspaper such as the *Times* begin to address such subjects as how Japanese fared in Seattle during World War II, or western coverage of the Plains Indian Wars, or the impact of Cambodian refugees on Florida race relations.

Passing the Torch: Teaching Students History in the Internet Age

Our final question must be how do we teach our students to use the Internet as a tool for historical research? Rosenzweig suggests that "future graduate programs will probably have to teach such social-scientific and quantitative methods as well as such other skills as 'digital archaeology' (the ability to 'read' arcane computer formats), 'digital diplomatics' (the modern version of the old science of authenticating documents), and data mining (the ability to find the historical needle in the digital hay)."[12] He is probably correct. But first I must learn these skills myself.

At the private Midwestern research university where I now teach, most of my students have grown up with computers. My experience suggests that while I can give my students guidance, they have far more to teach me about the Internet than I can ever hope to teach them. I believe that I must help them learn to distinguish a reputable source from a nonreliable one, to look for complexity where they find shallow simplicity, to see what is not there as well as what is readily apparent. In other words, I can teach them to use the Internet wisely by teaching them the same skills I taught before the Internet became a viable research tool. I have colleagues who believe this includes policing what students use, either by putting out lists of what web sites they are allowed to consult or by requiring students to electronically post the web sites they cite so that the professor can check them herself. But the time we have with students is limited and dear, and the energy and time we have for preparation is limited, no matter how dedicated we are to pedagogy. I do not see the value in sacrificing teaching valuable analytic skills in order to teach ones limited only to Internet research. The answer clearly is to bring the two together: to teach students "to think," as they say, always keeping in mind that their lives, academic and otherwise, are increasingly mediated by technology.

The Internet as an archive poses specific problems for undergraduate teaching. Unfortunately, the many .com sites sometimes confuse my students. The plethora of legitimate material is rivaled by the slew of web sites consisting of little more than celebratory prose that gums up my students' papers and leads them away from thoughtful analysis. The simple solution is to tell them to use only web sites with .edu or .org in the address. Even so, because students are often writing papers alongside web sites they are checking, my colleagues and I have noticed increased problems with plagiarism. I am not talking about the students who willfully steal from other sources—that happened just as frequently before the Internet came into our lives. I am speaking of students who sloppily cut, paste, and paraphrase documents they dredge up while writing the paper. They sometimes reproduce the language and even the organization of other sources, without apparently realizing that simply footnoting the material does not render it legal. I would argue that the boundary between the paper they are writing and the paper they are citing is rendered conceptually thin by a medium that places the two documents side by side. Discussing the problem in my classes has gone a long way toward reducing it, suggesting that while in the process of writing many of the students become confused about divisions between their own paper and the web sites they cite. They know the difference between a published paper and their own; this is not a problem of understanding, but rather one of perception and remaining aware.

Truthfully, I fully believe that the best thing I can teach them about the Internet is that it is not the only or even the best tool for the job. The more the Internet comes into usage, the more I find I need to urge (and sometimes even coerce) them to use the library and archives, to contact reference librarians and consult bibliographic sources, to keep in mind census records and microfilmed city directories. Because Internet sites, no matter how well constructed, are not the same as working with tactile artifacts, deciphering handwritten records, or talking with a knowledgeable curator. Losing oneself in a pile of textbooks in the back of a library brings a measure of contemplation that easily surpasses impatiently surfing the Web. Waiting while the computer thinks simply is not the same as wading through prose. My students are comfortable with the Internet; they need to be taught the virtues of the less entertaining but perhaps more useful physical repositories of information.

Raising the Bar

In my search for thoughts on the Internet and research, I found many comparing the emergence of the Internet to the advent of the printing press. Since we are clearly searching for similes to make the changes we face comprehensible, I offer up the car. Two decades ago in *More Work for Mother: Ironies of Household Technology from the Open Hearth to the Micro-wave*, Ruth Schwartz Cowan demonstrated that the American response to new "labor saving" technology is to raise the bar, not give ourselves more time off but rather to expect more production.[13] The impact of the Internet follows that trend. Like the automobile, the Internet shrinks distance and changes the relationship of the traveler and destination. The invention of the automobile has changed our everyday lives in every way. It has led to many wonderful things, but it has also contributed to a more stressful life: commuting, excessive travel, complex extracurricular schedules, and the possibility of cramming in many small errands at the end of a long day. The Internet acts much like the car, in that the World Wide Web is a complex network of highways and the computer acts as our vehicle for speeding from point to point at the rate of whatever access we have purchased. Our standards have gone up; a meticulous gathering of material that was once the mark of a seasoned historian is now expected in graduate level papers. Theoretically, it is too easy to find the information to expect otherwise. But let us also be honest: the computer often does not live up to the ideal, and because we are creating expectations that leave no room for technological breakdown, this can cause real problems.

My own experience with Menken has led me to see the Internet as adding to my workload, not lessening it. I do not see this as necessarily a bad thing. In terms of scholarship, it has its benefits. Finding all of those web sites featuring Menken forced me to reevaluate my work within a present-day context. The presence of the Internet community means that I work with greater awareness of others. And as more digitized materials find their way into Internet web sites (as opposed to subscribed databases), I will come to rely more on my computer as a site of research.

But however bizarre and interesting the materials I have found through my computer, they never send me on flights of imagination like paging through original newspapers and getting the dust of two centuries under my nails. A picture of Menken on the Internet is impersonal and uninteresting in a way that can never be said about an original carte-de-visite in the palm of my hand—especially if I find a bend in the corner or words scrawled on the back. After a few weeks of reading through private letters, I came to know Menken in a personal way I did not even try to describe in the book. I could eventually tell with a glance whether the letter would be emotional, flirtatious, or prim, before I began to decipher the spidery script. And it was these ephemeral and, to me, fascinating details that fueled my interest and kept it burning through all the slow, painful, and numerous stages of writing, revising, cutting, and rewriting. And perhaps, however rational I have tried to keep my argument in this essay, it is that human response to tangible artifacts that I have seen time and again in my students as well as myself that convinces me that virtual archives will never serve as more than a place to begin and end the research journey; never as a place to dwell.

Notes

1 Roy Rosenzweig, "Scarcity or Abundance? Preserving the Past in a Digital Era," *American Historical Review* 108, 3 (June 2003): 738.

2 Carolyn Hamilton, Verne Harris, Jane Taylor, Michele Pickover, Graeme Reid, and Razia Saleh, eds., *Refiguring the Archive* (Dordrecht: Kluwer Academic Publishers), 25.

3 Lorraine Daston, "Marvelous Facts and Miraculous Evidence in Early Modern Europe," in James Chandler, Arnold I. Davidson, and Harry Harootunian, eds., *Questions of Evidence: Proof, Practice, and Persuasion Across the Disciplines* (Chicago: University of Chicago Press, 1994), 243.

4 Peter Novick, *That Noble Dream: The "Objectivity Question" and the American Historical Profession* (New York: Cambridge University Press, 1988), 1.

5 Verlyn Klinkenborg, "Information That Humans Create," *New York Times*, November 12, 2003; see *New York Times* online archives.

6 Rebecca Seamen, AHR electronic discussion, letter of September 6, 2003, posted at http://www.historycooperative.org/phorum.

7 Rosenzweig, "Scarcity or Abundance?" 758.

8 See Renée M. Sentilles, *Performing Menken: Adah Isaacs Menken and the Birth of American Celebrity* (New York: Cambridge University Press, 2003), 268–80.

9 Roger A. Griffin, "Using the Internet as a Resource for Historical Research

and Writing," posted on the web site of Austin Community College's History Department, http://www.austincc.edu/history/research.html.

10 R. J. Morris, "Computers and the Subversion of British History," *Journal of British Studies* 34, 4: 511; posted on http://www.jostore.org.

11 See Proquest.com.

12 Rosenzweig, "Scarcity or Abundance?" 758.

13 Ruth Schwartz Cowan, *More Work for Mother: Ironies of Household Technology from the Open Hearth to the Microwave* (New York: Basic Books: 1983).

PART II

States of the Art

"OFFICIAL" ARCHIVES AND COUNTER-HISTORIES

Jennifer S. Milligan

"What Is an Archive?"

in the History of Modern France

Many, even great minds, remain unfamiliar with the meaning

of "archives."—Alphonse Huillard Breholles,

"Les Archives de l'Empire"

FOUNDED, LIKE THE MODERN FRENCH NATION, in 1789, the Archives nationales has stood at the center of debates over the proper relationship between state and society throughout French history. The revolutionary act of creating a national archive posed the question "What is an archive?" at the very founding of the new nation. The Archives outlived its Revolutionary architects and remained to testify to the fraught history of the French nation-state. Throughout its own history, the Archives has been the subject of intense debate, inside and outside its walls, over the meaning, function, and contours of this institution. Who should have access to the evidence of the state? Was the Archives nationales the proper location of historical information? What, indeed, was the meaning of the "archives" in modern France?

The meaning and the history of the Archives nationales have most often been subsumed under the sign of historical practice. The nineteenth century has been called the "century of history" for archival collections in general, and the Archives nationales in particular, characterized by efforts of historians to press its holdings and of archivists to classify documents and to publish inventories.[1] This history dovetails with the history of the historical profession in France and beyond, with its increasingly self-conscious and self-confident practitioners fanning out over the globe in search of official documents, eager to reveal the objective history of the nation-state.[2] And indeed, it was under the tutelage of the Second Empire (1850–70) that the National Archives (then called the Archives of the Empire) worked to publicize its historical riches and create comfortable working conditions for scholars. While the archivist Alphonse Huillard-Breholles could lament in 1863 that the meaning of "archives" remained obscured to many, today the "archive" stands as a metaphor for all things historical, thanks in no small part to the work in this period to fix the meaning of the institution in the Archives nationales.

However, while its contents were indeed pressed into the service of scientific history, the Archives nationales of post-Revolutionary France was not merely a documentary treasure trove for historians seeking to tell the story of the vicissitudes of politics and the glory of the French past. To be sure, the Archives nationales is a central institution for the production of histories of France, but it is above all an institution with a history of institutionalization: a history that is deeply implicated in the politics of the nation-state as well as the production of scholarship and the promotion of national memory and identity. To untangle this complicated archive story, this essay will look at the way that the question "What is an archive?" was posed at two key moments in the Archives' history: its founding in the Revolution and its reorganization under Napoleon III's Second Empire. While these moments could be considered "foundational" (the Revolution founded the modern Archives, and the Second Empire geared the institution toward historical research), they also suggest that such foundational narratives obscure central tensions at the heart of the Archives.

What emerges in this investigation is that the question of the Archives nationales became a question of control over the memory of the state's exercise of power over citizens; and of who had the power to mobilize or intervene in this memory to shape the body politic, to make as well as to write history. Thus arguments over the Archives' function, identity, or content would be as much about the shape of the French polity as about the nature of historical truth. Indeed, rather than accepting the idea that the Archives nationales (or any archive, as we see especially in the essays by Peter Fritzsche and John Randolph that follow) is first and foremost a collection of historical documents, this essay argues for the importance of history in understanding the complexes of ideas, practices, material, and power that make this collection and its communication to a variously defined "public" possible. The history of the French National Archives is an "archive story" of its own, one that forces us to consider the relationship between the history *of* the Archives, and the claims of historians, citizens, and the state on history *in* the Archives.

The Archives *dites nationales*

Before 1789, just as there were no citizens and no modern nation-state, neither was there an institution akin to a national archives of France. When the National Assembly moved to create its own archives on July 29, 1789 (within two weeks of the storming of the Bastille), official archival depositories were numerous and dispersed. The king had his *trésor des chartes* (the treasury of charters, a collection that contained treaties and other documents dating back to Dagobert and Charlemagne); each parish and monastery had its own charterhouse, with records of land holdings and registers; the courts held the records of their proceedings.[3] The Assembly's archives were at first closer to these Old Regime institutions, designed to hold the constitution and all acts emanating from the new Revolutionary government. The first (at least nominally) national archives came a year later, when the Assembly's archives became the National Archives (September 9, 1790) and were declared to be "the depository of all acts that establish the constitution of the kingdom, the rights of its public, its laws."[4] The National Archives would contain the constitution of the nation, the rights enjoyed by its citizens, the laws that emanated from and formed the state. The Archives, in other words, expressed the relationship between the people and government that founded the new French nation.

Regulating access emerged alongside the regulation of content as a modern archival issue. The Archives gained their modern legal and physical foundations under the Convention, with the law of 7 *messidor* year II (June 25, 1794). This law broke with the tradition of the Old Regime in two significant ways—in terms of centralization (vs. dispersion to repositories around the country) and of public access (vs. Old Regime secrecy). Article 1 declared the Archives nationales to be "the central depository for the entire Republic."[5] Legally, it prescribed the centralization of all papers from the former establishments of the Old Regime (such as the abolished institutions and the Church) and all documents pertaining to confiscated property and the personal papers of émigrés and former heads of state, thus also providing the Archives with its physical content and a link to the past and extending the claims to the "national."[6] It also made the right of access to these documents a right of all citizens: article 37 allowed that "all citizens can ask, in all depositories, at the dates and times fixed, communication of the pieces contained therein," without cost and provided that they remain on the premises. Although its prescribed techniques and the extent of its application would be debated throughout the Archives' history, the right of access was not officially rewritten until 1979.[7]

The law of 7 *messidor* seemed to legislate and institutionalize the separation of the "historical" from the "national" Archives. The Archives nationales were to contain the Constitution and acts of the new order based on the natural law of the Rights of Man; the National Library (Bibliothèque nationale) would be the seat of art, history, and the sciences, offering tools for the instruction of the citizen. Citizens would thus have access to the workings of politics through the documents contained in the Archives and access to "history" and its acceptable fruits in the Library. A triage committee was convened to continue the work of classifying and conserving (and when necessary destroying) documents and sending them to their proper institution.[8] This law could be read quite differently, however, for the meaning of "history" was itself subject to historical change, and the Archives held the evidence of a new nation that would have a history all its own. This history resided in archival records of the nation's birth, in papers charting the fits and starts of its early years, and in documents establishing a firm legal foundation for its growth. The law of 7 *messidor* thus stood as the knot that tied nation and state to its new, ever-emerging history—a history that evolved with the workings of government.

Standing at the gates of the Archives was the national archivist who managed this crucial institution. At its inception, the position of archivist was that of a government functionary, elected by the National Assembly and responsible for following its directives and answering its requests for documents. The nation's first archivist, Armand-Gaston Camus, was a well-known lawyer and spokesman for the legal profession (his *Letters on the Lawyer's Profession*, which appeared in 1772, remained a classic on the law well into the nineteenth century). He performed a variety of duties for his employers—both government and citizens. Camus's most important functions included the conservation and communication of essential documents to citizens and officials alike, but also the sorting and classification of the Archives described as *dépouillement*, which meant variously to inspect, to cast off, or to divest.[9] The ambiguity of this term and the results of its application would be debated throughout the history of the Archives, for it involved selecting what belonged in the Archives and determining how that content would be categorized.

With the shape of the nation-state and that of the Archives so intimately linked, it is not surprising that changes of regime would mean changes in the Archives. While the law of 7 *messidor* continued to govern the Archives, each new government attempted to make its mark on the institution. A most ambitious post-Revolutionary archival vision belonged, not surprisingly, to Napoleon.[10] With the help of Pierre-Claude-François Daunou, another lawyer and former representative appointed to replace Camus at his death in 1804, Napoleon theorized an Imperial Archives that would centralize evidence of the Empire and its memory, spread across time and space. In this way Napoleon's archive was very much a continuation of his Revolutionary predecessors' depository. Concerned with property titles as well as history, Napoleon ordered the capture of archives as well as lands on his foreign campaigns. Equally obsessed with constructing a government at home and a lasting legacy, Napoleon kept scrupulous notes, all to be held in the Archives (though kept in a separate office, away from the gaze of his ministers or the public).

Despite Napoleon's forays into archival policy, Daunou, who served until 1840, managed to continue the work started by Camus by focusing his efforts on the classification of those documents that made up the national documentary patrimony. He divided the archives into five sections—property and topography, judicial, administrative, legislative, and historical monuments, each with an alphabetic and numeric code. This move institutionalized the presence of the raw materials of "history" in the Archives: the monuments comprised mostly the *trésor des chartes* and treated them as "monuments" because of their antiquity and anachronism. This is not to say the Archives drew much in the way of interest from historians—from 1804 to 1816, there were only seven reported requests from scholars.[11]

This poor showing on the part of historians is not necessarily evidence that the institution was empty of "historical" information, materials, or interest. The boundary between the scholarly and the legal or administrative was hardly fixed in this period. Under the Bourbons and the July Monarchy François Guizot and Jules Michelet both found work in the administration of the Archives as well as in research in its contents. Michelet was appointed head of the Historical Section from 1830 to 1852; Guizot enjoyed significant power over the institution as the Minister of Public Instruction until 1848. For them, history and politics were intimately linked. While in the Old Regime royal historiographers, who were most often jurists or functionaries, had consulted documents and written histories in the service of the king, historians such as Michelet, Guizot, and Thierry (themselves functionaries or trained lawyers) were inspired by and participated in politics as citizens. They regarded politics as inseparable from the law, history, and future of the French nation. The issues addressed by these historians and the methods employed to address them were shared by the science of jurisprudence. The Archives embodied these shared interests in this period, paving the way for scientific history.[12] Camus and Daunou, both venerated as lawyers as well as for their active roles in politics, thus fit perfectly into the Archives' directorship.

It would be up to the next generation of directors to translate this interest in archival materials into changes in the institution. Increased interest from legal and historical study manifested itself in a public reading room, installed in 1847 by Daunou's successor, Jean-Antoine Letronne. A respected antiquarian and historian of art known for his prodigious scholarship, Letronne took up the post upon Daunou's retirement in 1840. Letronne was typical of a new generation of archivists that would head the central state depository: still not trained as an archivist but also not a jurist, he was a scholar experienced in the administration of institutions, having held posts as the inspector general of universities, administrator of the Collège de France (where he took Daunou's chair in history in 1831), and a conservator at the Royal Library.

The Archives changed names with each change of regime, and during the turmoil that brought the Second Republic into being, Letronne tacked up a sign reading "Archives of the Republic" to obscure the royal title it had acquired.[13] This hasty gesture symbolized the return of the Archives and the nation to their republican roots, but also underlined the Archives' relative stability. The institution of the Archives had not changed much in the intervening years. Despite his opening of the reading room, Letronne's short tenure failed to produce any substantial changes in the Archives' practices regarding public access. The gesture, however empty in practice, nonetheless signaled a will to welcome scholars to the institution. On Letronne's death in 1848 his post was given to François-Armand Chabrier, a functionary with a similar institutional experience, though lacking the scholarly reputation of his predecessor. Scholarship had not yet won the day at the Archives of France. The idea of a truly national Archives, however, had stuck, regardless of the distractions of political upheaval since the Napoleonic era.

It would take another Bonaparte, Louis-Napoleon, to revive governmental regard for the institution. It also took a Bonapartist regime to bring to fruition the republican dream of public interest in the Archives. The Bonapartist alchemy of quasi-democratic institutional forms suffused with the dictatorial exercise of administrative control was exercised on the Archives. Under Napoleon III, the Archives were transformed into an institution manifestly dedicated to the public interest, especially if that interest was in historical study. The archival policies of the Second Empire were devoted to treading the fine line between the increasing demands of the self-styled liberal professional historian and the indistinct and ever-changing (but nonetheless real and compelling) notion of raison d'état that guided the Archives administrative functions. The Archives—the Imperial Archives as of 1852—had a strong administrative pedigree and contained historical documents. However, administration and history proved to be a powerful and volatile mix under the Second Empire, for this combination pitted public against government and highlighted the distinctions that emerged in the as yet unstable nation-state.

Privacy, Privilege, and Public Interest: The Praslin Case

> Silence and obscurity may not be had for the asking. . . .
> It is your fate to be remembered against your will.
> —Rachel Field, *All This and Heaven Too*

François-Armand Chabrier directed the Archives of the Republic when Louis Napoleon Bonaparte made history with his coup d'état in 1850. The transition from Republican to Imperial Archives was, in general, a smooth one, though Michelet was eventually dismissed from his post as head of the Historical Section in 1852. In the few histories of the Archives of this period, any trouble in the workings of the institution is likely to be attributed to Chabrier's reputation as a curmudgeonly taskmaster. Whatever complaints there were about Chabrier's directorship, it can be said that he ran a tight ship. It seems that most of his lack of popularity stemmed from his refusal to allow archivists to work on personal scholarly projects during business hours and his insistence on attention to the archival duty. He yearned for earlier days when "order reigned in the establishment," before the influence of those who could not stand surveillance and supervision allowed abuses to be given free reign.[14] His tenure was for the most part punctuated by petty disagreements with staff rather than grand institutional efforts. Chabrier was continually frustrated with the institution and his lack of power to impose the kind of order on the Archives that he felt it required. This order, however, went beyond the organization of personnel and papers, as his vision of the Archives required the institution to be an expression of the social contract. This vision put him in direct conflict with individuals in high places in and out of government, and with the trajectory that the Archives were to follow in the Second Empire.

Chabrier's archival vision comes into view in a dispute over the status of a group of papers pertaining to an infamous murder case that caused much uproar at the end of the July Monarchy. In 1847, the duc du Praslin (or Choiseul-Praslin) apparently brutally murdered his wife. The case was particularly scandalous in that it was speculated that the duke was having an affair with a young governess charged with the care of his children.[15] The case never made it to trial, however, for the duke committed suicide in jail before being brought to justice. The public was riveted on the case, as it resonated with popular fascination with and repugnance at the private lives of the privileged classes, an interest that was as political as it was prurient.[16] This scandal stood out, however: as a particularly salacious example in a series of political and personal misdeeds of members of the French political elite, the Praslin case brought public disgust to a head, fueling the political and moral crisis that would bring on the Revolution of 1848.[17]

The volatile mixture of public, private, and privilege was not so easily contained even when the revolution was over. In 1854 Minister of the State Achille Fould approached Chabrier with a request to deal with the papers of the Praslin case held at the Archives. The Comte de Breteuil, guardian of the orphans of the duke and duchess (and perhaps more importantly, senator and father-in-law to Fould) had written to the minister to request "the return, or preferably the burning in my presence, of all the letters, family papers and miscellaneous that, in my view, belong to the nine children I represent." Loath to see the papers conserved and thus possibly consulted, Breteuil saw his request as "driven by propriety." This propriety went beyond the notion of personal conduct into the realm of law. He asked not for the court transcripts or the defendant's statement, for those without question belonged to the Court. Making this distinction between the public and the private, Breteuil appealed to the law and numerous precedents as well as the "justice of his Majesty and his government."[18] Because of their salacious and ultimately "private" content, the papers were legally the property of the children and the Praslin family, he maintained; thus justice in the public sphere of law as well as in the private sphere of reputation required the destruction of the papers.

The question of honor and its place in the regulation of the Archives turned out to be more complicated than Breteuil had imagined.[19] Fould did not simply order the destruction of the papers. Instead he went through proper channels and duly submitted the request to Chabrier, who found no legal basis for granting the request. As he sympathized with the Praslin children and Breteuil's faith in the law, he explained, he would like to respond positively. If the "law, his majesty's justice and government allowed for the return or destruction requested," then Chabrier might be willing to cast aside "other considerations, other reasons to object" in order to satisfy this "understandable, and completely legitimate desire, in view of the unhappiness and suffering of an honorable family." But the interests of family honor did not stand above the law, and granting the destruction would "unfortunately implicate the code and the justice of the Emperor."[20]

The law quite clearly required that documents in criminal cases remain the property of the courts that dealt with them. The question of privacy and family honor, however, raised a serious issue given the fact that there was no protection from public access to the papers. No specific body of Archives' legislation had yet approached the implications of access for the private life of the individual citizen. Access to the materials held in the institution was governed by the law of 7 *messidor* and had been modified in practice throughout the Archives' short history. Originally a democratic right (albeit limited to the limited category of the citizen), it had become a privilege granted to scholars and functionaries who sought access through proper channels.[21] This practice had not been challenged, however, as few frequented the Archives even for historical research. The guarantee of access, raised as a check against the secret workings of government, was designed to give the citizen power vis-à-vis government. Now the question was raised about the possibility of government providing individuals a window into the private affairs of their fellow citizens.[22]

The question of removing materials had likewise not been publicly raised. While the 7 *messidor* law also called for the distribution of documents throughout the institutions of the nation (as noted, administrative, judicial, and property matters would be stored in the Archives, while literature and history would be the province of the Library), it did not imply that these documents would ever leave the purview of the state. Papers had been confiscated from émigrés and men of state and their families had donated papers to the Archives, but the issue of removing papers from the record had not been legislated, nor so baldly posed. Rumors that the Bourbons had taken cartons from the Archives and had failed to return them would circulate into the twentieth century, drawing the ire of critics of that regime and its unlawful exercise of privilege on the documentary patrimony of the nation. Breteuil had alluded to precedents of papers being extracted from the Archives but did not seek to exercise privilege. To the contrary, he made his request as a citizen under the law and sought legal redress, claiming the primacy of family honor over the integrity of the archival record. The state held information about a citizen's private life that could be publicly damaging to that citizen's family. Thus, the danger came not from the state's possession, but from its Archives and the relationship between state, public, and private that the Archives arbitrated

Who, then, was responsible for policing the line between public interest and private honor? In a time of increasing state interest in society, the family, and the citizen, this potentially explosive question had not been subject to legal debate or modification of existing laws.[23] In the realm of the "social," nascent social science applied by moral reformers and state institutions such as the police and hospitals skirted the question of public and private. It instead was posed as a question of society and state: of population to be counted, disciplined, examined, known, and thus governed, shattering the concept of privacy of the individual into infinite pieces that matched up to aggregate categories. The archival question, though it implied understanding the terms of access to this knowledge, rested on similar assumptions of the nature of the public as a population, but one that was potentially dangerous to its individual members. Private honor had to be weighed against public curiosity, which in turn had to be measured against the public interest in a whole and accessible Archives.

Chabrier looked to the set of abstract principles that he imagined governed the Archives as an organ of government. Instead of social scientific notions of society or population, Chabrier appealed to the contract between state and citizen that governed the institution that held and expressed this contract.

The Archives, in this view, was thus more than a mere repository of governmental knowledge; it was an active articulation of the relationship of nation and state. The principles that animated the somewhat straightforward legal status of the papers were explained to Breteuil and the Emperor in a report from Chabrier. In order to guarantee the legal imprimatur of his decision, Chabrier engaged a lawyer, the liberal former president of the Paris Bar, Eugène Bethemont.[24] Bethemont's research concurred with Chabrier's judgment that the Breteuil request could not be satisfied within legal channels, because the request was for papers pertaining to a criminal inquest.[25] The individual in question had been interpellated by the law, and thus the papers were clearly property of the state. Criminality obliterated the line between public and private, a line ultimately guaranteed by the law and granted only to those who obeyed it.[26]

This question interested Bethemont and Chabrier only insofar as the state's sovereignty was legitimate in its just policing of this boundary between public and private. Sovereignty was guaranteed only by state ownership and conservation of documents that were evidence of the relationship between the state and its citizens. The conservation of legal documents by the state, according to Bethemont, was fundamental, and "the return or the destruction of documents that establish law and criminal justice as it was rendered . . . would sacrifice public interest to private interest." Governments that did so were thus acting illegitimately. These documents served an essential, legitimizing function for the state: "Power, when it is reduced to assert itself in such grave and difficult circumstances[,] can and must conserve the proof that its actions were not capricious." Breteuil's request was doubly threatening to the state: the state would both act capriciously (in sacrificing public interest to private) and relinquish evidence of its just exercise of power. The protection of this depository of evidence of the state's legitimacy was an "immense moral responsibility," and Bethemont argued that the state would make a fatal error in "casting off the proof that justifies the actions of its agents."[27] The moral issue was thus moved from the protection of family honor to the defense of state legitimacy that made family honor possible in its exercise of justice. The Archives' integrity was a moral imperative for the state that would govern justly in the name of the public it claimed to represent.

The "public interest" extended beyond the matters of justice and its administration into the realm of history, however, and here Breteuil's anxiety over access emerged. What about the right to one's reputation? What about the private interests of members of the public? Family and individual honor was a pillar of the increasingly influential bourgeois self-imagining.[28] Bethemont wondered if there wasn't an overriding "social interest" in conserving state papers, as "traces of the acts that belong to the history of our institutions, and of our society." Like the primacy of public interest over private in matters of state, the history of the nation should trump the concerns of an individual or family. Bethemont acknowledged that this was the risk that Breteuil worried over, but the lawyer again showed his faith in the state and its justice, calling the protection of the papers, "seized in the name of public interest," from "indiscrete curiosity." Public curiosity was the threat that the public could pose to its own public interest.

The boundaries of public interest and curiosity were never pinned down in Bethemont's brief and would reemerge throughout the Archives' history. Ironically, Bethemont's ultimate solution lay not in the immediate force of law but in the unfolding of history. Justice would bear out in time: "When the wounds of families have healed, when time has opened to the historian his due, when the depositors have made use of the archives that tradition has consecrated, then I will have nothing to say on this matter."[29] If the Archives were allowed to serve their purpose, they would act as a guarantee against the tyranny of government and the specter of "indiscreet curiosity." Governed by a mixture of law and good sense, a balance of conservation and access would be achieved, and state and public interest could find harmony in the Archives. The Archives created the necessary buffer zone between the state and citizen, between public and private, that the social contract required.

Establishing with the help of his lawyer the requirement of the Archives' role in the public interest in stability and sovereignty, Chabrier pleaded with the Emperor for hard legal safeguards to prevent this kind of conflict in the future. If there were indeed antecedents, as the Count Breteuil suggested, then Chabrier would see if these allegations were true. He would ensure that this kind of act would never be committed again. If papers had been removed in the past, these actions should in no way be

considered "precedents" but rather "under the guise of inoffensive indul-
gence, these acts constitute an usurpation of power, flagrant illegalities,
offences against public property, a violation of the depository."[30] In other
words, Chabrier argued that any government that would sanction the
removal of documents from the Archives would be acting against its people and thus would render itself illegitimate. Sovereignty required the
inviolability of the Archives, and Chabrier called for the government to
seize this occasion to confirm this fundamental inviolability in the law.
This put the director of the Archives and his staff in a precarious position:
the archivist was both guardian of the state's business and a watchdog
against the improper exercise of its power.

The Empire in the Archive: The Decree of 1855

Foud seized the moment to create a new legal foundation for the Archives
to deal with such issues, and in so doing fixed the relationship between
state and citizen in the Archives into law—with the state firmly in charge
under the sign of public interest. The decree of December 22, 1855, significantly restructured the Archives. In article 2 the depository was formally
declared to hold "all documents that the public interest deems useful," and
it made the deposit of ministerial papers that were "unnecessary to current affairs" a legal requirement; article 3 gave the power to authorize or
call for deposits to the minister of the state; article 4 made the papers held
in the Archives "inalienable" property of the state, unless a law was passed
under the recommendation of the minister of the state. The director, who
under article 6 was to be appointed (or dismissed) by and serve under the
tutelage of the minister of the state, was effectively circumvented by this
decree.[31] The power over the Archives and its contents thus resided completely in the Emperor's hands, making this legislation the archival equivalent of his coup d'etat, without the possibility of referendum.

Access to the public depository was not surprisingly a central issue in
this new archival regulatory scheme. Article 14 stated that the "conditions
under which documents will be requested, and the mode of communications to be made, either on the premises, or outside, to administrations
and to private citizens" would be governed by regulations to be drawn up
by the minister of the state. This was an imperial solution to the more
liberal interpretation of public interest raised by Bethemont, as it moved

the right of access out of the law and into the realm of administration. These attendant regulations passed in 1856 managed the inner workings of the Archives, most significantly and ambiguously the issue of access for citizens. Article 35 of these rules required requests for documents to be formulated in writing. These requests had to "describe the precise object that the requestor has in mind. Requests that do not contain this description are not accepted." Article 36 explains that the director general "authorizes or refuses [the requested] communication. In case of refusal, the requestor may appeal to the minister." Article 39 allowed that "members and laureates of the Institute of France, doctors of one of the universities, archivist-paleographers [graduates of the École des Chartes], and students of the École des Chartes will be given immediate attention to their requests" and would promptly receive either the requested documents or the reason for the refusal. This privilege was also granted to those having received authorization to work at the Archives, although the specifics of this authorization remain unexplained. Overwriting (but not abrogating) the law of 7 *messidor*, communication of documents could be practically limited to scholarship (laureates, archivists, professors, or other recognized scholars) or official business (functionaries).[32] Eased by the imprimatur of institutions (and thus the rules of propriety and professionalism observed by these men would reign in the Archives) and the exigencies of state administration, the gaze of "indiscreet curiosity" that threatened the families and the state was thus limited by administrative regulation.

Although this only put into new law what had been practiced over the history of the Archives, the decree decisively marked the direction of Imperial archival policy. Chabrier wholeheartedly agreed, despite his leanings toward institutional independence, with the concrete outlines of the director's responsibilities. According to Chabrier, all governments had been preoccupied with this "grave" responsibility, and none with success. Some governments had, "to the great detriment of our public archives," exaggerated the director's power, declaring him independent of ministerial control; others made the opposite error, threatening to abolish the directorship entirely. Chabrier considered the minister of the state to be a "born Conservator of state documents"; he warned, however, that the authority of the director general over his employees and "agents in whom he was obliged to trust" was essential to maintaining the proper balance.[33]

Chabrier was also pleased with the reiteration of an older decree (from 1809) that prevented employees of the Archives from publishing manuscripts. Article 15 required any employee of the archives to gain authorization before publishing "either documents confided to him in the performance of his functions or any work based on these documents." This permission would be granted by the minister, under the recommendation of the director, and violation would result in dismissal. Chabrier's enthusiasm for this article came from his concern that the archivists under his employ were more interested in personal scholarly glory than public service. It was not scholarship that bothered him so much as the shirking of duty. The article had a more direct impact on the creation of an inviolable depository, as secrets, state or family, could not be divulged in the press by those functionaries charged with the keeping of those secrets. With this decree, the archivist's duty to the Archives was to take precedent over the quest for scholarly glory, or even truth, as this set out another safeguard against threats from the public that took the form of functionaries with private interests.

Despite these points of agreement with the Archives' new regulatory footprint, this clearly was not the institution Chabrier had imagined. There was no archival independence and the language of public interest was ambiguous at best. Chabrier did not remain in the Archives, but was replaced in 1856 by Léon de Laborde. Laborde's name would become synonymous with the professionalization of the Imperial Archives.

While histories of the Archives are largely silent about this transition, a contemporary, the journalist Horace Viel-Castel, gives us a taste of the rumors that surrounded Chabrier's departure. According to Viel-Castel, Chabrier understood the new decree as a set of conditions for Imperial intervention in the depository, creating the possibility for precisely the kind of tampering with the history of governmental power that the Archives was established to prevent. Chabrier is reported to have burst into Fould's office, where he was meeting with the Emperor, and the director made his displeasure known. Understanding the implications of such a move, Chabrier apparently ended his outburst with a recognition of the new regime: "I know that in acting thus I've just handed Your Majesty my resignation." Whether or not this particular archive story, told by a notorious gossip of the Second Empire, is true, Chabrier's resignation was indeed accepted, thus canceling one of the voices of potential contest in the making of the Imperial Archives.

Viel-Castel ended his account with a portentous question: "Will Laborde deliver the documents?"[34] This question is difficult to answer, for there is no official order in the archives of the Archives. But as we will see, the possibility of such an archival history of the Archives took new shape under the regime that would make such a move imaginable by critics of the Empire. The ambiguity of the decree and regulations put the Archives squarely in the domain of the public interest, did not decisively rule out public access, and would make such decisions open for debate in the future. That was only if, of course, the public was made aware of these actions and more importantly of the significance of the institution. Conservation of papers in the public interest remained a vexing problem. Their classification and ultimately their communication to the public made this issue all the more complex and required a solution in keeping with Imperial imperatives. The epitome of Imperial Archives policy came in the form of a completely novel section that would serve as both a category of papers and an administrative organ. The secretariat would come to represent the political will of the Empire in the Archives.

The secretariat played a significant new role: It was designed chiefly to police public access and usage of the Archives, but it would also serve to monitor internal administrative movements as well. Article 12, governing the requirements for the appointment to heads of sections, specifically excluded the chief of the secretariat from such regulation. The head of this section was to be appointed by the minister with no requirements about the candidate's qualifications. In its administrative capacity and in its direction, this new section bore the marks of its Bonapartist origins.

The secretariat's main function was the policing of the Archives relations with outsiders: state functionaries, scholars, or other private citizens. Regulating communication involved a litany of new duties. The secretariat was responsible for the maintenance and staffing of the reading room, the delivery of communications and their refusals, classification of inventories and documents, reporting and recording the state and number of inventories held by the Archives, the reception and registration of and response to correspondence, dispensing information to individuals, putting the seal of authenticity and delivering expeditions of copies needed by government and public alike.

In its classificatory function, the secretariat represented both the Empire's recognition of the importance of the Archives to conserve papers and its ambivalence vis-à-vis its public nature. Along with its duty to regulate the Archives' contact with the public and government, this section would receive a highly sensitive group of documents that had belonged to the former secretariat of state (under Napoleon I and the Bourbons, an office abolished by the Second Republic), the contents of the infamous *armoire de fer*—a cabinet rumored to be originally the property of Louis XVI and supposedly containing the most precious and secret of documents held by the Archives—and future accessions from the minister of the state. Quietly, this section produced a zone of protection for a motley selection of documents that represented precisely the privilege that Chabrier and Bethemont had argued against. At the same time, the secretariat created the conditions for this new regime to protect its most precious secrets not only from public scrutiny, but from the eyes of other archivists as well.

Most striking was the secretariat's role as the archives of the Archives. The secretariat was to oversee the classification and conservation of all the acts, laws, decrees, bylaws, and instructions concerning the organization and service of the Archives; the collection of letters, reports, notes, titles, and any other papers concerning the "history of the formation and progress of the Archives"; copies of reports from the heads of sections and director general on the questions of service and interior order.[35] The archives of the Archives were their own entity, and from now on the Archives were to be seen as an object of history as well as an essential administrative organ. The secretariat section reproduced the state in the Archives: mirroring the state in its need to keep records and recognize itself in history, the secretariat also expressed the state's ambivalence about the Archives as a public institution. The Imperial Archives would respect the sacred triad of communication, conservation, and communication, but only under its own terms. The secretariat would now regulate these terms.

When Léon de Laborde assumed the directorship on Chabrier's resignation in 1856, the Archives of the Empire had a legal framework that defined the institution and its employees, an internal structure designed to protect the interests of the state, and a history whose interpretation would ultimately work to challenge the stability of this definition. Laborde's tenure would be devoted to the struggle to find the proper place for historical study between the needs of the state and the public in the Archives, within the limits of political possibility. These political possibilities, however, had been carefully circumscribed by the Bonapartist policies that aimed to dictate the terms of the relationship of state to nation.

History in the Archives

In fact, historians and archivists writing about the Archives of France generally credit Director General Léon de Laborde, a scholar of wide-ranging interest and institutional talent, with shepherding what amounted to a revolution in archival practice. Laborde oversaw the publication of inventories, the expansion of the archivist's duty to public service, the opening of a public museum of French history, and a tireless effort for public recognition, funding, and access to the institution. The archivist and archive historian Robert-Henri Bautier called this period a "crucial phase in the history of the archives, one which marked the transition from the institution's role as an 'arsenal of authority' and its attendant secrecy to a 'public' archive and laboratory of history."[36] This "transformation," however, did not go uncontested. In 1867, Henri Bordier, historian of France and former archivist in the Archives nationales de France, grumbled that policies of Napoleon III had unfortunately turned the Archives into "an office of history."[37] He decried the tendency to obscure the administrative nature of the Archives and its holdings in the name of a separate endeavor, that of historical study. Even today, the transformation of the Archives into an office of history is credited to the efforts of Napoleon III and his policies.[38] This so-called transformation, coinciding as it does with the professionalization of history, is taken as a given by most histories of the Archives, so much so that other possible meanings and effects of archival policies have remained unexplored.

Focusing on this transformation, and on the presumed incompatibility of the interests of science and administration, not only obscures the historical work of the Archives and archivists under Chabrier and in earlier periods, but it also ignores other important functions and developments in the history of the Archives. The Archives were an important administrative institution for the French state, but also the repository of administrative, judicial, and other government documents that were useful in the lives of its citizens, which in fact underwrote the relationship between state and citizens. This interpretation implies a clearly definable administrative will and a public interest that could be easily collapsed into the compound public-historian. In fact, the interests of the state and of the public were troublingly fluid abstractions rather than solid, recognizable foundations of politics and archival policy. This period of transformation was thus more a period of smoothing over disturbing conflict in the interests of an appearance of stability. I would argue that the divorce of administration and science emerged rhetorically because of deeper divides that would threaten not just the institution, but the legitimacy of the state as well.

Boundaries of archival access marked the outlying limits of democracy: How much and what kind of transparency could the state accept and society demand? If criticism of absolutism created the public sphere, the issue of *raison d'état* did not disappear with the monarchy. Setting the boundaries of the modern Archives was part and parcel of marking the limits of state power in the post-revolutionary nation. The regime of Louis-Napoleon provided peculiar ground to test these boundaries. The explosion of administration and his hybrid authoritarian–quasi-democratic techniques of government (which always risked downfall, for there was no historical evidence that the government and his dynasty would prevail) testified to the constant improvisation at the heart of politics. The institution of the Archives was emblematic of this improvisational exercise of power, and a test of the legitimate limits between state and citizen.

Thus we might think of Michel Foucault's and Jacques Derrida's philosophical reflections on archives as knowledge-power-history as intervening in a history of concern with the formation of subjects and society. The Archives nationales can be situated in this same genealogy: the regulation of historical patrimony and governmental information by a governmental institution in the name of the nation can be seen as an expression of the state-citizen (and knowledge-power) contract in modern France.[39] The "archive" was not merely a convenient metaphor: although it signifies more than the single institution, the archive is bound up in a history of political power as well as of the search for absolute historical truth.[40] Indeed, Derrida's *Archive Fever* is founded on the (often overlooked) premise that the question of the archive is, at base, a question of the body politic: "There is no political power without control of the archive, if not memory"; the archive in fact "determines politics from top to bottom as *res publica*."[41]

While history can indeed be found in the "archive," the place and shape of that history was imagined differently at different times; the institution of the Archives was itself a testament to particular regimes of power and knowledge, each marked by particular commitments to and rhetorics of secrecy and publicity. From here we can better understand the place of the historian in the Archives as performing a politics of the nation-state, the imbrications of the politico-ethical in the epistemological status of the official archive (both registers are present, but produced as separate); and the self-conscious moves by governments to both regulate and encourage archival access in the name of national history, a national history that was to be synonymous with the history of the state.

The use of the "archive" as shorthand for complexes of history and memory, power and knowledge, risks repeating the mythologizing gesture upon which the power of the "archive" is based. Reflections on the "archive" and archives thus need to be careful not to presume, indeed reproduce, the authority of the institution that they seek to describe and critique. Instead, such critical work might aim to uncover how the archive got to have that authority in the first place. As we will see in histories of disparate archival collections, practices, and impulses that follow, it is historical analysis of the archive that can best reveal the limits of the archive's power to speak in the name of history.

Notes

The chapter epigraph is from Alphonse Huillard Breholles, "Les Archives de l'Empire: Leur passé et leur état present," *Revue Contemporaine*, April 30, 1863 (2), 744. The author wishes to acknowledge the Penn Humanities Forum for its support.

1   Françoise Hildesheimer, "Les Archives de France, mémoire de l'histoire," *Histoire et Archives* hors-série 1997 [special issue, published out of series]: 45. See also Kryztof Pomian, "Les Archives du Trésor des chartes au CARAN," in Pierre Nora, ed. *Les Lieux de mémoire*, vol. 3, book 3 (*Les Frances*) (Paris: Gallimard, 1992), 192–200. Historians have started to investigate the history of the concept and practice of the archive; see Antoinette Burton, *Dwelling in the Archive: Women Writing House, Home and History in Late Colonial India* (New York: Oxford University Press, 2003); Nicholas B. Dirks, "Colonial Histories and Native Informants: Biography of an Archive," in Carol A. Breckenridge and Peter van der Veer, eds., *Orientalism and the Postcolonial Predicament: Perspectives on South Asia* (Philadelphia: University of Pennsylvania Press, 1993), 279–313; Arlette Farge, *Fragile Lives: Violence, Power, and Solidarity in Eighteenth-Century Paris*, trans. Carol Shelton (Cambridge, Mass.: Harvard University Press, 1993), 1–3, and her *Le Goût de l'Archive* (Paris: Editions du Seuil, 1990); Bonnie G. Smith, *The Gender of History: Men, Women, and Historical Practice* (Cambridge, Mass.: Harvard University Press, 1998), esp. 130–56; and Carolyn Steedman's *Dust: The Archive and Cultural History* (New Brunswick, N.J.: Rutgers University Press, 2002). Some of the early work on the "archive" comes from anthropology. See especially Michel-Rolph

Trouillot, *Silencing the Past: Power and the Production of History* (Boston: Beacon Press, 1995).

2 For the state of historical studies in nineteenth century France, see Pim Den Boer, *History as a Profession: The Study of History in France, 1818–1914,* trans. Arnold J. Pomerans (Princeton: Princeton University Press, 1998); C. O. Carbonell, *Histoire et Historiens: Une mutation idéologique des historiens français, 1865–1885* (Toulouse, 1976); Donald R. Kelley, *Historians and the Law in Postrevolutionary France* (Princeton: Princeton University Press, 1984); William Keylor, *Academy and Community: The Foundation of the French Historical Profession* (Cambridge, Mass.: Harvard University Press, 1975); Gérard Noiriel, "Naissance du métier d'historien," *Genèses* 1 (1990): 58 85; Smith, *Gender of History,* 130–56.

3 For a detailed study of the institutions and historians of the Old Regime, see Blandine Barret-Kriegel, *Les Historiens et la monarchie,* 4 vols. (Paris: Presses Universitaires de Paris, 1988); Donald R. Kelley, "Jean Du Tillet, Archivist and Antiquary," *Journal of Modern History* 38, 4 (1966): 337–54, and his *Foundations of Modern Historical Scholarship: Language, Law, and History in the French Renaissance* (New York: Columbia University Press, 1970); for the Revolution, see Keith Michael Baker, *Inventing the French Revolution* (Cambridge: Cambridge University Press, 1990), 31–106.

4 *Archives parlémentaires* (Paris, 1863) 50, 267.

5 Text of the law of 7 *messidor* year II quoted from copy in Archives nationales (hereafter AN), AB I, 1.

6 The confiscation of Church and feudal records had a specific political purpose: in order to alienate or confiscate Church and feudal lands and goods, it was necessary to possess the records of legal title. This project was of particular interest to the Convention as the wars fought in the name and in defense of the Revolution after the regicide drained the national treasury. It was in this context that the law of 7 *messidor* was passed. In January of 1794, the Convention set up a committee designed to review the Archive in order to devise a system of organization that would allow for the most expedient separation of those titles that would be of financial value to the state.

7 For a discussion of the Revolutionary legislation, see A. Outrey, "La notion traditionnelle de titre et les origines de la législation révolutionnaire sur les archives," *Revue Historique de Droit Français et Etranger* 5 (1955): 438–63. For an analysis of the legislation in light of current archival politics, see Sonia Combe, *Archives interdites: Les peurs françaises face à l'Histoire contemporaine* (Paris: A. Michel, 1994), 79–102. Michel Duchein and Françoise Hildesheimer argue a from different perspective with quite different political implications: see Duchein, "L'Accès aux Archives en France de Messidor an II à Janvier 1979: Libéralisme et frilosités," in *Histoires d'Archives: Recueil d'articles offert à Lucie Favier par ses collègues et amis* (Paris: Société des amis des archives de France, 1997), 59–69; Hildesheimer, "Échec aux Archives: La difficile affirmation d'une administration," *Bibliothèque de L'Ecole des chartes* 156 (1998): 91–106. The genealogy of the right to access—its history, its limits, and its possibilities—is central to current debates.

Whether or not the archives *really were* accessible does not diminish the rhetorical and political force of the historical question of the *possibility* of access introduced at the Revolution. Combe, *Archives interdites*, 79; Duchein, "L'Accès aux Archives," 60; Hildesheimer, "Échec aux Archives," 91. For an intervention into the current debate on the archives of the Algerian crisis that favors the revolution as revolutionary, see Marc-Olivier Baruch and Vincent Duclert, "Archives: Il faut une loi, il faut une politique," *Le Monde*, November 30, 2000, 18.

8 There was and is debate over the extent of the Triage Committee's impact on French archival holdings. Some argue that the committee, headed by Camus, partook of the general zeal of the day and destroyed many historical documents that smacked of Old Regime privilege, much to the horror and dismay of later historians. Others argue that the committee (a knowledgeable group that despite its manifestly political goal included former Benedictines and scholars familiar with the royal collections) in fact protected documents from their almost assured annihilation in Camus's or other patriots' possession. Although this makes some political sense—as the Revolution was often a screen for arguments about Republicanism vs. Bonapartism—the cultural or epistemological stakes (about the fate of the truth about history or about standards of evidence required to establish the existence of burned or disappeared documents, for example) are much more interesting than simple ideological battles. See Léon de Laborde, *Les Archives de France: Leurs viccissitudes pendant la Révolution, leur régéneration sous l'Empire* (Paris: Vve. Renouard, 1867) and Henri Bordier, *Les Inventaires des Archives de l'Empire: Réponse à M. le marquis de Laborde, Directeur Général, contenant un errata pour ses préfaces et ses inventaires* (Paris: Librairie Bachelin-Deflorenne, 1867), for the most representative and important texts in the debate.

9 *Archives parlémentaires* (Paris, 1863) 50, 267.

10 Napoleon planned a grand "Archives' Palace" to house his documentary spoils, but this like his other imperial projects remained only partially realized. For a discussion of Napoleon's vision of the Archives and First Empire archival policy, see Raymond J. Maras, "Napoleon's Quest for a Super-Archival Center in Paris," *Consortium on Revolutionary Europe, 1750–1850: Selected Papers* (1994): 567–78; and Frances E. Montgomery, "Tribunes, Napoleon, and the Archives Nationales," *Consortium on Revolutionary Europe, 1750–1850: Selected Papers* 19, no. 1 (1989): 437–59.

11 Hildesheimer, *Les Archives de France*, 44.

12 As Donald R. Kelley puts it: "the law required and inspired respect for documentary evidence that led, especially in the nineteenth century, to that assault on archival sources so essential to the new science of history." *Historians and the Law*, 9.

13 AN, AB Va 6.

14 AN, AB I, I, Chabrier, "Projet d'un decret Imperial portant règlement sur les Archives de l'Empire," March 1, 1855.

15 The Praslin case fascinated authors such as Flaubert (who included references to the scandal in *L'Education sentimentale*) and Hugo (whose archives con-

tain a slipper taken from the crime scene) and is the subject of a fictionalized account of the life of the governess, Henriette Desportes. See Rachel Field, *All This and Heaven Too* (New York, 1939). The book, which provides the epigraph for this section, was made into a popular 1941 film of the same name starring Bette Davis.

16 For a discussion of the role of the private life of the royal family in public discourse under the July Monarchy, see Jo Burr Margadant, "Gender, Vice, and the Political Imaginary in Postrevolutionary France: Reinterpreting the Failure of the July Monarchy, 1830–1848," *American Historical Review* 104, 5 (December 1999): 1461–96.

17 Ibid.

18 AN, AB Va 7, Letter from Breteuil to Achille Fould, November 15, 1854.

19 For a discussion of the interplay of interest, honor, and gender in postrevolutionary politics and the public sphere, see William Reddy, *The Invisible Code: Honor and Sentiment in Postrevolutionary France, 1814–1848* (Berkeley: University of California Press, 1997).

20 AN, AB Va 7, report by Chabrier, 1854.

21 There is a vast literature on the problem of citizenship and the question of the state in France. A few works that inform my understanding are Etienne Balibar, *Masses, Classes, Ideas: Studies on Politics and Philosophy Before and After Marx* (New York: Routledge, 1994); Rogers Brubaker, *Citizenship and Nationhood in France and Germany* (Cambridge: Cambridge University Press, 1992); H. S. Jones, *The French State in Question: Public Law and Political Argument in the Third Republic* (Cambridge: Cambridge University Press, 1993); Pierre Rosanvallon, *Le Sacre du Citoyen: Histoire du suffrage universel en France* (Paris: Gallimard, 1992), and his *L'État en France de 1789 à nos jours* (Paris: Seuil, 1990); Joan Scott, *Only Paradoxes to Offer: French Feminists and the Rights of Man* (Cambridge: Cambridge University Press, 1996).

22 The 7 *messidor* law, passed at the height of the Terror, probably implied this social transparency as well.

23 See Andrew R. Aisenberg, *Contagion: Disease, Government, and the "Social Question" in Nineteenth-Century France* (Stanford, Calif.: Stanford University Press 1999); Joshua Cole, *The Power of Large Numbers: Population, Politics, and Gender in Nineteenth Century France* (Ithaca: Cornell University Press, 2000); Jacques Donzelot, *L'invention du social: Le déclin des passions politiques* (Paris: Fayard, 1984) and his classic *La police des familles* (Paris: Éditions de Minuit, 1977); and Sylvia Schafer, *Children in Moral Danger and the Problem of Government in Third Republic France* (Princeton: Princeton University Press, 1997), esp. 26–42.

24 For more on the legal profession under the Second Empire, see Phillip J. Nord, *The Republican Moment: Struggles for Democracy in Nineteenth-Century France*, (Cambridge, Mass.: Harvard University Press, 1995), especially his chapter "The Republic of Lawyers," 115–38; Lucien Karpik, "Lawyers and Politics in France, 1814–1950: The State, the Market, and the Public," *Law and Social Inquiry* 13 (Fall 1988: 707–36; see also Kelley, *Historians and the Law*. For the longer history of

lawyers and politics in France, see David A. Bell, *Lawyers and Citizens: The Making of a Political Elite in Old Regime France* (New York and Oxford: Oxford University Press, 1994).

25 AN, AB Va 7, Brief by Bethemont excerpted in report by Chabrier, 1854.

26 Although "privacy" or "private" does not appear in this brief, this echoes Sylvia Schafer's observation (in this case, of abandoned children in Third Republic France) that "the beginning of 'history'—and the end of 'privacy'—was marked by an apparent deviation from the prescribed norms of family stability and internal cohesion." Schafer, *Children in Moral Danger*, 1.

27 AN, AB Va 7, Brief by Bethemont excerpted in report by Chabrier, 1854.

28 For a discussion of the complicated sinews of bourgeois identity in this period, see Robert Nye, *Masculinity and Male Codes of Honor in Modern France* (New York: Oxford University Press, 1993); Margadant, "Gender, Vice, and the Political Imaginary"; and Bonnie G. Smith, *Ladies of the Leisure Class: The Bourgeoises of Northern France in the Nineteenth Century* (Princeton: Princeton University Press, 1990).

29 AN, AB Va 7, Brief by Bethemont excerpted in report by Chabrier, 1854.

30 Ibid.

31 AN, AB I, Text of the law and regulations courtesy of Lucie Favier.

32 AN, AB I, 1, Chabrier, "Projet d'un decret Imperial portant règlement sur les Archives de l'Empire," 1 March 1855.

33 Ibid.

34 Horace Viel-Castel, *Mémoires du comte Horace de Viel-Castel sur le règne de Napoléon III, 1851–1864* (Paris: G. Le Prat, 1942), 42–43, entry from March 18, 1857.

35 AN, AB I, text of the 1855 Decree.

36 Robert-Henri Bautier, "La phase cruciale de l'histoire des archives: la constitution des dépôts d'archives et la naissance de l'archivistique (XVIe-debut du XIXe siecle), *Archivum* XVII (1968): 148.

37 Bordier, *Les Inventaires des Archives de l'Empire*, 14.

38 For instance, see Boer, *History as a Profession*, 86–87.

39 Jacques Derrida, *Archive Fever: A Freudian Impression*, trans. E. Prenowitz (Chicago: University of Chicago Press, 1995). Works drawing on Derrida's reflections include Steedman, *Dust*; and a special two-issue *History of the Human Sciences* devoted to The Archive, 12, 2 (1998 and 1999).

40 Foucault wrote about the archive as a figure that organized and represented relations of power and knowledge, but he also mined archives for evidence of the history of that relationship. His critical histories of governmental power vis-à-vis the production of the social and the individual subject were produced, in part at least, from the records of official archival institutions. Foucault performed this archival gesture as an essential technique in his own critique of historical knowledge. Genealogy is not genuflection at the altar of the archive; rather it is a powerful rereading of the official archive with a critical historical eye. Foucault's students, among them Arlette Farge and Blandine Barret-Kreigel, have used the archives of the French state complex (from local to national gov-

ernmental archives) to write about the power of history to give voice to or suppress subjects, a power that is as much about the historian's reading and valorization of documents (and the way these documents position subjects) as it is about a particular archives' holdings. See Kriegel, *Les Historiens et la monarchie*; Arlette Farge discusses the "emotion" of the archive in her *Fragile Lives*, 1–3 and *Le Goût de l'Archive*.

41 Derrida, *Archive Fever*, 4n.

Peter Fritzsche

The Archive and

the Case of the German Nation

"NO ONE," WROTE PASCAL, "dies so impoverished that he does not leave something behind." Setting the scene at the moment of a single individual's death and drawing attention to personal possessions, Pascal conjures up the material traces of a single lifetime. A lived life creates physical effects: a sheaf of letters, a lucky coin, a small fortune. These are things that construct correspondences between experience and materiality. Pascal's words work in a way that put stress on the larger world reflected in small objects. Pascal ennobles even the most modest lives, and he puts all individuals in the same passage from life to death. Every soul possesses an archive, and an archive exists to tell each individual story.

Nearly three hundred years later, Walter Benjamin reflected on Pascal's archive. To Pascal's things he added "memories too," and then went on to subtract from what he had just augmented: "although these do not always find an heir."[1] What Benjamin accents is not the material endurance of things but the inconstant operations of memory. There is no longer the unproblematic correspondence between life lived and life remembered, but the difficult endeavor of remembering and the more general prospect of forgetting. For Benjamin it is not so much what the dead leave behind as it is what the living end up recalling. He thereby poses the question of attentiveness, the historically situated presence or absence of the habit of cultivating memories. Moreover, the habits of cultivation operate across time: the heirs are daughters, grandsons. At the remove of a generation or two, they are the ones who undertake the work of recollection. And in place of the universal by which Pascal affirmed the material existence of all men and women, Benjamin implied particular heirs who need to make a connection to the past in order for memories to remain alive. In contrast to Pascal's materialism, Benjamin proposes a cultural interpretation of remembering in which traces are not simply left behind and recollection is not assumed, in which mental habits across time rather than physical things in the present are what bring the past into view, and in which specific heirs are necessary for the work of memorialization to succeed. Pascal refers to things and thereby builds an implicit archive of past lives, but it was Benjamin who imagined the space in which the specific historical archive was constructed in order to ward off forgetfulness and make the case for a particular historical subject.

The three hundred years that separate Benjamin from Pascal dramatize the historicity of the uses of history and suggest the specific historical circumstances under which so much of the past does not find heirs while other parts are energetically recollected. Benjamin writes in reference to a "memory crisis," a historical moment in the modern age when there is both a surfeit of unusable pasts and a deficit of usable history, when individuals die in the face of general indifference while self-appointed heirs anxiously look for particular memories.[2] It is in the distinction between Pascal and Benjamin that a history of the archive can be conceived. Archives are not comprehensive collections of things, the effects left behind by the dead—material testaments—nor are they arbitrary accumulations of remnants and leftovers—garbage pits. The archive is the production of the heirs who must work to find connections from one generation to the next and thereby acknowledge the ongoing disintegration of the past. The heirs must also distinguish themselves as such: they are a cultural group that cultivates a particular historical trajectory. This collection is very much about the activity of the heirs, how they identify themselves as such, confront larger political entities, and both construe and misconstrue the past. The heirs that most directly concern me here are the contemporaries that make up the nation, a collective imaginary that has been extraordinarily successful in creating a common, durable past within its borders and emphasizing the difference of cultural origins across its borders. The nation is a specific, historically contingent configuration of time and space and its effort at upholding its identity fuels what Jacques Derrida referred to in another context as "archive fever."[3]

A historical view, in which the distinction between Pascal and Benjamin is fundamental, reframes an institutional or structural reading of the archive. In what is not an authoritative conceptualization, the archive is widely recognized as one of an array of disciplinary institutions such as hospitals, prisons, and asylums that manage the technologies of power that are indispensable to the maintenance of social collectives and the enforcement of social norms. More than thirty years ago, Michel Foucault drew attention to the laws and practices of archival knowledge which determine what can and cannot be said, what will and will not be remembered. Since Foucault was primarily concerned with how records—and the categories by which those records were assembled—created subjects who could be identified, assessed, and (self-)mobilized in normative ways, his analysis has been extremely influential for understanding the archive.[4] However vast its holdings or capacious the collecting zeal of its administrators, a Foucauldian perspective insists, the archive sets limits on what is worth preserving. It defines and establishes categories by which documents and other materials are stored and can be retrieved. The archive thus functions as a machine that manufactures the pertinence of particular kinds of evidence and particular casts of historical actors. This ability to differentiate creates the boundedness that characterizes all historical subjects. In order to continually reinforce the viability of the collective subject—in the most pertinent case, of the nation-state—the archive must exclude evidence from the margins that would jeopardize the continuous instantiation of a common past. The archive, therefore, is "not a piece of data, but a status."[5]

What gets overlooked in the formal analysis of the archive, however, are the historical and epistemological origins of the problem of boundedness, the shifting definitions of pertinent evidence, and finally the extraneous features of any collection of the past. The archive was not simply constituted as a powerful way to contain the past but developed in relationship to a past that was regarded as fragmented, distant, and otherwise difficult to hold on to. The archive produced certain histories, but, at the same time, certain ways of looking at and believing to have experienced history also produced archives. If most conceptions of the archive emphasize how the archive has shaped history, I want to examine how history has shaped the archive.

At the most general level, archival production rests on the premise that the past is no longer the business of the present and must be handled carefully in order to retrieve its fragments and reveal its differences. But the energy of archival activity is founded on the assumption that artifacts and documents can be made to tell very special, if incomplete, stories about social identity. The arduous endeavor of provenance, the concern for getting right chronology and context, functions to establish particular trajectories of the past and thereby to create a common past (and a shared future) that is culturally distinct. The archive thus produces two effects: the boundedness of identity *in* time and space and the synchronization *of* time and space within those bounds. Precisely because they are the means by which the provenance of identity is established, archives are crucial to the infrastructure of the modern nation-state. The archive arrives at the nineteenth-century moment the state assumed responsibility toward the particular heritage of the past encompassed by its territory.[6]

The effort of one nation to distinguish itself from other nations or to resist the claims of supranational entities such as empires has important, if sometimes neglected, democratic ramifications. It is often the case that potential archive stories exceed state-sanctioned histories. This is because ordinary people increasingly recognized themselves as inhabitants of cultural territories distinguished by language and custom. Indeed, domestic settings—food at the table, the architecture of the farmhouse, the annual cycle of festivals—became primary markers of national identity, which had the effect of enfranchising citizens into history and authorizing their own vernacular versions of national history. Moreover, the busy work of heirs created intimacies among strangers who held in common a national past. As Germans, or Italians or Americans, came to regard each other as contemporaries they took interest in the tribulations of fellow citizens, tied their own autobiographies to the national epic, and thereby intertwined personal with national history. Precisely because the ordinary could stand for the national, and even became most evocative of the national, the story of the nation never existed in a single defining version. It was reworked into vernaculars, sub-versions that existed as potential subversions, as many of the authors in this collection suggest.[7] Thus collective disasters and, in particular, war had the effect of both intensifying the personal experience of the national and legitimizing individual and even dissident versions. Put another way, the onerous requirements for fighting war in the modern era necessitated upholstering a common past, while the sheer violence of war worked to jeopardize that unity, with both motion and countermotion adding to the paperwork of history.

The history of the archive is the recognition of loss. For archives to collect the past, the past has to come to mind as something imperiled and distinctive. This presumes a dramatization of historical movement that leaves behind temporal periods based on the radical difference between now and then, which, in turn, invites the recognition of radical difference between here and there. The feverish part of archival activity is to dis-

tinguish difference in order to create a bounded national subject characterized by a distinctive history that is held in common by its citizens. The
establishment of historical and cultural archives in Germany at the beginning of the nineteenth century well illustrates the effort to create the
particulars of national identity. This bounded identity was also the premise
for the vernacular archival activity of ordinary citizens in the insistently
autobiographical nineteenth century. Loss continued to facilitate the production of archives after the unification of the German empire. And in the
twentieth century, the world wars pushed the state to revisualize its citizens in order to more effectively mobilize them, producing new inventories of popular sovereignty in the Weimar period and finally racial archives
in the Third Reich. Yet the experience of mass death and the Holocaust
ended up creating dramatically divergent life stories that made it ever
more difficult to hold onto the idea of a common German past or find
shared memories among victims and perpetrators. After 1945, Benjamin's
heirs in East and West Germany, Israel, and the United States, picked up
separate strands of German history. At the beginning of the twentieth-first
century, the German archive can no longer be premised on the national
rehabilitation of loss. It can only provide testimony to the violence of the
attempt to do so.

The Recognition of Difference

It was not memory as such, but the specter of loss that constituted the
German archive and prepared for the reorganization of the German past.
The menace of French empire, the initial "German catastrophe" at the
beginning of the nineteenth century, is the point of origin for the German
archive, whose purpose was to establish the provenance of a specifically
German past, a genealogy called *Vaterland*. The French Revolution had the
fundamental effect of dramatizing the movement of history into distinct
periods separated by epochal breaks—1806 will be followed by 1871, 1914–
18, 1933, 1945, and 1990. With the disintegration of the Holy Roman Empire
in 1805–6, the continuities connecting past and present shattered, and the
past increasingly came into view as a vast field of ruins. This was a remarkable revolution in the way history was understood.[8] While Napoleon
endeavored to organize ruins in a way that would represent the historical
inevitability and endurance of the French Empire, literally by collecting

exemplars in Paris, German statesmen and intellectuals used medieval relics to signify the political defeat but also the historical existence of the German nation. This was a bold epistemological step because it took ruins out of natural time and resituated them in historical time in which traces of the past could serve as the particular evidence for political and religious confrontations, defeats, and occupations that represented apparently un-developed political alternatives. Ruins thereby acquired a half-life. If prop-erly preserved, catalogued, and analyzed, they could be made to speak for the nation (or any of the other collective subjects explored in this book).

In the early 1800s, the German art collector Sulpiz Boisserée made the most sustained case for the separate national development of Germany. He rejected Napoleon's assumption that the French Empire expressed the most complete development of universal history, a schema in which Ger-many's medieval ruins occupied the subordinate status of precursor. In-stead, he argued that the German masters and Gothic cathedrals repre-sented Germany's historical particularity that was no less credible than France's. He thereby reanimated the broken-down past as a national alter-native to empire. In contrast to the centrally deposited "exemplary speci-mens" in Paris, Boisserée made the case for the eloquence of "recovered relics" in context.[9] It was provenance that became the key to establishing separate national trajectories that resisted the logic of universal or colonial history.

Boisserée's journeys up and down the Rhine, in which he catalogued the ruins of medieval abbeys, cathedrals, and castles, thus were the first steps in the creation of a German archive. Medieval history—first in 1806 in the form of debris, then as archival material, and later reworked as narrative—became German history; old time was turned into new space that defined the nation and repudiated the center-periphery model of empire. With the defeat of Napoleon, the German states established the first official archives to house the huge numbers of documents that, with the end of the many sovereign entities of the Holy Roman Empire, had lost their practical value but could now be rearranged as the prehistory of the German nation. The preservation and analysis of these and other religious and local documents was overseen by the state-sponsored historical agency initiated by Baron vom Stein in 1819, the Monumenta Germaniae Historica, which published dozens of multi-volume editions of medieval documents.[10] The attention to Germany's medieval heritage is striking and absorbed most of the energies of Germany's historians for the rest of the nineteenth century.

One practical reason for this is that the persistence of the absolutist state meant that Prussian records even from the eighteenth century did not become properly historical until 1918 and so remained scattered in ministries rather than collected in central archives.[11] But the medieval past also functioned as the dominant metonym for the German nation as a whole because it provided the key marker for the difference on which German identity was based.

The establishment of Prussian state archives and Stein's Monumenta Germaniae Historica, as well as Boisserée's collection of early-modern German art, Karl Friedrich Schinkel's efforts to preserve German monuments, and also Jacob and Wilhelm Grimm's fairy tales, were attempts to create a common, durable, and specific German past. Of course, it would be senseless to argue that the great majority of inhabitants in the German states suddenly regarded themselves in terms of an encompassing German identity and recognized as their own the medieval past that Boisserée and others tried to put into view. Yet the extraordinary success of the Grimm fairy tales in the years after their first publication in 1812 indicates how well the German story resonated with German contemporaries. Despite their transnational appeal—the first English edition came out in 1823—the fairy tales are definitively the *Grimms'* fairy tales and evoked a particular idea of the German landscape. Moreover, the brothers insisted on the specifically Germanic origins of the tales. Indeed, the characters in the fairy tales were very much like the readers the Grimms hoped to find: they comprised locals rather than cosmopolitans, commoners rather than aristocrats, women and children as well as men, perfect examples of the vernacular culture the books came to represent. By the middle of the nineteenth century, the *Kleine Ausgabe*'s collection of fifty of the most popular tales had sold two million copies in the German-speaking realm of fifty million people.[12]

The fact that the Grimms' collection of old German tales stood on the shelves of so many readers suggests the ways in which even ordinary households established archives. Although the point should not be pressed too hard, the new historical context allowed Germans to see themselves quite literally as contemporaries (*Zeitgenossen*), Benjamin's heirs who shared history and historicized national territory. As a result, the most ordinary people came to take an interest in each other and to read their lives against the ordeal of the nation. The nineteenth century "was swamped with unremarkable self-revelations," notes Peter Gay. "Men and women with no claim to fame of any kind," wrote these up; "they left their memoirs moldering in attics or buried in local archives, or asked a job printer to make an unpretentious book."[13] Autobiographical supply flourished because it appealed to biographical demand. What authorized the histories of ordinary people was not simply notions of enfranchisement that came with the French Revolution but the tissues of connectedness that came with a historical worldview and national identity. The idea of the nation both sentimentalized and popularized ordinary stories. It served as a social and literary point of reconciliation, making the ordeal of the nation the vehicle for recognizing the fate of the individual. The immense paperwork of history in the nineteenth century struggled to bring the distress of the one into correspondence with the other.

The People's Archive

It is remarkable how the echoes of Napoleon's cannons continued to sound throughout the nineteenth century. The French Revolution, the Wars of Liberation, and the outsized figure of Napoleon dominated the production and consumption of popular German history; Napoleon lent his name to fictional antiheroes as late as 1918 in Heinrich Mann's *Man of Straw*. Nearly one hundred years after the event, Germans still drew attention to the imperial menace and the fragile nature of national relics. But it was the wars of the twentieth century that dramatically reconfigured the archive, because total war posed insistently the question of the survival and definition of the German people.

Almost immediately, World War I intruded into the lives of almost every German family. Between August 1914 and July 1918, more than thirteen million men served in the German army. Nearly 20 percent of the total population and 85 percent of all eligible males mobilized to fight. Since the rupture of war coincided with the unprecedented engagement of millions of actual individuals, the crisis had a remarkable autobiographical aspect. Germans from all walks of life knew relatives on the front and told tales about fighting the war, procuring food, and laboring in wartime factories. As a result, the war vastly expanded the people's archive. Although the German government produced thousands of war-related texts and histories, these cannot compare to the millions of letters, poems, and newspaper articles written and consumed in domestic settings.

All sorts of documents revealed this personal engagement. During the war, newspapers published hundreds of unsolicited poems every day; by one estimate fifty thousand German war poems were written on each day of August 1914.[14] Families pasted scrapbooks, and ordinary soldiers kept diaries and sent millions of letters home every day. Some twenty-nine billion pieces of mail were sent back and forth between the battlefront and the home front in the four years that followed mobilization: every day some ten million letters, postcards, telegrams, and packages reached the front, and every day nearly seven million were sent back home.[15] Although the political valence of this correspondence is unclear, given ordinary literary conventions, the increasingly centralized management of news, and military censorship, contemporaries prized their own vernacular knowledge of the war. By the end of the war, over ninety-seven separate editions of war letters had been assembled, published, and purchased, the most famous of which was Philipp Witkop's 1916 *Kriegsbriefe deutscher Studenten*.[16] The high command acknowledged the power of these completely ordinary, unauthoritative letters by incorporating them into the patriotic "enlightenment" the troops received in the last two years of the war.[17] What all this suggests is the degree to which the war was regarded as a distinctively people's war. It was legitimated in the name of the people rather than in the state or the monarchy, and it dramatized as never before the involvement of individuals in the larger movements of history. Archivists themselves recognized the importance of documenting popular sovereignty and called on citizens to preserve and turn over letters and other reports on the war.[18] Total war thus prompted an expansion of what constituted compelling historical evidence and reoriented the history of the war into social-historical streams.

It was on the basis of individual experience that Germans disputed among themselves the meaning of the war. Although the published editions of war letters retained a generally patriotic tone, private correspondence to pastors, mayors, and Reichstag deputies told other stories about injustices on the front and urged alternative courses of action.[19] And after the war, citizens returned again and again to the archives they had assembled to support their claims about the course of the war, the reasons for military defeat, and the justice of the November Revolution. Partisan newspapers on the Left and the Right were filled with recollections of frontline service, and recriminations forth and back were played out again when the flood of semiautobiographical war novels commenced in the late 1920s.[20] Indeed, one of the most compelling wartime diaries, written by the seaman Richard Stumpf and documenting the harsh discipline of naval authorities, was submitted as evidence in 1926 to a Reichstag commission examining the origins of the revolution and later published in polemical form.[21] No other war had been depicted in this unmanaged, democratic way.

The great consequence of World War I was the emergence of popular sovereignty as the organizing principle of German politics and thus the basis for the reorganization of the German archive. While Germans certainly did not agree on political questions, they justified their actions and expectations in terms of the nation. As a result, excerpts from the people's archive gained unprecedented political value: Witkop's edition of war letters is the primary example. At the same time, Germany's defeat and the convulsions of the revolution threw open questions of political liability. Did Germany's government mishandle foreign affairs before 1914? Did socialists on the home front stab the army on the front lines in the back? And what burden of responsibility did the military bear for the outbreak of the revolution? It was the sorry fate of the postwar nation that authorized enormous historical projects in the form of parliamentary commissions and protracted libel cases around the "stab-in-the-back" legend. The result was a massive reconstitution of the official archive in the public sphere, which signaled the unresolved nature of Germany's historical itinerary, even if massive editions such as the sixty-volume *Die grosse Politik der Europäischen Kabinette 1871–1914,* overseen by the "Central Office to Investigate the Causes of the War" in the Foreign Ministry, claimed to offer definitive statements about Germany's guiltlessness.

The importance of making the case for Germany, for both a domestic and an international public and by both critics and apologists of the Kaiserreich, prompted the establishment of a central archive, the Reichsarchiv, in 1919. As a central repository of German history, it was charged with documenting and preserving the national heritage of Germans in the wake of the nation's defeat—"wars trigger archives"—in 1806 and again in 1918.[22] Housed in a former military school on the Brauhausberg in Potsdam and largely staffed by decommissioned officers, the Reichsarchiv was central to the effort to justify Germany's national cause. That it opened its doors to the public and initiated the collection of war letters and other documents of the people's struggle in the war indicated how sovereignty had shifted from state to nation, and it thus enabled the production of alternative histories, but for the most part the Reichsarchiv served as the point of verification for Germany's national ordeal and for its refurbished future.[23]

As Bernd Faulenbach explains for the 1920s, "a flood of historical publications engaged contemporary themes. A significant part of the work capacity of modern historians was absorbed in writing the 'prehistory to the present,' whereby the experience of the war and its resolution was the primary motivation."[24] Most of this historiography was nationalist and conventional, but it was supported by exhaustive and unprecedented archival research. The same empirical foundation characterized as well the few historians such as Veit Valentin and Eckart Kehr who struggled to expose the authoritarian structure of the prewar German state. Entangled as they had become in German history, historians in Great Britain, France, and the United States vigorously joined the debate about the origins of World War I. (Bernadotte Schmitt and Sidney Fay are the key figures.)[25] This entanglement was, of course, far greater after World War II, by which time it was impossible to write German history without non-German historians. Ultimately, the huge inflation of archival sources and archival documentation corresponded to a deflation in archival authority and to the revival of historical hermeneutics.

The shift from an emphasis on state to one on nation was the consequence of Germany's total mobilization effort during the war. But military defeat left the German subject undefined. Weimar culture added to a relentless attempt to survey, inventory, and describe in order to revisualize the nation as an active, even triumphant political player in the future. This required a dramatic expansion of the archive. Historians and sociologists initiated comprehensive ethnographic surveys to establish the durability of German ethnic identity. Historians focused less on the achievement of German unification, as they had in the years before 1914, and more on the long-term and continuing struggle of the German people in Europe and thus operated in the subjunctive mode and put accent on what remained incomplete and broken.[26] Along the edges of the profession, younger historians pursued more energetically the attempt to write a deliberately new kind of history of the German people. In particular, they looked to the border regions, which were not only imperiled by the postwar settlement but had been neglected in the Second Reich. It was here that historians believed they had found the site of a pure, besieged Germandom. "The variety of German settlements in east-central Europe and even overseas," writes Willi Oberkrom about these social-historical studies, "seemed to hold the 'magical key' to the recognition of 'our' ethnic identity." A closer examination of "settlement patterns, house types . . . traditions and customs, clothing and food" promised to inventory "common generalities and regional particularities" and thereby uncover a "genuine folk life." Increasingly, "Volk was perceived as the constituent element and subject of social-historical evolution."[27]

In an almost obsessive practice of self-observation, Germans scanned the resources of the country and the makeup of the population, building up a cultural archive of items and types that would be needed to master the "altered world" of international instability and technological innovation. It was almost a game to identify the nation's new resources. Germany's largest weekly, Ullstein's *Berliner Illustrierte Zeitung*, introduced to the nation its "New Age Types": "the traffic policeman," "the radio operator," "the soundman," "the woman doctor," "the sports announcer," "the race car driver," "the driving instructor," and "the Alpine skier," all newfangled experts of one sort or another.[28] Weimar culture produced dozens of physiognomic surveys such as this one, each one surveying and taking measure of the new face (*Antlitz*, a favorite Weimar-era word) to the postwar world. Photographers such as Erich Retzlaff, Erna Lendvai-Dircksen, and August Sander scrutinized the faces and bodies of Germans to build galleries of strength, solidity, and rootedness at the level of the ordinary existence.[29]

Cultural activity in the Weimar years developed as an effort to identify the human types and biological and technological forces that would equip the regenerate nation. It constituted nothing less than an ever-expanding archive of German capacity. However, the instrumentalization of the archive in the first postwar years was never systematic and lacked political direction, despite its nationalist tendency and military accent. After 1933, with the National Socialist seizure of power, the archive assumed a much larger role in German political life.

The Racial Archive

For the Nazis to realize their aim of reconstituting the German public as a self-consciously biological body politic they had to be able to distinguish Jews from Germans and unhealthy elements from healthy ones, and had to discipline the Germans to conduct their lives according to new biological standards. This required not only the mobilization of existing records for political ends but the creation of new records that would recognize the biological categories the Nazis held to be so consequential. As the definitions of the political became more biological so did the official archive. Josef Franz Knöpfler, director of the Bavarian archival administration, stated the enhanced function of the archive in the National Socialist state quite clearly in 1936: "There is no practice of racial politics without the mobilization of source documents, which indicate the origin and development of a race and people. . . . There is no racial politics without archives, without archivists."[30] The first major step in the process of racial documentation consisted of directives that, beginning in 1933, instructed local health offices to identify those citizens who were deemed to be biologically unhealthy. These became ever more detailed and intrusive and provided the basis for the sterilization campaign that identified as many as one million Germans as biologically degenerate—a fifth of these were actually sterilized.[31] The second step was taken with the Nuremberg Laws of September 1935, which redefined German citizenry and excluded Jews from public life. But a comprehensive archive of who was German and who was not was only established with the census of May 1939.

   Conducted on May 17, 1939, after having been postponed for one year to include Austria, the national census established a relatively accurate count of who was German and who was Jewish. It counted a total of 233,973 so-called racial Jews within the borders of 1939. A much more comprehensive survey took place on August 13, 1939, and it was the data this produced that was stored on punch cards for subsequent retrieval. (IBM's German subsidiary, Deutsche Hollerith Maschinen Gesellschaft, produced as many as 1.5 billion punch cards a year to sort and resort Germany's population.)[32] Although the data were never reassembled on a national level, they were stored in local and regional card catalogs, or *Volkskarteien*, which allowed authorities to identify in the territory of their responsibility able-bodied workers, potential soldiers, and Jews. Handed out one week by thousands of volunteers and collected the next, the Volkskartei compiled data in fourteen fields that corresponded to fourteen punch holes at the top margin of each card; these were later tabbed with different colors to simplify the process of assessment. All legal residents—Jews as well as non-Jews— filled out the cards, providing information on trade (field 2), physical impairments (field 4), education (field 6), ability to speak foreign languages or travel experience in a foreign country (field 7), other skills and expertise (field 8), and the ability to drive, ride, and fly (field 9). It was no secret that this information was assembled in order to more perfectly mobilize Germans and make efficient use of their specific skills in the event of war. The types the *Berliner Illustrierte Zeitung* had introduced to readers in its Weimar-era photo series, the Nazi census had succeeded in identifying for political purposes across the entire population. Mobilization was also accompanied by exclusion: in the last field, field 14, authorities marked whether residents were Jewish; a black tab over the punch hole designated the cardholder as Jewish. It was on the basis of the catalog that local authorities identified and gathered up German Jews for deportation after 1941; all they had to do was pull the cards with the black tab on the last field.[33] Although not accessible from a single point, the Volkskarteien very nearly realized the goal of a systematic ethnographic and racial archive.

The Nazis also racialized vernacular archives since they obligated individual Germans to maintain extensive racial archives at home about their bodies, lives, and genealogy. The biological politics of the regime did not simply posit the applicability of new physiognomic categories of race and health but demanded that citizens strive to match their lives to those categories. "It is not a party badge or a brown shirt that makes you a National Socialist, but rather your character and the conduct of your life," announced the first issue of the eugenic journal, *Neues Volk*, in July 1933. A "spiritual revolution" had to follow the accomplishments of the political revolution, insisted Walter Gross, director of the Rassenpolitisches Amt of the Nazi party, in 1934: it would "fundamentally remodel and reform," "even all those things that seem today completely solid," he added.[34] What was necessary was to "recognize yourself" (*Erkenne dich selbst*), which meant following the tenets of hereditary biology to find a suitable partner for marriage and marry only for love, to provide the *Volk* with healthy children, and to accept "the limits of empathy" as a revitalized Germany weeded out racial undesirables.[35] Not only would the Aryan body have to be protected through vigorous eugenic measures, but the Aryan self had to be implemented by the individual's responsibility to the collective racial whole. This put the emphasis on the efforts of ordinary, racially desirable Germans to discipline themselves in order to conduct their lives in accordance with the precepts of the racial future.

The most important papers in the expanded archive of domestic life in the Third Reich were those that documented Aryan identity. With the publication of the Nuremberg Laws, the racial distinction between German (or "Aryan") and Jew governed the most important aspects of every-day life, particularly the permission to marry and the registration of births and deaths. Just how willingly the transformation of Germans into Aryans and Jews was accepted is not clear, but the categories worked their way into everyday life. Victor Klemperer, for example, was astonished to hear even non-Nazi acquaintances suddenly talk about *Sippe* or genealogical kin.[36] Since vigorous public interest in genealogy went hand-in-hand with legal requirements to prepare an *Ahnenpass*, or genealogical passport, there seems to have been broad legitimacy to the idea of kin and thus the notion of racial insiders and outsiders. Most contemporaries were familiar with a "family tree," in which relatives are organized from the oldest ancestors down several generations to the numerous family clusters of the living generation. But the table of ancestors that Germans had to include in the racial passport worked quite differently, from the contemporary individual backward to include all blood relatives in an inverted pyramid. "If the family tree is colorful and many-sided, depending on the number of children and the structure of the family," one genealogical expert commented, the table of ancestors "has an architectonic layout characterized by strict discrimination and mathematical uniformity." Beginning with the individual in question, it "reveals the direction of maternal and paternal bloodlines" in order to serve as a certification of blood purity and thus the inclusion of the individual in the "racial community."[37] The effort at certification was no easy task. Germans needed the "nose of an accomplished detective" in order to gather up all the data to track bloodlines into the past. "State archives and libraries have to be trawled . . . and also ranking lists, muster roles, telephone books, bills of lading, guild records. We also have to make our way to old cemeteries where tumble-down graves might reveal yet another clue."[38] "Tumble-down graves"—there is an uneasy resemblance between the effort to document Aryan identity before 1945 and the recovery of traces of Jewish life in Germany and Poland after 1945.

Beginning in 1936, anyone getting married also assumed an "Aryan" identity. Prospective husbands and wives needed to document their Aryan racial status with notarized citations of the registrations of the birth, marriage, and death of each of their parents and grandparents. Moreover, prospective newlyweds had to certify their genetic health, which, if local authorities believed it necessary, meant a visit to the local public health office and the acquisition of additional documents. (The law requiring such visits was drawn up, but suspended in practice.) In addition to hand-ing out *Mein Kampf*, the registrar's office provided couples with pamphlets on maintaining and reproducing good racial stock—*Deutscher, denk an deine und deiner Kinder Gesundheit, Handbuch für die deutsche Familie,* and *Ratgeber für Mütter*—and instructions on how to maintain proper genealogical records.[39] This constituted a broad effort to push Germans to document and comport themselves as Aryans. Piece by piece, ordinary Germans assembled their own private archives, and as they did they invariably became more recognizable as Aryans in Hitler's eyes and in their own.

Like the preformatted albums in which contemporaries during World War I pasted letters and photographs under patriotic and other sentimental headings, the racial passport or Ahnenpass was the axis around which the people's archive proliferated in the 1940s. For individuals to acquire the necessary passport entailed the reorganization and systemization of old family records that were lying around as well as the procurement of new documents, some going back to the early nineteenth century. A cardboard box in Berlin's Landesarchiv contains old Ahnenpässe. Many are in fact the one mass-produced by the Verlag für Stammbaumwesen, which included in its pages a handy "Reichsalphabet der Familie"; a list of permissible names for children, divided into recommended Germanic names from Adalbert to Wulf, for men, and Ada to Wunhild, for women, and acceptable non-Germanic names (Achim to Vinzent for men, Agathe to Viktoria for women); as well as the ubiquitous "Blutschutzgesetz" of 15 September 1935. New papers gathered inside the pages of the Ahnenpass: the mandated *Arbeitsbuch*; a four-leaf clover; a restaurant bill; a marriage certificate; birth announcements of children; baptismal certificates; inoculation records; divorce papers; insurance cards; Winter Aid stamps; and also correspondence with a son serving on the front; official confirmation of a soldier missing in action; a letter from a fallen man's comrade describing the whereabouts of the dead man's grave "in Aleksandrwoka (village center) . . . some 16 km s. of Olenin which is 60 km. w of Rshew"; a 1945 welfare card for bomb victims on which was also handwritten "refugees from the East."[40] Family archives, racial categories, and individual identities became increasingly calibrated with one another.

For German Jews, however, the process of archiving ran in reverse. Jews and so-called "racial Jews," converts to Christianity, were required to register themselves as Jewish with local authorities and to carry identification papers which labeled them as such. But otherwise, the paperwork they filled out at the command of the National Socialist regime was a prelude to the destruction of their private property and ultimately to their murder. In Dresden, Victor Klemperer spent the morning of Wednesday, June 29, 1938, "filling out forms: Inventory of Assets of Jews." An inventory of "household assets" followed in December 1941. Since "a house search can be expected immediately after the inventory statement," Klemperer resolved to part with his manuscripts and his diary, which his wife stowed with friends; thereafter, the additional entries that Klemperer made had to be secreted out of his rooms in small packets. As it was, the ability to maintain a private archive was already severely hampered by the shortage of paper and the prohibition on Jews possessing typewriters. Since the concentration of Jews in "Jew houses" usually preceded their outright deportation, Klemperer, like so many others, was forced to move into drastically smaller quarters, which meant the disposal of books and papers. "[I] am virtually ravaging my past," he wrote in his diary on May 21, 1941. "The principal activity" of the next day was "burning, burning, burning for hours on end: heaps of letters, manuscripts." Letters were still received: "today," wrote Klemperer on December 7, 1941, "I saw a postcard with the postmark: 'Litzmanndstadt Ghetto.' . . . The card bore yet another stamp: 'Litzmannstadt, biggest industrial city of the East,'" Klemperer added.[41] But soon that correspondence came to end as well. Incidentally, Jews had been prohibited from using German archives since 1938.

The racial archive reflected the ambitious efforts of the Nazis to shape a new collective subject; it at once required substantial self-archiving and recontextualization on the part of racial insiders and rested on the step-by-step exclusion and decontextualization of racial outsiders. It came with extraordinary systemization of provenance in order to manufacture a collective Aryan subject in such a way that the possession of the archive itself became the arbiter of historical existence.

Archives of Loss

The burning of his personal archive which Klemperer undertook in May 1941 indicates an entirely new dimension to modern archival practice. Even the vernacular archive had become dangerous and its maintenance impossible in conditions in which the Nazis sought to revisualize, reclassify, and reorder the world. Klemperer's activity on that spring day

reproduced in miniature the immense reconfiguration of the German
archive in the twentieth century. His arson followed the demolition of
countless politically risky archives already in 1933, when left-wing politicians and intellectuals burnt or otherwise disposed of their papers, a con-
flagration which the Nazis themselves fueled in their own book-burnings,
which they sponsored across Germany beginning in May 1933, and the
ransacking of the files of countless civic groups and trade unions.[42] The
emigration of German Jews also entailed the dispersion and loss of personal papers, libraries, heirlooms, photographs, and other family memo-
rabilia. Hundreds of synagogues were burned down in November 1938 and
with them the evidence of Jewish life in Germany over the course of many
centuries, a prelude to the willful destruction of the life and property of
Jewish communities across Europe after 1939. German history came to the
rest of Europe in the form of terrifying annihilation.

Klemperer's arson of May 1941 also anticipated the destruction that came
with the end of the war. As we know, Germans across the Reich destroyed
the evidence of their political complicity. These deliberate actions were
compounded by the furious end of the war in Germany, the expulsion of
twelve million Germans from eastern Europe, the bombardment of German cities, and thus the ruin of countless households. In his poem "Autumn 1944," Hans Magnus Enzenberger remembered watching Allied
bombers fly toward his hometown of Nuremberg and imagining the remnants of what amounted to his family's archive in the attic catching fire:

> to him lying in the grass
> they appeared magnificent
> shimmering high up
> in the wide open October sky
> these streams of bombers, and no great loss
> the souvenirs burning far away in the musty attic
>
> collector's teacups and angel's hair
> grandfather's Parisian postcards
> (*Oh là là!*) and his belt buckle
> from another war,
> petticoats full of holes, medals,
> doll houses, a plaster model of Psyche

and in a cigar box
some forgotten tickets to a shrine

but in the basement
the corpses are still there[43]

I do not cite Enzenberger's poem in order to dramatize the poignancy of the material losses of Germans in Nuremberg or elsewhere, but to indicate the radical discontinuity that past things came to stand for after the mobilizations of total war. Whether the ruins are Jewish tombstones in an overgrown plot, or faded Hebrew advertising in Berlin's Scheunenviertel or the suitcases in Auschwitz, or even a grandfather's postcards from an earlier world war, they are not contained in sensible narratives but speak out as the remains of irreparable loss and violent discontinuity. They are objects stranded in the present as the debris of broken connections. The end of the war thus reconfigured the archive once more, less because so few items survived the destruction of the war, although that is certainly the case, but rather because those items changed in signification, marking out the loss and dispersion of German and Jewish lives whereas before they had stood for former wholes within relatively stable narratives.

In the first decades after World War II, there was an attempt to reconstitute the German archive as a record of German loss and German victimization. In the 1950s, the West German government sponsored a massive Dokumentation der Vertreibung der Deutschen aus Ost-Mitteleuropa, which gathered up hundreds of eye-witness accounts of German refugees expelled from eastern Europe and cited the growing memoir literature. To some extent, this undertaking was innovative. It "took seriously the testimonies of individuals" and served as an acknowledgement, as Martin Brozsat argued, "that in modern societies 'the broad mass, society in its entirety, has itself become in large measure the subject of history,' not its object."[44] At the same time, *Dorfchroniken* and *Familienchroniken* of abandoned German places in eastern Europe detailed the broken legacies of collective lives. Throughout the post-1945 period, novels, magazines, chronicles, photo collections, and other documentations of German loss in World War II revealed a large, if parochial, publication industry. Like the autobiographical accounts that followed the Napoleonic Wars and flourished during World War I, this vernacular archive demonstrates that modern memory repeatedly fastens on to a moment of disruption and a prior duration of tradition.

However, this German archive reproduced the excisions that had taken place during the Third Reich. There was scant attention paid to the victims of the Nazis or the political origins of the regime and the war it pursued so vigorously and pitilessly. Of course, the Holocaust was acknowledged, but it was regarded as something that happened to non-Germans and was described in spare and impersonal terms. The evidence that the postwar archive collected on German suffering therefore rested on the archival rearrangements of the Nazi period in which German identity was limited to non-Jews. It thus raised the question of how German history could even be written in Germany. Although the paradigm shift in historiographical approaches that came with the 1960s revealed the insufficiency of Germany's postwar archive and gave voice to political dissidents and marginalized groups, the problem of how to represent a common past remained. If Jewish refugees could still write about "My Life in Germany" before 1939, it was much more difficult to do so after 1945.[45] One solution was to make the incompleteness of the story the story itself, to acknowledge the strain of and the limits to a common past, and to produce archives of loss.

Neither World War II nor the Holocaust destroyed the archive, but both transformed its epistemological status. The national archives live on, in the form of the Bundesarchiv, but they no longer make the pretense of speaking for the nation or its past and do not encompass the records of its experience. Its holdings cannot provide the answers to the questions about complicity, survival, and murder or even provide a record of loss. At the same time, the Bundesarchiv is no longer the only site where it is possible or necessary to research German history. German history no longer belongs to Germans alone: among the most moving Holocaust memoirs, for example, are those written by a Pole, an Italian, and a Spaniard. And historians of Germany must move beyond Germany to begin to account for its history: to the places to which European Jews fled while it was still possible, including the Wiener Library in London, the Leo Baeck Institute in New York, Yad Vashem in Jerusalem, and the National Archives in Washington, D.C. The forcible dispersion of European Jews and other refugees produced an archive of exile which encompasses semiofficial papers of institutions such as the American Friends Service Committee, the Central Zionist Archives in Jerusalem, the American Jewish Archives, and the American Jewish Joint Distribution Committee; private efforts at documentation from the autobiographies deposited starting in the 1930s at Harvard University; the oral interviews of the Yale Holocaust project; and most impressively, thousands upon thousands of memoirs, autobiographies, and other recollections of displacement passed on from generation to generation.[46] The global displacements of the Holocaust have created a massive archive of survivor accounts that is without precedent.

The point of origin of this last archive is discontinuity, which makes special demands on its users. It is plural, rather than authoritative; manifestly incomplete, rather than comprehensive; global, rather than local. This archive of loss thereby subverts the state-centered authority of the conventional archive. To even begin to adequately understand the history of exile and mass death in twentieth-century Germany, and to write against the idea of a common past, the historian needs to write narratives from a variety of perspectives and adopt techniques of intertextuality. At the same time, the histories of Germany are marked with a lingering deficit: the final impossibility of completely understanding or fully accounting for the loss. The great burden of German history is to recognize that the archive in Germany is broken; to use it as if it were not would be to reproduce the exclusions of the Nazi era. At the same time, the great opportunity of German history is to take the broken, dispersed archive of the twentieth century as a means of reflecting the storiedness of history, its excisions, and its means of self-representation, and to reconsider the displacements of life and death in the past. In the end, the German archive provides evidence for both the absence of a common past and the enormous violence entailed in the attempts to produce it.

Notes

1 Walter Benjamin, "The Storyteller," in his *Illuminations*, ed. Hannah Arendt, (New York: Schocken, 1969), 98.

2 On "memory crisis," Richard Terdiman, *Present Past: Modernity and the Memory Crisis* (Ithaca: Cornell University Press, 1993).

3 Jacques Derrida, *Archive Fever: A Freudian Impression*, trans. E Prenowitz (Chicago: University of Chicago Press, 1995).

4 Michel Foucault, *The Order of Things: An Archaeology of the Human Sciences* (New York: Pantheon Books, 1970).

5 Achille Mbembe, "The Power of the Archive and Its Limits," in Carolyn

Hamilton, Verne Harris, Jane Taylor, Michele Pickover, Graeme Reid, and Razia Saleh, eds., *Refiguring the Archive* (Cape Town: David Philip, 2002), 20.

6 Ernst Posner, "Some Aspects of Archival Development since the French Revolution," in Maygene Daniels and Timothy Walch, eds., *A Modern Archives Reader: Basic Readings on Archival Theory and Practice* (Washington, D.C.: U.S. General Services Administration, 1984), 5.

7 The word play is from Roberto Gonzalez Echevarria, *Myth and Archive: A Theory of Latin American Narrative* (Cambridge: Cambridge University Press, 1990), 175.

8 See Peter Fritzsche, *Stranded in the Present: Modern Time and the Melancholy of History* (Cambridge, Mass.: Harvard University Press, 2004). See also Reinhart Koselleck, *Futures Past: On the Semantics of Historical Time* (Cambridge: Cambridge University Press, 1985).

9 Stephen Bann, *The Clothing of Clio* (Cambridge: Cambridge University Press, 1984), 86. On Boisserée, see Fritzsche, *Stranded in the Present*, 108–20.

10 Wolfgang Ernst, *Im Namen von Geschichte: Sammeln—Speichern—Er / Zählen* (Munich: Wilhelm Fink, 2003).

11 Heinrich Otto Meisner, *Archivalienkunde vom 16. Jahrhundert bis 1918* (Göttingen: Vandenhoeck and Ruprecht, 1969), 125, 146.

12 Reimer Dänhardt, "Grimm-Editionen im Kinderbuchverlag Berlin," in Astrid Stedje, ed., *Die Brüder Grimm: Erbe und Rezeption* (Stockholm: Almqvuist and Wiksell International, 1984), 51.

13 Peter Gay, *The Naked Heart* (New York: Norton, 1995), 109. See also Clive Emsley, *British Society and the French Wars, 1793–1815* (Totowa, N.J.: Rowman and Littlefield, 1979), 172–73; and Gustav René Hocke, *Das europäische Tagebuch* (Wiesbaden: Limes, 1963),67, 201–02.

14 C. Busse, ed., *Deutsche Kriegslieder 1914 / 16* (Bielefeld: Insel Verlag, 1916), vi, cited in Klaus Vondung, ed., *Kriegserlebnis: Der Erste Weltkrieg in der literarischen Gestaltung und symbolischen Deutung der Nationen* (Göttingen: Vandenhoeck and Ruprecht, 1980), 13.

15 Bernd Ulrich, "Feldpostbriefe im Ersten Weltkrieg—Bedeutung und Zensur," in Peter Knoch, ed., *Kriegsalltag: Die Rekonstruktion des Kriegsalltags als Aufgabe der historischen Forschung und der Friedenserziehung* (Stuttgart: Metzler, 1989).

16 Philipp Witkop, *Kriegsbriefe deutscher Studenten* (Gotha: F. A. Perthes, 1916). See also Manfred Hettling and Michael Jeismann, "Der Weltkrieg als Epos: Philipp Witkops 'Kriegsbriefe gefallener Studenten,'" in Gerhard Hirschfeld and Gerd Krumeich, eds., *"Keiner fühlt sich hier mehr als Mensch": Erlebnis und Wirkung des Ersten Weltkriegs* (Essen: Klartext, 1993), 175–98; and Ulrich, "Feldpostbriefe," 40.

17 Gunther Mai, " 'Aufklärung der Bevölkerung' und 'Vaterländischer Unterricht' in Württemberg 1914–1918: Struktur, Durchführung und Inhalte der deutshen Inlandspropaganda im Ersten Weltkrieg," *Zeitschrift für Württembergische Landesgeschichte* 36 (1977): 215.

18 John Meier and Eugen Fischer, "Sammelt Soldatenbriefe!," *Mein Heimat-*

land: Badische Blätter für Volkskunde 3 (1916): 103–5, cited in Bernd Jürgen Warn-eken, *Populare Autobiographik: Empirische Studien zu einer Quellengattung der All-tagsgeschichtsforschung* (Tübingen: Tübinger Vereinigung für Volkskunde, 1985), 13–14 n.13.

19 Bernd Ulrich, "Die Desillusionierung der Kriegsfreiwilligen von 1914," in Wolfram Wette, ed., *Der Krieg des kleinen Mannes: Eine Militärgeschichte von unten* (Munich: Piper, 1992), 117.

20 Bernd Ulrich and Benjamin Ziemann, eds., *Krieg im Frieden: Die unkämpfte Erinnerung an den Ersten Weltkrieg* (Frankfurt: Fischer Taschenbuch Verlag, 1997).

21 Daniel Horn, ed., *War, Mutiny, and Revolution in the German Navy: The World War I Diary of Seaman Richard Stumpf* (New Brunswick, N.J.: Rutgers University Press, 1967). See also Wilhelm Dittmann, *Die Marine-Justiz-Morde von 1917 und die Admiralsrebellion von 1918* (Berlin: Dietz, 1926); and Richard Stumpf, *Warum die Flotte zerbrach: Kriegstagebuch eines christlichen Arbeiters* (Berlin: Dietz, 1927).

22 Ernst, *Im Namen von Geschichte*, 664.

23 Ulrich and Ziemann, *Krieg im Frieden*. See also Ernst Müsebeck, "Der Einfluss des Weltkrieges auf die archivalische Methode," *Archivalische Zeitschrift* 38 (1929): 135–50.

24 Bernd Faulenbach, "Nach der Niederlage: Zeitgeschichtliche Fragen und apologetischen Tendenzen in der Historiographie der Weimarer Zeit," in Peter Schöttler, ed., *Geschichtsschreibung als Legitimationswissenschaft 1918–1945* (Frankfurt: Suhrkamp, 1997), 31–34.

25 Sidney Fay, *The Origins of the World War*, 2 vols. (New York: Macmillan, 1928); and Bernadotte Schmidt, *The Coming of the War, 1914* (London: Scribners, 1936).

26 Bernd Faulenbach, "Nach der Niederlage," 31–34.

27 Willi Oberkrome, *Volksgeschichte: Methodische Innovation und völkische Ideo-logisierung in der deutschen Geschichtswissenschaft 1918–1945* (Göttingen; Vanden-hoeck and Ruprecht, 1993), 24–25, 32, 35, 99, 113. See also Ingo Haar, " 'Revi-sionistische' Historiker und Jugendbewegung: Das Königsberger Beispiel," in Schöttler, ed., *Geschichtsschreibung* 69, 71.

28 In order, *Berliner Illustrierte Zeitung*, no. 26, June 27, 1926; no. 4, Jan. 27, 1929; no. 32, Aug. 11, 1929; no. 34, Aug. 31, 1929, no. 41, Oct. 13, 1929, no. 4, Jan. 26, 1930, no. 33, Aug. 17, 1930; no. 2, Jan. 11, 1931.

29 See the discussion of portrait photography in Claudia Schmölders, *Hit-lers Gesicht: Eine physiognomische Biographie* (Munich: Beck, 2000), as well as Hans F. K. Günther, *Rassenkunde des deutschen Volkes* (Munich: J. F. Lehmann, 1922); Erna Lendvai-Dircksen, *Das deutsche Volksgesicht* (Berlin: Kulturelle Ver-lagsanstalt, 1932); Erich Retzlaff, *Das Antlitz des Alters* (Düsseldorf: Pädagogischer verlag g.m.b.h., 1930); August Sander and Alfred Döblin, *Antlitz der Zeit: Menschen des 20. Jahrhunderts* (Munich: Transmare Verlag, 1929); and "Antlitz der deutschen Stämme," *Berliner Illustrierte Zeitung*, no. 22, May 31, 1931. On "Antlitz" in general:

Ernst Benkard, *Das ewige Antlitz* (Berlin: Frankfurter Verlagsanstalt, 1927); Wilhelm Haas, *Antlitz der Zeit: Sinfonie moderner Industriedichtung* (Berlin: Wegweiser Verlag, 1926); Josef Hofmiller, *Das deutsche Antlitz: Ein Lesebuch* (Munich: A. Langer, 1926); Ernst Jünger, *Das Anltitz des Weltkrieges* (Berlin: Neufeld and Henius, 1930); Heinz Kindermann, *Das literarische Antlitz der Gegenwart* (Halle: Niemeyer, 1930); Karl Christina von Loesch, *Das Antlitz der Grenzlande* (Munich: F. Bruckmann, 1933); Karin Michaëlis, *Das Antlitz des Kindes: Bilder und Studien aus der Welt unserer Kinder* (Berlin: Neufeld and Henius, 1931); Alfred Wien, *Das Antlitz hinter der Maske* (Gütersloh: Bertelsmann, 1932); Arnold Zweig, *Das ostjüdische Antlitz* (Berlin: Welt-Verlag, 1920).

30 Cited in Wolfgang Ernst, "Archival Action: The Archive as ROM and Its Political Instrumentalization under National Socialism," *History of the Human Sciences* 12, 2 (1999): 26.

31 Gisela Bock, *Zwangssterilisation im Nationalsozialismus: Studien zur Rassenpolitik und Frauenpolitik* (Opladen: Westdeutscher Verlag, 1986).

32 Edwin Black, *IBM and the Holocaust: The Strategic Alliance Between Nazi Germany and America's Most Powerful Corporation* (New York: New Crown Publishers, 2001), 10.

33 Götz Aly and Karl Heinz Roth, *Die restlose Erfassung: Volkszählen, Identifizieren, Aussondern im Nationalsozialismus* (Berlin: Rotbuch, 1984), 47–49, who draw on Klaus Heinecken, "Die Volkskartei," *Allgemeines Statistisches Archiv* 31 (1942–43): 39–44.

34 Walter Gross, "Von der äusseren zur inneren Revolution," *Neues Volk* 2 (August 1934).

35 Hans F. K. Günther, "Was ist Rasse?" *Illustrierter Beobachter* 8, 32 (August 12, 1933); "Grenzen des Mitleids," *Neues Volk* 1 (July 1933).

36 Victor Klemperer, *The Language of the Third Reich: LTI, Lingua Tertii Imperii: A Philologist's Notebook*, trans. Martin Brady (Somerset, N.J.: Continuum, 2000; orig. pub. 1957), 80.

37 Oscar Robert Achenbach, "Eine Viertelstunde Familienforschung," *Illustrierter Beobachter* 9 (May 19, 1934): 812, 814.

38 Udo R. Fischer, "Familienforschung; ein Gebot der Stunde," *Neues Volk* 1 (July 1933): 20–21.

39 Reichsministerium des Innern, "Dienstleistungen für die Standesbeamten und ihre Aufsichtsbehörden" (1938), Bundesarchiv Berlin-Lichterfelde, R1501/ 127452.

40 "Ahnenpässe," Sammlung F Rep. 240 / 1, Landesarchiv Berlin.

41 Entries for June 29, 1938, May 21, 22, 1940, December 4, 7, 1941 in Victor Klemperer, *I Will Bear Witness 1933–1941: A Diary of the Nazi Years* (New York: Random House, 1998), 260, 338–39, 447–49.

42 Marion Kaplan, *Between Dignity and Despair: Jewish Life in Nazi Germany* (New York: Oxford University Press, 1998), 19.

43 Hans Magnus Enzenberger, "Herbst 1944," quoted in Jörg Lau, "Auf der

Suche nach der verlorenen Normalität: Helmut Kohl und Hans Magnus Enzens-
berger als Generationsgenossen," in Klaus Naumann, ed., *Nachkrieg in Deutsch-
land* (Hamburg: Hamburger Edition, 2001), 505–6.

44 Robert G. Moeller, *War Stories: The Search for a Usable Past in the Federal
Republic of Germany* (Berkeley: University of California Press, 2001), 60.

45 Harry Liebersohn and Dorothee Schneider, eds., *"My Life in Germany Before and After January 30, 1933": A Guide to a Manuscript Collection at Houghton
Library, Harvard University* (Philadelphia: American Philosophical Society, 2001).

46 See the series edited by Henry Friedlander and Sybil Milton, *Archives of
the Holocaust: An International Collection of Selected Documents*; Liebersohn and
Schneider, *"My Life in Germany."*

John Randolph

On the Biography of
the Bakunin Family Archive

I wanted to destroy all castles, burn absolutely all documents

throughout the whole of Bohemia, all administrative as well as

judicial, governmental, and manorial papers and documents, and

declare all hypothecs paid. . . . In a word, the revolution I was

planning was terrible, unparalleled, although it was directed

more against things than against people.

—*The Confession of Mikhail Bakunin* (1851)

SPATIAL AND CONCEPTUAL METAPHORS dominate recent scholarship on archives. Scholars routinely read archives as "sites" of memory or contestation, for example, or as "epistemologies" or Foucauldian "systems of statements."[1] As important as these metaphors are, however, archives are more than places or mental maps. They are also objects, or more precisely collections of objects, possessed of a physical nature that is crucial to everything archives make possible. We encounter archives physically. We build our policies, societies, economies, and histories around our sensible impressions of these objects, and in their physical exchange. Even in our analysis of archives' conceptual properties, we should not forget that archival claims purport to be like currency on the gold standard. They are made in reference to a thing.[2]

But things change, literally and inevitably. Though it may seem that archives are merely props in the action that turns around them, they are constantly impacted by it, and as they change their physical form, they assume a different role in society. Coins preserved for their luster in one era may be esteemed for their illustrative tarnish in the next. "Visionary" blueprints, altered over time, begin to testify to conceptual confusion and political wrangling instead (as Kathryn J. Oberdeck's study of the "unbuilt environment" in this book reminds us). Nor do the life-histories of objects fail to affect their meaning and subsequent social life. To take one famous example: refashioned over time as the "Elgin Marbles," a collection of sculptures from the Parthenon have helped define both British imperialism and Greek nationalism, changing and being changed in a process that continues today.[3] As objects, then, archives must have histories. The obvious question for our current collection is: How do the archives' physical lives relate to our own "archive stories"?

One might attempt to understand one's own archival experience by interrogating the history of the archive's hosting institution. Certainly, as Jennifer S. Milligan's analysis of France's Archives nationales in this book shows, many state archives seek to convince us that the institution is all: that they are "the" archive. Yet often the life of a collection begins before it enters such institutions; just as often, collections change hands; and in this sense the physical history of an archive is a story of production, exchange, and use across and among a number of social and institutional settings. For this reason "biography," rather than institutional history, suggests itself as a productive metaphor for thinking about the physical history of an archive and its relationship to lived experience, including our own.

Popular in recent anthropological research on material culture, the notion of the "biography" of an object has at least two distinct advantages.[4] First, it underscores the point that archives as objects gather meanings over time—in their exchange and physical transformation—and have meaning for us today through this process and not in isolation from it. Second, biography as a heuristic metaphor should help remind us that archives, as objects, are also subjects of history. Their evolving historical presence makes certain kinds of actions and meanings possible—even as their direct involvement in these processes insures their own continuing transformation. In this sense, all archives are like the Elgin Marbles. They lead social lives and have characters defined as much by their exchange and evolution as by their essence.

If taken too literally, of course, this biographical metaphor may be accused of vitalism and an artificial coherence.[5] A composite object—made of many discreet things—an archive is not a unified, autonomous agent; its identity is conceptual and contingent; at any point it is subject to dismemberment and integration into some new entity. In all of this, however, the archive only seems more, rather than less, like the fractured self posited by recent philosophy—a self which despite these fractures remains open to biographical research as a unity produced in culture. Indeed, for archives as for objects and as for people, one essentially biographical question is how an identity forged out of many heterogeneous elements sustains or loses coherence over time.[6] And because archives make us, it is important to know how any given archive has been and continues to be made. Though Peter Fritzsche is undoubtedly right to say in his essay in this book that "the history of the archive is embedded in the recognition of loss," we ourselves are embedded in what has survived.

What follows, then, is something of a thought experiment, an attempt to understand my own archive story through the life of an important acquaintance of mine: the Bakunin family archive. An influential noble family, the Bakunins were iconic figures for Imperial Russia's liberal party, famous for their culture as well as for their political activism. Mikhail Bakunin (1814–76), the anarchist, was one of the nineteenth century's greatest celebrities, a tireless rebel who terrorized bourgeois Europe with the claim that all new worlds begin with destruction. What sealed the historical reputation of Bakunin and his family, however, was that his planned "revolution against things" never succeeded and his family's archive survived. A gargantuan collection that helped form the empirical spine of Russian intellectual history, the Bakunin archive has supported the careers of generations of scholars and historians and inspired many novelists as well.[7] But how was this archive itself made? By whom, and for what purpose? What are the eras of its social life, how did it change the societies it entered and how was it changed by them? In what follows, I hope to sketch some answers to these questions. The result should illuminate which sides of the past a biographical approach to archives reveals.

The main source for my inquiry will be the evidence provided by the Bakunin archive itself, both textual and physical. My main goal will be to describe the life and activity of the Bakunin archive across the cycles of its production, exchange, and use (the main periods or chapters of its "biography"). But since the subject at hand still exists—and since part of what I am trying to explain is my own lived experience—perhaps I ought to begin with a memoir of my own acquaintance with the archive. Its biographer, I am also its contemporary.

At Home in Pushkin House, Part One

I first encountered the Bakunin family archive in the early 1990s. Then, as now, it was *fond* number 16 of St. Petersburg's Institute of Russian Literature (IRLI), an institution more popularly known as "Pushkin House." Built by the commission organized to celebrate the centennial of modern Russia's most famous poet in 1899, Pushkin House was designed as "something of a literary mausoleum, preserving not only Pushkin's relics, but those of all the actors of nineteenth-century Russian literature."[8] Interment in Pushkin House marks the Bakunin archive's status as one of Russia's national treasures, destined for public preservation and study. That said, the rooms in which the Bakunin papers make their limited public appearances are in fact quite intimate. Normally stored in large preservation boxes, the Bakunin papers can be seen either on the desks of archivists—themselves tucked away in an off-limits sector of the building—or on one of the green, felt-lined tables of the Institute's small manuscript reading room. In either location, the archive is distributed and guarded by the Institute's specialists, the majority of whom are women. During working hours, one of these specialists sits and reads with the readers while her colleagues work back in the sector.

In keeping with my biographical metaphor, I might say that the archive had reached a solid middle age when I first encountered it. On the one hand, it had acquired a certain organizational maturity and respectability. Its thousands of manuscript pages—for the most part personal letters, with an admixture of poetry, diaries, and domestic projects—were subdivided into 661 distinct "units of preservation," by author. Each page was neatly numbered in pencil according to this system. Yet myriad lines and creases testified to another, earlier life. Alongside the pagination provided by Pushkin House, there were two, sometimes three alternate systems of numeration. Undated letters often had dates penciled in by anonymous researchers. Likewise, there were many paratextual underlinings and exclamations, made by previous generations. For example: "This is the result of Fichte" was written in large red pencil across an 1836 letter from Mikhail Bakunin's sister Tatiana.[9] The archive also contained copies of itself, notebooks of letters carefully transcribed for remote use and returned later. Last but not least, and hardly noticeable at first, the Bakunin papers were punctured by thousands of tiny needle-holes, running up and down their folds. Like the alternate paginations and manuscript copies, these holes testified to now-outgrown systems of organization, binding, and use.

The Bakunin family archive when I first made its acquaintance was thus the product of generations of archival work, both physical and conceptual. Physically, the archive had undergone several radical alterations. It had passed through different societies with different rules of engagement (no current archivist would think of writing "This is the result of Fichte" directly across an original), and emerged from this process a changed object. Yet on the conceptual level its continuity and identity as a domestic archive had been carefully maintained. Labeled fond 16, "The Bakunins," by Pushkin House, the archive is generally called the "Bakunin archive" or the "Priamukhino archive" in scholarly literature. Both names highlight the domestic origins of the collection (Priamukhino being the name of the Bakunin family's former estate in central Russia's Tver Province). For convenience's sake in what follows, I will generally use the phrase "the Bakunin archive" to refer to this collection.

Though easy to miss, the conceptual work involved in maintaining this domestic identity should not be taken for granted. After all, in many senses fond 16 is demonstrably not the Bakunin family's archive. Not only has the collection been reorganized several times since leaving the family's hands in the early twentieth century, but only a part of the Bakunin household's papers actually entered the collection in the first place. Such, at least, was the conclusion of a revolutionary archaeological commission in 1918, which found a "mountain" of paper on the floor of Priamukhino's office after the family itself fled the estate. (These papers were not subsequently incorporated into fond 16).[10]

The moral I would draw from this brief memoir is this: the life of an archive is not merely the story of its physical "preservation," but of a capillary interplay between conceptual continuity and objective change. In the case of IRLI fond 16, the collection's conceptual identity as a family archive was sustained precisely by means of the collection's physical transformation. The labor of maintaining the Bakunin archive—as well as the work of altering it—must have had meaning for the societies through which the archive passed, as well as for the individual actors involved. It is this meaning—and this activity—that the biography of an archive allows us to explore. Setting aside the archive's current life for a moment, let us consider the history of its production, exchange, and use in more detail.

The Creation of the Priamukhino Archive

If it is not simply a collection of the Bakunin family's papers, but rather a carefully fashioned subset, where and how did the Bakunin archive first come to be made? The best evidence on this question suggests that although the archive's domestic identity is misleading in some respects, it is revealing in at least one. The archive was made by and through noble domesticity on the Bakunins' serf estate.

The Bakunin family first purchased Priamukhino, their home in central Russia's Tver Province, in the late eighteenth century.[11] There is little evidence today—in any archive—that the Bakunins had collected much paper before then. The family's two-century career in Russian service was not documented in any records the family itself held; nor did this branch of the family have records of earlier home life or of the management of previous estates.[12]

Shortly after the purchase of Priamukhino, however, this changed. First, the family began to write more. Sentimental correspondence and domestic projects became an inextricable part of family life, filling the Bakunin household with paper. Second, the Bakunin women assumed responsibility for organizing and preserving this "epistolary commerce." Domesticity, in other words, added a new, affective economy to their traditional task of estate-management.[13] Keepers of the family's books, they also became keepers of its new intimate documents. What has come down to us as the Bakunin family archive was then fashioned from these papers—a process that quite likely began in the estate office as well. As evidence, one may again cite the fact that the discarded remainder—the part of family paper that did not enter the archive we now know—was later found on the floor of Priamukhino's office. (From the early nineteenth century on, this space was romanticized in Bakunin family lore as "our kind mistress's cabinet.")[14]

As long as the Bakunin family papers remained at Priamukhino, the borders of the collection now known as the Priamukhino archive seem to have remained fluid. Letters from the mid–nineteenth century identify not one but several collections of family papers, stored in corners and cupboards of varying intimacy. In the early 1870s, for example, one cache of precious letters is reported as being "on the top shelf of the library bookshelf—where I hid them—on the right side of the divan, as you go through the doorway from the salon."[15] Yet by the end of the nineteenth century, a specific "Bakunin archive" began to have a public profile. In 1899, the liberal historian Aleksandr Kornilov made a glowing reference to it in Russia's celebrated Brockhaus-Efron encyclopedia.[16] This public acclaim prepared educated society for the notion that "the" Bakunin archive could and perhaps should leave the family's hands and enter national institutions as a relic of national culture. In the next few years, that is exactly what happened. What guided the final fashioning of this new public actor, and how did its final debut occur?

Like any good good, the Bakunin archive seems to have been fashioned at a confluence of supply and demand. In the mid–nineteenth century, liberal Russian journalists and historians began to approach the family, seeking access to its papers. Meanwhile, the family and its "archivists"—the Bakunin women—proved willing and able to satisfy this historical curiosity. Since the interests of all sides helped shape the archive for its public debut, it seems wise to pause to consider them in detail here.

The first historians to approach the Bakunin family were the liberal journalists Pavel Annenkov (1811?–87) and Aleksandr Pypin (1833–1904).[17] A generation apart, Annenkov and Pypin shared at least one common despair. They believed that censorship and social backwardness had corrupted the modern Russian historical record. Activity that never found public expression in Russia's regressive public sphere—either because of lack of space or lack of permission—had simply gone undocumented.

In particular, Annenkov and Pypin were vexed by the fate of a group of Moscow University students known in historical literature as the "Idealists of the 1830s." The Idealists were credited with being the first to translate the modern philosophies of Schelling, Fichte, and Hegel into compelling Russian terms. That said, their reputation exceeded their documented accomplishments. Some (such as the philosopher Nikolai Stankevich) had died young without publishing anything. Others (such as the literary critic Vissarion Belinsky) published voluminously but somewhat cryptically, leaving later readers to guess what exactly it was that lay "behind" their articles and expressions.[18] In either case, the Idealists' ethereal reputation could be read as a symptom of a larger problem: the limitations of Imperial Russia's public record.

The Bakunin archive came to represent one solution to this dilemma.

Since Mikhail Bakunin and his sisters had been close friends of the Idealists, Pypin and Annenkov hoped that the family's papers might have captured these men's activity more fully than the public record. Thus, it was precisely as a private archive, free from the flaws induced by Russian public life, that the Bakunin papers particularly interested historians. At the same time, it is important to observe the foreboding with which these historians began their research. As political liberals, Annenkov and Pypin were reluctant to violate what they regarded to be the essential privacy—and implicit ahistoricity—of home life.[19] At the turn of the century, their colleague and successor Pavel Miliukov likewise bemoaned the consequences of knowing one's heroes too closely. Such "excessive familiarity" boded ill for the rights of the individual in Russia, Miliukov claimed.[20] (Of course, it also undermined gendered assumptions about historical agency and activity, by revealing the private home as a theater of history. But having built their vision of liberty around such gendered assumptions, late-nineteenth-century liberals were much less willing than later feminists and cultural historians to problematize them.)[21]

The trick, then, was to find a private archive that was both indisputably historical and comfortingly exceptional—an archive that would allow historians to conceptualize and document a case in which private life had been historical without radically historicizing the home itself. The Bakunins and their family archive fit this bill perfectly. Prolific preservers of paper, uniquely involved in important cultural and political movements, the Bakunins were also clearly and comfortingly atypical. They were not every family but "that historical family"—as Annenkov punningly nicknamed the Bakunins in recognition of their dual service to intellectual history as both actors and archivists.[22]

For "that historical family" to play this delicate role, however, it had to have an archive and be willing to share it. Fortunately for the historians, both of these conditions applied. The Bakunin home by the mid–nineteenth century was alive with historical activity. As early as 1842, Mikhail Bakunin's sister Tatiana began work on a family history, never completed. Yet by her death in 1871 she and her sisters and nieces had organized much of the family's correspondence by year. Belinsky's letters to the family—lengthy philosophical communications running to some four hundred manuscript pages total—had been painstakingly copied into a hand-sewn notebook. Even before they were approached by historians, then, the Bakunin women had begun organizing a historical subset of the family papers for preservation and limited circulation.[23]

What historical vision guided the creation of this artifact, from within the family? The answer to this question seems to lie in a combination of obligation and opportunity. Responsible for the family's record keeping, the Bakunin women were of course aware of the reverence the personal papers in their possession evoked. As committed philosophical Idealists themselves, they were also appalled by the materialist and empiricist turn Russia's public life had taken during the Era of Great Reforms in the 1860s. Given the restrictions on female participation in this public life, they could not defend their ideals in this arena themselves. Fashioning the Bakunin archive, however, offered an opportunity to create a public role for themselves as the family's archivists. Getting into the new history on the ground level, they then used their stewardship of this much-sought-after archive to project their values into institutions (the Academy, the press) that resisted their direct participation.[24]

Illustrative in this regard is the career of Natalia Semenovna Bakunina (1828–1914)—Mikhail Bakunin's sister-in-law and the family's chief consultant to late-nineteenth-century historians. A fervent convert to the Idealist "religion" for which Priamukhino was famous, Natalia Semenovna copied and sewed countless private documents, gradually gathering together what she and her sisters-in-law saw as the most sacred and enduring of the family's papers. Advising and assisting the historians who came to visit, Natalia Semenovna received public thanks in their works. When he praised the richness of the Bakunin archive in the Brockhaus-Efron encyclopedia in the late 1890s, Kornilov also underscored the debt Russian society owed to Natalia Semenovna for its preservation.[25]

Nor was distinction Natalia Semenovna's only reward for making the Bakunin archive. Control over the papers also allowed her to intervene in the scholarship being created through the home. In the early 1900s, the liberal activist and historian Pavel Miliukov visited the Bakunins to inspect the philosopher Stankevich's letters, presented to him as part of the family archive. The result was an essay on the interconnections between the history of Stankevich's heart and the history of his mind. Miliukov examined the impact of Stankevich's broken engagement to one of Mikhail Bakunin's sisters, Liubov' Bakunina, on his intellectual development. In the end, he concluded, Stankevich's rejection of Liubov' Bakunina was a symbol of his gradual abandonment of Idealism. Even as his former fian-cée remained faithful to the philosophy's artificial and otherworldly doc-trines, Stankevich turned to the here and now, as represented by his next love, a buxom German woman. According to Miliukov, the evolution of Stankevich's heart from Idealism to Realism—and his turn from Liubov' to Berta—anticipated a new epoch "in the development of educated society as a whole."[26]

This interpretation, however, gravely dismayed Natalia Semenovna. First, it implied the ideals she and her sisters-in-law believed in had been outmoded by history. It was also factually wrong. According to letters by Stankevich in the Bakunin family's possession, the philosopher's final ro-mance had not been with a "pretty German girl named Berta," but rather with Liubov's resolutely spiritual (and married) sister Varvara.[27] Regarded by the family as particularly intimate, Stankevich's love letters to Varvara Bakunina had been kept out of the archive shown to Miliukov. Yet it was important to Natalia Semenovna that Miliukov's conclusion be refuted. Transferring Stankevich's letters to the Imperial Russian Historical Mu-seum in Moscow, Natalia Semenovna allowed them to be edited and published in full. This corrected Miliukov's neat narrative, albeit at the cost of shrinking the size of the Bakunin archive itself.[28] Deleting from the family papers one of their most famous treasures, Natalia Semenovna used her authority over the archive to shape the scholarship that emerged from it.

The Bakunin archive was thus fashioned at the intersection of historical interests, interests which established its initial identity and shaped its com-position and form. It was of utmost importance to outside scholars that the Bakunin archive be a private archive, since it was precisely the deficien-cies of Imperial Russia's public record that drove their somewhat guilty interest in personal papers in the first place. At the same time, the family and in particular its female record-keepers shaped this artifact according to their own historical visions. Indeed, the Bakunin archive had no set form as long as it remained in the family's hands—a fluidity that enhanced the Bakunin women's influence on historical scholarship. All the while, how-ever, the historical reputation—the identity—of this unstable relic grew, becoming strong enough that it could survive outside Priamukhino, when the collection left the family's possession. This happened during the revo-lutionary era.

The Bakunin Archive Changes Hands

In 1905, fearing radical arson near her home in the Crimea, Natalia Bakunina sent her carefully crafted collection of family papers to an estate in central Russia, owned by her good friends the Petrunkevich family.[29] The Bakunin archive remained there for several years, before being claimed, with the Bakunins' permission, by the historian Kornilov.[30] He would then serve as its keeper throughout the violent decade that followed. Midwifed by revolution into its first independent form, the archive thus began its circulation as an object outside of the family's hands. Though the family itself could no longer add to or subtract from the archive, the capillary interchange between its conceptual formation and physical evolution did not end. The Bakunin archive still helped create archivists and historians even as they refashioned it. Let us now look at this process.

The first to work with the Bakunin archive was Aleksandr Kornilov himself. As a founding member and leader of Russia's liberal Kadet Party, Kornilov saw his scholarly and political career ruined by the October Revolution. Briefly brought to power by the collapse of the Romanov dynasty in 1917, the Kadets rapidly lost influence as that of Russia's socialist parties grew. The Bolshevik seizure of power then forced many Kadet leaders into the White cause and eventual emigration. Kornilov, however, stayed in Russia, keeping the Bakunin papers with him as he sought refuge around the country.[31]

For Kornilov, personal possession of the Bakunin archive during the revolutionary era meant being able to continue his scholarly research even as the profession of history writing as he knew it ended. Far more than his audience changed during this time: the institutional framework of history itself was warped. Most obviously, the roles of outside historian and intimate archivist suddenly collapsed into one. Kornilov had unprecedented access to and freedom with the Bakunin archive. Censorship no longer banned the use of the Bakunin name; likewise the Revolution rendered moot many notions of privacy and decorum. As Kornilov's feverish work with the archive and publication of its contents would testify, politesse was less important than affixing the history of a society now turned upside-down.

Kornilov seized this unique moment to try to reconceptualize Russian intellectual history. He did so in ways that depended on his ability to preserve the reputation and identity of the collection in his hands even as he altered its physical form. As shown above, earlier historians had used the Bakunin archive to shore up the history of intellectual circles (e.g., the Idealists of the 1830s). Biography, rather than the history of private life, was at the center of their scholarship.

Taking advantage of his unprecedented liberty with the Bakunin archive, however, Kornilov sought to reimagine the evolution of Russian social thought through the prism of noble family life. Taking the Bakunin family life as a kind of artistic "work," Kornilov's investigations placed the home itself at the center of historical analysis, examining its role as a stage for historical activity.[32] The resulting work, *The Bakunin Family* (2 vols., 1914–25), was read by contemporaries inside the Soviet Union as a memorial to Old Regime society. In particular, Kornilov's chronicle sought to draw back the curtain and reveal the close ties between noble family life and the development of social thought in Imperial Russia.[33]

The Bakunin Family achieved this effect by systematically baring the family's secrets. This repudiation of politesse changed the picture entirely. Previous histories written from the Bakunin archive had imagined their male heroes against a backdrop populated by "ideal women," whose names were concealed by circumspect initials. Kornilov's focus on family life inevitably foregrounded the latter's identity and activity. Kornilov named all names, bringing the Bakunin women out onto the historical stage as actors (as opposed to archivists) for the first time.[34]

Kornilov's close and physical interaction with the Bakunin archive made this radical historiographical turn possible. Fashioning a running narrative from thousands of pages of family correspondence was a formidable task. It not only required living with the archive, but altering it for increased legibility—as the numerous paratextual marks made by Kornilov testify. Undated or unsigned letters rarely escaped the historian's scrawled attributions. Dates and authors (sometimes incorrect) were assigned to each document. Kornilov highlighted themes in red: the rude "This is the result of Fichte" mentioned earlier is likewise his.[35] As a result, the Bakunin women's carefully sewn reliquary seems to have taken on the appearance of a well-thumbed paperback while in Kornilov's possession. Indeed, its spine cracked under the investigation. According to Iurii Steklov, the historian who inspected the archive on its arrival at Pushkin House in the early 1920s, Mikhail Bakunin's papers—one of the archive's constitutive artifacts—arrived from Kornilov in a state of "chaotic disorder."[36]

Much of this "disorder" undoubtedly resulted from Kornilov's difficult personal and intellectual odyssey during the Russian Civil War. Living on the road and on the brink of starvation in Petersburg, Kornilov was in no position to care properly for the large collection. Along the way, his grander historical design gave way under changing circumstances. As his health failed and Bolshevik power stabilized, Kornilov abandoned his broader theoretical and even narrative interests in favor of simply publishing the Bakunins' domestic documents.[37] Like the previous archivist, Natalia Bakunina, only on a grander scale, Kornilov in the end turned to the simple mechanism of introducing family documents into the public record as a way of completing his chronicle. In this sense, there is a logical symmetry between the disintegration of the archive while in his hands and its virtual incarnation through the published volumes of *The Bakunin Family*. To bring its contents fully into the open, Kornilov relied on his ability to take the archive apart.

Kornilov died, however, before his running chronicle of family life could be completed. By prior arrangement, his widow transferred the Bakunin archive to Pushkin House, where it was eagerly received.[38] Almost immediately, the archive entered the hands of another historian with big ambitions: Iurii Mikhailovich Steklov (1873–1941).

Steklov was a high-ranking Soviet scholar and journalist, charged by the Bolshevik leadership with preparing a complete academic edition of Mikhail Bakunin's works. Inspired by the fiftieth anniversary of Bakunin's death in 1926, this new edition was also part of the larger effort, ongoing in those years, to create a new communist history of the revolutionary movement in Russia.[39] Yet collecting and publishing Bakunin's works posed at least two formidable difficulties. First, Bakunin's manuscripts were scattered across several continents (some were in South America, where the reform-socialist Max Nettlau was attempting an edition of Bakunin's works in Spanish). The second obstacle to fashioning a complete works was the essential intimacy of Bakunin's writings. Bakunin was, as Steklov noted, a "writer of letters first and foremost," a comrade-revolutionary rather than a publicist-theoretician like Marx. This meant that one had to deal with the privacy concerns of Bakunin's addressees and their legatees—many of whom were likewise abroad, in the capitalist countries.[40]

The Soviet Academy's acquisition of the Bakunin family archive changed this rather dismal picture dramatically. Steklov had earlier assumed—and publicly announced—that the "Priamukhino archive burned during the course of revolutionary events after 1917."[41] Its unexpected survival meant that it was suddenly possible to publish hundreds of Bakunin's letters in one fell swoop. This not only illuminated Bakunin's early intellectual development as never before; it gave the whole project of memorializing Bakunin by means of a complete works a shot in the arm. This breakthrough was particularly important because there were important adversaries to the publication of the anarchist's works in communist Russia, as would become increasingly evident as Steklov continued his project.

Despite the windfall the Bakunin archive represented for his efforts, Steklov struggled with the archive's physical form. In his foreword to volume one of the collection, Steklov described these struggles in detail.[42] On the one hand, the archive's "chaotic disorder" set science back (for which Steklov placed the blame squarely on Kornilov). More generally speaking, the archive's condition fuelled debate over whether it had been completely transferred to Pushkin House. Steklov accused Kornilov's liberal friends and relatives, such as the heritage publisher P. Shchegolev, of withholding documents from their proper place in the "All-Union repository." In this sense, Steklov presented the archive's recent history as one of covert political resistance on the part of noble liberals and old anti-Marxists. Unreconciled to the idea that the Bakunin papers belonged to the new Soviet nation, bourgeois families and scholars were now preventing the birth of Soviet historical science.[43]

Though he bemoaned the Bakunin archive's physical condition and questioned its integrity, one should not underestimate the degree to which these anxieties actually helped Steklov's cause polemically. Most fundamentally, they allowed him to portray the preservation of Mikhail Bakunin's legacy as an important front in the class struggle. This was particularly significant at the time, in as much as the main opposition to Bakunin's enrollment into Soviet heritage came not from noble liberals, but from the ranks of the Communist Party itself. For many party loyalists, Bakunin's name stood for "petit-bourgeois socialism" and anarchist opposition to Marx. Although the Bolshevik party leader L. B. Kamenev had commissioned Bakunin's works, Steklov found money difficult to raise and had to wait almost ten years for the first volume of his collection to appear.[44] Both to redeem Bakunin and to defend his reputation as a respectable Soviet historian, then, it only behooved Steklov to dramatize the uncertainty and political struggle suggested by the "chaotic disorder" of the Bakunin archive. Such a history of struggle, in dialectical terms, suggested the continued actuality of Bakunin's legacy.

Even so, Steklov's work, like Kornilov's, was not fated to see completion; only four of its proposed twelve volumes were published. In 1935, its funding agency, the All-Union Society of Political Prisoners and Exiles, was liquidated. Shortly thereafter the *Stalinist Short Course*, a lethally rigid history of the Communist Party, denounced anarchists as principled enemies of Bolshevism. Steklov's attempt to present Bakunin as "one of the founders" of the Russian revolutionary movement was fully repudiated. As for Steklov himself, he was arrested in 1938 and died in prison in 1941. No other attempt at rehabilitation of Bakunin occurred in the Soviet Union until the Thaw.[45]

During the revolutionary era, then, the Bakunin family archive evolved rapidly as it changed hands. It became the basis of two major scholarly projects. The archive's evolving physical form—and continuing historical reputation—were crucial for both. Kornilov radically altered the archive in the service of his intimate portrait of the mental world of the old regime. Steklov, on the other hand, used the fate of the fabled "Priamukhino archive"—and the results of Kornilov's tampering—to symbolize the political battles attending the birth of Soviet history.

As for the archive itself—its distinctive identity reinvigorated by these interpretive struggles—it settled into its new home at Pushkin House. There, it was gradually reorganized into its current form. Judging from the logs each researcher has to sign before using the archive, no reader since Kornilov and Steklov has had such broad access to it.[46] Certainly, no new grand projects were mounted: most researchers, no doubt for practical as well as political reasons, simply settled for the evidence marshaled by Kornilov and Steklov. For decades, the main identities the Bakunin archive helped fashion were those of Pushkin House and its archivists. Only recently, following the collapse of the Soviet archival regime in the late 1980s, has the Bakunin archive resumed its physical evolution and been enrolled in broad scholarly projects. It is time to return to this life, Soviet and post-Soviet, at Pushkin House.

At Home in Pushkin House, Part Two

No fair history of Pushkin House or its archival sector yet exists, and this history, when it emerges, will surely be a complex and ambiguous one. Conceived as an extension of Imperial Russian intellectual culture—and the national-progressive historical vision of the Russian intelligentsia— Pushkin House became a part of the Soviet Academy in the 1920s. From this time on, it shouldered an overtly ideological role within the life of the world's first socialist state. (According to an official history of the institute written in the 1980s, Pushkin House's main job was to help form "the personality and world-view of the Soviet individual—a builder of communism.")[47] As a guardian of both Imperial and Soviet traditions, Pushkin House was no doubt often a house divided, and the archives within it undoubtedly lived dual lives.

Even in advance of detailed histories of the IRLI, however, it seems fair to say that the Bakunin archive was very well suited to the Pushkin House's split personality. The Bakunin collection had both national and revolutionary credentials; it was controversial enough to require close supervision and disheveled enough to plausibly require decades of slow and largely secret reorganization. The possession of such a well-known artifact helped maintain the national and international profile of Pushkin House, even during a time when access to the Bakunin archive—for Soviet and non-Soviet researchers alike—was utterly restricted.

By the early 1990s (the time of my first acquaintance with the collection) all this was changing. As Soviet political censorship ended, new challenges to the intelligentsia's influence on Russian cultural life emerged. Pushkin House was both free to present its materials to a much broader audience and forced to do so in order to maintain its national and international profile. The number of foreign visitors accepted and archival publications permitted exploded. Yet the economic collapse of the Russian Academy left many Russian academics wondering if they would have any successors.

As far as the Bakunin archive was concerned, the most immediate impact of these changes was the resumption of the large, synthetic scholarly projects undertaken on its basis in the 1910s and 1920s. On the one hand, the Bakunin papers were employed in popular-scientific "heritage" publications undertaken as correctives to the Soviet revolutionary canon. Kornilov's vision of noble family life as a crèche of nineteenth-century culture and philosophy was revived, complete with glowing portraits of the now-destroyed Bakunin home.[48] On the other hand, the International Institute of Social History in the Netherlands became the first to fulfill Steklov's project of publishing Bakunin's *Oeuvres complètes*. Taking advantage of the Soviet reorganization of the Bakunin files, the Institute copied a complete run of Bakunin's letters and manuscripts. These images were then published alongside the works themselves on a CD-ROM.[49]

Supporting and sustaining these renewed scholarly initiatives were the coworkers of Pushkin House's archive sector, mostly women. No longer subject to the "leading role of the Party," they remained subject to the administrative, economic, and gender hierarchies of the new Russia. Their pay is miniscule; their labor heavy and sometimes dangerous. (Not long ago, the hastily installed fire prevention system exploded, shooting shrapnel and flooding the preservation room with toxic flame retardant.) At the same time, as they gather for tea every day in the sector, the personnel of this archive aspire quietly to fashion the new Russia's notions of tradition and heritage. In an atmosphere suggestive of the estate office of a noble home, the archive's specialists thus take up the role pioneered by Natalia Bakunin in the late nineteenth century.

Like many foreign researchers, I experienced this cultural trusteeship firsthand, partly through the ritual of taking tea with the archivists. Kindly invited into the sector, where I could witness the careful labor behind the scenes, I was gradually instructed in the culture of the archive. This involved both my table manners and my sense of intellectual tradition. I came to partake in knowing conversations about the Institute's founders and their interaction with its various archives. Soviet days were rarely discussed, except in their more positive material aspects (rarely did a birthday go by without a discussion of Soviet champagne). As I became a member of this archive society, I was shown more intimate relics of the Bakunin archive, secreted, as at Priamukhino, in the corners of the archive's cabinets. In this sense, the Bakunin archive as object remains integral to the maintenance of the traditions of intimacy which have characterized and continue to characterize the production of Russian social thought. As the Bakunin archive ages and is published, it will be harder and harder to ignore this intimate frame.

The Unburned Letter

Revolutionary by the mere fact of its completion, the final publication of Mikhail Bakunin's *Oeuvres complètes* by the International Institute of Social History is remarkable in another respect: it includes images of Bakunin's manuscripts. These images openly display for the first time the marks that score the Bakunin archive. Such virtual reproductions will undoubtedly thematize the biographies of archives in the future, as their physical evolution becomes visible to a broader range of audiences.

Take, for example, the image of Mikhail Bakunin's letter to his friends the Beyer sisters, written on June 24, 1837. Well known from Steklov's previous print publication, this letter details the germination of what became Bakunin's first conspiracy—a plot to "liberate" his sister Varvara from her marriage. (Made famous in scholarly circles by Kornilov's work, Varvara's "liberation" features as an episode in Tom Stoppard's recent play *Voyage*.)

As the new CD-ROM makes plain, however, audiences outside the archive have heretofore only known part of the story this letter tells. First and foremost, the letter bears the paratextual markings of several generations of archivists. What is folio page 7 according to the current system is page 35 according another, with yet a third, indecipherable digit circled in the top right corner. The existence of these several paginations points to several ruptures, moments in time when a judgment was made to keep the record in question even as the archival system surrounding it changed. No matter how it changed, however, the archival system surrounding this letter never honored the simple command that lines its left-hand margin, in capital Russian letters: "TO BE BURNED."

The command seems to be in Bakunin's handwriting. But neither the old nor the new editions of this letter identify it as such or even mention this injunction at all. Instead Bakunin's editors have simply ignored this "TO BE BURNED," as well as the running battle it wages with the letter's serial archivalization and publication.

Yet this is exactly the sort of biographical text that the virtual reproduction of archives will increasingly reveal. Whether or not historians choose to be interested in archives' stories, the lives of collections are becoming more visible; the need to incorporate their biographies into our own, more plain.

Notes

The epigraph is from Robert C. Howes, trans., *The Confession of Mikhail Bakunin*, with an introduction by Laurence D. Orton (Ithaca: Cornell University Press, 1977), 111.

1 Broadly speaking, Michel Foucault and Jacques Derrida (and the dialog among their positions) remain the theoretical and metaphorical touchstones of much recent writing on archives: see, among others, Jacques Derrida and Eric Prenowitz, "Archive Fever: A Freudian Impression," *Diacritics* 25, 2 (summer 1995): 9–63; Michel Foucault, *The Archaeology of Knowledge and the Discourse on Language*, trans. A. M. Sheridan Smith (New York: Pantheon, 1972); Krzysztof Pomian, "Les Archives: Du Trésor des Chartes au Caran," in Pierre Nora, ed., *Les Lieux de Mémoire*, vol. 3, part 3, *Les Frances*, (Paris: Éditions Gallimard, 1992), 166–233; Sandhya Shetty and Elizabeth Jane Bellamy, "Postcolonialism's Archive Fever," *Diacritics* 30, 1 (spring 2000): 25–48; Carolyn Steedman, "The Space of Memory: In an Archive," *History of the Human Sciences* 11, 4 (1998): 65–84; Ann Laura Stoler, "Colonial Archives and the Arts of Governance: On the Content in the Form," in Carolyn Hamilton Verne Harris, Jane Taylor, Michele Pickover, Graeme Reid, and Razia Saleh, eds. *Refiguring the Archive* (Cape Town: David Phillip, 2002), 83–100. Most of the contributors to two major collections of essays (*History of the Human Sciences*, 11, no. 4 [1998] and Hamilton et. al., *Refiguring the Archive*) use "site" or "system" as their dominant metaphors for understanding archives. For reflections touching more heavily upon the life of archives as objects, see Mike Featherstone, "Archiving Cultures," *British Journal of Sociology* 51, 1 (January–March 2000): 161–84; Kenneth E. Foote, "To Remember and Forget: Archives, Memory, and Culture," *American Archivist* 53 (summer 1990): 378–92; and Sarah Nutall, "Literature and the Archive: The Biography of Texts," in Hamilton et al., eds., *Refiguring the Archive*, 283–99; as well as Roy Rosenzweig, "Scarcity or Abundance? Preserving the Past in a Digital Era," *The American Historical Review* 108, 3 (June 2003): 735–62, http://www.historycooperative.org/journals/ahr/108.3/rosenzweig.html, December 13, 2003.

2 Arguably, new digital technologies make possible ethereal, "virtual" kinds of archive; but as has been recently pointed out, we ignore the physical properties of the "virtual" world only at our own peril. Like other kinds of knowledge, digital information still exists in physical and social contexts. See John Seely Brown and Paul Duguid, *The Social Life of Information* (Boston, Mass.: Harvard Business School Press, 2000), 2–35; Rosenzweig, "Scarcity or Abundance?"

3 See Yannis Hamilakis, "Stories from Exile: Fragments from the Cultural Biography of the Parthenon (or "Elgin") Marbles," *World Archaeology* 31, 2 (October 1999): 303–20.

4 On the biography of objects, see Chris Gosden and Yvonne Marshall, "The Cultural Biography of Objects," *World Archaeology* 31, 2 (October 1999): 169–78, whose generalizing discussion poses many of the questions that follow; see also

J. Hoskins, *Biographical Objects: How Things Tell the Story of People's Lives* (London: Routledge, 1988); I. Kopytoff, "The Cultural Biography of Things: Commoditization as Process," in A. Appadurai, ed., *The Social Life of Things: Commodities in Cultural Perspective* (Cambridge: Cambridge University Press, 1986), 64–91. In "Archiving Cultures," Mike Featherstone sees the current crisis of archives as in part a crisis of "objective culture," though he does not delve into the biography of archives per se.

5 See the critiques of the "lives" of forms and objects in recent art history, in Richard Cándida Smith, "The Other Side of Meaning: George Kubler on the Object as Historical Source," *Intellectual History Newsletter* (2001): 87, 92–95.

6 On attempts to rethink the biography of people along these lines, see Jo Burr Margadant, "Introduction: Constructing Selves in Historical Perspective," in Margadant, ed., *The New Biography: Performing Femininity in Nineteenth-Century France* (Berkeley: University of California Press, 2000), 1–32.

7 Among notable works that depend on the Bakunin family papers, one may list (chronologically) A. N. Pypin, *Belinskii, ego zhizn' i perepiska* (St. Petersburg: Tipografiia M. M. Stasiulevicha, 1876); A. Kornilov, *Molodye gody Mikhaila Bakunina: Iz istorii russkogo romantizma* (Moscow: M. and S. Sabashnikov, 1915); E. H. Carr, *Michael Bakunin* (London: Macmillan, 1937). To the list of Russian novelizations of the Bakunin family life, one may add Tom Stoppard's recent play *Voyage*, which opens on the Bakunin's veranda at their estate Priamukhino (*The Coast of Utopia*, Part 1 [London: Faber and Faber, 2002]).

8 From the memoirs of E. P. Kazanovich, as quoted in B. N. Baskakov, *Pushkinskii Dom*, 2nd ed. (Leningrad: Nauka, 1988), 19.

9 Here and throughout this paper, I will refer to manuscript materials from the Russian Academy of Sciences Institute of Russian Literature (Pushkin House) using standard Russian archival notation form: archive, *fond* number, *opis'* (description) number, *delo* (folder) number, and *list* (or manuscript page). IRLI, the acronym for the Institute of Russian Literature and so for Pushkin House, refers throughout to the manuscript reading room of that institution. This letter is T. A. Bakunina to M. A. Bakunin, [spring 1836?], IRLI f. 16, op. 4, no. 582, l. 8. The attribution to 1836 is my own, based on context.

10 That, at least, is the testimony of a post-revolutionary scholar sent to investigate the Bakunin estate in 1918; see Vladimir Sysoev, *Bakuniny* (Tver: Sozvezdie, 2002), 84.

11 The best general history of the Bakunin family remains Kornilov, *Molodye gody*; Priscilla Roosevelt discusses Priamukhino and its history in *Life on the Russian Country Estate: A Social and Cultural History* (New Haven: Yale University Press, 1995).

12 I discuss archival holdings of Bakunin papers in John Wyatt Randolph, "The Bakunins: Family, Nobility, and Social Thought in Imperial Russia, 1780–1840" (Ph.D. diss., University of California, Berkeley, 1997), 49–53.

13 On the broader role of Russian noblewomen as estate managers, see Michelle Lamarche Marrese, *A Woman's Kingdom: Noblewomen and the Control of*

Property in Russia, 1700–1861 (Ithaca: Cornell University Press, 2002). I take the term "epistolary commerce"—and the idea of exploring women's role in managing it—from Dena Goodman's *The Republic of Letters: A Cultural History of the French Enlightenment* (Ithaca: Cornell University Press, 1994), 136.

14 Within the Bakunin family's own tradition, "our kind mistress's office" was romanticized as the heart of the home's economy in Aleksandr Bakunin's ode to family life, "Osuga," composed in the first half of the nineteenth century (Dmitrii Oleinikov, "Aleksandr Bakunin i ego poema 'Osuga,' " *Nashe nasledie* 29–30 [1994]: 57). Aleksandr Bakunin (1768–1854) was Mikhail Bakunin's father. For a broader discussion of the Bakunin family's domestic idyll at Priamukhino, see Randolph, "The Bakunins," and Sysoev, *Bakuniny*.

15 Thus Natalia Semenovna Bakunina (1828–1914; see below) to her husband Pavel, an undated letter seemingly from October 1871, IRLI f. 16, op. 5, no. 114,II. 49–490b.

16 See A. Kornilov, "Bakuniny," in *Novyi entsiklopedicheskii slovar'*, vol. 4 (St. Petersburg: Tipografiia Auktsionernogo obshchestva "Brokgauz-Efron," n.d.), s.v.

17 In what follows, I abstract from a longer exploration of Pypin and Annenkov's interest in the Bakunins, in John Randolph, " 'That Historical Family': The Bakunin Archive and the Intimate Theater of History in Imperial Russia, 1780–1925," *Russian Review*, 63, 4 (October 2004): 2–21. See also the works produced by Annenkov and Pypin using materials from the Bakunin family: P. V. Annenkov, *Nikolai Vladimirovich Stankevich* (Moscow: Tipografiia Kat'kova, 1857) and A. N. Pypin, *Belinskii, ego zhizn' i perepiska* (St. Petersburg: Tipografiia M. M. Stasiulevicha, 1876).

18 A. N. Pypin to P. V. Annenkov, letter of February 1, 1874, as cited in T. Ukhmylova, "Materialy o Belinskom iz Arkhiva A. N. Pypina," *Literaturnoe nasledstvo* 57 (1951): 305.

19 Both Pypin and Annenkov resorted to circumspect abstractions and euphemisms when speaking of Bakunin family life in their works, partly but not solely under the pressure of censorship. In his own correspondence with the Bakunins, Pypin assured them that he had no desire to touch upon "purely intimate" details and would avoid them in favor of "general considerations." See A. N. Pypin to A. A. Bakunin, letter of February 11, 1874, cited in Ukhmylova, "Materialy," 313.

20 Nonetheless, Miliukov once again turned the spotlight on "Love Among the 'Idealists of the Thirties' ": see P. Miliukov, "Liubov' u 'idealistov tridtsatykh godov,' " in *Iz istorii russkoi intelligentsii: Sbornik statei* (St. Petersburg: Tipografiia A. E. Kolpinskogo, 1902), 73–74.

21 On the public-private distinction as a liberal response to the disappearance of human rights during the French Revolutionary Terror, see Lynn Hunt's famous analysis in Michelle Perrot, ed., *The History of Private Life*, vol. 4, *From the Fires of the Revolution to the Great War*, trans. Arthur Goldhammer (Cambridge, Mass: Harvard University Press, 1990), 13–45. On the "sexual system" of liberal

politics more generally speaking, Isabell Hull, *Sexuality, State, and Civil Society in Germany, 1700–1815* (Ithaca: Cornell University Press, 1996), 299–333. Miliukov's anxieties about intruding into private life, just cited, fit comfortably within this broad, post-revolutionary framework.

22 For the nickname, see S. Ia. Dolinina, "Pis'ma P. V. Annenkova k V. P. Botkinu i A. V. Druzhininu," in *Russkaia literaturnaia kritika* (Saratov: Izdatel'stvo Saratovskogo universiteta, 1994), 174, 182.

23 On the role of the Bakunin women and Tatiana and Natalia Bakunina in particular as the Bakunin family's archivists, see Kornilov, *Molodye gody*, vi–xii; see also Tatyana's aborted history (IRLI, f. 16, op. 6, no. 9, l. 71) and the recopied notebook of Belinsky's letters, dated 1871 (IRLI f. 16, op. 9, no. 542).

24 On women's difficulties and successes in Imperial Russian public life, see the introduction to Barbara T. Norton and Jehanne M. Gheith, eds., *An Improper Profession: Women, Gender, and Journalism in Late Imperial Russia* (Durham: Duke University Press, 2001).

25 Kornilov, "Bakuniny"; Miliukov also credits N. S. Bakunina in "Liubov,' " 82.

26 Miliukov, "Liubov," 81.

27 See N. S. Bakunina's letter to Aleksei Stankevich of December 14, 1902, State Historical Museum (or GIM) f. 351, op. 1, no. 3,ll. 68–69.

28 See N. S. Bakunina's letters to the librarian of the Historical Museum, Aleksei Stankevich, of May 26, 1904 (GIM f. 16, op. 1, no. 3,ll. 105–105) and December 21, 1914 (ibid.,ll. 114–115). The letters to Varvara Bakunina appeared in N. V. Stankevich, *Perepiska Nikolaia Vladimirovicha Stankevicha*, ed. A. I. Stankevich (St. Petersburg: Tipografiia A.I. Mamontova, 1914).

29 See N. S. Bakunina's letter to A. A. Kornilov of April 4,1905, State Archive of the Russian Federation (or GARF) f. 5102, op. 1, no. 413,ll. 14–15.

30 A. A. Levandovskii, *Iz istorii krizisa russkoi burzhazno-liberal'noi istoriografii: A. A. Kornilov* (Moscow: Izdatel'stvo Moskovskogo gosudarstvennogo universiteta, 1982), 144–45.

31 On Miliukov's political fate see Melissa Kirschke Stockdale, *Paul Miliukov and the Quest for a Liberal Russia, 1880–1918* (Ithaca: Cornell University Press, 1996); on Kornilov's, see Levandovskii, *Iz istorii*.

32 Levandovskii quite properly underscores the innovative quality of Kornilov's work in *Iz istorii*, 132–33; Kornilov identifies family life at Priamukhino as a self-conscious "work" (created in the late eighteenth century) in *Molodye gody*, 30.

33 See the comments of D. I. Shakovskoy in his letter to B. I. Modzalevsky of September 17–18, 1926, in G. E. Potapova and T. V. Misnikevich, "Pis'ma D. I. Shakhovskogo k B. L. Modzalevskomu i L. B. Modzalevskomu," *Ezhegodnik Rukopisnogo otdela Pushkinskogo Doma* (1996): 561 and 563, n.4. Only the first two of the three planned volumes of Kornilov's work appeared: *Molodye gody* and *Gody stranstvii Mikhaila Bakunina* (Leningrad-Moscow: Gosudarstvennoe izdatel'stvo, 1925). They bear the common series title *The Bakunin Family*, volume 1 and 2, though this is not how they are generally listed.

34 Compare the use of anonymous euphemisms and initials in the works by

Annenkov, Pypin, and Miliukov cited above with the explicit discussions of the identities and opinions of the Bakunin women in Kornilov's *Molodye gody* and *Gody stranstvii.*

35 I base these judgments on my physical inspection of hundreds of documents from the Bakunin archive, IRLI f. 16.

36 See Iu. Steklov, "Predislovie," in Steklov, ed., *Sobranie sochinenii i pisem 1828–1876*, Dogegelianskii period, 1828–1837 (Moscow: Izdatel'stvo Vsesoiuznogo obshchestva politkatorzhan i ssyl'no-poselentsev, 1934), 18.

37 See Levandovskii on this shift from analysis to publication in Kornilov's work, *Iz istorii*, 144–45.

38 See Steklov, *Sobranie sochinenii*, 18–19; Kornilov's letters of February 1, 1924 and February 8, 1925, IRLI f. 184 (unnumbered), ll. 2–3; as well as the collection history *(delo fonda)* of IRLI f. 16 (the Bakunins). At the time Pushkin House was trusted by many old regime intellectuals because of the honorable reputation of its head archivist, Boris Modzalevskii.

39 Steklov describes the commissioning of his work in "Predislovie," 6.

40 Steklov discusses the scattering of Bakunin's papers and the difficulty of dealing with their holders' privacy concerns in his preface to the first volume of Bakunin's works he produced: *Sobranie sochinenii*, 7–18.

41 Steklov, "Predislovie," 18.

42 A vast majority of the papers contained in volume one of *Sobranie sochinenii* were from the Bakunin archive.

43 See especially Steklov, *Sobranie sochinenii*, 9–11, 13–15 for his discussion of the political battles being fought around Bakunin's legacy.

44 Steklov describes these difficulties in "Predislovie," 6.

45 N. M. Pirumova's works are a touchstone for postwar rehabilitations of Bakunin; see her *Bakunin* (Moscow: "Molodaia gvardiia," 1970). See also *Istoriia vsesoiuznoi Kommunisticheskoi Partii (bol'shevikov)* (n.p.: Izdatel'stvo TK VKP(b) "Pravda," 1938), 3. Steklov tries to establish Bakunin's place in the revolutionary movement in "Predislovie," 5; he does so in qualified terms, but even these failed. See also N. M. Pirumova, "Iu. M. Steklov," in E. M. Zhukov, ed., *Sovetskaia istoricheskaia entsiklopediia* (n.p.: Izdatel'stvo "Sovetskaia entsiklopediia," 1971), s.v.; and K. A. Zalesskii, *Imperiia Stalina: Biograficheskii entsiklopedicheskii slovar'* (Moscow: Veche, 2000), 429.

46 I base this on my own inspection of the logs, contained in each folder.

47 The main history of Pushkin House remains Baskakov, *Pushkinskii Dom*, which describes the Institute's communist mission on page 8.

48 Among the publications in this mold: N. Pirumova and B. Nosik, "Premukhino Bakuninykh," *Nashe Nasledie* 3, 15 (1990): 143–58; E. Sorokin, *Priamukhiskie romany: Povestvovanie, osnovannoe na podlinnykh pis'makh* (Moscow: "Sovetskaia Rossiia," 1988); Sysoev, *Bakuniny.*

49 This edition is International Institute of Social History, *Bakounine: Oeuvres complètes* (Amsterdam: Royal Netherlands Academy of Arts and Sciences, 2000), CD-ROM.

Laura Mayhall

Creating the "Suffragette Spirit"

BRITISH FEMINISM AND THE HISTORICAL

IMAGINATION

FOR THE GENERATION OF WOMEN creating the discipline of women's history in the 1970s, the archive posed logistical difficulties: How, they asked, given political history's emphasis on the actions of famous men, could evidence of the lives of ordinary (or even extraordinary) women be retrieved? The emerging field of social history supplied some answers, for in its championing of "history from below," a generation of scholars learned how to read sources in new ways. Looking for—and finding—women as witnesses in court proceedings, to cite just one example, historians of women interrogated primary documents creatively in order that women's pasts might become visible. Despite this productive shift in perspective, however, the archive itself remained essentially unproblematic, imagined as a fundamentally unbiased universe of potential histories.[1] But who makes the archive? How do the circumstances under which an archive is formed shape the stories it may tell? How does the meaning of the archive change over time?

This article explores one episode in archive formation by examining the narrative strategies employed by a number of British activists who wrote about their participation in the Edwardian women's suffrage movement in the years following the First World War. It charts the emergence of what came to be known as the "Suffragette Spirit," a heady combination of self-sacrificing devotion to the Cause and to one's sisters in the movement. Largely the self-conscious creation of a small group of former suffragettes in the 1920s and 1930s, the "Suffragette Spirit" enshrined a narrative of authentic suffrage militancy that has remained surprisingly coherent ever since. While this narrative had been fiercely contested throughout the duration of the Edwardian "Votes for Women" campaign, it came to dominate subsequent discussions of the movement.

This narrative gathered adherents when a new generation of feminist activists and scholars, in the process of writing women into history, accepted the self-assessments of a small group of women active in the Edwardian suffrage movement—members of the Women's Social and Political Union—and interpreted those assessments as evidence of an unbroken trajectory of women's political activism linking the early twentieth century to the 1970s. Members of the Women's Social and Political Union placed the militant suffrage movement, and indeed, the women's movement in Britain, at the "storm-centre" of an international movement, and they were quick to assert the singular authenticity of certain political practices, in particular, violence against property and the suffragette hunger strike.[2] Second-wave feminists in Britain and the United States, especially those identifying themselves with radical feminism, consistently took the narration of experience by former members of the Women's Social and Political Union—notably the suffragette hunger strike and forcible feeding—as the origin of knowledge about the women's suffrage movement. Alternative narratives were simply subsumed by a meta-narrative in which authentic suffrage militancy became the precursor of radical feminism.[3] More recently, some critics have interpreted the suffragette hunger strike and forcible feeding as a critical site of identity formation for prewar feminists, a location where individual subjectivities were reconstituted into the collectivity of suffragettes.[4] What all these interpretations share is a belief in the centrality of the suffragette experience as told from one perspective—that of the Women's Social and Political Union under the leadership of Emmeline and Christabel Pankhurst. This article, then, addresses the contexts within which certain narratives of the women's suffrage movement were produced and how they gained legitimacy. It asks, by what means, within what contexts, and for what purposes was the evidence produced which scholars use to analyze the women's movement?[5]

Participants' accounts of the prewar suffrage movement in Britain proliferated in a number of texts in the years between 1914 and 1935. Paralleling the prodigious output of war memoirs by combatants were autobiographies and histories produced by former members of a variety of suffrage organizations. These can and should be discussed in terms of individuals' organizational affiliations, with members of the Women's Social and Political Union (WSPU), the Women's Freedom League (WFL), and the National Union of Women's Suffrage Societies (NUWSS) producing accounts differing widely in format, content, and scope of analysis. Several of these memoirs have been reprinted by feminist presses over the last twenty years and have come to serve as a basis for much of the current scholarship on the women's suffrage movement.[6]

Largely neglected, however, has been the extent to which the exigencies of postwar feminism shaped the subject of suffrage in the 1920s and 1930s. The contours assumed for the prewar women's suffrage movement— contours familiar to us today—owe a great deal to the ways in which women who participated in that movement shaped their experiences in the years following the Great War. This was due largely to the fact that it was in the 1920s and 1930s that the foundations were laid for a historical record of the women's suffrage movement. While organizations and libraries had accumulated pamphlets and newspapers from the Edwardian movement during the campaign, a disproportionate number of documents later used to describe and interpret the activities of the WSPU, in particular, were created in the years following World War I. These documents form the basis of the Suffragette Fellowship Collection, now housed at the Museum of London. This collection and certain postwar memoirs and histories serve as the primary body of evidence upon which historians and critics have drawn to discuss the "militant" suffrage movement.[7] The Suffragette Fellowship Archive and postwar memoirs of former suffragettes have a great deal in common. As accounts of the suffrage movement, they support a postwar construction of the subject of suffrage by establishing as fixed two intertwined narratives. These narratives posit, first, a static distinction between "constitutional" and "militant" women's suffrage organizations, and second, a sequence of action defining authentic suffrage militancy. Subsequent historical and critical treatments of the prewar suffrage movement have relied extensively upon these narratives without considering the conditions under which they were produced or how their narrative strategies have shaped what we know of that agitation.

Certainly, a case could be made for a crude characterization of suffrage organizations as either militant or constitutional. After all, these were the terms some members of these organizations attached to themselves in the years 1906–14.[8] Ultimately, however, the terms are unsatisfactory as a way of describing the movement as a whole because they are defined so as to elide all forms of militancy other than those identified with the WSPU: property damage, including arson, window-smashing, and painting-slashing; the suffragette hunger strike; and the forcible feeding of hunger-striking prisoners. Such a definition precludes strategies such as passive resistance and tax resistance, pursued by large numbers of women prior to the outbreak of war in 1914. Such a definition excludes also those women who rejected the WSPU's narrowed definition of militancy after 1912. Further, to characterize Edwardian suffrage organizations in this fashion is to ignore the fact that many women belonged to, and / or contributed money to, one or more suffrage organizations. Indeed, even if it be granted that the polarities of "constitutional" and "militant" mark the boundaries of the suffrage movement, there remains a significant, and largely unexamined, continuum of thought and activity between the two.[9]

One of the most influential postwar works to articulate a rigid distinction between "constitutional" and "militant" organizations was not written by a former "militant" at all, but by Ray Strachey, secretary to Millicent Garrett Fawcett, leader of the NUWSS. Strachey's history of the women's movement, *The Cause*, established the constitutional NUWSS as heir to a tradition of women's political agitation stretching back well into the nineteenth century.[10] As Kathryn Dodd has shown, Strachey used the political vocabulary of liberalism to position the militant wing of the suffrage movement in opposition to that of the constitutional and to demonstrate how constitutional tactics were responsible for the parliamentary victories of 1918 and 1928. Strachey reinforced this dualism by enlisting a number of binary oppositions—constitutional is to militant as civilized is to uncivilized, as rational is to irrational. Strachey's history attempted, Dodd argues, "[to cast the militants out] of the making of women's history because of their reckless activity, their passion for change, their angry propaganda, and their autocratic organization."[11] The WFL, a self-proclaimed militant organization careful to distinguish itself from the WSPU on the basis of its democratic ideals, and the United Suffragists, an organization composed of men and women determined to redefine militancy after Christabel and Emmeline Pankhurst intensified the use of violence in 1912, thus become erased with a definition that renders synonymous the "reckless activity" of the WSPU with suffrage militancy.[12]

Strachey was not alone in conflating these organizations under a rubric of militancy that obliterated all distinctions between them. By the late

1920s, former members of these organizations themselves had a vested interest in being identified with the WSPU—as they came to believe their very existence within the historical record depended upon that identification. This was due in part to a codification of the constitutional versus militant dualism, which forced women who had been active in the movement to choose between the two poles in characterizations of themselves. But it was due also to the creation of a narrative of militancy promulgated through the privileging of one trajectory of experience while devaluing and obliterating any other.

The text central to the creation of this second narrative, Constance Lytton's *Prisons and Prisoners: Some Personal Experiences*, was published in 1914 and later reissued in 1976 and 1988. Lytton's work enshrined the narrative of authentic suffrage militancy, a story that has come to serve as the archetype for the true militant autobiography. The basis of Lytton's claim to authority as speaker for the militant suffrage movement was precisely her experience of authentic militancy, that is, her experience of imprisonment, hunger strike, and forcible feeding. An analysis of the form, argument, and emplotment of Lytton's memoir suggests the ways in which her text would come to stand as the representative experience of militancy, and indeed, participation in the suffrage movement.

Lytton's account was employed originally as suffrage propaganda, as an elaboration upon a story already known to those active in the movement and one whose telling reinforced suffragettes' sense of embattlement and urgency.[13] Despite Lytton's insistence upon the primacy of experience, her text assumed a community of women whose reading of her account would unify them in her hard-fought understanding of the historical necessity for WSPU-style militancy. Her text was written to reconstitute the lived experience of militancy within a community of readers.[14] Chapter 1 serves as prologue to the central drama of Lytton's life, the WSPU's campaign for women's enfranchisement. Remaining chapters detail police court trials, describe Lytton's various imprisonments, or present her observations of prisoners and prison conditions. As Liz Stanley and Ann Morley have observed of the autobiographical writings of another notorious member of the WSPU, Emily Wilding Davison, Lytton's account consists almost entirely of "arrestable and punishable militant events."[15] For Constance Lytton, as for Davison, there is precious little to life "before militancy." Thus, the form alone of Lytton's account attests to the primacy of the struggle for the vote in her life, with personal sacrifice on behalf of that struggle a key element in her self-fashioning.

In contrast, the autobiography of one-time WSPU, later WFL-member Hannah Mitchell, points to a different conception of the significance of the suffrage movement for its participants. The structure of Mitchell's autobiography, *The Hard Way Up*, more conventionally follows the stages of her life, with chapters entitled "Child," "Woman," "Wife," "Suffragette," "Socialist," "Councilor," and "Magistrate." While Mitchell, like Lytton, asserts that "all [her] previous life had been a preparation" for the suffrage movement, her account of years of municipal service, both before and following her suffrage agitation, substantially undercuts that statement.[16] Quite in contrast to Lytton's memoir, and those of various WSPU members following her, Mitchell's autobiography points to an understanding of her own multiple identities over the course of a lifetime.

The argument implicit in Lytton's account is that one trajectory of experience alone constitutes authentic suffrage militancy. This trajectory extends from the act of militancy to the subsequent arrest, imprisonment, hunger strike, and forcible feeding of the suffragette prisoner. Central to Lytton's account is the assumption of personal sacrifice and voluntary exposure to bodily humiliation. For Lytton, personal sacrifice was manifest in the relinquishment of class privilege, something she undertook when she disguised herself as Jane Warton, Spinster, in an attempt to experience imprisonment as an unknown suffragette. Lytton's testimony to that end was compelling, as she did, in fact, experience far worse treatment in prison under an assumed name. As Constance Lytton, daughter of the Earl of Lytton, a congenital heart defect was given as justification by prison officials for releasing her from prison after she had initiated a hunger strike. In contrast, as Jane Warton, she received no medical examination before her first forcible feeding and only a cursory one thereafter.

Personal sacrifice, and the experience of what was presented as a form of state-sanctioned torture, formed the critical aspect of Lytton's narrative. Both the activity leading to imprisonment and the initiative involved in undertaking to hunger strike were given considerably less emphasis. Lytton carefully framed her experience of forcible feeding in such a way that the reader continually confronts not the prisoner as actor, but the prisoner's body as acted upon. However, our horror at Lytton's portrayal of being forcibly fed—her graphic depiction of the violation of her body's boundaries by individual doctors and, by extension, the state—draws our attention from her brilliant and manipulative rhetorical strategy. *Prisons and Prisoners* is, in fact, suffrage propaganda at its most effective, and its structure should be analyzed for what it was: a justification of the policies of the WSPU at a time when that organization was most under attack from the government, the press, the public, and other women suffragists.

Analysis of the form and argument of Lytton's narrative alone fails to account for the manner in which it has become synonymous with militancy. Lytton's text appeared originally with a disclaimer by its publisher, William Heinemann, that worked to contextualize it more fully as part of a volatile public debate about militancy. Heinemann's statement merits full inclusion:

> The Publisher hopes that fault will not be found if he disclaims agreement with some of Lady Constance Lytton's views expressed in this volume, notwithstanding the fact that he is glad to offer it to the public. He feels that personal disagreement over details should not hinder him from publishing this splendid story of heroism and unselfishness.

While unclear about the nature and extent of the "disagreement over details," Heinemann clearly places Lytton's account within the context of a contemporary debate about the utility of the strategies she describes. Lytton's readers would have understood that debate to exist both within the ranks of suffragists and the larger public. In contrast, in her introduction to the 1988 reissue of Lytton's text, Midge MacKenzie defined Heinemann's "details" as "public acts of daring of the suffragettes" such that all women suffragists are cast unequivocally on one side against the government. MacKenzie's introduction suggests that one side of a contentious debate—that taken by the WSPU under Christabel and Emmeline Pankhurst—and not the debate itself, has come to characterize subsequent discussions of the suffrage movement.[17] MacKenzie's comments indicate that between the original publication of Lytton's memoir in 1914 and its reprinting in 1988, Lytton's text had formalized an identity around which other former suffragettes, and indeed later feminists, would construct their own. In other words, Lytton's experience of militancy had become the archetype of suffrage militancy.

The means by which Lytton's text became synonymous with militancy owes a great deal to the emplotment of her account.[18] A number of critics have suggested that the plot of the romance lies at the center of the suffragette narrative. A much stronger case could be made, however, for the significance of the romantic plot for the suffragette story as told by Constance Lytton: this accounts both for its popularity among former participants in the suffrage movement and its enduring fascination for contemporary feminists.

According to Northrop Frye's typology, the narrative structure of the romance draws upon the reader's familiarity with three stages of what is essentially a quest: from a perilous journey and preliminary minor adventures, through a crucial struggle between the hero and the enemy, during which one of them must die, and finally, to the exaltation of the hero. Essentially a dialectical conflict, the romance pits the hero against an enemy in a struggle in which the reader's values become intertwined with those of the protagonist. The romance presents a story that is neither subtle nor complex in its characterization of the struggle between protagonist and antagonist; as a reader, one is forced to identify either for or against the protagonist.[19]

The narrative structure of the romance can be read easily within Lytton's text. As protagonist, she must first decide to undertake the quest, a decision she veils in Christian symbolism. In the opening chapter, entitled "My Conversion," Lytton relates the process by which she came to feminism. While on holiday at "The Green Lady Hostel" in Littlehampton, she came into contact with Annie Kenney and Emmeline Pethick Lawrence, two prominent members of the wspu. Long conversations with the two women, who she felt "represented something more than themselves, [for] a force greater than their own seemed behind them," provided a context within which she came to understand herself in relation to the world. Lytton recounts how the actions of a group of villagers encircling an escaped sheep revealed to her by analogy "the position of women throughout the world" (13–14). Lytton's realization of the marginality of women around the world thereby propels her conversion to feminism, a process she describes while simultaneously providing a history of the previous forty years' agitation for women's suffrage, agitation whose lack of success, she argues, ultimately justifies the use of militant tactics.

Lytton then embarks upon the perilous journey towards sex-equality through a series of minor adventures that includes a deputation to the prime minister, resulting in her first imprisonment. The crucial struggle, however, unfolds after Lytton's attempted hunger strike during her third imprisonment reveals to her the protection afforded her by her class. She begins a hunger strike but is released on grounds of ill health. Her subsequent actions, which as noted, are to disguise herself as Jane Warton, Spinster, commit offences for which she will be arrested, and undertake to hunger strike yet again, provide the backdrop against which it pitched a battle between a passively angelic suffragette and an actively demonic government.

Lytton's account sought to draw attention to the brute force exercised by the government against women for daring to claim political rights and to downplay the popular image of the militant suffragette as axe-wielding arsonist. Consequently, the actions culminating in the arrest of Jane Warton, Spinster—actions that led ultimately to horrific scenes of forcible feeding—appear harmless. Lytton is arrested in Liverpool for, in her words, "limply dropping" stones into the garden of the governor of the local prison (245). Although recounting an incident from 1910, Lytton's text appeared in 1914—at the height of WSPU assaults against property. As such, its emphasis upon the passivity of the protest leading to her arrest drives home her point that it was the government that leveled the distinction between the militant practices of the WSPU and what she and numerous other suffragettes perceived to be truly violent and, indeed, unpatriotic forms of militancy such as those undertaken by striking workers and men and women on both sides of the Irish Question.

The crucial struggle in Lytton's account, however, unfolds in the account of her hunger strike and forcible feeding once incarcerated as Jane Warton. The predominant imagery Lytton uses to describe her hunger strike is paradisiacal. She recounts dreaming in prison of "fruits, melons, peaches and nectarines, and of a moonlit balcony that was hung with the sweetest smelling flowers, honeysuckle and jessamine, apple blossom and sweet scented verbena; there was only the sound of night birds throbbing over the hills that ranged themselves below the balcony" (264). Forcible feeding, in contrast, presents a vision of hell: confinement, violation, and humiliation. Perhaps the best-known insult proffered a suffragette is the slap a prison doctor contemptuously gives Lytton at the conclusion of her first forcible feeding as Jane Warton (269–70).

Part of the success of Lytton's narrative lies in her use of recognizable tropes. Throughout the text, Lytton's narration of her experience relies on an engagement with the reader that draws upon readily available cultural assumptions about women's passivity and their powerlessness in relationship to men. Overlaying her narrative of violated innocence is an analogy

between her imprisonment and the crucifixion. She recounts a vision of
three crosses appearing in the wooden moldings of the window in her cell:

> It looked different from any of the pictures I had seen. The cross of Christ, the
> cross of the repentant thief, and the cross of the sinner who had not repented—
> that cross looked blacker than the others, and behind it was an immense
> crowd. The light from the other two crosses seemed to shine on this one, and
> the Christ was crucified that He might undo all the harm that was done. I saw
> amongst the crowd the poor little doctor and the Governor, and all that helped
> to torture these women in prison, but they were nothing compared to the
> men in the Cabinet who wielded their force over them. There were the up-
> holders of vice and the men who support the thousand injustices to women,
> some knowingly and some unconscious of the harm and cruelty entailed.
> Then the room grew dark and I fell asleep. (276)

In this passage and elsewhere, Lytton enlists the Christian narrative of
righteousness wrongfully persecuted to elevate a narrative of the violation
of female innocence. The conclusion to her vision—"then the room grew
dark and I fell asleep"—evokes the classical rendering of sleep as death's
twin brother, making explicit her analogy between suffering women and
Christian martyrdom by raising the specter of Emily Wilding Davison,
who had died after colliding with the king's horse at the Derby the previous June.

The poignancy of Lytton's account as a romance lies in its lack of completion: Having suffered mightily for the good, redemption for the heroine
is not to come in this text. Instead, the memoir concludes with an impassioned plea: "I hear the cry go up from all parts of the country, 'How long?
How long?' The time is fully ripe, when will women be fully represented
in Parliament by the vote, equally with men?" Lytton's emplotment of the
romance, while departing from Frye's typology in its inconclusiveness,
thus issues a call to arms to women on a crusade for justice that had yet to
reach its conclusion.

Lytton published her account in 1914, while the WSPU still struggled with
the Liberal government. Consequently, her memoir provided both a justification for militancy and an argument for its continued necessity. It is a
text specifically situated within the context of a political movement in
process, an agitation not yet ended. Published just months before the
outbreak of war, Lytton's autobiography created a narrative of the suffrage movement that was to have tremendous significance in the postwar

production of suffrage narratives, as it came to define the quintessential suffragette experience, one that honored the act of militancy—narrowly defined as violence against property—and the trajectory from that act, to arrest, hunger strike, and forcible feeding. Simultaneously, it defined the quintessential suffragette experience within a narrative structure with much resonance for its readers. Lytton's memoir, with its open-ended conclusion, lent itself easily to new readings and uses in the postwar period. Most significantly, the placement of forcible feeding at the pinnacle of the hierarchy of suffragette experience received legitimation from Lytton's account; that placement would be challenged and accepted in the years to come.

Following World War I, key aspects of this interpretation were reinforced through narratives that followed Strachey and Lytton in adhering to a rigid dichotomy between "militant" and "constitutional" suffrage organizations and memorializing a particular form of militant experience that alone was considered definitive. These two narratives came together in an explicit way in an organization founded in 1926 by former members of the WSPU and WFL, known as the Suffragette Fellowship. Edith How Martyn, a founding member of the WFL, played a critical role in the establishment of the Fellowship and served as its secretary for many years. The Fellowship's stated purpose was "to perpetuate the memory of the pioneers and outstanding events connected with women's emancipation and especially with the militant suffrage campaign, 1905–1914, and thus keep alive the suffrage spirit."[20] While the distinction between constitutional and militant was made overtly—by the Fellowship's very statement of purpose— the elevation of authentic militancy occurred at every level of the organization's activity.

The Suffragette Fellowship instituted a number of public forms of commemoration in the 1920s. Through a calendar of celebrations, the Fellowship created a timeline of events purporting to be central to the history of the militant movement. Events celebrated annually included the birthday of Emmeline Pankhurst on July 14; the first militant protest, of October 1905, when Christabel Pankhurst and Annie Kenney interrupted a Liberal Party meeting at the Manchester Free Trade Hall; and the suffrage victories of 1918 and 1928, celebrated in February and January, respectively.[21] This timeline created the lineage of the militant movement by honoring as

its progenitor Emmeline Pankhurst, and as its heroines Christabel Pankhurst and Annie Kenney, while establishing a causal relationship between
suffrage militancy as practiced by the WSPU and the extension of the
parliamentary franchise to women in 1918. These celebrations extended
from the late 1920s until the 1980s, receiving regular press, television, and
radio coverage.[22]

These commemorative events worked to shift emphasis from Lytton's
narrative of bodily suffering towards a narrative of the suffrage movement
that celebrated the comradeship and community found within the WSPU.
This was most clearly articulated by Fellowship member Geraldine Lennox, in a 1932 lecture on "the Suffragette Spirit." In her words:

> The Suffragette Spirit! What was it? It was an unswerving loyalty to an ideal—
> the political emancipation of womanhood, with all that implied; obedience to
> leaders; a thorough discipline and denial of self, with all its petty weaknesses; a
> sharing of work and hardships and a magnificent enthusiasm which made all
> loss and suffering of no account. It was a spirit that would not sit down under
> injustice—a spirit meant to get things done.[23]

Obedience to leaders is the significant phrase in Lennox's definition, for
here she conflates the qualities demanded of political activism—denial of
self—with unwavering devotion and loyalty to Emmeline and Christabel
Pankhurst. Lennox's invention, "the suffragette spirit," would be incorporated in perhaps the most significant project undertaken by the Suffragette
Fellowship—its archive—defining both its purpose and acquisitions policy.

Aside from suffrage pamphlets and a few contemporary records, a great
number of documents in the collection were created for the archive in
response to a questionnaire distributed by Edith How Martyn in 1929.[24]
This questionnaire framed its investigation around the experience of imprisonment, requesting information on dates and details of prisoners' incarceration. The implication of this line of enquiry was that suffrage militancy, in any true sense, was impossible without imprisonment. How
Martyn's questionnaire revealed, as did Lennox's formulation of the "suffragette spirit," that while forcible feeding remained the highest form of
militancy to which one could aspire, by the 1930s a shift in emphasis was
under way in the narrative of authentic suffrage militancy. The prewar
significance of women's passivity in the face of the brutality of forcible
feeding, as manifested in Lytton's autobiography, was giving way to a

postwar interpretation of prewar activism that exalted the comradeship of the movement, embodied in suffragette's imprisonments, adherence to the organization, and the act of militancy itself.

Above all else, inclusion in the community of militant suffragettes rested upon the defining act of imprisonment. Numerous documents generated in the formation of the collection attest to this shift in the narrative. A fund, established by the Fellowship to assist former suffragettes, had, as its prerequisite for borrowing, a certain pedigree, that of imprisonment. Writing to another member of the Fellowship in 1932, How Martyn expressed her unease with the application to the fund of a Miss Sprott. How Martyn explained that, "in this case we are not quite certain about the imprisonment . . . if you have any opportunity of ascertaining what Miss Sprott's record is said to be, we might be able to verify the details." A more telling example is found in correspondence between How Martyn and another former suffragette. Writing from Australia in 1932, Louise Cullen prefaced her account of participation in the militant movement with the lament that "I have always regretted that through ill-health my activities had to cease just when 'real' militancy started—i.e., window smashing and hunger-striking."[25] Cullen defines real militancy in active terms: window smashing and hunger-striking. While the latter clearly could lead to the forcible feeding of a prisoner, Cullen's emphasis lies not upon the suffering of the prisoner, but upon the activity of the protest leading up to imprisonment, and the refusal, once incarcerated, to accept that punishment passively.

For Cullen, as for How Martyn and other members of the Suffragette Fellowship by 1930, the first criterion of militancy had become imprisonment. As a consequence, the Fellowship recognized as militant only those actions likely to result in the arrest and jailing of a suffragette, actions typically represented as violence against property. Assaults against individuals, in which several prominent WSPU members had participated between 1909 and 1914, never appear in accounts of prewar protests.[26] And it became axiomatic in the years following that "the militancy of the suffragettes was not just an assertion of their rights; the fact is that they used force which ultimately hurt none but themselves."[27] Other forms of resistance less violent received no honors. As the government's policy had been to distrain the property of tax resisters, incarceration as a consequence of tax resistance and certain other forms of civil disobedience rarely occurred. The contribution these forms of protest made to the Edwardian campaign, perceived as vital at the time, would play virtually no role in post-war analysis. Thus, despite a wide range of protests arguably "militant," it is significant that imprisonment alone bestowed the imprimatur of authenticity upon acts of militancy.

The culmination of the narrative of authentic suffrage militancy came with publication of the Fellowship's "Roll of Honor of Suffragette Prisoners." Conceived in the late 1920s as the "Book of Suffragette Prisoners," the original plan called for the compilation of short biographical notices, alongside photographs of each man and woman known to have been imprisoned during the campaign. Such a publication would have provided marginally more information about those arrested in service of the Cause than that ultimately made available in the *Roll of Honor: Suffrage Prisoners, 1905–1914*, published in the mid-1950s, which simply presents a list, in alphabetical order, of those known to have suffered arrest and imprisonment on behalf of the Cause. The Roll of Honor served to cement further the distinction frequently made by former participants, between those who had suffered imprisonment and those who had not.[28]

Members of the Suffragette Fellowship actively promoted this interpretation of women's suffrage in yet further ways. In addition to creating the documents by which historians were later to reconstruct and analyze the women's suffrage movement, members of the Fellowship undertook to control the content of numerous cultural productions treating the suffrage movement during their lifetimes. This became a stated goal of the Fellowship in 1936, when it was asserted that "the Fellowship endeavors to correct all false or damaging stories which may be circulated, not only about the militant movement, but of the women who took part in the militant campaign. In this way, the Fellowship hopes to hand down to posterity a true and accurate account of the Militant Movement and its leaders."[29] Successes in this department were claimed when members of the Fellowship lobbied to have incorrect passages excised from forthcoming memoirs or removed from subsequent editions of accounts already published. Members also acted as consultants to various film productions, including *Royal Cavalcade* in 1935.[30]

As the Bakunin archive has done for Russian intellectual history (see John Randolph's essay, above), the Suffragette Fellowship, in effect, created a master narrative of the militant suffrage movement, one that privileged the sequence of events leading from action on the part of women to their arrest and incarceration. This narrative, embodied in the Suffragette Fellowship Archive, elided other forms of militancy that had been pursued by large numbers of women, such as passive resistance and tax resistance, and had the effect of limiting discussion of militancy to forms practiced by the wspu. This story elided also the debate within the Edwardian women's movement over the question of what constituted militancy and how most effectively to resist a government denying women citizenship. The consequence of this second elision has been to freeze militancy into a static either / or proposition, one that loses sight of militancy's dynamic and evolving nature and, more importantly, its significance within the suffrage movement as a point of discussion and tool for exclusion.

This narrative has implications both for how historians have interpreted the suffrage movement and for how former suffragettes constructed their political identities as feminists in the 1920s and after. Perhaps the most pernicious effect has been the equation of wspu-style militancy with radical feminism, "radical" meaning both the most authentic expression of women's political activism and the historically specific movement of the 1960s and 1970s. Beginning in the 1970s in Britain and the United States, new editions of suffrage memoirs, particularly those of Christabel, Emmeline, and Sylvia Pankhurst, and Constance Lytton, introduced a new generation of feminists to their foremothers. Christabel Pankhurst especially has been celebrated as a forerunner of radical feminism.[31] An unbroken connection between the suffragettes and second-wave feminism was asserted, despite the fact that many former suffragettes denied any such affiliation.[32] These historical accounts failed to examine earlier narratives as political fictions, in some cases going to great lengths to establish Christabel and Emmeline Pankhurst and their followers as feminist heroines with no blemishes.[33]

More recently, a spate of works examining feminist subjectivities, particularly the role played by the hunger strike and forcible feeding in shaping a collective suffragette identity, threatens to reinscribe the romance at the heart of Lytton's narrative. Women's bodies in pain lie at the center of many recent analyses, enticing us voyeuristically to imagine the suffering of Edwardian women activists and to comprehend it as the defining moment of their political consciousness. As a narrative strategy, this proves problematic as it again occludes the debate within the Edwardian movement over how to represent women in the political nation while simultaneously elevating the narratives of certain wspu members over those of all other activists. In addition, privileging the reproduction of the female body in pain—both as a contemporary critical strategy and as a historical tactic undertaken by the WSPU—overlooks the danger of a feminist political practice dependent upon the exhibition of women's bodies. Unintended consequences follow women's production of themselves as spectacular; only a very limited reading of those practices would suggest that women always control the reception of images they produce about themselves.

Of course, I am not arguing that the narrative of authentic suffrage militancy is a misrepresentation, for that would imply that there is an "accurate" representation elsewhere. But I am arguing for an approach that contextualizes the emergence of a new discursive identity, that of the Suffragette Spirit, in the 1920s and 1930s, one in which an archive and various autobiographies and memoirs actively produced meanings that have come to stand for the totality of the experience of militancy. To contextualize the Suffragette Spirit means listening to its exclusions as well as its inclusions, to its silences as well as its expressions. It requires that we subject feminist histories to the same scrutiny that we employ in reading more traditional histories, that we excavate, in Antoinette Burton's words, "the narrativization of our history—how we end up with the stories about historical feminism upon which we rely."[34] And it requires that we remember that the archive itself is both a physical collection of objects and the material through which political agendas are performed.

Notes

1 See for example, the recent article by Jill Liddington, "History, Feminism and Gender Studies," published as e-paper 7, Centre for Interdisciplinary Gender Studies, http://www.leeds.ac.uk/gender-studies/epapers/liddington.htm.

2 This characterization of the British women's movement is frequently attributed to Teresa Billington Greig, "The Storm-Centre of the Woman Suffrage Movement," *The International* (September 1908).

3 On the political uses to which stories about the suffrage movement could be put, see Kathryn Dodd, "Cultural Politics and Women's Historical Writing: The Case of Ray Strachey's *The Cause,*" *Women's Studies International Forum* 13 (1990): 127–37.

4 Barbara Green, *Spectacular Confessions: Autobiography, Performative Activism, and the Sites of Suffrage, 1905–1938* (New York: St. Martin's Press, 1997).

5 Joan Scott, "The Evidence of Experience," *Critical Inquiry* 17 (1991): 773–97.

6 A complete list of autobiographies and memoirs by former participants in the suffrage movement is too long to reproduce here. The most frequently cited works by former WSPU members include: Constance Lytton, *Prisons and Prisoners* (London: William Heinemann, 1914; reprinted East Ardsley: E. P. Publishing, 1976, and London: Virago, 1988); Christabel Pankhurst, *Unshackled: The Story of How We Won the Vote* (London: Hutchinson, 1959; reprinted London: Cresset Library, 1977); Emmeline Pankhurst, *My Own Story* (New York: Hearst's International Library, 1914; reprinted Westport, Conn.: Greenwood Press, 1985, and London: Routledge / Thoemmes Press, 1993); E. Sylvia Pankhurst, *The Suffragette Movement* (London: Longman, 1931; reprinted London: Virago, 1977, 1984, and 1988).

7 The Suffragette Fellowship Collection is housed at the Museum of London, Barbican, and is available to researchers—even at the museum—in a microfilm collection published by Harvester. (See note 24 below for its evolution and history.) All references to the Suffragette Fellowship Collection are to the microfilm version (hereafter referred to as Suffragette Fellowship). The availability of the collection on microfilm may have contributed to its heavy use by researchers. Other collections containing contemporary documents relating to the suffrage movement that provide different narratives include the Sylvia Pankhurst papers (International Instituut voor Sociale Geschiedenis, Amsterdam, now also available on microfilm from Harvester); Pethick-Lawrence papers (Trinity College, Cambridge); Women's Suffrage Collection, Archives, Manchester Public Library; and numerous collections at the Women's Library, London, particularly the papers of Teresa Billington Greig and Millicent Garrett Fawcett.

8 As Sandra Stanley Holton has shown, these were categories that many in the suffrage movement resisted, but which were embraced readily by the press and public; see her *Feminism and Democracy: Women's Suffrage and Reform Politics in Britain, 1900–1918* (Cambridge: Cambridge University Press, 1986).

9 See Krista Cowman, " 'Crossing the Great Divide': Inter-organizational Suffrage Relationships on Merseyside, 1895–1914," in Claire Eustance, Joan Ryan, and Laura Ugolini, eds. *A Suffrage Reader: Charting Directions in British Suffrage History* (Leicester: Leicester University Press, 2000), 37–52.

10 Ray Strachey, *The Cause: A Short History of the Women's Movement in Great Britain* (London: G. Bell & Sons, 1928; reprinted Bath: Chivers, 1974, and London: Virago, 1978 and 1988).

11 Dodd, "Cultural Politics and Women's Historical Writing," 134.

12 For discussion of the range of militant protest in the Edwardian movement, see Laura E. Nym Mayhall, *The Militant Suffrage Movement: Citizenship and Resistance in Britain, 1860–1930* (New York: Oxford University Press, 2003).

13 See for example, WFL president Charlotte Despard's review of *Prisons and Prisoners*, in *The Vote*, March 27, 1914, 266–67.

14 I draw here upon Kate Flint's discussion of reading communities in *The Woman Reader 1837–1914* (Oxford: Oxford University Press, 1993).

15 Liz Stanley with Ann Morley, *The Life and Death of Emily Wilding Davison* (London: The Women's Press, 1988), 74.

16 Hannah Mitchell, *The Hard Way Up* (London: Faber and Faber, 1968; reprinted London: Virago, 1977).

17 Midge MacKenzie, "Introduction," to Lytton, *Prisons and Prisoners* (Virago, 1988), p. xii; all further references are to this edition.

18 Here I borrow from Northrop Frye, *The Anatomy of Criticism* (Princeton: Princeton University Press, 1957), and Hayden White, who defines emplotment as the "encodation of the facts contained in the chronicle as components of specific kinds of plot structures," in *Tropics of Discourse* (Baltimore: Johns Hopkins University Press, 1978), 83.

19 Frye, *The Anatomy of Criticism*, 186–203.

20 The organization began informally in 1926 as the Suffragette Club. By 1930, it had become known as the Suffragette Fellowship and undertook to create a Women's Record Room, wherein relics and memoirs of the militant movement would be housed. The statement of purpose quoted comes from the Suffragette Fellowship Constitution, post-1940, in the Teresa Billington Greig papers, Box 401, The Women's Library.

21 As reported in the *Suffragette Fellowship Newsletter* (1936), Women's Library.

22 For example, movie footage of the October 13, 1936, Prisoners' Dinner was shown in movie theaters around the nation; see *Suffragette Fellowship Newsletter* (1936). The last of these celebrations organized by former suffragettes appears to have been in commemoration of Emmeline Pankhurst's birthday, on July 14, 1986; see Victoria Lidiard papers, 7 / xxx5 / 1, Women's Library.

23 Geraldine Lennox, "The Suffragette Spirit" (London: Suffragette Fellowship, 1932), 3.

24 An early version of the questionnaire circulated in the form of a letter from two organizers of the Suffragette Club, Edith How Martyn and Florence Bright, to men and women prominent in the prewar campaign. See Florence Bright to Hugh Franklin, November 5, 1929, Franklin / Duval papers, Box 226 (5), Women's Library. The Suffragette Fellowship Collection consists not only of the documents reproduced in the Harvester microfilm collection, but also of posters, banners, buttons, badges, scarves, soap, games, and many other products designed to "sell" the women's movement to a wider audience. For a fuller accounting of the collection's contents, see Diane Atkinson, *Suffragettes in the Purple, White and Green* (London: Museum of London, 1992). The collection was first exhibited in 1935 as the Women's Record Room, housed in the Minerva Club of the Women's Freedom League, 28a, Brunswick Square. In 1939, the Record Room moved to a house owned by former WSPU member Rose Lamartine Yates, at 6, Great Smith Street, Westminster. During the war, the collection was stored in the home of WFL member Mrs. Sparrow, 43, Black Lion Lane, Hammersmith. By 1948, the Women's Record Room was reorganized as the Museum and Record Office at 41, Cromwell Road, South Kensington. The Fellowship successfully

obtained the consent of the London Museum to house the collection later that year. The collection was accessioned in 1950, first displayed at Kensington Palace in 1951, and relocated with the rest of the Museum (now Museum of London) to the Barbican in 1976. My thanks to Diane Atkinson for discussion of the collection and her research on the wspu with me.

25 Edith How Martyn to Miss Margaret McPhun, May 24, 1932, Suffragette Fellowship, 57.116 / 56, reel 1, group c, volume III, p. 111; Louise Cullen to Edith How Martyn, March 13, 1932, Suffragette Fellowship, 57.70 / 23, reel 1, group c, volume III, p. 9.

26 Working with the documents in the Suffragette Fellowship Collection, it is nearly impossible to ascertain that wspu members had, on several occasions, physically assaulted individuals, including cabinet ministers, the prime minister, a Holloway Prison medical officer, and a newspaper editor with whose opinions they disagreed. Nor is it made evident that early window-breaking involved not smashing plate glass windows of government buildings or even privately owned shops, but throwing bricks through windows of public halls while ministers spoke to capacity audiences. For details of these events, see Andrew Rosen, *Rise Up, Women! The Militant Campaign of the Women's Social and Political Union, 1903–1914* (London: Routledge and Kegan Paul, 1973), 122–26, 171, 235. My thanks to Ian Christopher Fletcher for stressing this point.

27 Elsie Bowerman and Grace Roe, *Calling All Women*, February 1975, 18.

28 Suffragette Fellowship, *Roll of Honor: Suffragette Prisoners, 1905–1914* (c. 1955), Women's Library. The compilation of this list grew out of a practice of both the wspu and the wfl of awarding prisoners with badges upon their release from prison. The original plan was outlined in a flier put out by the Suffragette Fellowship, Franklin / Duval papers, Box 226 (5), Women's Library.

29 *Suffragette Fellowship Newsletter*, 1936, p. 3.

30 Memoirs thus claimed included one then forthcoming from the Bishop of London (*Suffragette Fellowship Newsletter*, 1936). The film success was reported in the *Suffragette Fellowship Newsletter*, 1935.

31 Elizabeth Sarah, "Christabel Pankhurst: Reclaiming Her Power," in Dale Spender, ed., *Feminist Theorists: Three Centuries of Key Women Writers* (New York: Pantheon Books, 1983), 256–84.

32 See the analysis of the Women's Liberation Movement by former wspu members Elsie Bowerman and Grace Roe, in which the militant suffrage movement's "spiritualism" is set in opposition to the "materialism" of the newer movement; in *Calling All Women*, February 1975, 18–22.

33 June Purvis, "A 'Pair of . . . infernal queens'? A Reassessment of the Dominant Representations of Emmeline and Christabel Pankhurst, First Wave Feminists in Edwardian Britain," *Women's History Review* 5, 2 (1996).

34 Antoinette Burton, " 'History' Is Now: Feminist Theory and the Production of Historical Feminisms," *Women's History Review* 1 (1992): 26.

Kathryn J. Oberdeck

Archives of the Unbuilt Environment

DOCUMENTS AND DISCOURSES OF IMAGINED SPACE

IN TWENTIETH-CENTURY KOHLER, WISCONSIN

It seems to us in all hard-headed common sense that it is well

worthwhile to have allowed room and opportunity for such a dream

at any rate, because then we are sure we have an opportunity for

the real thing which, when it happens, presumably will be smaller

rather than larger than our dreams. — Henry V. Hubbard,

Landscape Architect, Olmsted Bros., to Jerry Donohue,

Engineer for Kohler Village, 1928

IN 1916 A VISIONARY industrialist, Walter J. Kohler, Sr., began to develop a "garden industrial village" adjacent to his factory in Sheboygan County, Wisconsin. A manufacturer of plumbing fixtures, Kohler had inherited the business at the turn of the century, shortly after the factory had moved out of the city of Sheboygan to expand in a rural setting four miles to the west, at a hamlet called Riverside. As a hodgepodge of workers' homes gradually grew up around the new plant, Walter Kohler turned to town-planning ideas to try to prevent the neighborhood from developing into a squalid industrial district. Conceived at a moment heady with town-planning ambitions, Kohler's project blossomed into a model industrial community, Kohler Village, that connected him with leading lights in urban planning. Throughout the development of the village Kohler would wrestle with the artistic conceptions these landscape architects and planners proposed, as well as the competing community visions of Kohler employees who lived and worked in the village.[1] In the midst of these conflicts, Kohler, his descendents, and the planning professionals they employed repeatedly redesigned the village in response to new landscape visions and user practices.

Documents of such planning histories necessarily lie largely in archives of what I am calling here the "unbuilt environment": paper streets, imaginary blocks, fantasy buildings, and vividly described neighborhoods that remain unrealized. The production processes of design professionals are partly responsible for this—architects, landscapers, and planners draw, describe, and map countless unused designs as part of their advisory roles with clients. The comprehensive town plans envisaged by planning professionals of the early twentieth century were all the more prone to remain imagined spaces because the practicalities of urban politics and development, dominated in the United States by private developers and ward politicians, eluded grand urban planning schemes.[2] In planning histories, these plans are used principally to document the process that produced a final built result, to chart an individual architect's or planner's style and vision over the course of a design career, or, more recently, as a central document that illuminates the politics of planning, usually with lessons for current planning strategies.[3]

This essay reflects upon documents of the unbuilt environment to an alternative end. I ask how the kinds of archives generated at Kohler can contribute to the history of a spatial imaginary that includes but also extends beyond the specific activities of planning professionals and the powerful elites who commission their services. And I argue that this spatial imaginary has a history—or more properly histories—simultaneously illuminated and shrouded by archives of the sort generated by the planning processes at Kohler. To interrogate these archives for their histories of the unbuilt environment and the imaginary discourses that generated it is necessarily to question their mobilization as testaments and confirmation of the built environment. In the process, it becomes possible to sketch the outlines of an elusive conversation in images and visions about what spaces might have been—the dreams that become smaller realities, as the landscape architect Henry Hubbard, who worked for decades on Kohler's plans, put it in my epigraph. Such a conversation engages anachronistic continuations of styles that evoke residual spatial projects; efforts to harmonize planning visions that are socially at odds; and responses to vernacular lived experiences of built space that express the limits of the built environment for various social purposes. By putting Kohler's planning designs in dialogue with related documents of the unbuilt environment—including the visions of those who commission plans as well as those of village residents and factory workers—I try to suggest how they might provide windows on such wider spatial imaginaries.

Such imaginary histories of place engage wider concerns regarding the nature of archival work because the unbuilt environment necessarily confounds the "inevitability" of the identities associated with the materiality of local places. As Martin Hall has observed in an essay on the relation between local places, archives, and the violently contested identities of deterritorialized nationalism, narratives of group identity tend to aggrandize themselves by co-opting the materiality of specific places read back in time as the local bedrock of an inevitable history. Spatial visions imagined for a specific place but never built disrupt this materiality, unveiling a process whereby place and its implied identities are constructed through a process of alternative imagined geographies. Documents of this kind of history escape the conventional archival mandate of proving something "that actually existed," in favor of unfolding what might have been. These might-have-beens generate, in turn, their own questions about the processes that preserved them and rendered them more or less accessible, more or less available to the interwoven histories of the built and the unbuilt. In the case of Kohler Village, traces of the unbuilt environment left in company, planning, union, and other archives need to be weighed against authorized histories of the materialized village that prefer certain versions of the imagined village—and their attendant identities—over others. Such records open up an archive and a process of historical construction that compares what was once possible to powerful versions of the inevitable. Through such comparisons, imagined spaces can become measures of the boundaries around authorized histories of why materialized spaces came to be.[4]

Kohler Village's own peculiar history accounts in part for the wealth of imaginary spaces its official archives offer as a self-reflexive commentary on the town's built environment. Funded by a visionary entrepreneur, the early stages of urban planning in the village enabled the application of otherwise politically impracticable planning visions, albeit in conditions centrally shaped by entrepreneurial concerns.[5] The town's longevity, moreover, permits especially intriguing perspectives on the history of planning as they appear through the filter of the entrepreneurial ambitions of successive generations of the Kohler family as well as conflicts generated by the changing project of the village itself. The result is a revealing twist on existing narratives of the planning professions that helped shape the design of Kohler. Here, discarded ideals of planning and styles of urban design reemerge in later eras, often translated into the language of clients and users who stake new claims on the old visions because of the exigencies of emergent quandaries regarding the purposes and meaning of previously built spaces. At the same time, those built spaces themselves served a variety of public relations purposes for the company. These purposes tended to shape the mobilization of the archive to celebrate achieved plans and built spaces and submerge alternative imaginary, unbuilt environments.

With planning for the Village of Kohler about to enter its second century, the town's history and archives offer a vast range of unbuilt spaces and narrative constructions. To foreground the nexus of unbuilt space and social identity, I focus here on episodes of planning, development, and discord centered on problems related to envisioned public civic spaces for Kohler Village. Such spaces generated questions about the social identity of the village as a place for a number of reasons. Since Walter Kohler's original vision emphasized the provision of homes offered for sale to workers to generate "American" pride in home ownership, the town's identity was formulated around privately owned spaces from the start. This generated debates as to what aspects of these private comforts the company was to provide as a civic gesture as well as what kinds of local identities would adhere to public civic spaces. The problem was exacerbated by town planners who tended to wax exuberant over the design of public civic spaces and monuments that often jarred the sensibilities of Kohler company officials interested in the village's private meanings. Residents and workers themselves, in turn, had alternative visions of the "public" character and meaning of their town. In the proposals, counterproposals, and complaints surrounding unbuilt public spaces in Kohler can be read a wide conversation about the contested identities associated with space in a model company town.

To explore such visionary alternatives contained within archives of spaces "that actually existed" is to reflect upon the importance of spatial identity implicit in the fractures and self-critique that contributors to this volume have identified in many official archives. Contemporary as well as historical—and even many a historian's—notions of the archive often lay claim to a spatial universe of the "real," as Antoinette Burton's reflections on archival concepts both popular and scholarly richly suggest, particularly in the case of the "universe" of spaces archivally available to the young Obi-Wan Kenobi. But the narratives produced here about the construction and use of archives attest to the ways in which the space of official archives, as well as their descriptions of space, contain internal conflicts undermining universalist myths in favor of contested spatial imaginaries. Jennifer Milligan and Peter Fritzsche provide acute critiques of the contradictions implicit in archival spaces devoted to one of the most powerful spatial constructs constituted by archives, the nation. In Milligan's account of the Archives nationales, the French nation-state and its wider imperial vision repeatedly shape and reshape archival spaces fraught with questions of access and use that come to define French civic identities in ways intriguingly analogous to the spatial visions that define more local identities in Kohler. For Fritzsche it is less who than what gets into the space of the German archives that raises profoundly moving questions about the trajectory of national identity, with the archive sometimes generating and at other times brutally expunging stories from diverse spaces whose presence or absence the archive historians must themselves imaginatively ponder.

In other cases conflicts over participation in national politics generate the enforcement of smaller spatial "scales" to shape an archive to a particular historical purpose. This is particularly apparent in Laura Mayhall's suggestive critique of "the body" as the spatial scale at which protest identified with the "Suffragette Spirit" of the Women's Social and Political Union occurred and could be documented—a scale enforced against the wider spaces (home, court, legislature, etc.) in which other women's suffrage activists imagined the making of their civic identities. John Randolph charts the biography of the Bakunin archive across multiple spaces that shaped and marked its contents, from the family estate that helped generate interest in the archive as a collection of "private" documents weighed against an impoverished "public" life to its current existence in the redefined "public" of cyberspace. Such spatial distinctions of public and private resonate with the valorizations of household space that, as we shall see, animated conflicts over the significance of civic space in Kohler. They find poignant resonance as well in Marilyn Booth's account of Zaynab Fawwaz's fictional inversion of the gendered spaces of nineteenth-century Lebanon, which renders as centers of power the female domestic spaces ignored by conventional archives while radically opening public space to women. Such counter-archives insist on what even the official archives in this collection divulge when mined for their own unbuilt spaces—the fissured and fortuitously included documents that attest to both the incompleteness of archives and their inclusion of visions that exceed their own official boundaries.

It should be noted, finally, that the unbuilt archives considered here address imagined spaces ventured before Kohler Village's latter-day transformation into a luxury golf and spa resort tangentially available to visitors shopping for the company's well-known upscale plumbing fixtures. To be sure, this transformation itself raises myriad issues of public spaces and social identity along with steadily accumulating unbuilt plans to document them. While the overall intention of making the town into a monument of company commitment to craftsmanship, comfort, and home life continues in the retooling of the town toward hospitality and the marketing of "gracious living," its shift away from the purposes of worker housing has necessarily changed the stakes of envisioning unbuilt private and public spaces there.[6] Therefore, while I will gesture at ways in which Kohler Village's archives contain visions forecasting this later transformation, I leave the more detailed analysis of "Destination Kohler"—a reality that might have surprised Henry Hubbard by exceeding his dreams—for a later day. My focus here will be on conflicts and connections among the unbuilt visions for the village as it developed from its inception in the 1910s under the direction of the German planner Werner Hegemann through several decades of planning advice by the Olmsted Brothers firm of Brookline, Massachusetts, from the 1920s through the 1950s, a period in which two hard-fought labor battles further agitated issues of the identities associated with private and public space in the village.

After touring garden city and industrial housing examples in Britain and Germany in the early 1910s, Walter J. Kohler returned to Wisconsin and found ready-to-hand some eager planners steeped in the ideas that informed such models. Foremost among these was the German planning theorist Werner Hegemann. In his early thirties at the time, Hegemann was already well established in international planning circles. He had served as housing inspector in Philadelphia, organized planning exhibitions in Boston and Germany, and toured extensively throughout the United States to lecture on planning. He had settled into a private practice of planning consultation in Milwaukee in 1916 when Kohler engaged him in planning for Kohler Village, Hegemann's first practical planning project.[7]

Hegemann's early plans for Kohler reflect his immersion in a nexus of broad-ranging planning inspirations that span stylistic and political aspirations that seem, at first blush, mutually antithetical. Influenced by graduate training in economics that had included a stint at the University of Pennsylvania under the progressive economist Simon Patten, Hegemann was sensitive to social relations and conditions underlying the different aesthetic appearances of European and American cities. But his economic concerns did not preclude his insistence on the importance of aesthetic considerations in town planning, which he saw as the prime concern of professional planners. Thus he wove into the political-economic and sociological concerns that made him interested in Kohler's industrial village project an enthusiasm for monumental beauty—a preoccupation that many narratives of planning history see being supplanted by more functional concerns in the 1910s. A frank admirer of Daniel Burnham's monumental Beaux-Arts style "White City" at the 1893 World's Columbian Exposition in Chicago, Hegemann advocated city and town plans that integrated such "civic art" into urban and suburban conceptions while also addressing social issues like crowding, access to parks, and free space. He wanted to embed the "City Beautiful" at the heart of the "city functional." Hegemann's peripatetic gathering of planning visions and his expansive philosophy of the sociological aspects of planning generated ideas that would echo throughout the village's development, both built and unbuilt, over the next several decades.[8]

At Kohler, Hegemann styled his role as that of an aesthetic consultant to an enlightened entrepreneur who was interested in realizing his peculiar combination of social and aesthetic. His early sketches of new blocks of homes redirected his eclectically functional and monumental urban visions to apply to residential sections for a garden industrial community. Reflecting Hegemann's appreciation of the teachings of the Austrian architect Camillo Sitte, who saw in Europe's finest plazas a lost tradition, Hegemann's plan for a block of Kohler homes reproduced a Sittesque plaza emphasizing uniform style, careful siting for light, and the integration of imagined public buildings. Such aspects of his vision for the Village of Kohler show up in other early planning documents for the town as well. Lists of proposed features for the village prepared by Hegemann and his partner, the landscape architect Elbert Peets, included such monumental

"City Beautiful" features as "Entrance Gates to the City," "Museum," "Monuments," and "Theatre," alongside the more sociologically motivated provisions for schools, kindergarten, baths, and an Altenheim for pensioners.[9]

These heady plans for Kohler remain among the first and most interesting "unbuilt environments" that would linger in the archives of the town. Significantly, Hegemann's plans emphasized public facilities in Kohler— and indeed the development of the "private" residences as a public service—as much as the private homes on which Walter Kohler focused his attention. These competing imaginary spaces provoked apparently unresolvable tensions between the planner and the entrepreneur. Their differences derived in part from Hegemann's sheer visionary zeal—his dreams of the unbuilt village far exceeded his practical competence to draft plans for the parks and neighborhoods he and Peets imagined. Kohler complained that work on the village had encountered costly delays while Hegemann tried to acquire these necessary skills from Peets. But correspondence between Hegemann and Kohler also reveals disagreements related to Hegemann's very conception of his role in village development.

As his planning works indicate, Hegemann saw the planner's aesthetic expertise as a crucial antidote to the fundamentally commercial concerns of bourgeois civic leaders who dominated U.S. planning in the absence of a nobility of the type that could assemble artistic experts to develop nineteenth-century European estates and urban centers. The opportunities offered by an industrial garden city like Kohler Village were thus enhanced, for Hegemann, by the peculiar influence a planner could exert over a single entrepreneur with the leverage to plan an entire small municipality. In Hegemann's correspondence with Kohler, such advice extended to the role of artistic steward he urged the plumbing magnate to cultivate. According to Hegemann, such a role required Kohler to absorb a considerable amount of the cost of planning for the town, which Hegemann worried that the entrepreneur would fold into the price to workers of individual houses. Incensed at Hegemann's impertinence in advising him on management and perplexed that the planner expected him to patronize future residents despite a stated opposition to employer paternalism, Kohler responded with an angry missive repudiating Hegemann's interference in such matters. Though Kohler never sent this letter, relations deteriorated, and Hegemann and Peets disappeared from the project in 1917.[10]

The break between Hegemann and Kohler had important repercussions for the company's subsequent narratives about the town and, consequentially, for the mobilization of company archives as a narrative of town development. The break was so bitter that the industrialist virtually erased Hegemann and Peets from the village's early planning history. Company and village publicity awarded the credit of early planning to the Olmsted Brothers firm, which took over in 1924. Not until company officials and planning historians rediscovered Hegemann's and Peets' involvement in the 1970s was their role in the planning of Kohler recognized, and even in the 1980s they were often ignored in preference to the better known Olmsted planners.[11] When recognized, Hegemann's and Peets's influence was relegated to design elements that were partially realized (in the construction of the "Lincoln Circle" cul-de-sac and "Ravine Park") in the first subdivision of Kohler Village, West I, but ultimately enveloped by more comprehensive plans attributed to the Olmsted Brothers. Only at the beginning of the 1990s did a company official, John Lillesand, develop a narrative of village history that fully incorporated Hegemann's and Peets's visions as enduring influences in the town's development. Placed in a wider context of archives of Kohler's unbuilt spaces, however, Hegemann's visions appear not only as the enduring contributions to Kohler's spatial imagery that Lillesand recognized, but also as prescient records of ongoing debates over the identity of Kohler village.[12] Many of his preoccupations would haunt later documents of Kohler's unbuilt environment.

Indeed, documents of correspondence between Kohler Company officials and the Olmsted Brothers planners who guided village development after 1924 indicate that competing visions of private and civic space and their relations continued to confound the work of design professionals involved in the project. Though celebrated in company histories as the source of planning counsel that translated Walter Kohler's visions into practicable plans realized in the materialized village, Olmsted's planners generated volumes of unbuilt designs and reams of disregarded advice that they unsuccessfully urged on Kohler officials. At the crux of many of their differences with Walter Kohler and his aides and successors was the balance between private and civic spaces as they promised to embody, in built form, the meaning and identity of the village as a place. Three topics of dispute in particular can serve to illustrate these conflicts: a difference over the provision of parking space on Kohler streets to accommodate visitors to the village's central "Nature Theatre," plans for commercial districts in the town, and the long-envisioned and repeatedly revised plans for a Kohler Civic Center.

Walter Kohler initially approached the Olmsted firm for planning advice in 1924 and began a long correspondence with Henry Vincent Hubbard, and later Carl Rust Parker, regarding Kohler planning. Since 1917 the Kohler company had been pursuing village development on the basis of the Hegemann and Peets plans of 1916–17, which charted the neighborhood of West I immediately west of the Kohler plant as well as the small South I neighborhood south of the plant. With a surging plumbing fixtures business based on the boom in 1920s real estate development, Walter Kohler envisioned plant expansions that warranted further housing for a growing population of workers. He wanted the Olmsted firm to develop a master plan for an expanded village, incorporating schemes for traffic, parks and recreation, schools, well-designed neighborhoods, commercial sectors, and public spaces. On the basis of this plan Hubbard and his associates would formulate more detailed proposals regarding logical next directions for development, street layouts, and housing groups. A preliminary report on the master plan forwarded to the company in January 1925 outlined the grand scale of the mutual Kohler-Olmsted vision: a town of 30,000 people (grand by the measure of the population of roughly 1,300–1,800 that Kohler Village would maintain throughout the twentieth century), a network of central and subordinate business centers in various neighborhoods, a system of ten grammar schools feeding into one or two high schools, and an imposing civic center.[13] So far the planners and the entrepreneur concurred. However, as correspondence moved in the latter half of 1925 to designing the details, visions of the unbuilt town diverged and multiplied around boundaries of civic and private space.

Hubbard was eager to forge ahead immediately on a civic center equal to the ambitions of the master plan, but Kohler repeatedly demurred and refocused their correspondence on planning for new neighborhoods of private homes to house the workmen he sought to attract to his plant. He was not deaf to needs for civic life in the emerging town. But he thought the immediate needs for public assemblies could be served by the "Nature Theatre" his engineers and construction workers had sculpted out of the northern end of Ravine Park, which cut across the western edge of the village's first developed neighborhood. "Located in the center of the city," Kohler explained to Hubbard, the Nature Theatre "affords such unusual

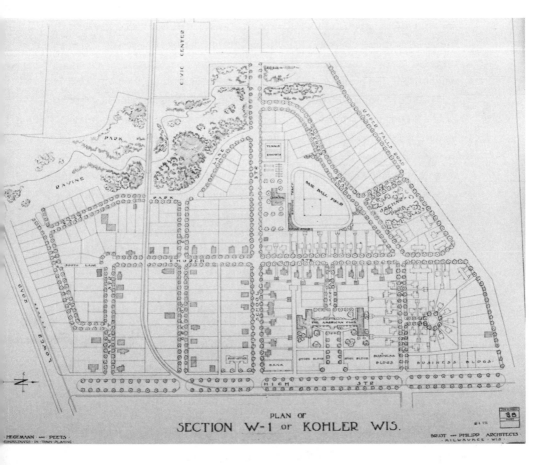

PLAN OF
SECTION W-1 OF KOHLER WIS.

The early plan drafted by Werner Hegemann and Elbert Peets for the West I Section of Kohler Village. Note the Civic Center and store and business buildings. *Photo by William Munro, Kohler Archives, courtesy of Kohler Co.*

and exceptional opportunity for large civic affairs that it must be featured to the utmost and provision made for accommodating the crowds." This meant that "we must utilize the parking facilities of West 2," the next neighborhood to be developed. Recent experiences with the well-attended concerts put on at the Nature Theatre by John Philip Sousa's band inspired Kohler's concerns, while also reflecting the kind of civic culture he imagined for Kohler's public spaces. In line with his overall purpose of developing an "American" planned community that mingled coordinated design with individual ownership and initiative, Kohler emphasized the provision of civic events like Sousa's concerts that rallied village residents around a shared patriotism.[14]

Kohler's conception of the American identity expressed in civic affairs like the Sousa concerts had implications for the relation between private residences and public streets that ran counter to Hubbard's visions, however. Specifically, Kohler wanted to widen the streets in the unbuilt West II neighborhood enough to accommodate parking spaces for the Nature Theatre. While this arrangement of space accorded to a certain extent with Hubbard's more general ideas of civic space, detailed below, in other respects Kohler's parking provisions ran completely athwart the planner's notion of how to integrate public and private space. Hubbard was aghast that Kohler would compromise the Olmsted firm's aesthetic designs by running broad ribbons of bland pavement through the intimate neighborhoods and carefully configured house groupings he and his associates had mapped out for West II. He thought that, for the few occasions when extra parking was needed, the lawns of individual residences would suffice. But Kohler was adamant:

> We are confirmed in our opposition to utilizing the residence grass plantings for parking of cars on any occasion. . . . The beautiful appearance of the village, which is the result of the personal maintenance on the part of the residents, is a cause of pride to all of us identified with the community and cannot be disturbed by any of the activities emanating from this company.[15]

This would not be the only case in which Hubbard's efforts to design spaces that would be pleasing year-round to the entire community and visitors clashed with Kohler's notion that the pride, comfort, and independence of home-ownership operated as an inalienable principle in village planning. Hubbard complained repeatedly that his efforts to design aesthetically attractive house groupings and coherent "vistas" down streets were scuttled in favor of Kohler's rigid adherence to village rules for house setbacks and space between homes.[16] The results in terms of the built environment were usually a compromise of the two principles. Discarded unbuilt visions mapping Hubbard's principles were consigned to the archives of both companies, where they remain to document not only the processes that produced what got built, but also, as we shall see, spatial visions that were later retraced in wider discourses and differences regarding what the space of Kohler might be and mean.

Efforts to plan space for commercial enterprises in Kohler provoked further arguments between Hubbard and Kohler over issues of public space and local identity. Sites for such enterprises as retail stores, restaurants, and taverns had been woven into Hegemann's earliest visions of Sittesque blocks integrating private and public purposes. In the more official plans he drew up with Peets these became more distinct commercial districts but were still scattered throughout their neighborhood designs for West I and South I.[17] As he expanded and revised Hegemann and Peets's designs into a master plan for the town, Hubbard maintained substantial space for commercial purposes. He reshaped this space into a commercial center that would serve as a site for shopping, resting, and informal public congregation: "In the central plaza there is an opportunity to secure good architectural treatment, a fair sense of enclosure and a plaza effect which provides a setting for the surrounding buildings and a shaded retreat for those who wish to rest and wait in this vicinity."[18] A further appeal of his planned commercial center, Hubbard noted, was its location at an important crossroads central to the already developed area of the town, the intersection of High Street, which ran between the factory and West I, and Upper Falls Road, a thoroughfare running on the northern edge of West I and the factory.

Hubbard's plan to run Kohler's commercial section into the factory zone aroused immediate opposition from Walter Kohler. Never enthusiastic about independent commerce in the town (a restaurant and tavern established in the early years of South I had been rapidly transformed into a music studio and women's club), Kohler was particularly averse to sacrificing space he envisioned for industrial expansion to commercial development.[19] In light of impending expansion of the Kohler Company's industrial enterprises, Kohler informed Hubbard, it was very possible the company would close the Upper Falls Road east of High Street, so business development would have to locate elsewhere. Hubbard objected that such disruption of traffic circulation would stymie the proposed commercial development and adversely affect the road and highway system from a regional planning standpoint. In reply, Kohler respectfully but firmly asserted his own concept of the town's spatial imperatives:

> We will not argue against your position that, from a town planning standpoint, the arrangement of this as a business center is most desirable. However, this community depends upon this industry, and nothing must interfere with the orderly growth and efficient operation of the manufacture. . . .
>
> There is no objection to the business section as you planned it for High Street and north Upper Road, but we may never complete it as indicated, due to our industrial expansion. . . . Should we ever utilize the northeastern quadrant for industrial purposes, it would mean the elimination of part of the Upper Falls Road, as we could not permit any public thoroughfare running through and interfering with our industrial planning.[20]

This perspective on planning for a commercial center accorded with Kohler's wider vision of the town as a model community that made the comfort and pride of owner-occupied homes available to workers as a component of efficient industrial planning. As he would quip to a reporter featuring Kohler Village in a 1931 *New York Times Magazine* article, "I think the day must come when industrial engineers will give as much attention to building an attractive plant and community as they do today in making a plant efficient. The two things really are one. It is part of the bigger task of stabilizing industry."[21] Here the contours of town and community planning were subordinated to and guided by the imperatives of private industry, as opposed to Hubbard's wider regional vision that included industry in an integrated town plan blending private and public interests. But Hubbard's vision of a commercial center offering public respite and through traffic, though unbuilt, would resound later in the dissatisfactions engendered by some of Kohler's coordinated industrial and community engineering.

No imagined unbuilt public space endures as persistently in the archives of Kohler planning as the dream of a monumental civic center. Hegemann located this feature in his early plans as a plaza just west of Ravine Park and figured into his written visions a range of educational, entertainment, and civic institutions. Hubbard enthusiastically embraced this vision but moved it to the edge of South I, on a site that would command stunning vistas over the Sheboygan River (the site is visible at the lower-right edge of

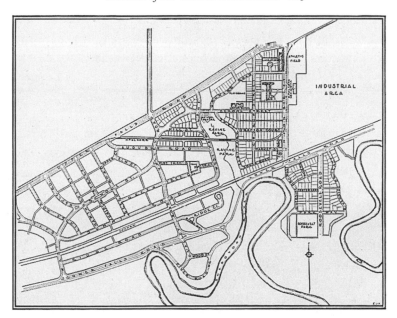

The Olmsted Brothers Master Ground Plan for Kohler Village, c. 1920s. Note the more residential character of West I. (This view is rotated 90 degrees counterclockwise from the preceding figure.) *Photo by William Munro, Kohler Village: A Town-Planned Wisconsin Industrial Community American in Spirit and Government* (Kohler, Wisc.: Kohler Col, 1928).

this figure). Throughout the 1920s Hubbard urged Walter Kohler to undertake a massive civic center on this site. Even the entrepreneur himself briefly embraced the idea of a civic center imagined on a grand scale. Though he had been pressing Hubbard to design yet another residential neighborhood, West III, in the latter half of 1926, Kohler abruptly reversed himself in December and asked instead that plans for a "splendid and outstandingly beautiful" civic center take precedence. Arranged around a plaza some two to four hundred feet wide and several thousand feet long, Kohler's imagined civic center featured an array of cultural institutions. A large combination auditorium-bath anchored the north end of the plaza, closest to the existing town; with seats for ten thousand people for dramatic and musical events, it could also be converted to aquatic activities. A junior university would connect Kohler to the expanding Wisconsin state university system, giving shape to the campus-like character of the factory itself, with its clock tower and vine-covered buildings. A city hall, post office, hospital, and central fire station would serve the political, communication, health, and safety needs of the community. A hotel would welcome visitors while clubhouses for fraternal organizations would facilitate the camaraderie of residents. A theater, a movie house, and a public library would serve the town's cultural needs, and a union church would draw together its various religions denominations.

Hubbard moved immediately to elaborate the description and planning of a civic center imagined on this scale, taking the opportunity to warn Kohler against any diminution in his vision. He had rearranged the components, he explained, in order to "embody your idea in a way which might challenge comparison with the really big things of this kind now in the world." But this meant maintaining the relative proportions of the large building masses involved. "It would be a fatal mistake," Hubbard warned, "to undertake so magnificent a composition as that which might be made out of this group related to the auditorium, if it should then prove that for practical and financial reasons it was impossible to construct building masses big enough to be worthy of their assigned sites."[22]

That this vision momentarily engaged even Walter Kohler's imagination says much about the kind of public space that accorded with his vision of the village's identity. Massive, worthy, world-challenging—this was the kind of civic space associated with capital-C Culture that Kohler could imagine associating with his town. As he opined in a 1920 speech before the Massachusetts Sanitary Club, "We have felt that the citizen's social life need no more be absolutely distinct from the plant than the social life of a student be a thing apart from the university."[23] To Kohler, the factory, homes, and eventual civic center were a kind of university, providing for workers an uplifting *Bildung* that could be well materialized in a monumental civic center.

As Hubbard's simultaneously "hard headed" and wistful 1928 commentary on the prospects for the civic center suggests, however, the project remained a dream he knew was likely to diminish in execution. In his letter to the engineer Jerry Donohue, who supervised the actual grading, cutting, and digging of Kohler earth to accommodate the projects that developed out of Hubbard's dreams and Walter Kohler's strictures, Hubbard was trying to maintain "room" for the civic center by providing a grading plan for the site and directing Donohue to fill it accordingly with earth cut for other more pressing projects. But the dream kept receding for a number of reasons. Walter Kohler was elected Wisconsin's governor in 1928 and became more preoccupied with affairs of the state than with Kohler Village development. In the same year, the home construction industry began to falter in an early warning sign of the full-scale Depression that would scuttle many of Hubbard's dreams for Kohler development.[24]

Remarkably, however, the unbuilt civic center persisted as an imaginary space well after both Hubbard and Walter Kohler had ceased directing development in Kohler Village. When Carl Rust Parker took over supervision of Kohler planning at the Olmsted firm in the 1940s, the topic of a civic center, "perhaps less pretentious than originally planned," dominated his correspondence with Herbert V. Kohler, who headed the Kohler Company following his half-brother Walter's death in 1940.[25] At this point the focus of the civic center idea was a "Kohler Memorial" building provided for in Walter's will as a tribute to his father, the company's founder John-Michael Kohler. The groupings Parker imagined for this building, in collaboration with Kohler architect Richard Philipp, kept alive the Beaux-Arts style of civic monumentality that made the imagined Kohler Civic Center a long-term inheritor of such grand turn-of-the-century visions of civic uplift as the "White City."[26] Like that monument to patriotic uplift, the civic group proposed for Kohler in the 1940s—incorporating a pool and gymnasium into a civic institution featuring an auditorium and museum—would embed entertainment in ennobling cultural self-improvement. Only when Kohler residents' plans for a municipal pool closer to the center of town threatened to compete with the dream of a civic center was this monumental vision abandoned. Hubbard's dreams gave way to the "smaller" reality that residents wanted: a distinctly modernist Kohler Memorial that combined an auditorium with an indoor-outdoor pool at the site of the Kohler school, conveniently located in the middle of the town's oldest district, West I.[27]

If the practicality and immediacy of residents' desires ran athwart the more monumental vision of public space represented by Hubbard's civic center, in other cases Kohler residents and workers tendered visions that echoed some of the planners' unbuilt dreams. While successive Kohler executives and Olmsted planners ventured competing visions of the ways private and public space embodied identity in Kohler Village, they were not the only sources for imaginary spaces giving that identity local shape and meaning. As they bought up the houses that embodied Walter Kohler's conception of the town's importance—an identity imprinted in 1920s Kohler advertising that featured line drawings of Kohler homes as an emblem of Kohler craftsmanship—village residents, along with their fellow factory workers, conceptualized private and public space in Kohler according to their own needs and imperatives. During periods of labor strife at the plant in particular, these imperatives could crystallize into spatial conceptions that retraced some of the planners' and company officials' unbuilt spaces from the perspective of everyday—and not so everyday—use.

Some of the dissatisfactions that gave shape to these alternative visions for the town derived from Walter Kohler's somewhat idiosyncratic approach to the rigors of Depression industry. Devoted to an ethic of steady employment to support the steady home lives he tried to cultivate in the village, Kohler endeavored to keep his workforce employed by filling up storerooms and then gradually cutting back hours rather than laying off workers. When layoffs did begin in the early 1930s, village homeowners were often retained to enable them to continue paying on their mortgages. But this favoritism did not necessarily assuage the villagers' frustrations, as the company required them to sign documents promising the first cut of their reduced wages to the Kohler Building and Loan Association that financed their homes. As a result many were reduced to paychecks of little or nothing to meet other living expenses. These and other frustrations with the authority wielded by the company over employees' lives gave rise to an organizing effort in the plant by the American Federation of Labor and a tumultuous strike that began in July 1934.[28]

In both the 1930s strike and another more tenacious United Auto Workers (UAW) conflict that followed in the 1950s, the spaces of the village and the company's control over them became important arenas of contest for strikers and Kohler officials. While not all of these conflicts bore on the design of the village, many did echo the thorny issues of the prominence of private versus public space in the identity of the town that had often brought Walter Kohler into conflict with his planning advisors.[29] Whether they lived elsewhere and felt betrayed when Kohler favored village residents to retain jobs or lived in the village and chafed at Kohler's control over how they spent their meager Depression paychecks, workers in the 1930s raised the question of what kind of relation between an employer and his workers the planning and construction of a model town implied. Few unionists would have accepted either Hegemann's or Kohler's view of this problem as they had expressed these views almost twenty years before. The paternalism of Hegemann's view of the entrepreneur as a civic patron would have grated against workers' demand for an independent voice in company and village decision making, a voice that Hegemann, enamored as he was of Progressive-era expertise, found unequal to the task of industrial or civic planning. But Kohler's counter-vision of the village as an exercise in "American" independence rather than "Old-World" paternalism rang hollow as well. When "Americanism" was cultivated as a decorous style of independent "garden city" suburban life detached from the economic stratagems of small-scale farming or animal-raising whereby workers survived in less regulated neighborhoods, the "independence" of American "homeownership" became a tenuous status. In the 1930s and when they struck again and finally won union recognition in the 1950s, Kohler workers wanted industrial relations that involved less surveillance over worker behavior and a more democratically constructed commitment to worker welfare than Hegemann or Kohler conceived.

Nor did strikers regard the front yards of private homes as inviolate as Kohler had maintained they were in his struggles with Hubbard over parking spaces. Especially in the long and fierce strike of the UAW against Kohler in the 1950s, strikers boldly marched up sidewalks and front yards to impel "scabs" to stop taking their jobs at the Kohler plant. Far from the factory's supporting serene islands of domestic independence, these workers saw private yards as legitimate spaces to engage industrial disputes (though in observance of the heavy policing of Kohler's residential districts they tended to enact such interpretations of space in neighboring Sheboygan rather than in the village).[30]

Striking workers advanced their own visions of the proper alignment of public and private space within the village as well. Early on in the 1950s strike the union's daily strike bulletin noted with frustration the absence of commercial spaces such as taverns or restaurants where strikers might have rested and regrouped within the town. From their perspective the design of Kohler around interdependent industrial and private residential spaces deliberately thwarted efforts of residents and workers to form their own civic associations independent of the company's civic visions. Their complaints recalled Hubbard's unrealized commercial center with its provision for more space outside the industrial and residential areas to rest, wait, and congregate. In the strikers' view, as less militantly in Hubbard's, "civic" space implied an independence from private industrial and residential control.[31]

The contrasting views of public versus private space as part of local identity that the Kohler strikes provoked were deeply divisive. The two strikes, especially the long 1950s battle, rent community feeling between the company, workers, and village and even divided neighborhoods and families in the village. Vigorous as strikers were in advancing their unbuilt visions of village space that would accommodate public debate, they never represented a vision of development common to all users of village space. Plenty of worker-residents in Kohler continued to embrace the vision of independent home ownership in a company-orchestrated civic life that Walter Kohler had imagined from the inception of the village. But even these more contented workers might venture new spatial demands at odds with the visions of the company and its planners, as when their plans for a swimming pool redirected the long debated designs for a more grandiose civic center. An example more prescient with respect to recent developments was the golf course proposed by the Kohler town council in the midst of the second strike (partially realized in a small golf facility by the early 1960s). Here users again echoed unbuilt visions of the early twentieth century—both Hegemann and Hubbard had proposed golf courses as part of their Kohler development plans, while Walter Kohler demurred in favor of letting local demand accumulate. At the same time, the resident-initiated golf course looked forward, ironically, to the village's late twentieth-century transformation into a resort dramatically reshaped for a public of luxury hospitality guests far removed from the home-owning workers for whom Walter Kohler had planned.[32]

Which brings us back to Henry Hubbard's efforts to make room for dreams and, finally, their status as historical archives. Though historians of Kohler's well-known industrial disputes have seen the industry's strikes as arising in part from dissatisfactions with arrangements in the village, few have looked to the strikers' archives for commentary on the spaces Kohler and his planners designed as they bore on the locality's identity. Even Hubbard's and Parker's many cast-off plans have been relegated to dusty drawers and distant archives, despite their firm's acknowledged leadership in planning the built environment at Kohler. To so subordinate the archives of the unbuilt to the materialized shape of the village itself—whatever one's assessment of its virtues or flaws—demonstrably diminishes our access to the varied identities that interested officials, planners, and users mobilized in their visions for the shapes the village might take. For many participants in Kohler's history, imaginary spaces gave shape to identities no less "real" than those that powerful actors were able to realize in directing the "actual" shape of the village. Historians of the built environment ignore these visions at the peril of restricting their narratives to a "reality," as Hubbard said, much smaller than the dreams for which the unbuilt environment has always made ample room.[33]

Notes

1 See Kathryn J. Oberdeck, "Class, Place, and Gender: Contested Industrial and Domestic Space in Kohler, Wisconsin, USA, 1920–1960," *Gender and History* 13 (April 2001): 97–137.

2 See for example Peter Hall, *Cities of Tomorrow: An Intellectual History of the Planning and Design of Cities in the Twentieth Century* (Oxford: Blackwell, 1988).

3 See for example Greg Hise and William Deverell, *Eden by Design: The 1930 Olmsted-Bartholomew Plan for the LA Region* (Berkeley: University of California Press, 2000).

4 For archival inevitability and the materiality of the local, see especially Achille Mbembe, "The Power of the Archive and Its Limits," and Martin Hall, "Blackbirds and Black Butterflies," both in Carolyn Hamilton, Verne Harris, Jane Taylor, Michele Pickover, Graeme Reid, and Razia Saleh, eds., *Refiguring the Archive* (Dordrecht: Kluwer Academic Publishers, 2002), 19–26; 333–61.

5 Margaret Crawford, *Building the Workingman's Paradise* (London: Verso, 1995).

6 On continuities and changes brought about by resort development, see Herbert V. Kohler, Jr., speech to Young Presidents Organization, American Club, Kohler, Wisconsin, December 7(?), 1982, Kohler Archives (hereafter KA) 5–160, 711: Village of Kohler, Master Plan #2 (1977), Speeches.

7 J. M. Hasenstab speech to Sheboygan County Board of Realtors, KA 5–100 659.2 Folder: Village of Kohler, Speeches; Christiane Crasemann Collins, "Hegemann and Peets: Cartographers of an Imaginary Atlas," introductory essay for Werner Hegemann and Elbert Peets, *The American Vitruvius: An Architects' Handbook of Civic Art* (New York: Princeton Architectural Press, 1988), xiii–xiv; Werner Hegemann, *Report on a City Plan for the Municipalities of Oakland & Berkeley* (Oakland and Berkeley: The Municipal Governments of Oakland and Berkeley and others, 1915) and *City Planning for Milwaukee: What It Means and Why It Must Be Secured* (Milwaukee: Wisconsin Chapter of the American Institute of Architects and Others, 1916).

8 Hegemann, *Report on . . . Oakland & Berkeley*, 11–16; Hegemann and Peets, *American Vitruvius*, 99–101; on Hegemann's blending of the preoccupations of the "City Beautiful" and the "City Functional," see Alan J. Plattus, "The American Vitruvius and the American Tradition of Civic Art," introductory essay for Hegemann and Peets, vii–xi.

9 KA 5–140 711; Village of Kohler; Folder: Early Plans 1916–1917.

10 Hegemann, *Report on . . . Oakland & Berkeley*, 15; Werner Hegemann to

Walter Kohler, December 20, 1916, KA 5–140 711, Village of Kohler, Folder: Early Plans—Hegemann & Peets; Walter J. Kohler (WJK) to Werner Hegemann, January 15, 1917, KA 5–140 711, Village of Kohler, Folder: Early Plans, 1916–1917.

11 On the rediscovery of Hegemann and Peets in Kohler history, see 1970s correspondence between the librarian and Peets scholar Caroline Shillaber and the Kohler official Richard Lemmerhirt, KA 5–140 711, Village of Kohler, Early Plans—Hegemann & Peets; Arnold R. Alanen and Thomas J. Peltin, "Kohler, Wisconsin: Planning and Paternalism in a Model Industrial Village," *Journal of the American Institute of Planners* 44 (1978): 145–59; Hasenstab speech to Sheboygan County Board of Realtors.

12 John Lillesand speech to Friends of Wisconsin State Historical Society, May 8, 1990, KA 5–100, 659.2.

13 Olmsted Brothers, "Preliminary Report on the Development of Kohler, Wisconsin . . . ," 16 Feb. 1925, Reel 373, MS 20,112.8, Container 417, Job File 7384, National Archives, Washington D.C. (hereafter Olmsted Records).

14 WJK to Henry V. Hubbard (HVH), July 27, 1925, Reel 373, MS 20,112.8, Container 417, Job File 7384, Olmsted Records; on Kohler's enthusiasm for Sousa's concerts in general, see extensive report on Sousa concert at dedication of Nature Theater in *Kohler of Kohler News*, Sept. 1919, 3–4; on Sousa's patriotic band fare, see Neil Harris, "John Philip Sousa and the Culture of Reassurance," in his *Cultural Excursions: Marketing Appetites and Cultural Tastes in Modern America* (Chicago: University of Chicago Press, 1990), 198–232.

15 WJK to HVH, Aug. 10, 1925, and for general discussion of parking, HVH to WJK, Jul. 13, Aug. 4, Aug. 19, 1925, Reel 373, MS 20,112.8, Container 417, Job File 7384, Olmsted Records.

16 HVH to WJK, Dec. 14, 1925; WJK to HVH, Dec. 21, 1925; HVH (or assistant) to WJK, Jan. 26, 1926; Reel 373, Container 417, Job File 7384, Olmsted Records.

17 Hegemann and Peets, Plan of Section W-1 of Kohler Wisconsin, June 6, h1917, Stack 5, Fl 5, KA; "Sketch Plan for the Development of the South Section of Kohler," Nov. 1, 1916, Stack 5, Fl 5, KA.

18 HVH to WJK, Jun. 9, 1926, Container 418, Reel 374, Job File 7384, Olmsted Records.

19 On the history of the "Greenleaf Tavern," see correspondence and historical material regarding its 1982 sale, KA 1–200 Kohler Co., 621.5 Dept. Files HVK Sr Exec.-WJK, 1930–1984.

20 WJK to Olmsted Bros., Jul. 16, 1926, Container 418, Reel 374, Job File 7384, Olmsted Records.

21 James C. Young, "A Model Town That Grew on a Prairie," *New York Times Magazine*, Oct. 11, 1931.

22 WJK to HVH, Dec. 15, 1926; HVH to WJK, Jan. 24, 1927; container 418, Reel 374, Job File 7384, Olmsted Records.

23 Walter J. Kohler address before Annual Dinner Meeting of Massachusetts Sanitary Club, Boston, November 10, 1920, prepared October 10, 1920, KA 5–100, 659.2, Village of Kohler—Speeches.

24 HVH to Jerry Donohue, Sept. 29, 1928, Container 418, Reel 374, Job File 7384, Olmsted Records.

25 Carl Rust Parker (CRP) to Herbert V. Kohler, Sr. (HVK), June 14, 1940, Container 418, Reel 374, Job File 7384, Olmsted Records.

26 Preliminary Plan showing Proposed Auditorium, Swimming Pool and Gymnasium, Olmsted Brothers, November 30, 1940; "Perspective of Proposed Memorial Auditorium," Olmsted Brothers, Nov. 30, 1940; KA.

27 On Kohler Memorial see KA 5–300, 625.8, Village of Kohler, Recreational Buildings, Kohler Memorial; on planning concern over the competition between the town's planned pool and the civic center see CRP to HVK, May 15, 1946, Container 418, Reel 374, Job 7384, Olmsted Records.

28 On the prelude to this strike see Walter Uphoff, *Kohler on Strike: Thirty Years of Conflict* (Boston: Beacon, 1966).

29 I have dealt with the particulars of such conflicts, elsewhere; see Oberdeck, "Class, Place, and Gender."

30 Walter Uphoff, *The Kohler Strike: Its Socioeconomic Causes and Effects* (Milwaukee: privately printed, 1935); on the existence of restrictive deeds forbidding the raising of animals, see 1943 correspondence between Herbert V. Kohler, Sr., and E. Albrecht, village president, on residents raising chickens during the war. KA 5–100.811 Village of Kohler Folder 38A, HVK, Sr. Files—Village Board 1926–49.

31 Kohler Local 833, UAW-CIO *Daily Strike Bulletin*, 1954.

32 On village requests for a golf course see especially W. Wandschneider to Herbert V. Kohler, October 8, 1957, in KA 5–100 Village of Kohler, Box 711, HVK Sr. Files—Village Board 1950–1963, Folder 38B. The golf course is pictured in the Kohler Co. pamphlet "Kohler of Kohler" (Kohler, Wis.: Kohler Co., 1963).

33 The author would like to thank Cheryl Prepster of the Kohler Archives for assistance with the Kohler Company materials from which some of this paper is drawn; Angela Miller, archivist for the Kohler Company, for permission to publish this material; and Ruth and Robert Maschke for their help and hospitality.

Marilyn Booth

Fiction's Imaginative Archive

and the Newspaper's Local Scandals

THE CASE OF NINETEENTH-CENTURY EGYPT

IN 1893, ZAYNAB FAWWAZ, an immigrant to Egypt from south Lebanon, declared that she would send her 500-page biographical dictionary of famous women, *Scattered Pearls among the Generations of Mistresses of Seclusion*, to Berthe Honoré Palmer for inclusion in the much-publicized women's library at the Chicago World Exposition. There, few browsers would have been able to read Fawwaz's Arabic-language biographies of Jeanne d'Arc, Maria Edgerton, or Eugénie of France, let alone her lives of Hani'a bt. Aws and many other renowned Arab women. But the tome itself constituted a representation, an object to be read: of contemporary Arab women's intellectual activity, of their awareness of and participation in a "women's world history," of their activism in a colonized metropole far from the capitals of Western feminisms at a moment shaped locally by European imperial and missionary reach as well as by local histories. For Fawwaz, that library as an archive of women's literary acts would have been incomplete without her contribution.

Fawwaz publicly inscribed her biographical dictionary as an alternative archive, grounds for and stemming from a differently inflected writing of history, when she complained in the preface that lives of "the most important renowned men of the past" had been written many times over, yet "amidst all this activity I have observed no one going to the other extreme, reserving even a single chapter in the Arabic tongue for half the human world, in which one might assemble women who attracted fame for their merits and shunned bad traits." Indeed, inscribing women's biographies, she also archived myriad contemporary essays by women as part of her prefatory material, to offer "a semantically full contemporary scene of Arab women writing and reading."[1]

But if Fawwaz was interested in materially representing Arab women's literary labor to an audience that was imagining "Egypt" not as a writing woman but rather as the belly dancer at the Exposition's Midway café—a representational scandal that shocked and distressed commentators in Egypt at the time—she was at least equally intent on giving local readers new maps around which to think gender politics. She chose to do so by publishing not only fierce essays in Cairo's nationalist press but also two historical novels. In this essay I consider one of those novels as a gendered rewriting of local history. If, in the late nineteenth century, female heroes were at the center of many Arabic literary narratives (those by men as well as those by women) and historical romance was a dominant fictional presence among Arab readers, how did the novel act as an archive for the writing of history? Excluded by virtue of gender assignment from the possibility of writing authoritative histories—chronicles, that other narrative form—what uses did Arab women begin to make of fiction in rewriting political histories of the Middle East from a (differently, and overtly) gendered perspective—a practice that has once again, at the end of a later century, emerged as a significant strand of Arabic fictional discourse?[2]

Highlighting the novel in this way also highlights by contrast the dependence on narrative of archival material that is assumed—by virtue of its presence in the archive—to be nonfictional and thereby somehow uncontaminated by the interested pressures that shape narrative. Laura Mayhall (in her essay in this volume) notes that even as researchers seek new ways of reading the archive, "the archive itself remain[s] essentially unproblematic, imagined as a fundamentally unbiased universe of potential histories." Of course, as Mayhall's history of the shaping of a preeminent suffragist archive reveals, the specific emplotments on which archives and their scholarly consumers silently rely are anything but "untainted" by story line. Furthermore, Middle Eastern archives have long been a source of contention, a space suspected by its constituents, scholarly and otherwise, as politically interested whether they are the spaces of colonial record or of local governmental entities keen to shape their own legacies. To see fictional narrative as an alternative site of archival imagining simply highlights the shifting and suspect nature of the archive.[3]

I set this analysis against the rise of another archive in Egypt, the site whence Fawwaz wrote: the daily newspaper, *not* as an archive of political narratives, economic fortunes, and "great-man history," but as a vehicle for and a shaping force in the emerging discursive centrality of gender politics in the public order. How were the public spaces of everyday negotiation constructed as gendered spaces through the rhetoric—and not simply the content—of the newspaper? Nationalist dailies of the 1890s, in their news items from the provinces, construct the female subject (whether adult or child) as both disruptive force and precious national commodity, in particular through items on prostitution and urban space on the one hand, and girls' education on the other. How did fictions and local newspapers formulate emergent definitions of a new female subject appropriate to a post-imperialized society wherein "modernity" was a capacity both desired and debated? The productive simultaneity of novel production and news addiction—in the form of the consumable daily newspaper with its multiple running narratives—has been remarked on for European nation-states as well as for colonized-and-emerging-nationalist societies: As alternative sources for the deeply gender-striated formation of a public sphere, were they mutually constitutive? What did they *tell* people about how to read?

Fawwaz's novel also acts as an archive of reading praxis. It is thus a doubled archive: one that the author of fiction built as a house of counter-histories and one that the literary critic reads now as a (rather one-sided) dialogue between an early novelist and her envisioned readers, a set of instructions on how to read fiction when the reading public for fiction was new and the routes were uncertain.[4] For the awkward doublings back and explanatory asides to the reader—leaving nothing at all to the reader's imagining or ability to read gaps in the plot—suggest more than Fawwaz's lack of experience, trying her hand at a form emerging from the historical chronicle, the belletristic anecdote or longer narrative, and the oral tale, while also nourished (if badly) by translations of European popular fiction circulating in Egypt. These structural features suggest also a communication act aimed at a very new audience for fiction, perhaps one that was substantially female.[5] This was a moment when narrative forms were especially fluid, when the same term, *riwaya*, could label what later became the distinctive genres of novel, playscript, and nonfiction account, and at a time when the boundaries of the nation and its future were equally unstable. Fawwaz's imagined history ignored customary boundaries of genre, fictionality and facticity, geography and gender, perhaps enacting Antoinette Burton's reminder that "women's historical memory has evidential status when and if it is read as an interpretive act: as neither truth nor fiction . . . but as a continual reminder of the historicity—and of course the political valences—of all traces from the past."[6]

In her essay in this volume, Kathryn Oberdeck draws a link between "spatial imaginaries" and the disruption of assumptions about material "truths," about the seeming inevitability that a built environment projects; other possibilities lurk in alternative archives that "escape the conventional archival mandate of proving something 'that actually existed' " and that forms the substance of conventional archives. Oberdeck argues that "traces" of what might have happened but did not "open up an archive and a process of historical construction that compares what was once possible to . . . versions of the inevitable[;] . . . imagined spaces can become measures of the boundaries around authorized histories of why materialized spaces came to be." I want to suggest that the historical novel can act similarly, as a ghost-archive, a record of alternative possibilities and alternative visions that also, through divergent narrative, highlights and shows as arbitrary the boundaries of the official record, in this case the chronicles of an event in south Lebanon. Fawwaz's version, animating the possibility that gender politics was central to this event, highlights the narrowly political boundaries of official historiography and marginalizes them in favor of other possibilities. Not only what *might* or could have been, but what indeed *may* have been.

A Shi'i Muslim from a south Lebanon non-elite family, Zaynab Fawwaz (1846?–1914) traveled to Egypt possibly as a servitor, inserted herself into the Islamic nationalist strand of public discourse in the era, and made herself into a fierce presence in the women's and nationalist presses.[7] Her two novels and one play were elements in her manifold public intervention in the realm of gender politics in Egypt, Lebanon, and Syria as the nineteenth century turned into the twentieth. Responding in her newspaper essays to male commentators on gender politics and national identity, Fawwaz argued not only for expanded female education funded by the state but also for women's right to waged employment outside the home and—enunciating her own visibility through her consistent interventions in the press—the imperative of including women's voices in a national and nationalist dialogue. Fawwaz's first historical novel, *Good Consequences, or The Lovely Maid of al-Zahira* (1899), emplotted a gender formation in process while subtly arguing against conservative challenges to its blueprint for gender relations.

When Fawwaz's novel came out in 1899, the magazine *Anis al-jalis* praised it as "full of exemplary lessons, worthy of the highest praise for its fine author whose likes, we hope, will multiply in this country."[8] Fawwaz prefaced her novel with a plea for the moral utility of fiction that was, she insisted, proximate to historical "truth." Her diction, molded in rhymed phrases that traditionally signaled learned prose, the "high" practice of literature, appeared intent on securing for this fiction a greater measure of respect than she feared might come its way:

> Since literary narratives are eminent among compositions whose perusal gives sheen to the mirror of thought, and whose pleasure disperses clouds by anxieties wrought; and since to the measure of their minds people derive from them remembrance and contemplation of their lot; and furthermore since those of greatest value and status are novels broaching the actual or representing events that are factual, I aimed to publish this pleasant account (which in its benefits is a veritable fount), because of its era's proximity to the age of presence and possibility, and its truancy from caravans on the paths of talk-of-what-once-was. I named it *The Lovely Maiden of al-Zahira* with an eye to the manifest events it enfolds, and I titled it *Good Consequences* for the wondrous developments it holds.[9]

Fawwaz insists on the worthy fiction's adherence to "the actual" and "the factual," and its proximity and relevance to the present, "the age of possibility." Writing history, it cannot dissociate itself from maps of the modern: the text announces self-distancing not from its inscription of the past but from (other) ways history had been imagined, from those "caravans on the paths of talk-of-what-once-was." Like *Anis al-jalis*'s announcement, the preface suggests that the novel is of moral benefit, as a work that will draw people to "contemplation of their lot." If Fawwaz's rhetoric was conventional and modest, it was also language that fiercely connected historical narrative to contemporary experience.

And what "exemplary lessons"—in the words of *Anis al-jalis*—would the novel teach? Trajectories of its characters suggest detours not so much from events of the past as from regimes of gender organization associated with a local past and equally with discourses of nostalgia shaping constructions of that past—the novel as "truant": as mapping an alternative route to present and future possibility, one that takes up available historical narratives to suggest that they codified moments of political failure and weakness but avoided their imbrication with customary, and outmoded, gender regimes. Rewriting this history was urgent for its temporal proximity to "the age of presence and possibility." An announcement appended to the preface warns that new narratives of a very recent past are obliged to exhume and examine a struggle over "honor" that left real victims and demarcated a villain:

> In this novel I deliberately changed the names of people and places, to avoid mention of those who are still alive and to protect the honor of noble houses sullied by one of their sons, for whom it was a matter of little consequence to abase his honor for the sake of obtaining his earthly desires. He clothed his family in a garment of shame, a garment reworn each time that events tested him. May God protect and shield us [from such events and people]. (2–3 [37])

In fact, if the novel rewrites recent history, names are barely concealed, while Fawwaz's allusion to living souls teases the reader with its assertion of proximity. The struggle plotted in the novel mirrors an attested rivalry between 'Ali Bek al-As'ad (1821–65) and his paternal cousin, Tamir Bek Husayn, for the regional rule (*'imara*) of Jabal 'Amil, south Lebanon (the text's Jabal Husn), during the widespread social unrest of the early 1860s. 'Ali Bek (like Fawwaz's hero Shakib), had succeeded his uncle Hamid, and Tamir Bek (like Fawwaz's hero Tamir b. Hasan), who was the elder (as in the novel), challenged 'Ali's right in a series of confrontations.[10] Although Fawwaz does portray rivalries and alliances among clans of both "Jabal Husn" and Hawran (the Syrian agricultural plains to the Jabal's east), she does not introduce the political maneuverings of the Ottoman governors of the area, who appear (according to conventional sources) to have exploited the rivalry between 'Ali and Tamir.

Fawwaz, it seems, preferred to focus on internal family politics and the contours of the local. *Good Consequences* gives the rivalry a gendered dimension lacking in conventional histories of this struggle; in the novel, women and the question of patriarchal right motivate the conflict's sustenance and its demise. Fawwaz gestures toward the archival possibilities of fiction in setting up—and defending—her project: if these are not the "scattered pearls" of Fawwaz's biographical dictionary, they are stories rooted in a family whose very names she maintains in this "fiction," thereby raising the question, through her coy naming practices, of what indeed differentiates the historical novel from the historical chronicle. The women were lost in that more official historical memory of this feuding family. Here, it is the women who become the center of the story, the pivots of Fawwaz's alternative rendering of history. Fawwaz takes it upon herself to make an intervention in writing this history, somewhat in the way that the Bakunin family archive, as John Randolph tells its life story in this volume, was a product of the Bakunin women's active shaping, for "restrictions on female participation in . . . public life [meant] they could not defend their ideals. . . . Fashioning the . . . archive . . . offered an opportunity to create a public role for themselves as the family's archivists"—a point that indicates the critical and elusive role of women as archivists of a nation.

The novel begins with a direct address to the reader as traveler, drawing on the familiar Arabic genre of travel and discovery literature while suggesting that to read is to take a voyage of displacement in space and time. The reader—as "visitor" and "scout," as someone who "travels" and "roves" (*sa'ih, ta'if;* 8 [41])—is participant in the narrative. We are to set our countenances for Syria and Palestine, and to "listen": an invocation echoing women's legacies of oral storytelling to signal a path divergent from those of written chronicles that gave these events their official rendering. With this imagery the narrative echoes the preface's metaphor, playing truant from the pliable caravans of yore and instead setting out to trace its own path through time and space. And in fact this novel abounds in the spatial movements of its female characters, who are not restricted by the *harim*, the demarcated space of idealized elite female experience, the domestic space wherein women and children were protectively separated from men to whom they were not closely related (though the position of first cousin, a relation and yet also a potential marriage partner and indeed traditionally often the ideal prospective marriage partner, is in a sense liminal, both "inside" and "outside" the family, a point with which Fawwaz plays, as we shall see). These female characters map the spaces beyond the paternal household as paths traversable by the female subject; what was then Ottoman Syria is mapped here as feminine space, countering the construction of histories as the public deeds of men and the existing construction of this particular family history as that of political feuds between men. At the same time, the harim is inscribed as a space of power, wherein men come to seek the counsels and decisions of women.

The story proper opens with a description of the citadel or *qasr* of Tibnin (the town of Fawwaz's birth), erected by Crusader forces in 1104 C.E. Despite the text's insistence on its historical provenance, the setting that birthed this family feud is fairy-tale-like. Yet even the fairy-tale is shaped thoroughly by the modern. The beautiful palace, surrounded by gardens, so high that it lies within the clouds, shelters a great emir within, father to four sons who were "given the finest upbringing." This phrasing echoes nineteenth-century Arabic discourse on the crucial contribution of knowledgeable and responsible child rearing to the community's political future; even more so is this articulated in the description of the emir's daughter-in-law as a princess not only "of the finest beauty" but also "superbly able in the management of a household" (8–9 [41]). The fiction thus takes up the era's polemics on the exemplary modern woman—among them biographies of "Famous Women" as guides to right conduct that Fawwaz's biographical dictionary introduced into Arab elites' gender debates, for the exemplary "Famous Woman" was always a consummate home manager.[11] Fawwaz announces through this figuration that she will weave contemporary conceptualizations of gender politics into the fabric of her novel.

It is the grandchildren of the patriarch-emir who enact this tale; Fawwaz constructs a detailed genealogy of the players, three sets of cousins whose fathers, all but one of the four well-brought-up brothers, have died. Tamir—"oldest and wiliest" of the cousins—resents their living uncle's preference for cousin Shakib. Fearful that Shakib will inherit the princedom, Tamir recruits a gang to kill him, explaining to them that since he, Tamir, is the eldest—idiomatically, "the one most guided by reason" an epithet that resonates ironically throughout—he should succeed his uncle.[12]

Fawwaz sets up the plot according to a succession struggle that must have been known through oral narratives in her birthplace as well as having been recorded in chronicles. Yet it is not the male cousins' rivalry that animates the plot but rather their female cousin Fari'a's struggle to avoid Tamir's pursuit of a marriage that he also regards as his birthright, although it is the alliance thereby cemented with Fari'a's elder brother Aziz which Tamir wants.

Tamir's henchman Talib, "craftier than a fox, more perfidious than a leopard," offers to kill Shakib and asks for payment, which Tamir promises (12 [44]), setting up an opposition consistent throughout the novel whereby male characters fall on either side of a divide: villains operate for material gain whereas "good masculinity" is equated with working for "honor." A gunshot from beyond the interlaced tree branches wounds Shakib, who is carried to his cousins' home. His cousin Fari'a is instructed by her older brother to care for "the son of her paternal uncle" (customarily the perfect prospective marriage partner, first cousin on the father's side!). She is to avoid leaving him "to the female servants." The text thereby articulates another common trope within turn-of-the-century elite polemics on the exemplary woman who, no matter how wealthy, was to be able and willing to assume every household task, a discourse that attacked and then denied the modern household's dependence on the labor of other women.[13] When the girl complains to her mother—for she has never met this cousin—her mother tells her to do her family duty, preserving the cousin's comfort "as she would her brother's" (18 [47]).

When Shakib awakes, he deduces that this is his cousin, for "he believed it impossible that any women from outside the family [*nisa' ajnabiyyat*] would have come to him without a veil, and there was nothing in the appearance of this fine young maiden that would lead one to think she was a servant of the palace." Shakib is strongly attracted to his cousin's "sensitivity and gentleness," to her protestation of sisterly loyalty, and perhaps to the shyness she manifests. But there is more. "He found her speech pleasant, and began to question her, to elicit the breadth of her knowledge and the geography of that region, and she answered every question he put to her, with her strong and quick intelligence and her eloquent phrasing, and she took possession of his heart" (18–19 [48]). The sequencing is crucial, for it is only after Fari'a passes this geography test that Shakib's sentiments move from attraction to love; it is the educated and articulate young woman who inspires the strongest emotions. Fari'a seems to carry the lineage of the ancient Arab female poets, yet she epitomizes the modern educated girl whose trained abilities both console and save her. Weeping at Shakib's departure, she soon breaks into poetry, but finds ultimate solace in a book. Throughout, her ability to write and to read letters is crucial. And after Fari'a has been abducted by Tamir, as Shakib searches for traces of her at a ruined campsite (a gesture to Arabic poetry's ancient heritage, wherein the lover begins his lament at the abandoned campsite), he finds a book "that she had been reading to make time pass, an entertainment in her exile, a means to lighten the agonies of loneliness" (186 [158]). As the novel refracts a local politics of succession through a narration of feminine authority, it institutes reading, writing, and mapping territory as feminine acts that order local society, instituting a series of mutually agreeable companionate marriages and expelling a political practice premised on force, competition, and sequestration.

Through a convoluted sequence of abductions, disguises, shootings and stabbings, letters gone astray, head gardeners amenable to bribery, a near-drowning, meetings coincidental and planned, mysterious horsemen, elusive near-resolutions, tribal raids, escapes, and heart-stopping poetic declamations, Fari'a escapes from and manages to elude Tamir, crisscrossing the mountains and plains of Lebanon and Hawran. The protagonist's movement through space—outside the home, away from the spaces of female seclusion—maps a female subjectivity inscribed within companionate marriage as the proper future of the national-cum-nationalist female, but one that deploys its own desire to shape that future as demarcated by female desire and not by patriarchal will—and as a future not determined by seclusion or compelled marriage. It thus marks a moment, in the 1890s, when elite Arab women were speaking up on behalf of their own interests, and collectively through writing, arguing their own agenda for insertion into the nationalist modernist project of family building.

While the marriage is introduced as a scheme to further Tamir's political ambitions, as the novel progresses the marriage story takes center stage, subsuming the more overtly political conflict among men. Whether this tale, too, was one that Fawwaz might have heard from her aunts or women in the neighborhood—whether it was part of a feminine archive of local genealogies—is open to question, but what is clearer is that this story has not made its way into the written annals of southern Lebanon, and it may well be invention. In either case, that Fari'a's tale and those of her friends increasingly organize the narrative is indisputable. Twice abducting Fari'a, Tamir is pursued by her brothers and by Shakib, not for his political schemes, but for his transgression of family honor, while it is Fari'a herself who vocalizes his crime and suggests her threatened suicide as a sacrifice on behalf of other women:

> Don't you see that with this act [of abduction], you have lost your honor and your ancestors' as well, behaving like untamed folk of the mountain who lack conscience and religion, when rights of relationship and family honor require you to ward off from me anyone who aims to mar my honor, and to protect me in need with your blood and property?. . . . I am astonished to see how you can speak to me of marriage when I am far from my family. . . . To commit this crime . . . gives you eternal mention on history's pages. As for me, my death means life for women of purity and mistresses of chastity. (160, 168 [142, 147])

In her essays in the press, Fawwaz carefully marks out the spaces of a nationalist and Islamic modernist female subjectivity that did not dispute the outlines of an Islamic modernist state program but sought to urge attention to ways the project was not (yet) a smoothly and painlessly attainable one for women. In line with that program, this narrative comes to a tidy close with five simultaneous weddings (arranged by the hero's and heroine's mothers) and the disappearance and later death of the villain. Alliances and friendships instituted during the long quest are molded into the service of the new emir, thereby maintaining a prior sociopolitical hierarchy, albeit one cleansed of villains. The new reigning pair's closest friends—those characters nearest in social rank to the wedded cousins—are given residence inside the fairy-tale *qasr*, becoming the couple's retinue and companions.

If, in the end, Fari'a and her female companions disappear inside the walls of the patriarchal qasr—domestic space, political center, a fortress in every sense—they are seen to have rewritten society according to their vision of gender relations. The contest between "good" and "evil" here is one between good ruler and tyrant only in the sense that the very definition of each hinges on adherence to a specific concept of the gender order. Tamir's patriarchal absolutism (portrayed, interestingly, as garnering loyalty only through mercenary means) is resisted specifically through the symbolic siting of the book as the mark of modern femininity, which institutes Shakib's sexual desire but also locates his legitimacy to rule. In contrast, Tamir knows only of Fari'a's physical beauty, not of her mental prowess. Female desire inscribes a modern masculine subjectivity formed around mutual respect, consent, intellect, and monogamous heterosexual desire. In this context, other male players in the drama are key, especially brothers. Fari'a's elder brother (according to customary patriarchal practice, her de facto guardian), to whom Tamir goes expecting help, voices what is often the role of the father or elder brother in the era's biographies of "Famous Women": "I must seek her opinion in this," he tells Tamir. "If she accepts, that will be my wish. If she objects, I cannot force her to do what you want, because she has a mind, and often I have relied on her in my own serious concerns. And the question of marriage is important: upon it depends the sphere of her life" (36 [59]). Disappointed, Tamir "had hoped Aziz would give the command [to marry him] without consulting her" (36 [60]), in other words, that he would exercise patriarchal prerogative, disregarding her wishes. Further critique of forced arranged marriages ensues when Zarifa, Fari'a's loyal maid and companion, tells Tamir: "A covenant does not happen in this way. No, by God, for if marriage took place by force, you would not find a single flourishing home in this world" (42 [63]).[14]

Devoid of Aziz's ambivalence as the elder who must struggle with the pull of duty since he is effectively head of the family, the younger brother, Khalid, is Fari'a's loyal supporter throughout, insisting both on her right to decide on her marriage partner and on Tamir's villainous qualities, while also acting the astute observer. "[Tamir] is in love with himself, and can't distinguish today from yesterday"; "All his acts are despicable, and there is nothing lovable about him" (37, 67 [60, 80]). The younger brother derives little benefit from a patriarchal system that privileges age as well as maleness; Fawwaz sketches perceptively a subordinate elite masculine position that permits both vision and sympathy, while his status as a son gives him at least a voice. He is able to support his sister unambiguously and rejects the use of deception that their mother and elder brother consider. "With the eye of perception," insists Khalid, "she has learned . . . that which requires his rejection" (66 [80]). With the freer social status of a subordinate in the ruling system, Khalid has been able to find out the truth: Tamir's "morals have become widely known, but you don't know because you don't sit with those who would tell you, and if you do, they are too awed by you. But I sit with whomever I want, and they tell me" (66 [80]).

The novel inscribes an ideal of masculinity that sites legitimate political authority in the individual who cedes authoritarian patriarchal privilege, first and foremost through deference to an emerging notion of feminine selfhood predicated on bodily self-discipline and a public performance of modesty that allow the expression of newly sanctioned desires for mobility, (limited) autonomy, intellectual development, and exchange. The ideal masculine, here, is also implicitly an elite construction, one that enacts a beneficent patriarchal social role eschewing coercion in favor of kindly suasion across a broader social canvas: able to inspire followers rather than having to pay them off, this figure treats individuals lower on the social hierarchy with respect, follows established rules of fair play in combat, whether collective or individual, and offers infinite generosity to those of all social strata rather than only the lodging of necessary guests.[15] The novel archives a modern displacement of the notion of "honor" in a patriarchal system: repeatedly, characters voice the claim that Tamir does not show proper regard for "honor" in the sense of his duty to protect his female cousin Fari'a. If this is a received notion of gender relations, though, "honor" is inscribed here as respect for Fari'a and her desires rather than as the policing role of keeping her secluded from non-related men. Indeed, Fari'a and the other female characters come in repeated contact with such men; it is the women themselves who preserve their "honor," inseparable from their own goals and desires.

In the text's spatial mapping, its cultural geography as articulated through the movements of female characters, Fawwaz questions the gendered distribution of space as integral to formation of the gendered subject. The space of the harim—private space, that in which family honor is protected through the separation of women and children from men to whom they are not related—is not the only space in which the young elite female subject moves. Furthermore, the harim is the heart of the household, that space where decisions are made. The narrative's sons and male cousins enter the harim to pay respect to their mothers and aunts—but also to seek decisions. Fawwaz draws upon a long and well-attested history, across Islamicate societies, of powerful elite women whose voices were politically determinative.[16] Meanwhile, one marker of Tamir's base character is his lack of respect for boundaries of gendered sociality: repeatedly, he bursts into the harim without seeking permission.

A tempered rejection of patriarchal right as experienced by elite Arab women thus organizes this novel, as does construction of a new notion of desired masculinity that is evidently in formation across numerous forms of writing in this era. I argue elsewhere that this changing masculine subjectivity—or ideal—is implicit but unspoken in elite men's writings "on women," the unacknowledged "man question" that Fawwaz's novel reveals to be at the heart of her historical imaginary and suggests as crucial to new imaginings of social space.[17]

One sign of that unnamed discourse on masculinity that pervades texts of the time is the prevalence of female protagonists in the late-nineteenth-century novel, and indeed their centrality is posed as the very titles of those novels. To juxtapose this novel with one by Fawwaz's contemporary and fellow Syrian, Jurji Zaydan (1861–1914), is instructive.[18] Zaydan's ambitious series of historical novels, spanning Arab-Islamicate history, featured female heroines, who more often than not provided Zaydan his titles, though significantly these are more often epithetic labels than individual names, the heroine as representative of her station in life rather than an individualized character: *The Virgin of Quraysh, Young Woman of Ghassan, Girl of Karbala', Bride of Farghana, Young Woman of Qayrawan*—as well as the named *Armanusa the Egyptian, al-'Abbasa sister of Rashid, Shajarat al-Durr*. The abundance of these epithetic titles suggests at the least a recognizable nationalist implantation of the female—and of the nation—at the heart of novel-writing in that era. But these novels differently archived the nation as a gender-ordered entity, for the gender order of Zaydan's *Armanusa al-Misriyya* (1896 or 1898) is one based on the dutiful daughter; its female protagonist is far more passive than is Fawwaz's Fari'a, and I see in these two figures alternate renderings of historical moments and divergent mappings of a national future around differently imagined father-daughter axes. If "archive" suggests a fixity, a fixing of boundaries around what counts as history, then Fawwaz's novel revisits those boundaries and demolishes them through the movement across space of her female characters. Fawwaz's archive is that of the absences in the available historical narratives of that family, as they have been remembered in national histories.

What does it mean that Fawwaz chooses to set the novel, not in the urban space of Cairo or Damascus, in both of which she had dwelt by this time, but rather in the mountains of south Lebanon and the plains of Hawran? The narrative enacts female presence and vocality in a manner directly in contrast to public inscriptions of female presence in Egypt's urban social space, in the pages of the daily newspaper, a political presence less than three decades old in Egypt when Fawwaz's book appeared.[19] Women in urban space were overwhelmingly written into the newspaper as negative presences. Perusing letters and regular dispatches of local news from around the nation—a collocation of stories that mapped a new nation as subject to parallel issues of regulation from the far south to the northern tip of the Delta—elicits concern about women's performance in public, their "interruptions" of male space, although it is important to note that young men were also a target of criticism. Fragments from one nationalist newspaper—one in which Fawwaz occasionally wrote—sketch this mapping of female space, as in a letter from an Alexandria resident:

> I sought to attend Friday prayers on the 27th of Ramadan at the mosque of Sidi Abu al-Abbas, but this large mosque was jammed with worshipers and I found no space. I resolved to perform my religious duty adjacent to the mosque with a group of worshipers. As the collective prayer commenced, worshipers could hear nothing but the talk of women who were pressing in on the men at prayer, giving them headaches with the racket they were making. One woman was quarreling with another, while over here another shushed her children, and still another complained to her companion about how bad things were with

her husband. . . . No sooner did the prayer end than I saw . . . about six women surrounding two youths, one a sailor in the Egyptian Navy and the other in civilian clothes. They were all party to this flirtatious exchange, fully in sight of these worshipers at the mosque in their state of piety.

Since this is contrary to right conduct and religious practice, I wanted to address these people, but I feared that the results of my intervention would cause general discomfort or would set the worshipers against them. So I left the mosque area promptly to fetch a policeman who would thwart this inde-cent act. Indeed, I found Sergeant no. 1348 near the mosque entrance, on his way out. . . . He appeared concerned, but as soon as he reached the gate his pace slowed. After all, he claimed, the government man talking to and teasing the women at the mosque was also a member of the police, and his own orders did not permit him to call off the man since they were of the same service and rank. . . . I draw the attention of the authorities to this sort of thing, unbefitting as it is to public conduct, especially at times of worship. (Name withheld)[20]

Concern about "public conduct" was still more starkly represented in an ongoing commentary on prostitution, or rather, on prostitutes' claim-ing of public space. In the town of Zaqaziq, "People are complaining about prostitutes who go about the city streets with their faces uncovered, speak-ing words that breach moral bounds. We direct the authorities' attention to such matters."[21] Three years before, a particularly assiduous correspon-dent from the Fayyum, an oasis town south of Cairo, had noted that prostitutes

have so multiplied and pervaded the town that a person can hardly walk through the streets without seeing a great many around him. They compete to exchange words with him, and if he is a man of upright and honorable na-ture, making no response, they pelt him with the stones of foul language. . . . It is astounding that some have procured sites alongside respectable people on the pretext that they are women of chastity and protected honor, innocent of all that has been attributed to them. If a neighbor remonstrates against them for the immoral ways in which they conduct themselves, they shower him with curses . . . if he goes looking for the help of a policeman, he finds none nearby. . . . Everyone knows the harms that come to good folk when such women are left to do as they please, for most are afflicted with syphilis, whose outcome cannot be other than bodily destruction, weak bones, and corrupted reproduction. . . . We hoped to see a law at whose boundary they would stop, in the name of protecting the sanctity of morals. But this hope was lost at the gate of the freedom they enjoy. . . . On the public's behalf we demand from the authorities a law on these women.[22]

From towns across the country came complaints that prostitutes were moving into "respectable neighborhoods"; the anxiety centered not on the existence of prostitution but on a perceived lapsing of boundaries wherein prostitutes are the agents of spatial chaos and moral decay:

> Women [falsely] claiming chastity and the protection afforded by good family have grown numerous near the domiciles of respectable women. It is now a daily occurrence to hear reports of their acts and ugly plans, comprising reprehensible behavior and transgressions of honor and morality. . . . It is not sufficient that those female tricksters embellish their words, flatter and dupe individuals in their acts, and attach themselves to scions of eminent family and lineage. . . . The tricks they devise . . . have proliferated so that now we have come to expect the greatest evils.[23]

The rhetoric of the female trickster played on the long-established trope of "women's wiles," deflecting responsibility from customers, pimps, or the socioeconomic circumstances (whether in Europe or locally) that had landed these women in prostitution. This was a rhetoric of female agency as weakening the nation through the communication of physical disease to men and a corrupting proximity to women "of good families," all spatially represented in women's movement into public space. Women who broke gender custom were part of the everyday social fabric the newspaper archived:

> A woman who claims she is among the chaste and protected got in the habit of going into one of the foreigners' bars every night and getting drunk, so that word got around and her deeds were on every tongue. The police mounted a watch to seize her as she came out in a state of intoxication, her judgment gone and her mind lost. They filed the obligatory report, and we anticipated her punishment at the hands of the law on the basis of the warped behavior, licentiousness, and corrupt morals for which she was notorious. It is beyond doubt that her presence among the respectable is unsupportable to good manners, especially since her slyness and cunning have damaged many who know nothing of reprehensible behavior.[24]

The newspaper becomes an advocate, a mediator between populace and government, as these correspondents offer mundane events on the local street as proof of government irresponsibility and inaction. That such stories often appear juxtaposed to news of national and international political affairs, and are not relegated to back pages, reminds us that conventions of journalistic proportionality to which we are accustomed are both recent and arbitrary. Perhaps the newspaper's "failure" to prioritize stories through spatial placement unwittingly centers the local skirmishes of gender politics appropriately. But if the organized nature of the newspaper— like the official archive—makes it appear that everything is *there*, that no other stories are necessary, then Fawwaz's novel, like other writings by women at the time, reminds the reader of the gaps that categorizations of information mask.

The paper also, if rarely, archives an emergence of new institutions of gender formation, for the other site where females appear is the school. One week after Fayyum's correspondent complained of being surrounded by prostitutes, he noted:

> Among praiseworthy feats is that of Khatun Maryam Gabriel in founding a girls' school in Fayyum, in which will be taught the foreign languages, French and English, and sorts of hand work. May God reward her generously for her service to the girls of our nation. What amplifies our delight is this project's swift success; the number of students has grown, and all are daughters of Fayyum's eminent and notable men.[25]

So new were girls' schools that their end-of-year rituals were reported in the national press—and on this occasion, on the front page, perhaps because the orator was the daughter of an extremely prominent, politically active family in Cairo.

> Yesterday, the Khayriyya Girls' School located on Darb al-Gamamiz . . . was decked out with banners, flowers . . . and His Majesty the Khedive's portrait. . . . There attended the ceremony many eminent men who were shown [student] handwork. . . . After recitation of verses from the Noble Qur'an the ceremony opened with a speech delivered by one pupil, Ulwiyya, daughter of Abd Allah Basha Yakan. . . . A literary narrative was acted, with music performed during it . . . and the attendees left talking of this school's fine qualities.[26]

Again the press acted as advocate, urging fathers (and, rarely, mothers) to send their daughters to school, repeatedly advertising opportunities in their dispatches, consonant with nationalist rhetoric on the patriotic duty

of parents: "Some time ago a girls' school was started here. . . . It has manifested the signs of success and progress. Many notables have sent their
daughters. . . . We urge the eminent to concern themselves with training
their daughters, for tomorrow they will become the mothers of the country's sons, household managers who need training and economy."[27]

In the sense that the novel and the news both serve as supplications, as
statements of the relation between the subject and the state but as seen
from the subject's perspective as applying to the state for legitimacy—for
the authority to speak and the right to be heard—*Good Consequences* and
these news items are differently genre-d and gendered claimants to the
same public discursive space. Fawwaz's novel situates itself in the space
between the stories of prostitutes in respectable neighborhoods and the
announcements of girls acting in skits in new schools. Fawwaz's narrative
is the story that the newspaper does not archive. It is a story of female
agency that emanates from but does not remain within the harim. It is a
story of young women reading and writing.[28] It is a story of women
insisting, if not on transgressing all boundaries of customary practice, then
on redefining some.

Moreover, Fawwaz rewrites the trope of "women's wiles." In her narrative it is wily women who know how to resist and thwart the violent acts of
men taking patriarchal privilege as absolute right. (And the dangerous
"wiles" are men's.) Fawwaz draws on stock characters of oral narrative.
Paralleling the two aristocratic mothers who impress familial duty on their
children (and remain within their qasrs) are the *'awagiz*, elderly women
who mediate for good or for ill. The two elderly women in *Good Consequences*—one aids the villain's attempts to kidnap his cousin, and the other
competently harbors escaping women—are figures from Arabic oral storytelling. Though formulaic characters, they are not gratuitous. As social
mediators they are able to blur class and gender boundaries. Umm Zahida,
a cultivator married to a shepherd, uses her age-derived freedom—and the
greater liberty afforded non-elite women—to help younger women, while
her daughter carries letters between friends and lovers.

The accumulation of detail—sometimes tedious and perhaps partly due
to Fawwaz's inexperience as a fiction writer—fills out a gender and status
regime more fluid than that of the city. Thickly described within the
Bedouin and agrarian world of the Hawran especially, social practices
infusing the novel suggest not an invading regime of "modernity" but

rather a system that is always already present, inevitable, and indigenous, though laced with elements of modernity such as the *assumption* that girls read and write.[29] Women's prerogatives take on a protective role. The Bedouin emir Musaylima, to whom Tamir brings Fari'a and in whose encampment he plans to forcibly marry her, resists Tamir's demand for a wedding with the reminder that he can only write the marriage contract after preparations for the *zafaf* (bridal procession) are completed, and "that can only be done by the women, since it is one of their specialties, not men's. It is most suitable that she join the women now." This keeps Tamir away from Fari'a. "Tamir obeyed, but he was angry . . . seeing that Musaylima had taken away his freedom" (194 [164]). Fari'a is drawn into this harim as a protective space, a fluid one, the women's tent.

> She found their reception tent beautiful, furnished with Persian carpets and Indian cushions. There were the daughters of the Bani Khalid, in their beauty, wearing headcloths adorned with gold, strings of pearl and amber round their necks, bangles and bracelets on their arms, and anklets on their legs.
>
> They welcomed her warmly and were dazzled by her beauty. . . . The servant girls brought coffee, and they drank; and food, and they ate. From the time she had left al-Zahira, Fari'a had not eaten well, except on that day, and that was due to the warmth and gentleness of the women of Bani Khalid. (196 [165])

The women's tent with its objects and practices offers a temporary home where Fari'a can nourish herself. The tent's interior—unlike the paternal home's harim—is described; it is not nebulous space. The women's tent, an archive within an archive, is a reminder of other histories.[30] Its furnishings inscribe a cosmopolitan nomadic life where the amenities of trade—Persian carpets, Indian cushions—not only are the stuff of daily life but also gesture east rather than west. Fawwaz's female characters are emphatically not "tainted" by the objects of dangerous Westernization, consumption draining a national economy and fueling the unhealthy freedoms and desires of modern youth, as the faraway newspapers of Cairo were already bemoaning in this decade. Those accounts, like the stories of prostitutes and girls' schools, are part of the archive against which Fawwaz writes, an archive as "the cultural record of texts and contexts bringing these stories into relief." For, as Randy Bass also notes, "Knowledge-making depends on the creative straining of the story against the archive. That's where meaning lives."[31]

Roberto González Echevarría traces a path of "archival fiction" as sedi-
menting the history of the novel in Latin America. The novel emerges as
an obsessive search for origins, as "prefigur[ing] the economy of loss and
gain of the Archive, the origin unveiled."³² Though Echevarría is firmly
historicizing his inquiry, I find his mapping of the Latin American novel's
trajectory suggestive for the different history of Arabic fiction under colonial constraints. The novel's mimetic act for Echevarría is a rewriting of
"truth-bearing" texts that assert their role as "mirroring" social reality; the
novel thereby exposes these authoritative texts (which bring European
colonizing authority, as specific forms of writing, to bear on and discipline
target locales) as "simulacra" of the authority to speak, to name. If the
novel—in the Arabic as in the Latin American tradition—rewrites history
to construct "origins," and if those "origins" are imbricated with the law as
determinative language, in Fawwaz's novel it is the law of the father that is
exposed as an "origin" to be rewritten for and by the future. Outside the
house of the father—and perhaps outside the legislature of the urban elite
male nationalist—this law is rewritten through the resistant remappings of
the young female subject as protagonist of the text.

That Fawwaz situates this story far from Cairo's newspapers may suggest a desire to imagine an alternate space of possible female agency and
national efficacy, as well as to dwell in the forests of her childhood, which
she lovingly describes. It may also be a gesture to imagining a space larger
than, or different than, the nation. That she chose a historical framework
set in a moment of political crisis in her homeland but emphasized a family
story wherein the politics of gender displaced the politics of national,
ethnic, and religious division might be an archival gesture to a new balance of historical imaginaries. Zaynab Fawwaz found this rewriting crucial
to imagining her own future and those of other women—a future of
alternatives for Fari'a's "women of purity," a future of *Good Consequences*.

Notes

1 Marilyn Booth, *May Her Likes Be Multiplied: Biography and Gender Politics in
Egypt* (Berkeley: University of California Press, 2001), 8, 5. I want to thank Antoinette Burton and the participants in the Research Workshop, Center for Middle East Studies, New York University, as well as an anonymous reader, for their
contributions to this essay.
2 On fiction and gender-centered historiography in and on the Middle East,

see Marilyn Booth, "Middle East Women's and Gender History: State of a Field," special issue on "New Directions in Women's History," *Journal of Colonialism and Colonial History* (e-journal) 4, 1 (2003), http://muse.jhu.edu/journals/cch.

3   I am grateful to Elizabeth Frierson for pushing me on this point.

4   Antoinette Burton points to the double archiving that narratives of memory enact: domestic space acts as the archive from which the author constructs her histories of home-and-nation; this narrative of home space in turn produces, for the historian as its reader, "an archive from which a variety of counter-histories of colonial modernity can be discerned." *Dwelling in the Archive: Women Writing House, Home, and History in Late Colonial India* (Oxford: Oxford University Press, 2003), 5.

5   Space constraints preclude analysis of the novel's rhetorical underpinnings, but this is an aspect of the text's historicity I want to mention.

6   Burton, *Dwelling*, 25.

7   Much of Fawwaz's life remains elusive; I am chasing it as part of a substantial study on her. On women's journals see Beth Baron, *The Women's Awakening in Egypt: Culture, Society, and the Press* (New Haven: Yale University Press, 1994).

8   *Anis al-jalis* 2, 6 (June 30, 1899): 236.

9   Zaynab Fawwaz, *Riwayat Husn al-'awaqib aw Ghadat al-Zahira* (Cairo: Matba'at Hindiyya, 1899 [1316]), 2 [37]; reprinted as *Husn al-'awaqib (riwaya)/al-Hawa wa'1-wafa' (masrahiyya)*, ed. Fawziyya Fawwaz (Beirut: al-Majlis al-thaqafi li-Lubnan al-janubi, 1984). References to the republished version appear in brackets.

10   Muhammad Jabir Al Safa, *Tarikh Jabal 'Amil* (Beirut: Dar al-Nahar, 2nd printing, 1981), 51–61, 158–62.

11   Booth, *May Her Likes*, chap. 5.

12   "The one most guided by reason," *al-arshad (sinn al-rushd*, age of majority).

13   On this classed discourse in biography, see Booth, *May Her Likes*, chap. 5. Burton notes a similar troping in the elite family history of Janaki Majumdar, whose focus on the household does not include family servants' work (*Dwelling*, 46).

14   This novel is fascinating in its construction of socioeconomic and status boundaries as permeable especially among women, a subject beyond this essay's scope.

15   A distinction made explicitly between Shakib and Tamir (chap. 28). Numerous times, "good guys" and "bad guys" are contrasted through opposing behaviors.

16   On this trope in "Famous Women" biography, see Booth, *May Her Likes*. On women, power, and the harem, see Leslie Peirce, *The Imperial Harem: Women and Sovereignty in the Ottoman Empire* (New York: Oxford University Press, 1993).

17   Marilyn Booth, "*Woman in Islam*: Men and the 'Women's Press' in Turn-of-the-Century Egypt," *International Journal of Middle East Studies* 33, 2 (2001): 171–201.

18   Marilyn Booth, "On Gender, History . . . and Fiction," in Israel Gershoni and Amy Singer, eds., *Narrating History: Histories and Historiographies of the*

Twentieth-Century Middle East (Seattle: University of Washington Press, forthcoming).

19 Although an official government paper appeared in 1828, the major daily independent newspapers existing in the 1890s were mostly products of the 1880s.

20 *Al-Mu'ayyad* 1, 141 (May 24, 1890): 1.

21 *Al-Mu'ayyad* 5, 1225 (March 1, 1894): 2.

22 *Al-Mu'ayyad* 3, 556 (Dec. 1, 1891): 2.

23 *Al-Mu'ayyad* 3, 521 (Sept. 10, 1891): 2.

24 *Al-Mu'ayyad* 2, 313 (Dec. 23, 1890): 2, "Min akhbar al-Fayyum."

25 *Al-Mu'ayyad* 3, 563 (Dec. 10, 1891): 2.

26 *Al-Mu'ayyad* 1, 201 (Aug. 11, 1890): 1.

27 *Al-Mu'ayyad* 3, 597 (Jan. 19, 1892): 2.

28 I have not the space here to set this narrative against another archive, that of the discourse on girls reading and writing, in school and at home, properly and improperly; a discourse that sketches anxiety about the effects of female literacy and is evident for other modernizing societies. See Booth, *May Her Likes*, 110–15.

29 I am not suggesting that before the modern era females did not read or write. The *assumption* that they would do so seems new.

30 I am inspired by Carolyn Steedman's chapter on histories that "fictional objects" carry; see *Dust: The Archive and Cultural History* (New Brunswick, N.J.: Rutgers University Press, 2002), chap. 5, "What a Rag Rug Means."

31 Randy Bass, "Story and Archive in the Twenty-First Century," Symposium: English 1999, *College English* 61, 6 (July 1999): 660, 661.

32 Roberto González Ecchevarría, *Myth and Archive: A Theory of Latin American Narrative* (Durham: Duke University Press, 1998), 2.

PART III

Archive Matters

THE PAST IN THE PRESENT

Helena Pohlandt-McCormick

In Good Hands

RESEARCHING THE 1976 SOWETO UPRISING IN THE

STATE ARCHIVES OF SOUTH AFRICA

The tragedy is that the former government deliberately and

systematically destroyed a huge body of state records and documentation

in an attempt to remove incriminating evidence and thereby

sanitise the history of oppressive rule. — Truth and Reconciliation

Commission of South Africa, *Report*

WITH THIS STATEMENT IN 1998, the South African Truth and Reconciliation Commission confirmed what many historians had known to be true for many years: that the South African state archives, charged with minding the documentary records of the nation, had instead engaged in their methodical destruction during the apartheid years. The institution called upon to safe-keep the records of the South African state was the State Archive Services (SAS).[1] Responsibility for the proper management of state records was governed by national archival legislation and included the authorization for their destruction.[2] During the years of apartheid, the SAS had essentially done the bidding of the state, using its extensive powers to govern access to documents and to destroy those potentially injurious to the reputation of the state. There are many brown manila files in the archives that, while retaining the shape of the documents they must once have held, are now filled only with a small slip of paper upon which are written the ominous words: "*Vernietig* / Destroyed."[3] Mechanisms of control—access and destruction—initially put in place to protect individuals and evidence were thus progressively used to control access to knowledge.

On the other hand, the African National Congress (ANC), vulnerable to official sanction and suppression of information, had tended to hide the documents it produced. Many were taken abroad and only repatriated after 1990. The state confiscated large amounts of non-public records from people and organizations opposed to apartheid. In many cases such records were destroyed, although some survived in the archives. Nevertheless, such practices by government officials had a considerable impact on the record-keeping practices of anti-apartheid organizations. Activists became increasingly reluctant to commit certain kinds of information to paper and destroyed records preemptively rather than allow them to fall into the hands of the police or state security.

This was the context in which I began my graduate studies in history in 1989. It seemed unimaginably difficult to do critical research in South Africa. In the repressive, authoritarian context of apartheid South Africa, official or publicly sanctioned memories and histories were shaped around silences and lies. Archivists carefully controlled access to the records that remained in the archives according to strict rules and pro-government biases of which I knew my research agenda would run afoul. Committed to political change in South Africa, I respected the ANC's call for a cultural and academic boycott of South Africa.

But in 1990 Nelson Mandela was released from prison, and, in the end, my dissertation on the multiple constructions of historical memories of the Soweto Uprising on June 16, 1976, was written and researched in a time of change.[4] After an increasingly violent period of transition South Africa held its first democratic universal elections in April of 1994, ending the rule of the Afrikaner government and bringing the African National Congress (ANC) to power. By 1996 the new government had entrusted a powerful, if temporary, institution, the Truth and Reconciliation Commission (TRC), with the task of investigating the worst crimes against humanity under apartheid.

At times it seemed events in South Africa were moving so fast that the speed of change seemed also to accelerate historical time. Suddenly, the Soweto Uprising itself was seen as the beginning of the end of apartheid. What happens to historical research under such circumstances? What effect does the rapid movement from violent repression through political upheaval to the establishment of democracy and new institutions for historical accountability have on historical evidence, on the memory of historical experience, and on the writing and research of history? This essay will describe my experience doing research on the history of the Soweto Uprising during the 1990s. It will consider how researcher, historical experience (the event and the memory of the event in the minds of participant witnesses), institutions, and evidence are intertwined in a changing relationship that seeks to reconstruct the past but that is also revealing of the past's living, active, negotiated existence in the present.

This essay will consider three things: (1) the legacy of violence; (2) the historical context and moment of history in which the research was conducted, which had consequences for the actual "collection" of oral histories *and* for their peculiar character as shaped not only by the historical context (the present) in which they were recorded, but by the *pace* of historical (social and political) change in which they were embedded; and (3) the terrain of power in which the South African state's archives were embedded and that determined how historical evidence was collected and preserved, and, as a consequence, how historical knowledge was produced. Together these shaped the perspective and voices of those who stood at the center of the uprising; the shifting historical terrain in which I was working; differential access to evidence; and my understanding of the relationship between the events of the Soweto Uprising, the changing memory of these events, and the present.

Violence. In the three decades before 1994, South Africa had seen increasing violence. Physical violence and forms of discursive, rhetorical violence had become entrenched in the processes and institutions of the state and acted in collusion with silence to shape what the apartheid government wanted to be remembered into history. Pervasive violence shaped memories over time and the way in which people remembered and spoke. It also led to the destruction of historical records, and the disappearance of people and, with them, their stories.[5] The authoritarian and repressive nature of apartheid produced individual memories formed by the personal experience of violence, and disrupted or destroyed the ability of the individual to think historically.[6] Considerable damage was done, not only to individuals, but to society, when those who did the physical violence—in this case agents and institutions of the South African state—erased the histories of their victims and contrived to create histories that denied their culpability.

Historical Context and Oral Evidence. From the beginning it was clear to me that oral interviews—the stories of those who had not been heard before—would be an essential part of my research if I wanted to create a space for those narratives that had been excluded both in the official versions of what had happened and in the few, but important, historical studies of the event. This shift in perspective to the stories of those who participated in these events, the historical actors themselves, was inspired by South Africa's radical historiography and its methodology. History from below, oral interviews, life histories would recover the African voices, the stories that the official narratives of the state and of the ANC, as I argue, sought to suppress and silence. I took seriously the charge that "the people . . . *should speak for themselves.*"[7] A central principle of Black Consciousness—"It is only when the historical subjects speak as agents of history that they shape the direction of society"—it also rang true for the undertaking of the kind of history I wanted to write and discover.[8]

In the early 1990s, oral history research in South Africa was a project troubled with problems that can be ascribed to the politics of the day, even seventeen years after the Soweto Uprising. I made two short research planning trips to South Africa in 1991 and 1992, and spent six months in South Africa in 1993. During the period before the 1994 elections, social and political tension in the country was high, marked by such events as the assassination of Chris Hani, increasing violence, especially in the African townships, and mounting fears of change among whites. People were extremely suspicious of my motives and credentials, cautious, reluctant, and unwilling to talk, and it took an extraordinary amount of time to win their trust sufficiently to begin a conversation. History, especially personal history, was too full of tragedy.

When I returned for the second year of my fieldwork in mid-1994, after the elections, much of the tension had been replaced by relief and a new willingness to think about the past. Where there had been suspicion and guardedness before, interviews now were tinged with humor and cast into a new historical light by the heady feeling of victory. The tragedies of the past had become the building blocks of a future. Once again, history was something to reflect upon. Within the space of a few months and a new dispensation, many of those who had been "victims" of apartheid were drawn into the multiple efforts to rebuild and rethink, while those who had fought against it for so many years and with so much consequence found themselves taking their place in parliament and sitting on the many committees of transformation. Despite a new readiness to remember, now it was often difficult to get people to commit to long interviews as they were overextended in their new tasks and often exhausted from the drawn-out battle over the elections.

Archives and Documentary Evidence. I also intended to investigate the differences between how people remembered the events of the Soweto Uprising in the present and how they might have represented those experiences closer to the time. For the proxy voices of the young participants and witnesses of the uprising and for voices closer in time to 1976, I sought to find pamphlets, posters, signs, letters, testimony, speeches, newsletters, and flyers produced by students themselves. The search for such documentary sources took me to the archives.

The early 1990s were closely linked to the time of apartheid and many of its mechanisms of control were still apparent in the archives. I faced the prospect of closed archival holdings, a somewhat unyielding archival staff, and the secretive nature of government, all of which continually intruded upon my research design and hopes. As I focused my topic and placed it in the time of the Soweto Uprising of June 16, 1976, I came up against what, at the time, seemed like the intransigent barriers of the South African archival system and the laws that—not unlike those in other countries— prevented insight into documents younger than thirty years. It was clear that the archives were also rooted in a historical context and reflected the conventions and habits of the apartheid past as much as the rapid pace of historical change in South Africa during the 1990s.

Background: The Uprising

Memories of Soweto begin with police violence. For black South Africans the confrontation with police officers who shot at students, immediately killing two of them, transformed a demonstration march by school pupils into a violent and raging uprising. For several weeks, students in Soweto schools had disputed a policy change that would have forced them to study certain non-language subjects such as mathematics through the medium of Afrikaans. Not only did urban Africans consider Afrikaans a difficult language, but few teachers were qualified to conduct classes in that medium. In addition, as the language of the police, administration, and the hated apartheid government, its imposition as the language of instruction in African township schools was entirely suspect. Class boycotts and other forms of lower-key protest in upper primary and high schools had been either subdued, discounted, or ignored.[9] Finally, students from several schools in Soweto had organized the protest march.

As the students converged from all directions on Orlando West High School in Soweto, the police hurriedly prepared to counter them. The two groups came to face each other in Vilakazi Street, in front of the school. It was 10:30 on the morning of June 16, 1976. Six thousand pupils in school uniforms sang, shouted and waved placards bearing slogans such as "Away with Afrikaans," "Afrikaans is the language of the oppressors," and "We are fed the crumbs of ignorance with Afrikaans as a poisonous spoon."[10] Their weapons were the stones that lay on the ground before them. Opposing them, forty-eight policemen under the command of Colonel Kleingeld, "duty bound" to stop them and to restore order, carried revolvers, pistols, three automatic rifles, tear-gas grenades, and riot batons.[11] They had come in four police cars, three heavy armored vehicles, and two patrol cars with police dogs. There is conflicting evidence on almost every incident and aspect of what happened next, but within the hour two African children lay dead: 17-year-old Hastings Ndlovu and 12-year-old Hector Pieterson.

The students were filled with fury and frustration by the police violence that ended the march. The uprising swelled, and widespread violence raged on throughout the afternoon and the night. Liquor stores and West Rand Administration Board offices, buildings regarded as symbols of oppression, and other buildings as well, were burned down and looted, vehicles and several white people were attacked, stoned, and burned. Four people died in the "riots" that morning—the two black schoolchildren and two white officials. During the afternoon and evening eleven more people died, four of them under eighteen. All of these died of bullet wounds, and the police were responsible for their deaths.

The initial phase of the uprising lasted only a few days, but the unrest and clashes with the police continued with sporadic outbursts and new deaths through to the beginning of 1978. The violence was not contained to Soweto. By August 11, 1976, the uprising had spread to Cape Town, where things had remained relatively calm. But then the Cape townships of Guguletu, Langa, and Nyanga exploded, and by December over one hundred people had been killed there and more than three hundred "youngsters" arrested. Within two months after June 16, violence had swept into 80 African communities, townships, and rural Bantustans (homelands). Two months later still, the number stood at 160.[12] Soweto was everywhere.

As a result of the unrest in Soweto, 312 schools with 180,000 African pupils were immediately closed. In Alexandra, another township on the northeast side of Johannesburg, the closing of fourteen schools affected 6,000 pupils.[13] Ninety-five black schools in Soweto, four in Alexandra, and twelve in the Cape Peninsula were destroyed or damaged during the uprising. The uprising claimed at least 176 lives in the first two weeks, and according to one careful analysis, "The total number of *publicly recorded* deaths arising out of the disturbances between June 1976 and October 1977 is 700."[14] Interviewed in January of 1977, Tebello Motapanyane, former student and secretary-general of SASM (the South African Students' Movement, whose members were primarily students in higher primary schools) at Naledi High School, put the number considerably higher.

> I think they exceed one thousand two hundred (1,200) because after the first few days the Black Parents Association had a Commission of Inquiry. We discovered that in Baragwanath alone we had something like 238 people dead. There were others in the police stations, mortuaries and so on. The official figure of 176 is clearly a lie. And people are still dying.[15]

The South African Institute of Race Relations reported that eighty-nine of the dead in the West Rand Area were under twenty years old, sixty-nine between twenty and thirty, and forty-six over thirty years old.[16] There were many very young children who took part in the demonstrations, and the Institute identified twelve children under eleven who had died. Long lines of appalled and frightened parents trying to find their children formed in front of the Medico-Legal Laboratories and Morgue of the South African Police. A boundary had been shamelessly crossed. The violence of "Soweto," regardless of its agents, radiated across spatial and geographic, generational and racial boundaries

Looking for Evidence

The Commission of Enquiry into the Riots at Soweto and Elsewhere from the 16th of June 1976 to the 28th of February 1977

Immediately after the outbreak of the uprising, the Minister of Police, Jimmy Kruger, announced that the state president would be appointing a one-man commission of inquiry into the causes of the "riots." Just as in the debate over frontier violence in Tasmania, which Ann Curthoys discusses in "The History of Killing and the Killing of History" in this volume, at the heart of this investigation was alarm about the nature and extent of violence during the uprising. The opposition party member Colin Eglin cautioned that a multiracial commission would prevent a one-sided or superficial approach. The Soweto (Black) Parents' Association also appealed for the active participation of one or two black representatives. Kruger dismissed all of these appeals for the reason that a larger commission would need more time, whereas a small commission assisted by advisers would provide better insight and background. Indeed, the commission, under the chairmanship of Supreme Court Judge P. M. Cillié, convened almost immediately and held its first sitting on July 27, 1976. But it took the commission (henceforth the Cillié Commission) two years to complete its hearings and collecting of evidence, and its final report—severely marked by the "selectivity driven by a political agenda" with which Curthoys charges *The Fabrication of Aboriginal History*—would only be officially submitted in 1980, long after other events had overtaken those in Soweto. Until then, any questions in parliament about the proceedings of the commission, about its report, and about any substantive information linked to the uprising could be and were put off repeatedly.

As a government commission, the officers of the Cillié Commission charged with the investigation of the events of Soweto had the power to command information from any and all government institutions as well as from most nongovernmental organizations, many of which no doubt pursued their own political and social agendas when they submitted their reports and memoranda to the commission. Where simple requests or subpoenas failed, material was simply seized by South African Police officers who raided the offices of such organizations as the South African Students' Organization (saso, a student movement based in universities and tertiary institutions) and others. As a result, the evidence and the testimony of the commission represented—from an official or government point of view—as complete a set of documents as were generated by the multiplicity of organizations and institutions that had anything to say or contribute to a report and opinion of the uprising. The evidence gathered by the commission to support its findings was extensive (ten thousand pages of oral testimony alone) and included memoranda and other statements and reports from the government and its various institutions (such as the South African Police, the Bureau of State Security, but also Child Welfare services), from nongovernmental organizations, including those that clearly opposed the government, and from individuals from all walks of life. Nevertheless, it remains only a "sliver of a window" into the story of the uprising. What the Cillié Commission did not include were the voices of those who stood at the center of the uprising: the students of Soweto. Of the 563 witnesses the Commission heard, only 15 [3 percent] were persons under the age of 18.[17]

An informal list of the holdings relevant to this commission fell into my hands in the stacks of the Central (State) Archives Depot in Pretoria in the very early stages of my fieldwork when, battling against the slow pace of oral history research, I had turned to the archives in search of documents produced by students.[18] Like other archival holdings younger than 1960, the records of the Cillié Commission were closed to research. Although the hearings were held in public and reported on widely in the media, all the evidence that was gathered, as well as the transcripts of the hearings, was secured under South Africa's archive laws which closed such material for thirty years.[19] In the same way that the voices of the participants had been rendered almost completely indistinct, or had been silenced or ignored, the documented sources too had become inaudible and hidden. All that remained in the public realm were copies of the Cillié Commission *Report*, presented to parliament in 1980. Access would require special authorization. I decided to take on the bureaucracy, and in late 1993, with the help of the senior South African historian Charles van Onselen, I applied for permission to see the evidence and transcripts of the testimony. In the meantime, I waited and sought alternatives.

Four months after my application, permission was granted to use both the evidence collected by and the testimony heard and transcribed before the Cillié Commission of Inquiry. I was allowed to look at all materials except "in camera" (secret) testimony, but was permitted only to take notes by hand. My access to this source was unique, since no one had looked at it since 1978 when the Commission ended its proceedings, and where historians and others *have* commented, it was only with reference to the *Report* that the commission submitted to the state president several years later.

By 1994 another year and many pages of hand transcription had passed, but a more profound shift was beginning to happen in the archives. The old *Vierkleur* South African flag in the corner of the reading room had been replaced by the new South African flag, its bold black and gold resonant of the ANC's colors and imbued with a new and proud symbolism—the changing architecture of the space reflecting the regime change of 1994. Behind the counter sat the same archive attendants, those dealing with researchers mostly white and Afrikaans speaking, those fetching and carrying the document cases in their large green steel wheelbarrows mostly black. But above their heads new portraits of Nelson Mandela, F. W. de Klerk, and Thabo Mbeki adorned the wall.[20] Suddenly—and perhaps reflecting the "serendipity of bureaucrats" that Burton writes about in the introduction to this volume—I was granted permission to photocopy documents, without a formal waiting period and in response to an informal application on my part, which was immediately walked "upstairs" by a reading room assistant and signed by the senior in-house archivist. The archivists gradually became less guardians of the archives and more facilitators of research, and slowly began to actively help rather than hinder my research.[21]

From the transcripts and correspondence of the Cillié Commission I knew that the commission had received, from the police, many posters and banners that had been confiscated during various student marches in 1976. None of them would have fit into a traditional archive document box, and, though mentioned on the list of evidence associated with the Cillié Commission, they were initially not to be found. I continued to request that archivists search the repositories—without success. Then, one day, perhaps exasperated by my persistence or wanting finally to prove to me that there was nothing to be found in the space associated with K345, the archival designator of *my* Soweto materials, one of the archivists relented and asked me to accompany her into the vaults—otherwise forbidden to researchers—in order to help her search for these artifacts of the uprising, thus allowing me literally to go "backstage" in the archives (see Burton's introduction to this volume). To be sure, there were no posters to be found in the shelf space that housed the roughly nine hundred boxes of evidence associated with the Cillié Commission. But then, as my disappointed eyes swept the simultaneously ominous and tantalizing interior of the vault, I saw a piece of board protruding over the edge of the topmost shelf. There, almost nine feet into the air, in the shadowy space on top of the document shelves lay a pile of posters and banners.

No longer inhibited by the slow pace of transcription, I could quickly copy relevant sections of testimony before the Cillié Commission and leave them for later close analysis while I moved more quickly through the many thousands of files in the archives. Gradually I uncovered a wealth of documentary evidence.

I followed the Cillié Commission's lead and went through the records of as many court cases as I could trace to the Soweto Uprising. Court cases often proved to be true treasure troves of original documents by student activists and other people involved in the uprising, as the police obtained many of them in their brutal raids and submitted them to the courts as evidence. Among these were, for example, the records of SASO, found at their headquarters in Lekton House in 1977.[22] These collections—often preserved as "evidence" in cases against individual participants in the uprising—hid some of the texts that students themselves produced. Some of these were essentially private, never intended for the eyes of the police or other officials, nor even of the researcher.[23] Many are not explicitly political, although part of politically engaged lives. Because the government amassed anything and everything it could in its search for evidence, confiscating entire household inventories and everything they found during raids on student organizations, there was a lot of "raw" data that was not necessarily tarnished by the mere fact of its inclusion in government or police evidence rooms.[24] The Cillié Commission has, therefore, not unlike *Delgamuukw v. British Columia* (see Perry, this volume) created "an entirely new sort of archive" in which "all sorts of goodies" are on record.[25]

The Student Documents

When the pace of events threatened to overwhelm the students, with many killed, arrested, or detained, and police everywhere, they wanted to explain themselves and did so. The students were well aware of the need to communicate their stories and their political agendas and to show a strong leadership if they wanted the community to continue to support them. They produced many documents that attested to this, among them notes for speeches, pamphlets, press releases, flyers, and newsletters. As the schools were closed, robbing student organizers not only of their vital constituency, but also of the infrastructure of the classrooms, libraries, assembly halls, and playgrounds that had been so vital to their gatherings and meetings, it became imperative to find new gathering places and new ways of communicating. Many were killed in those first six months of the uprising, many were detained, and many more had fled into exile across the borders into Botswana and Lesotho. They were quickly replaced by others. Each new student leader imposed his mark on the organization while trying to continue the work that had been started by his predecessors.

The documents produced by students in the year after June 16 reveal how people, especially young people caught up in events that must at times have seemed overwhelming, thought of themselves. There was evidence that individuals and groups were in an ongoing process of defining themselves, especially in response to what they conceived of as attacks on their integrity. Young people identified themselves by their actions, by their differences from others and possibly from generations that came before them. They rejected the definitions imposed on them from the outside and by adults. They were different because of the particular historical context within which they emerged as a group.

Letters, confiscated by the police at the time of a young female activist's arrest, permitted a rare glimpse into the private turmoil of the young participants in the uprising, and clearly reveal how she was less able to protect her private life from the impact of her involvement in public politics. Even the most public events of the uprising brought private pain: the boy who had picked up the dying Hector Pieterson from the ground on the first day of the uprising, Mbuyisa Makhubu, was her nephew. In a letter to her sister, Mbuyisa's mother, Nombulelo Makhubu, she wondered, with reference to his disappearance for fear of the police, "what he might be going through, am I proud of that boy is a hero [sic], a soldier that never turns back on his pledge or vows, 'Vivat, Mbuyisa KaMakhubu.' "26

There were many attempts to sow dissent and destroy the Soweto Students' Representative Council (SSRC) by detaining students and leaders. Just before the anniversary of June 16, 1976, a series of pamphlets appeared in Soweto, authored anonymously by "A Black Parent," which called on "The People of Soweto" to stand firm and "resist the servants of darkness who are being paid by *communists* to spread death, chaos and suffering in the black community." A second pamphlet signed simply "TO HELL WITH S.S.R.C!!" was a direct attack on the SSRC and prevailed upon "all our people in Soweto and other African townships" to "stand fast" against

THE VANDALS AND THEIVES OF THE SOWETO STUDENTS REPRESENTATIVE COUNCIL AND OTHER ORGANISATIONS LIKE IT THAT SEEM DETERMINED TO PLUNGE THE BLACK RACE IN SOUTH AFRICA INTO A NEW DARK AGE OF MISERY, DEATH AND DESTRUCTION.27

The students *had* to counter such representations, and in a press statement by Gordon Trofomo Sono, who had just become leader of the ssrc after its former head, Daniel Sechaba Montsisi was arrested on June 10, 1977, the ssrc replied to the "slanderous" pamphlet:

> What a slanderous way to discredit people. We, the ssrc do not wish to argue in vain with a voice that has no identification. But to put a few things straight we openly and with no bitterness in our hearts challenge the writers of this insufficient pamphlet to strike the truth. To our dear parents, brothers and sisters we say your leaders will not be disheartened by anonymous vandals who are opposed to the dignity and respect of the Black man.[28]

The students were intensely sensitive not only to the way they were being portrayed by the government and its spokesmen (the ideological and discursive designs), but also to the way this was related to and connected with the practices of the government and the establishment of actual physical control, through detentions, of the protagonists in the uprising:

> We are also aware of the system's conspiracy:
> 1. To discredit present and past leadership with the hope of distracting the masses from the leaders.
> 2. To capture present leadership with the hope of retarding the student's struggle and achievements.[29]

The students responded to detentions and police harassment with fast changes in leadership, but these changes too needed to be explained. In 1977, after the arrest of Montsisi, the ssrc published a newsletter in which past leaders of the students were fully acknowledged with small biographies. Each new student leader needed quickly to establish his identity, and the documents—letters, notes, diaries—students produced during this time reveal much about those identities. Similarly, student organizations repeatedly asserted their identities through the publication of "histories" and by publicizing both policy and strategy. Sensitive to the fact that dissent and differences might divide the student movement, one document urged the activists within the ssrc to reflect on their own role and identity within it:

> To assess their genuineness and devotion in the struggle as such. To motivate non-participants and boost the moral of the Junior Secondary School students' leaders, i.e. if they suffer from inferiority complex or lack of expression etc. To

expose and eradicate arrogance and vanity from all council members including the able chairman of the ssrc. All members shall be treated equally irre-
spective of their intelligence, standard, status, or age and experience.[30]

In their documents, the students of Soweto invoked the names of those
who had led the movement since its beginnings on June 16 as well as those
who had suffered and died, clearly aware of the power that these names
evoked. When Montsisi was arrested on June 10, 1977, just days before the
anniversary of the uprising, Sono, a Form IV student at Madibane High
School who was described as a "brilliant student," faced a daunting challenge as the newly elected leader of the ssrc. In his notebook he wrote:

> I don't know how I became a leader, but it was neither guts nor intellect—yet
> suffering. My sufferings are not the kind of suffering that I suffer because of
> my suffering as an individual—yet a national suffering of all black man. A black
> man know suffering today—because of oppressive measures at each and every
> stinking corner of South Africa.[31]

Sono made his first public appearances at the various commemorative
services for the June 16 anniversary and at a series of student funerals.[32] At
one of these he addressed the deceased and asked her to deliver a message
to all the others "who have sacrificed their lives for social change." The
words reflected both the broader struggle and the immediate fears for
Daniel Sechaba Montsisi, whose detention was all the more ominous for
the knowledge of what had happened to others in detention:

> Tell Hector Petersen that we are still sweating with the educational crisis and
> the discriminative measures. . . . Do not forget to Mathews Mabelane that
> Sechaba has been detained. Detained to bring social changes in this country,
> detained to solve the educational crisis of this country and of course, for
> them to rest in hope. Tell Ntshuntsha that we do not know what will be
> happening to Sechaba—he might decide to suffer from heart attack, he might
> start playing with vests around his neck, he might make a mistake by taking
> his soap along to the shower, or rather—jumping from the peak of John
> Vorster Square. Tell all of them not to allow him to do all this, for he has not
> yet finished serving the people.[33]

There is, as Ranajit Guha has pointed out, little that will protect against the
"distortions" that inevitably alter the stories of the past because of the passage of time between the event and the telling of it or against the inter-

ference of the historian's own consciousness. But the old letters, pamphlets, and speeches from the time of "the trouble" described above, combined with interviews and other voices that come to us more indirectly through recordings, transcriptions of testimony, recorded statements, and affidavits, allow us, through their rich diversity and their indisputable authenticity, to see something of a past consciousness that has so often been seized and claimed for narratives that were not the participants' own. In these stories, and with this shift, the participant is no longer "only a contingent element" in a narrative that otherwise belongs to the government, the resistance movement, or the historian. She (he) is instead an active, thoughtful, and spirited agent of her (or his) own history. If the participant directs and speaks the story herself (or himself), just as she (he) made the history and experienced the events—however eloquently or competently—what emerges is the complexity of the historical experience with multiple and intricate layers of meaning. Accounts of the experiences of ordinary people create a historical picture that may not be neat or straightforwardly argued but that is a little closer to the multiple realities of historical experience. The shift in perspective that is a consequence of the presentation of the stories of the Soweto Uprising through the eyes of its protagonists allows us to see certain things differently, correct heretofore partial presentations, and complicate or enrich past explanations or interpretations.[34]

Creating a Space for Memory

The Truth and Reconciliation Commission

Between 1996 and 1998 the Truth and Reconciliation Commission (TRC), charged with investigating human rights violations during the time of apartheid and laying the groundwork for reconciliation by undoing some of the secrecy and repression of those years, created a new context for memory and history in South Africa. The TRC signaled a profound shift away from the secrecy and lies of the apartheid years to a new and deliberately revelatory encounter with the past. The TRC created a new space of individual and collective memory, and perhaps even a new respect for the past or history. It also partially wrested the past out of the exclusivist hands of academic historians and put it into the hands of those who had suffered this history. The TRC also created the institutions and the mechanisms (spaces in which to talk, a new archive), as well as the need for some forms of continuation of this work beyond its own mandate.[35]

Among its many investigations, the testimonies of the Soweto Hearings of the Truth and Reconciliation Commission in 1996 were produced in a much less antagonistic, but no less traumatic context than those of the Cillié Commission hearings. They are a historical record beyond compare, backed up by a vast archive of supporting materials. But they also posed dangers in the way they deliberately created heroes, drawing them into a larger national narrative of heroic resistance.

The presence and work of the TRC also changed my work. Most importantly the TRC created another set of oral testimonies, a new layer in time through which I could follow the changing memories of those who had spoken closer to 1976 and since then. Murphy Morobe, Sam Nzima, Sophie Thema, Nombulelo Elizabeth Makhubu, Daniel Montsisi, Ellen Kuzwayo, Antoinette Sithole-Musi (Hector Pieterson's sister), Elliot Ndlovu . . . these were all people who were witnesses to or participants in the uprising, who had spoken before, and who now eloquently spoke of these events again in a new setting deliberately designed to make these stories part of the public record. Although they were significant as a historical reference point and will endure in people's memories, in the end, the so-called Soweto Hearings were overshadowed by more compelling, perhaps more prominent and more historically recent topics such as, for example, those into the actions of the Mandela United Football Club, and so were relegated to larger summary chapters of the TRC *Report*.[36]

The TRC also articulated the idea that memory is not just carried by individuals but that institutional memory too is contained in countless documentary records. This is the purview of the archives. In the course of its work, the TRC inquired into the ongoing destruction of records because it needed to access documents relevant to the human rights violations it was investigating, documents which were important to the research and investigative work of the TRC and which would have a significant impact on its findings. The work of the TRC made clear that institutions such as archives play an important role in preserving the documentary record of historical memory. Its focus on the culpability of archives and other government institutions in the destruction of records highlighted the importance of such institutions in relation to public memory and history, and brought into focus that individual experience interacts with the discursive and political power of institutions in the process of articulating, preserving, inventing, silencing, and destroying memory.

The hearings of the TRC created a historical moment in time, when the work of memory accelerated and became both more self-conscious and deliberate.[37] The processes of societal remembering took place at many levels—public and private, individual and collective.[38] Usually these processes are gradual, and changes in interpretation and meaning, imperceptible. The "truth . . . will, in the very nature of things, never be fully revealed," wrote Archbishop Desmond Tutu in the Foreword to the TRC *Report*.[39] Nevertheless, in the search for clues to that truth, for authenticity among the multiplicity of accounts, both individual memory and institutional memory needed to be tapped. Susan Geiger suggests that "collective" memory—an elusive, changing concept whose constituent parts we more easily recognize than its definitive whole—is the consequence of the relationship between a widely shared social sense of an authentic past and the individual's process of remembering and storytelling—a creative act in itself.[40] I would suggest that there are potentially many and competing historical actors and institutions that participate in the processes of creating a shared sense of what constitutes the authentic past. It is therefore important to investigate those many historical actors and institutions—the archives prominent among them—that participate in the process, not simply the stories themselves. As individuals stepped forward into the public forum of the TRC to tell their story, the work of memory became simultaneously more public (official?) and private, and with each voice, with each document, "a new piece of the jigsaw puzzle of our past settles into place."[41]

It was in this context that I completed the work on my dissertation. Suddenly, the importance of the texts that students and pupils themselves had produced—which must have seemed forever lost to police raids and destruction—seemed more clear, as was the relationship between institutions that were charged with preserving the documents of the past and those who had actually experienced that past.

The Gutenberg-e Image Archive

The TRC also created a new context for the retrieval and dissemination of historical evidence. Shortly after delivering a copy of my dissertation to the archives in fulfillment of my obligations as a researcher to that institution, I began preparing the manuscript of " 'I Saw a Nightmare . . .' Doing Violence to Memory: The Soweto Uprising, June 16, 1976" for publication (with Columbia University Press) as a book in electronic format. Among the documents of the Cillié Commission, there was also a large collection of black-and-white photographs, many of them painstakingly pasted into large hard-board books, divided geographically by region in South Africa and by neighborhoods in townships, beginning with Soweto, but including photographs from many other townships around South Africa as well. With the funding provided by the Gutenberg-e Prize (2000), and with the full support of the National Archives and its then chief, Verne Harris, I began compiling a new electronic archive of 1,300 digital images of the 1976 Soweto Uprising from the historical collections.[42] These documents—the placards, posters, and handwritten letters, as well as historical police documents and black-and-white police photographs produced at the time of the uprising—provide a unique and rarely seen record both of the violence of the uprising and of its brutal suppression, and give a strong sense of "Soweto" as a place in time and geography. A collection of photographs from 2001–2 (also digital) complements the historical images and creates both connections and comparisons with the present. An inventory with detailed information about each image and document is part of a searchable database connected to the electronic book. The database and the documents and images it contains will be an accessible and rich resource for researchers as well as for those whose history this is.

Prominent in the collection are police statements and affidavits. Police statements, as much as police testimony, have an agenda, and despite their apparent formality and what perhaps may even have been their original intent (under "normal" conditions) to set out the facts of an incident, they are not simply evidence and quite certainly not uncompounded proof. In the South African case, because of the complicity of the police in the implementation of the racist order, such files were inherently tainted. They were, in this particular case of the uprising, further contaminated by their underlying purpose: to provide a record that would allow proof of the appropriateness, legitimacy, and justifiability of police action. While the extent of the taint may have been novel, its existence certainly was not. Documents are never innocent. These documents reveal something of the efficiency with which their fierce biases combined with their claim to authoritativeness to produce powerful official statements. To ignore such sources would be, amongst other things, to ignore the main axiom of historical research, to use all sources possible, but to treat none uncritically. It would also mean that we would fail to see historical actors and witnesses standing their ground and contradicting, countering, and contesting the institutions that sought to disempower them—not always successfully. Finally, these statements—from inside the belly of the beast—allow some insight into how coercive structures of thought and practices functioned. These too are voices of participants in the uprising—those on the other side of the political divide. Police statements, much like other sources produced by government officials, were constrained by their own experiential context, shaped by their own worldview, and carried their own assumptions within them.

The police photographs are now part of the public record in the archives. Collectively, the photographs present a complex picture of the consequences of the physical violence of the uprising and the material damage that was its end result: destroyed government administration buildings, burnt-out delivery trucks, ransacked beer halls and bottle stores, shattered windows, hijacked public buses, hastily scrawled graffiti. But there are also images of confrontations between police and students, shattered bodies, smoking buildings.

Some of these documents fill gaps in oral testimonies. Three full folders of photographs preserved a very suggestive list of demonstration slogans from which to study the echoes and influences from the writings, movements, and antecedent cultural forms, as well as to garner some insight on their historical relevance. For most young demonstrators at the time, resistance and political protests were a memory and experience of their parents. From the historical perspective, it is relevant that slogans were often re-invented by the young people and schoolchildren and used in a radically new context, with changed significances, with simultaneously new allusions and old references, and sometimes with different meanings.

Finally, autopsy reports conducted by the government's medical examiners and autopsy photographs in this collection are sources that provide some of the most graphic and inescapable evidence of the physical violence that confronted the participants in the uprising. In the face of evidence contained in these reports, neither the identity of the victim nor the fact of his or her death could be challenged or remain hidden. In addition to the irrefutable factual evidence they contain, these harsh documents at last provide a vocabulary so stark in its implications that it is equal to the task of rendering the violence of Soweto. The meticulousness with which autop-

318

sies were tracked through the bureaucracy of death leaves no doubt as to the capacity for painstaking exactitude of procedure on the part of the responsible authorities. This must of course raise grave suspicions about the frequency with which bodies disappeared temporarily or permanently, and suggests deliberate procedure rather than mistake or confusion.

In response to recent discussions, particularly in South Africa, but certainly relevant elsewhere, about the appropriation of archival and other historical materials by scholars based outside of Africa, I have deposited a digitized copy of these materials at the National Archives in Pretoria and at the new Hector Pieterson Memorial Museum in Soweto, where they will form the basis of a new historical images archive to be made available there to the community and to scholars. The documents—especially those of student participants in the uprising—belong in South Africa, where those who produced them and whose history this is must have untrammeled access to them. The creation of this database is but a small return for the many stories of the uprising South Africans have shared with me. Images from this collection have already been used by the curatorial team of the Hector Pieterson Memorial Museum Project to select photographs for the museum. The National Archive will use the collection as part of its archives' outreach program for young scholars in South African high schools and universities.

Although the presentation of all of these image and text materials in the electronic format of an e-book may raise the possibility of the appropriation or misuse of the materials, it is my understanding that this archive and my work will counter the history of concealment and exclusion in South African archives, which echoes other forms of silencing. The material will be adequately, I hope, protected by the licensing agreement which controls access to the archive through my electronic book on the one hand, and by the ethics of good research among scholars and students in archives and museums on the other.

Archival Memory, Archival Responsibility

By the time I completed the research for my dissertation in mid-1995, South Africa was one year into its new democracy. During my last weeks in the archives the archivists had put together a public exhibit of documents representing the time of struggle against apartheid in its hallways.

The 1995 exhibit of original documents of the Soweto Uprising, National Archives, Pretoria, South Africa. *Photograph by the author.*

Visitors to the archives were now greeting by a large poster, fashioned out of a piece of cracked blackboard, which proclaimed: "TO HELL WITH AFRIKAANS!"

In the years since 1994, South Africa has seen the emergence of an essential and vigorous sense of responsibility towards the past(s). Through institutions such as the Truth and Reconciliation Commission, efforts to rewrite the history curriculum, as well as cultural projects such as theater productions, memorials, and both autobiographical and literary writing, South Africans are building a strong culture of collective and individual remembering. Not surprisingly, the years since 1994 have seen South Africa emerge as a complex and conflicted nation, burdened still with the legacy of apartheid and resistance. The legacy is visible in the poverty that now determines most of the divisions in the country. The destruction of historical archives and the concealment or exclusion of materials must be included in the repertoire of the state's efforts to change what was known and remembered of South Africa's past. Less visible, but no less dangerous, are complex patterns of behavior (habits of secrecy, control, dissimulation, accountability or lack thereof) that have as much to do with apartheid bureaucracies as with resistance politics, most of all in the way they replicate each other, tie into each other. A new culture of remembering and accountability brings new evidence and historical understanding into the open, but it also brings with it new challenges. The documents and photographs of the Gutenberg-e collection raise important issues about the further damage such materials can do to those who have survived these ordeals when they become truly public again. Though for perhaps the wrong reasons, archival procedure protected these documents and protected people from them. The same is true of the personal documents that the police confiscated during raids and that their authors must long since have believed lost. It is crucial that researchers recognize and take into account the emotional weight of these materials even as it is crucial that the materials do not remain hidden as a consequence of old government secrecy or of new institutional inertia or discomfort with the notion of transparency.

The notion of archival custody has undergone profound changes in the past fifteen years of South African history. By the time of the publication of the TRC *Report* in 1998, its authors were proud to report that documents and correspondence it had fought hard to retrieve were "now in archival custody," as if the institution of the archive could be relied upon to keep such records safe. But we know that institutions are only as good or as bad as the people who run them and that archives, in particular, "do not act by themselves."[43] Danger comes, even now, when controls put in place to protect people or evidence are suddenly used to control access to information and to restrict knowledge.

Notes

The epigraph is from Truth and Reconciliation Commission of South Africa, *Report*, vol. 1 (New York: Grove's Dictionaries Inc., 1998), 201.

1 The State Archives Service was converted into the National Archives on January 1, 1997, in terms of the National Archives Act, No. 43 of 1996.

2 The Archives Act of 1953, No. 22 of 1953, and the Archives Act of 1962, No. 6 of 1962.

3 Perhaps one of the most prominent examples of the destruction of records in the State Archives is that of Magistrates Court Records, which held evidence of the many eviction, removal, and relocation proceedings under pass law and influx control violations in the 1970s and 1980s and which were destroyed for lack of space despite the willingness of other archives (for one, William Cullen Archives at the University of the Witwatersrand) to house them. As the epigraph

to this essay makes clear, the government deliberately destroyed records and thereby falsified the historical record of apartheid. The TRC devoted an entire chapter of its *Report* to its investigation of "The Destruction of Records," although this focuses more prominently on the records of South African security structures, such as the Defence Force, the Police, and Secret Service. See TRC, *Report*, 1: 201–43.

4 Helena Pohlandt-McCormick, " 'I Saw a Nightmare . . .' Doing Violence to Memory: The Soweto Uprising, June 16, 1976" (Ph.D. diss., University of Minnesota, 1999).

5 Such loss, damage, and willful destruction are noted also by Jeff Sahadeo in the history of the Uzbeki archives and by Ann Curthoys in the colonial record of Australia. It is only different by degree and method to the dismissal and silencing of the oral record noted by Adele Perry for Gitksan and Wet·suwet·en history. See their respective essays in this volume.

6 See Helena Pohlandt-McCormick, " 'I Saw a Nightmare . . .': Violence and the Construction of Memory (Soweto, June 16, 1976)," *History and Theory*, Theme Issue 39 (December 2000): 23–44.

7 N. Barney Pityana, Mamphele Ramphele, Malusi Mpumlwana. and Lindy Wilson, eds., "Introduction," in *Bounds of Possibility: The Legacy of Steve Biko and Black Consciousness* (Cape Town: David Philip, 1991), 3; emphasis added.

8 Ibid.

9 C. W. Eglin and R. M Cadman, House of Assembly, June 17, 1976. Hansard.

10 "The Commission accepts that shortly before the confrontation there were at least six thousand people, but that more were joining their ranks continually." P. M. Cillié, *Report of the Commission of Inquiry into the Riots at Soweto and Elsewhere from the 16th of June 1976 to the 28th of February 1977* (Pretoria: Government Printer, 1980), 112 (cited hereafter as Cillié *Report)*. Conflicting estimates put the number as high as twelve thousand and as low as one thousand, but many students had not yet reached the agreed upon gathering place.

11 Cillié *Report*, 114.

12 John Kane-Berman, *Soweto: Black Revolt–White Reaction* (Johannesburg: Ravan Press, 1978), 5.

13 House of Assembly, *Questions and Replies: 21 January to 24 June 1977*, Hansard, 70: 373–74.

14 See Kane-Berman, *Soweto*, 27–28; emphasis added.

15 Tebello Motapanyane, interview January 1977 in *Sechaba: Official Organ of the African National Congress South Africa* 11, Second Quarter (1977): 58.

16 Muriel Horrell et al., eds., *A Survey of Race Relations in South Africa, 1976* (Johannesburg: South African Institute for Race Relations, 1977), 58, 85.

17 Verne Harris, "The Archival Sliver: A Perspective on the Construction of Social Memory in Archives and the Transition from Apartheid to Democracy," in Carolyn Hamilton, Verne Harris, Jane Taylor, Michele Pickover, Graeme Reid, and Razia Saleh, eds., *Refiguring the Archive* (Cape Town, David Philip: 2002), 135. See also Jeff Sahadeo's essay in this volume, which uses Harris's metaphor to

describe the "significant voids" in the Central State Archive of the Republic of Uzbekistan.

18 An annotated list of the inventory of this commission has since been published.

19 John Kane-Berman attended many of the commission's sessions and commented repeatedly on its findings and on testimony given before it in his book, *Soweto: Black Revolt–White Reaction*.

20 Note the parallels here to Sahadeo's description (this volume) of the sign above the archive door which "symbolized the troubled relationship between past, present, and future in post-Soviet Uzbekistan." The presence of former apartheid Prime Minister F. W. de Klerk's portrait here—de Klerk and Mbeki were both deputy prime ministers under Mandela—reflected both a real accommodation of the white electorate and a symbolic gesture of reconciliation during the transition.

21 This was especially true after I attended, as one of only two historians, the annual South African Society of Archivists conference in 1993.

22 The university-based South African Students' Organisation (SASO) grew out of university student dissatisfaction with their role vis-à-vis white students in the National Union of South African Students (NUSAS) and the University Christian Movement (UCM). SASO was closely identified with the Black Consciousness Movement and its most prominent spokesman, Stephen Bantu Biko.

23 Although I realize that these documents are now accessible, where the material seemed of too personal a nature, I have chosen either to disguise the identities of the authors or not to use the document in my own work.

24 Sahadeo (this volume) uses a term similar to "raw" data to describe what I would call primary documents.

25 Not unlike Adele Perry's ("The Colonial Archive on Trial," this volume) careful treatment of *Delgamuukw v. British Columbia*, and Ann Curthoys's analysis of Windschuttle's *The Fabrication of Aboriginal History*, I have closely analyzed the working of the Cillié Commission as an apartheid institution as well as its multivolume *Report* in *"I Saw a Nightmare . . ." Doing Violence to Memory: The Soweto Uprising, June 16, 1976* (New York: Columbia University Press and the American Historical Association, 2005), chap. 3, with particular attention to contentions of the "untrustworthiness" of student witnesses, the use of expert witnesses, testimony as performance, selectivity with regard to evidence, and reception. The similarities between Cillié's and McEachern's (in *Delgamuukw*) exposure and sense of being overwhelmed at the "scale and scope of evidence" is striking, as is the tone of their analysis in the Report and Judgment respectively.

26 Private letter to Nombulelo Makhubu, September 9, 1976. WLD (Civil Case) 6857 / 77, WRAB v. Santam, vol. 427. WLD documents are located at State Archives Service, Pretoria.

27 Pamphlets. Documents confiscated by the South African Police, during the raid of SASM headquarters at 505 Lekton House, October 19, 1977. WLD (Civil Court Case No.) 6857 / 77, vol. 413.

28 Press release by Gordon Sono, handwritten, undated. Documents seized by security police at the time of the arrest of Masabatha Loate, 17/6/77. WLD (Civil Case) 6857/77, vol. 413, evidence in WRAB v. Santam.

29 Minute Book belonging to Nana Sabela, detained on June 10, 1977, together with Daniel Sechaba Montsisi; see South African Institute of Race Relations, *Detention without Trial in South Africa: 1976–1977* (Johannesburg: South African Institute of Race Relations, 1977), 27. The document was seized by security police at the time of her arrest, signed and dated 17/6/77. WLD (Civil Case) 6857/77, vol. 436, evidence in WRAB v. Santam.

30 "To Hell with S.S.R.C.!!" pamphlet (1977). Documents confiscated by the South African police, during the raid of SASM headquarters at 505 Lekton House, October 19, 1977. WLD (Civil Court Case No.) 6857/77, vol. 413.

31 Notebook of Trofomo Sono, found at 1590 Jabulani by Major Visser, at the time of the arrest of Chief Wilson Twala, September 17, 1977. WLD (Civil Court Case) 6857/77, vol. 411.

32 "Amandla! The Story of the Soweto Students' Representative Council, Part Four," *Weekend World*, Sunday, August 21, 1977.

33 Handwritten notes for a funeral service, Trofomo Sono, undated. Documents seized during the arrest of Chief Twala, September 17, 1977. WLD (Civil Court Case) 6857/77. Matthews Mabelane, age 23, fell to his death from the tenth floor of John Vorster Square on February 25, 1977. Horrell et al., *Survey*, 156.

34 Ranajit Guha, "The Prose of Counter-Insurgency," *Subaltern Studies* no, 2 (Oxford: Oxford University Press, 1983), 32–33.

35 "The volume of material that passed through our hands will fill many shelves in the National Archives. This material will be of great value to scholars, journalists and others researching our history for generations to come. From a research point of view, this may be the Commission's greatest legacy." Archbishop Desmond Tutu, TRC, *Report*, "Foreword by Chairperson," vol. 1, chaps. 1, 2.

36 Winnie Mandela's involvement in the killing of Stompie Sepei on January 1, 1989, was investigated as part of the United Football Club inquiry.

37 On "certain moments" in time, see Patricia Davison, "Museums and the Reshaping of Memory," in Sarah Nuttal and Carli Coetzee, eds., *Negotiating the Past: The Making of Memory in South Africa* (Cape Town: Oxford University Press, 1998), 147.

38 I have borrowed the concept of "processes of societal remembering" from Elizabeth Jelin and Susana G. Kaufman, "Layers of Memories: Twenty Years After in Argentina," paper presented at the conference on "Legacies of Authoritarianism: Cultural Production, Collective Trauma, and Global Justice," University of Wisconsin, Madison, April 3–5, 1998, 1.

39 TRC, *Report*, "Foreword by Chairperson," vol. 1, chap. 1, 4.

40 Susan Geiger, "Introduction," *Tanu Women: Gender and Culture in the Making of Tanganyikan Nationalism, 1955–1965* (Portsmouth, N.H.: Heinemann, 1997).

41 TRC, *Report*, 4.

42 Such a "connection with the archive director" (see also Sahadeo, this volume) highlights the necessary, sometimes complicit, sometimes conflicted relationship between historians and archivists, a relationship that is part of every researcher's story but very rarely examined.

43 Verne Harris describes the several "conduits" through which the archives act: "the people who created them, the functionaries who managed them, the archivists who selected them for preservation and make them available for use, and the researchers who use them in constructing accounts of the past" ("The Archival Sliver," 136).

Adele Perry

The Colonial Archive on Trial

POSSESSION, DISPOSSESSION, AND HISTORY IN

DELGAMUUKW V. BRITISH COLUMBIA

BRITISH COLUMBIA HAS A HISTORY—and by necessary extension a politics—of Indigenous dispossession that is anomalous within both the geographical context of North America and the imperial framework of the
British empire. Treaties were the central mechanism in the dispossession
of migratory peoples by Britain in the nineteenth century. As both legal
documents and as Talmudic symbols of an imagined imperial symbiosis,
treaties have served the colonial projects of Canada, the United States, and
New Zealand with remarkable efficacy. Canadian Indigenous people have
routinely pointed to disjunctures between the written and oral records of
treaties and to the colonial state's selective and self-serving interpretation
of their meaning. Yet they have also treated treaties as "sacred contracts,"
a powerful archive that acknowledges Indigenous people's centrality to
the nation and provides them the practical means to leverage rights and
benefits from the reluctant settler states.[1] For reasons that remain unclear,
only a handful of treaties were signed in British Columbia. The absence
of an official archive pronouncing and regulating Aboriginal dispossession
and European repossession has rendered tangible and painfully persistent questions that, given the overwhelming weight of settler geopolitics,
are politically charged but practically hyperbolic elsewhere in the settler
world—namely who owns the land.[2]

Archives have played a significant role in the "Indian Land Question"
since it was first named in the late nineteenth century. The debate has
been in part produced by the absence of one particular kind of colonial
archive—treaties—and it has been negotiated through competing sets of
archives and ways of interpreting of them. This paper deals with the work
of archives, documents, and history in contemporary politics about pos-

session and dispossession in British Columbia. It does so through a close of reading of what is, to local scholars at least, a familiar source, and that is the 1991 decision by the then Chief Justice Allan McEachern in the provincial Supreme Court case on Aboriginal land rights known as *Delgamuukw v. British Columbia*. In his almost-four-hundred-page judgment, McEachern dismissed the argument of the Gitksan and Wet·suwet·en peoples for "comprehensive title" to an area of more than fifty-seven thousand square kilometers in northwestern British Columbia, and relied heavily on documents, archives, and the discipline of history to do so. The claims of the Gitksan and Wet·suwet·en to the land, McEachern argued, were impossible to verify given the absence of adequate documentary evidence. Oral evidence was suspect, as was the work of scholars who relied upon it. The written archive and scholars who worked within it were, on the other hand, reliable sources of knowledge and, in essence, the appropriate arbiters of who owned the land.

The McEachern decision thus provides a vivid and telling example of the work of archives in postcolonial struggles in Canada. As Ann Curthoys argues in this volume, debates about the past have had particular import in settler colonies "where they are prompted and prolonged by deep psychic concerns about the morality of the nation itself." Like *Mabo* in Australia, *Mashpee* in the United States, and the *Witangi Tribunal* in New Zealand, *Delgamuukw v. British Columbia* has come to symbolize the fractious politics of settler societies reckoning with their imperial pasts and the place of archives in adjudicating those politics and that past. Superficially, *Delgamuukw v. British Columbia* indicates the unmitigated triumph of history and archives in the service of empire. Connections between orality and savagery and literacy and civilization that are generally associated with the high imperialism of the nineteenth century display an enduring and ominous political shelf life well into the allegedly postcolonial twentieth century. Likewise what we might call the "voice of history"—the putatively dispassionate cataloguing of the documented activities of European men acting on behalf of nation-states—lives on in McEachern's decision. Decades of Aboriginal arguments about the validity of oral tradition's distinctive archive, scholarly vogue for ethnohistorical methodology, or critical analyses of historical narration appear to have had little or no lasting effect, all to the material and political detriment of Aboriginal peoples and the disappointment and embarrassment of professional historians.

Yet the twelve years that stand between the immediate present and

McEachern's ruling on *Delgamuukw v. British Columbia* suggest that the archive is at best an unreliable ally in postcolonial struggles. McEachern may have tried to harness the archive in the service of empire, but even the Chief Justice could not make it work easily or effectively in defense of colonialism's past or, by implication, its future. The unequivocal fury of Aboriginal peoples and the highly critical scholarly response foreshadowed both the overturning of McEachern's decision by the Supreme Court of Canada in 1997 and, with that, the significant recognition of oral history as admissible evidence in land-claims cases throughout Canada. However unlike the South African Truth and Reconciliation Commission *Delgamuukw v. British Columbia* may be, both remind us how the colonial archives can alternately and sometimes simultaneously work to defend or challenge the states that create and sustain them.[3] McEachern and the settler society he represented may have wanted written documents to replace the Aboriginal past and ways of knowing it and thus dislodge Indigenous claims to British Columbia's present and future. But this knowledge and all that it represents, like Carolyn Steedman's archival dust that is "about circularity, the impossibility of things disappearing, or going away, or being gone," would not and could not disappear.[4]

Colonialism on Trial

The Gitksan and Wet·suwet·en are two distinct peoples that inhabit the territories around the Skeena, Bulkely, and Nechako rivers in what is now northwestern British Columbia. Like most North American peoples, Gitksan and Wet·suwet·en societies convey meaning, knowledge, and history through material and oral mediums. The most significant document in the oral archive of the Gitksan is the *adwaak*, the verbal records of a house and its history. The Wet·suwet·en *kungax* or song-series serves a roughly analogous function. The Gitksan and Wet·suwet·en have a substantial history of contact with and resistance to European encroachment, but little of it is documented with the kind of legal archives that have regulated dispossession elsewhere in northern North America and the antipodes. Europeans began a trade in ideas, knowledge, and material goods with the Pacific Coast of northern North America in the eighteenth century.[5] Proto-colonialism in the form of the Hudson's Bay Company (HBC) arrived with the establishment of its Fort Kilmaurs in 1822.[6] In 1849, the adjacent terri-

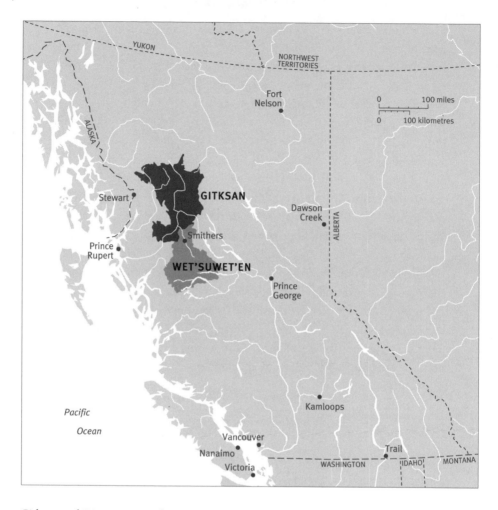

Gitksan and Wet·suwet·en claim area (approximate boundaries).
Image by Eric Leinberger.

tory of Vancouver Island was made a British colony, and between 1850 and 1854, Governor James Douglas negotiated fourteen "land purchases" with Indigenous nations there. These agreements—later interpreted by Canadian courts as treaties—mirror Douglas's provisional mode of imperial administration and bear only light marks of the advice he received from the Colonial Office, which in turn principally reflected the New Zealand experience.[7]

After 1854 no more formal treaties, agreements, or purchases were made between Indigenous peoples and the state.[8] The mainland territory of British Columbia was made a colony in 1858, and officials continued to lay out "Indian reserves," but did not seek to extinguish Aboriginal title in the ways of either the antipodes or the rest of British North America. In 1869, the Minister of Lands and Works did not seem to anticipate that this would be a problem. Regarding *"Indian Titles"* he wrote that "In most of the Districts from North Saanich to Sooke, & that in the Vicinity of Nanaimo Town, the Indian Title has been Extinguished by the payment to them of certain Blankets &c. The Book bearing on this subject is in the safe."[9] Yet the "safe" and the "books" it contained proved uncertain guides. The colony joined the new nation-state of Canada in 1871. British Columbia's idiosyncratic mode of managing Indigenous claims came into conflict with Canada's, which were governed by the Royal Proclamation of 1763's mandate that Indigenous title be ceded by treaty before settlement. Intergovernmental wrangling produced a flurry of letters and reciprocal recrimination between the capitals of Ottawa and Victoria, but little concrete change. British Columbia's Indigenous people in general and the Gitksan and Wet·suwet·en in particular entered the twentieth century with their Indigenous rights unacknowledged by the state and the particular archive—the treaty—that elsewhere marked colonialism's small though significant recognition of Indigenous loss.

From the 1860s onward, Aboriginal people and, if to a lesser extent, settlers alike demanded that the government formally acknowledge and extinguish Aboriginal title through treaty. Cole Harris's argument about the virtual absence of settler support for treaty rights correctly acknowledges the pervasive and highly strategic denial of Indigenous presence in British Columbia. Less helpfully, it accords an enormous and perhaps undeserved agency to the hero of Harris's thoughtful narrative, Gilbert Sproat.[10] This interpretation simplifies the uneven but still dialogic conversation about Indigenous land rights that circulated throughout the British empire and within British Columbia.[11] In 1860 a Victoria newspaper called on the example of one of the Douglas treaties and asked that "so easy or so inexpensive an arrangement" be replicated lest "the discontent and grasping avarice of the savage" be felt.[12] The expediency of treaties was a commonplace piece of settler wisdom throughout the 1860s. The *Colonist* newspaper, also of Victoria, lived up to its name with cheerful celebrations of the "Caucasian race" and vicious attacks on both Indigenous peoples and non-white settlers. Yet even this newspaper saw the acknowledgement of Indigenous rights through treaties as part of an ethical and, perhaps more importantly, a strategic colonial practice. "Indian Claims," they explained, needed to be settled so that Aboriginal people had "no excuse for entertaining ill feelings against the whites."[13]

Indigenous people argued for recognition of their claims on less calculated and equivocal grounds. From the 1850s to the 1870s they complained to local and colonial officials when settlers occupied local territory or when it was claimed in the name of the crown. By the 1880s these complaints had crystallized into an Aboriginal rights movement that pressed provincial, federal, and imperial governments to acknowledge Indigenous title, generally by treaty. Speaking to government officials gathered at the Nass River in 1888, Neils Puck named Indigenous people's problem as one of documentation. "I am the oldest man here," he explained, "and can't sit still any longer and hear that it is not our fathers' land. Who is the chief that gave this land to the Queen? Give us his name, we have never heard it."[14] The precise vehicles changed to reflect prevailing patterns of organization and communication, ranging from the localized complaints of the mid–nineteenth century, to the lobbying of the 1880s, to the first province-wide Aboriginal organizations of the twentieth century and the large, relatively powerful Pan-Indigenous groups of the late twentieth century. But the message—namely that Aboriginal people deserved and required recognition and settlement of their territorial claims and that this recognition should be acknowledged in an official archive—remained tellingly consistent.[15]

From the 1960s onward First Nations looked to the institution that has been so closely hewn to the imperial archive, the court, to articulate these grievances and seek redress. Thus when fifty-four Gitksan and Wet·suwet·en hereditary chiefs filed suit on behalf of their matrilineal houses in the British Columbia Supreme Court in October 1984 they were taking part in a relatively long-standing tradition. This case, as Louise Mandell, counsel to the chiefs, explained in her opening address in 1987, was unto itself historic, the culmination of efforts that "span the last century."[16] It was not their grievance but the scope of their claim that was new: the Gitksan and Wet·suwet·en asked the court to acknowledge their continued ownership and jurisdiction over a substantial part of British Columbia. This case rested on the argument that Aboriginal sovereignty was intact unless explicitly otherwise agreed, documented, and archived; since the archive contained nothing that documented Gitksan and Wet·suwet·en people ceding their land to settlers or the state, Indigenous sovereignty remained in force. This argument had implications well beyond the local. At stake was British Columbia's long history of denying Aboriginal land claims and, ultimately, its status as a legitimate settler state.

What was also different was the way the Gitksan and Wet·suwet·en and their counsel argued their case. As Joel R. Fortune points out, history has long been a staple of land claims cases in Canada and elsewhere. Yet *Delgamuukw v. British Columbia* engaged history in a newly explicit way by calling for a "self-aware and critical approach to historical understanding," one that both named and critiqued history's centrality to legitimating colonial knowledges and undermining or rendering invisible subaltern ones.[17] Mandell explained in her opening address that the case was not simply a request for recognition, but a challenge for the Court to overcome notions of the superiority of Western culture and its methods of communication, preservation, and legitimation of knowledge: "For the Court to deny the reality of Gitksan and Wet·suwet·en history except where it can be corroborated by expert evidence in the western scientific tradition is to disregard the distinctive Gitksan and Wet·suwet·en system of validating historical facts."[18] A direct result of this contention was that *Delgamuukw v. British Columbia* was the first Aboriginal title case in Canada to be argued primarily from the evidence of Indigenous peoples themselves.[19]

For Delgam Uukw, the Gitksan chief who was first named in the original suit, colonial denial of Aboriginal title and colonial denial of Aboriginal history and archives were one in the same. "The Europeans," he explained, "did not want to know our histories; they did not respect our laws or our ownership of our territories."[20] Their case sought dual redress for what were dual problems. *Delgamuukw v. British Columbia* was thus a literal challenge to the realpolitik of settler hegemony and a direct questioning of the historical methodology that documented, legitimated,

and sustained it. It was, in the apt words of some local observers, colonialism on trial.[21]

The Archive on Trial

The trial was a long one that was not only about archives but productive of
one unto itself. There were 374 days spent in court and 141 days spent
taking evidence out of court. It began in the northern community of
Smithers in May 1987 and concluded in the southern metropolis of Vancouver in June of 1990. Sixty-one witnesses gave evidence, many using
translators and others relying on "word spellers" to assist with the Gitksan
and Wet·suwet·en orthography. Another ninety-eight provided testimony
through affidavits or other out-of-court means. After the trial's completion
McEachern commented on the vast amount of paper produced: 23,503
pages of transcript evidence from the trial, 5,898 pages of transcript evidence, 3,030 pages of commission evidence, and 2,553 pages of cross examination on affidavits, all preserved in hard copy and diskette. Roughly 9,200
exhibits were filed at trial, comprising an estimated 50,000 pages; there
were 5,977 pages of transcript of argument. The province of British Columbia alone submitted twenty-eight of what McEachern called "huge bind-
ers" with excerpts of exhibits referred to in argument, while the plaintiffs
filed twenty-three.[22]

Chief Justice Allan McEachern was overwhelmed by the scale and scope
of the evidence. He explained in his judgment:

> As I am not a Royal Commission, and as I have no staff to assist me, it will not
> be possible to mention all of the evidence which took so long to adduce, or to
> analyze all of the exhibits and experts' reports which were admitted into
> evidence, or to describe and respond to all the arguments of counsel. In these
> circumstances I must do what a computer cannot do, and that is to summa-
> rize. In this respect I have been brutal. I am deeply conscious that the process
> of summarizing such a vast body of material requires me to omit much of
> what counsel and the parties may think is important. (14)

The volume and breadth of evidence led McEachern to modify some of his
initial decisions, including his important preliminary judgment that oral
testimony about property ownership would be admissible (55).[23] The
judge found himself in the disquieting position of the overwhelmed ob-

server of a massive archive, one not unlike the imperial archive analyzed by Thomas Richards in form, if so profoundly different in character, intention, and provenance.[24]

Yet it was not the scale and scope of the archive produced by the trial that led McEachern to reject the Gitksan and Wet·suwet·en case. It was what the plaintiffs knew about the history of British Columbia and how they knew it. Like Delgam Uukw, McEachern drew the conclusion that the content and methodology of the colonial past were irrevocably yoked. McEachern deemed the Gitksan and Wet·suwet·en view of the past too emotional and too political. "I have heard much at this trial about beliefs, feelings, and justice," he wrote, deeming these "subjective consideration" that courts of law were unable to deal with (13). McEachern here adopts an analytic stance that privileges dispassionate and above all "objective" accounts, a stance that is tellingly familiar to historians.[25]

The oral archive was the special target of the Chief Justice's disapproval. Jorge Cañizares-Esguerra has shown that the centrality of alphabetic scripts to European knowledge in general and history in particular was contested well into the eighteenth century.[26] But by the nineteenth century, the crisscrossed and mutually reinforcing connections between orality and savagery and writing and civilization were firm and politically charged. It is of course no accident that the ontological link between orality and savagery on the one hand and literacy and civilization on the other occurred simultaneous to the rapid expansion of European territorial control and cultural hegemony over the non-Western world, including North America and the antipodes. By the closing years of the nineteenth century the absence of written records was used to validate European claim to the so-called new world and to consign Indigenous people to what Anne McClintock memorably dubs "anachronistic space."[27] In 1894, Alexander Begg, an early historian of British Columbia, used the documentary stick to explain that First Nations people, however numerous and present, lacked a history:

> Of the pre-historic period, that is, prior to the arrival of Captain James Cook, on the north-west coast of America, little need be said. The fact, however, is well established that when Captain Cook and other early navigators visited the shores of the Pacific in this latitude, a very large population of aborigines existed on the coast. Alexander Mackenzie, in his expeditions across the unexplored portion of the North American continent to the Pacific, in 1793, also

found along his route a numerous population in the interior. But, like their brethren on the coast, they did not possess any written records. Their traditions were mythical; and, though carved emblematically on totems of enduring cedar in their villages along the seaboard, these emblems have not been deciphered so as to throw any light on the origins of the native tribes.[28]

Those who write and preserve their writing in what Begg calls "records" have history and those who do not have only the misty netherworld of myth. The written archive is here the adjudicator of empire, deciding whose histories, and thus territorial claims, are legitimate and whose are not.

The tight binds between literacy, archives, and colonial authority in the making of history are reinforced by and reflected by the legal traditions of the British common law, most especially by the hearsay rule. The hearsay rule deems information not given directly by a witness unworthy of legal consideration. The result is that oral tradition, which necessarily circulates between individuals and generations, is, for the purposes of the courts, invalid. The hearsay rule thus codifies and puts into legal language the same distrust of orality that historical methodology is premised upon. The difficulty of holding up this rule in a court case primarily about the past of an oral culture was grudgingly recognized by McEachern, who in a preliminary ruling decided the "the oral history of the people based on successive declarations of deceased persons was admissible." He made this decision, not because he had any particular faith in the oral archive, but because of the pragmatics produced by the legal pluralism that generally characterize imperial regimes.[29] "Where there is no written history," he wrote, "such evidence satisfied the test of necessity." Here McEachern does not validate the oral archive as much as he accords it a limited utility in instances where there is no documentary alternative. Thus the practice of colonialism forced a modification in documentary regimes, but it was only a partial one. Oral evidence was also singled out for special considerations of weight. Evaluating oral testimony, according to McEachern, necessitated a distinction between history, myth, and anecdote, one he insisted on making in the face of the Gitksan and Wet·suwet·en's counsel's exegesis of E. H. Carr.[30]

However grudging and partial, McEachern's initial ruling on the admissibility of oral testimony had enormous implications for *how* Aboriginal peoples and their supporters could conceptualize and argue the historical narratives that have been and will continue to be so central to Aboriginal rights litigation. Intense postcolonial struggles over the past have failed to conclusively dislodge the written as the real arbiter of history. Brent I Iarris writes in the South African context that the oral archive is valued only to verify that which is known from textual sources. This, as Harris notes, is not simply about inclusion and exclusion or the validation of textuality and the denial of orality—it is a function of the " 'reality effect' in the production of History," the complex process whereby some history is produced as real and some is rendered invalid or simply invisible.[31]

That orality is the precise mechanism that is used to render certain pasts unreal is not coincidental. That McEachern found himself literally unable to maintain his initial decision is a telling testament to something that Bain Attwood and Fiona Mcgowan point out in the Antipodean context and Gerald Torres and Kathryn Milun in the American one: that Indigenous modes of narrating and preserving history pose a genuine challenge to the form, content, and character of history as it is understood in the Western tradition and used in the courts.[32] Arguments about the equivalency of oral and written archives are a necessary corrective to methodologies and practices that are premised, if only implicitly, on the greater truth-value of documentary evidence. Yet easy analogies between written and oral history also can seriously underestimate how bound Western historical practice is to the written word and its preservation in archives. At the same time, it can understate the varieties of historical resources and knowledges within oral archives and, as Luise White's astute reading of African vampire stories suggests, downplay the interpretative possibilities of re-reading and recontextualizing colonial archives.[33] The competing modes of preserving and narrating the past proved fundamentally untranslatable in *Delgamuukw*. As in the *Mashpee* case analyzed by Torres and Milun, the existence of untranslatable examples and modes of communicating them rendered the entire cultures of which they were a part "unreadable."[34] McEachern explained that the court could not know Gitksan and Wet-·suwet·en history because of their archive. The trial challenged his faith in the "convenient but simplistic distinction between what European-based cultures would call mythology and 'real' matters" (47) but reinforced his conviction that textuality was a crucial signpost of civilization. "The evidence suggests that the Indians of the territory were, by historical standards, a primitive people without any form of writing, horses, or wheeled wagons," concluded the Justice (30).

But what of the massive archive that the plaintiffs had so exhaustively marshaled for the court? McEachern was unsettled when provided with ample evidence that the Gitksan and Wet·suwet·en archive was more than just lack. He was troubled by their archives' apparent embeddedness in culture and by its quotidian and distinctly female character. "Indian culture," McEachern explained, "pervades the evidence at the trial for nearly every word of testimony" (50). It was bound up with Indigenous cultures and their suspicious custodians, women. An archive that was "passed on orally from generation to generation, often it seems, by grandmothers who tell these things to their grandchildren often as 'an everyday thing'" was a dubious one (56). Here, women's words and Indigenous words are conflated, replicating not only the invalidation of subaltern history, but, as Antoinette Burton has recently written, the "longstanding template of fiction / feminine–history / masculine."[35]

McEachern was disturbed by the form of the archive as well. He experienced the Gitksan and Wet·suwet·en performance of their oral archive in court as unseemly and profoundly disquieting. Mary Johnson wanted to sing her adwaak in the witness box. According to one observer, the Justice responded by asking that it be written out, since "To have witnesses singing songs in court is not the proper way to approach the problem." After she had completed the adwaak, the Justice asked the Gitksan and Wet-·suwet·en counsel to explain why it had been necessary "to sing the song." In telling words he explained that "This is a trial, not a performance."[36]

The content of this oral archive met with similar disapproval and confusion. McEachern's final judgment argued that the adaawic and kungax lacked a consistent method, mixed myth and history, contained too many historical anomalies and inaccuracies, and often were at odds with each other and scientific evidence. A lengthy appendix to the ruling detailed these affronts, offering transcriptions of court testimony alongside careful notations of their mentions of moose, buckskin tents, and copper in oral testimonies meant that they could not be authentic documentary evidence of the years before European contact (*Judgment*, Schedule Four). Such was the basis of the Court's conclusion that he was "unable to accept adaawic, kungax, and oral histories as reliable bases for detailed history" except where they could be corroborated by historical knowledge generated from the usual repositories of Western knowledge, most notably written documents and their chosen scholarly interlocutors (78). Thus oral sources were acceptable when they played second or corroborative string to the documentary archives. It is not incidental that this relational positioning of oral and written archives mirrors that found in most current mainstream historical scholarship on North American history. This work, including my own, tends to pepper analysis rooted in the written archive with brief nods to oral sources. This scholarly approach, not unlike the legal one adopted by McEachern, is one that simultaneously acknowledges and submerges the critique of Indigenous history and archives.

The Court's unwillingness or inability to translate the Gitksan and Wet-·suwet·en archive and the epistemology it was premised on was matched by a concomitant inability to contextualize—or, in Dipesh Chakrabarty's lexicon, provincialize[37]—hegemonic EuroCanadian methods of understanding and narrating the past. In his judgment McEachern takes on the voice of the imperial traveler who, in Mary Louise Pratt's phrase, positions himself as the "lord of all he surveys."[38] He views the land not from within or upon it but from above it, finding it, as had so many European observers of North America and Australasia, "beautiful, vast and almost empty" (13). The land is reduced to a means for his visual pleasure, deemed too large to be known, and, most significantly, dispossessed of people, something that Elizabeth Vibert, via Pratt, calls a "routine textual strategy to separate the land from the people who inhabited it."[39]

McEachern adopts the voice of the historian as well as that of the traveler. He dispassionately chronicles events and recounts the actions of European men acting on behalf of nation-states. The human past that is not recorded in this archive is deemed unknown and unknowable, while the archive's inconsistency, polyvocality, and partiality slips below the radar. The *Judgment* begins, where it must, with the finding on the case. The legal discussion is quickly followed with a "Summary of Findings and Conclusions." These are distinctly historical. The first point is that "The last Great Ice Age, which lasted many thousands of years, covered nearly all of British Columbia. It ended about 10,000 years ago." The land is unknowable below its vaguely dated ice; so too are its inhabitants, the topic of McEachern's second point. Deeming Aboriginal peoples' origins "unknown" dislodges even their most basic claim of Indigenousness. This is echoed in McEachern's third point, that archaeological evidence is limited in scope and does not establish who the early inhabitants were or if they were simply "visitors," presumably not unlike the Europeans who would name the territory in the name of Britain (7).

Placing the land and its people outside the scope of human knowledge challenges their relationship and, at heart, their claim to each other in profound ways. The counterpoint to this is McEachern's loving and enthusiastic recitation of the actions of European men, a recitation marked by copious detail and more copious faith in the reliability of the archive that preserves their past. The *Judgment* includes two lengthy historical narratives that might well be taken for a textbook of British Columbia history written between 1880 and 1945. Using what he admits to be " 'scissors and paste' format" (98), the Justice reconstructs the past. The first historical narrative begins with a dismissive nod to "the fascinating questions of Viking or other Norse-type explorations" and quickly moves on to what has traditionally been the originary point of European histories of North America and the "new world" in general, and that is European men's "discovery" of them. The *Judgment* then discusses, in turn, maritime exploration, inland exploration, the establishment of European colonies in eastern North America, and, finally, the early colonization of British Columbia. The establishment of an HBC post marks the emergence of a "historic" period (29). Discussions of the fur trade, the establishment of colonies, colonial policies, and a digest of relations between Aboriginals and settlers in the nineteenth and twentieth centuries follow. This narration of the British Columbian past is eerily familiar to readers of general histories of British Columbia and other parts of the "new world," and it ultimately serves the same function: to shore up the supposed naturalness of European occupation in the fact of Aboriginal presence and, in McEachern's case, the Gitksan and Wet·suwet·en challenge to it.

In his *Judgment* McEachern becomes not only a historian but an appreciative audience for them. The Chief Justice had initially worried that "history is constantly being 'rewritten' " and raised questions about the reliability of archival documents.[40] The course of the trial allayed these fears about written history just as it amplified his ambivalence about the oral archive. McEachern did not make a simple distinction between European and non-European knowledge as much as he made a more complicated one rooted in this schism. The non-Aboriginal anthropologists called by the plaintiffs he found dubious, especially if they utilized the methodology of participant observation. Antonia Mills, Hugh Brody, and Richard Daly were deemed unreliable, not because they did know enough about the Gitksan and Wet·suwet·en, but because they knew too much and in inappropriate ways. "These anthropologists studied the Gitksan and Wet·suwet·en people intensively," he explained, adding that "Drs. Daly and Mills actually lived with the Gitksan and Wet·suwet·en for 2 and 3 years respectively after the commencement of this action" (51). Just as the oral archive is compromised by its embeddedness in the culture of its tellers, anthropological knowledge is compromised by its proximity to and, more dangerously, its possible affection for and respect of Aboriginal peoples. In court, the Crown asked Brody if he "liked Indians" and tried to have him disqualified as an expert witness. Heather Harris, a non-Aboriginal woman with an anthropology degree who had married into a Gitksan family, was also suspect. The Canadian government's counsel suggested that she might have "gone native" and thus lost her expert knowledge.[41]

The final *Judgment* positioned historians as good academics just as it positioned anthropologists as bad ones. The Justice expressed a genuine admiration for historians' work on both sides of the case, one rooted in his conviction that historians were essentially passive custodians of the archival record:

> Lastly, I wish to mention the historians. Generally speaking I accept just about everything they put before me because they were largely collectors of archival, historical documents. In most cases they provided much useful information with minimal editorial comment. Their marvelous collections largely spoke for themselves. (52)

William Brown, an HBC trader who kept records of his interaction with Gitksan and Wet·suwet·en people in the early nineteenth century, can therefore be deemed "one of our most useful historians" (29). The work of the historian in imagining and interpreting the past is rendered invisible. So too is the fact made so eloquently by Julie Cruikshank's analysis of gold-rush narratives: that mainstream historical writing, just like oral narrative, relies "on conventional, culturally specific narrative genres that help members construct, maintain, and pass on an understanding of how the world works or should work," or, as Judith Binney has argued in the case of Maori and Pakeha histories of New Zealand, that both oral and written history are "structured, interpretative, and combative."[42] That the Gitksan-Wet·suwet·en legal team decided that the historical-geographer Arthur Ray should work in isolation from the anthropologists suggests that they anticipated but were unable to successfully challenge the extent to which historical scholarship would be favored by the court.[43] In 1991 history thus found itself firmly positioned in its nineteenth-century place, as a positivist discipline rooted in the archive and a muse to the nation and the state and the practical keeper of the empire.

History as a Judge

When it was handed down in 1991 McEachern's judgment was greeted with shock and, by and large, disapproval. Its substantive findings went against a long-standing trend in Canadian courts toward more generous interpretations of laws and histories concerning First Nations peoples.[44] It was widely anticipated that McEachern would, given this trend and his preliminary findings, produce a different ruling. Yet McEachern not only delivered a ruling that went against the grain but did so in the language of what Paul Tennant identifies as a "traditional" or "old" white view of British Columbian history and Elizabeth Furniss characterizes as commonsense racism. The response was immediate and sharp. *Delgamuukw*, Tennant explains, received "more immediate public attention than any previous aboriginal rights judgment, and indeed, quite possibly more than any other judicial ruling in the history of this province."[45]

It is no surprise that Indigenous response was weary yet enraged. Gitksan and Wet·suwet·en observers emphasized that *Delgamuukw* was one incident in a long history of imperial betrayal and that McEachern was merely the most recent colonial authority to refuse to acknowledge the existence and validity of Indigenous cultures, claims, and archives. "We view this judgment for what it is," explained Satsan (Herb George), "a denial and a huge misunderstanding and ignorance of the First Nations across this country."[46] This was a studied ignorance that some saw in distinctly gendered terms. A member of the litigation team, Dora Wilson-Kenni, remarked that the fact that McEachern's decision was delivered on International Women's Day was highly symbolic, "just like slamming our matriarchal system."[47]

It seemed an especially galling insult in light of the process that led up to it. McEachern's was not an innocent ignorance, but a willful one, constructed in spite of, rather than in the absence of, meaningful contact with Gitksan and Wet·suwet·en peoples. Medig'm Gyamk (Neil Serritt) explained:

We did have a certain expectation. The expectation was partly created by Judge McEachern himself. He sat in his chair and the witnesses were in the witness box, elders with who he formed a relationship. They thought he was forming a friendly relationship, that there was something there, but you realize when you read his judgement that he saw our people as "cute." He didn't understand us.[48]

This combination of outrage and disbelief reflects the extent to which *Delgamuukw*, like so many other moments of postcolonial reckoning, put First Nations people in an enormously contradictory place that they inevitably could not resolve. "Our people have been asked over and over: 'How can you substantiate who you are? Who are you to say you have ownership by what we call territories' "? explained Miluulak (Alice Jeffrey).[49] Demanding that an Indigenous people prove their very existence in evidentiary terms that they lack is reminiscent of the predicament Elizabeth A. Povinelli identifies in contemporary Australia, namely the incessant yet unanswerable demand that Aboriginal peoples demonstrate "tradition." The result is that Indigenous people and their claims against settler societies are forever and necessarily found insufficient, impartial, and inauthentic.[50]

Scholarly communities also voiced strong objection to *Delgamuukw*, if for different reasons and in different voices. Anthropologists did so with the most amount of ink and of vigor. Their outcry was informed both by McEachern's uniformly pejorative evaluation of anthropological scholarship and the historic and continuing connections between anthropology, Indigenous peoples, and more especially Indigenous rights cases.[51] Historians also worked to publicly disassociate themselves from McEachern's view of the past and historical scholarship. That they did so reflects professional historians' newly significant role within Indigenous land struggles throughout the settler world.[52] In Canada, laments for historians' increasing public irrelevance are belied by their increasing prominence in Aboriginal rights litigation, where archival research and historical interpretation have been and will likely continue to be central.[53]

Delgamuukw thus forced historians to reckon with the implications of what was undeniably an explicitly politicized role in court and on the witness stand. Ray reflected publicly on his experience as an expert witness, explaining how ethnohistorical methodology and observations were easily misunderstood and manipulated in an adversarial courtroom environment. He despaired that after 374 days of trial covering all aspects of

Gitskan-Wet·suwet·en history in depth, Justice McEachern still held the "same Eurocentric view of native people that had been an unfortunate judicial and political tradition in British Columbia since the colonial era."[54] Robin Fisher argued that despite his putative praise of the discipline, Mc-Eachern "paid very little attention to historians," harked back to an old view that documents were self-explanatory and that history must necessarily be rooted in an examination of written records, and produced a decision based on "loose and shoddy use of historical detail."[55] Others turned to that special tool of social and postcolonial historiography, the contrapuntal reading of mainstream texts. Tennant, a political scientist, pointed out that evidence that McEachern assumed indicated colonial hegemony—in this case a colonial official's vigorous and repeated denial of Indigenous title—could be read against the grain as a telling indication that alternative views existed.[56]

For historians, *Delgamuukw* became a powerful symbol of how historical scholarship could be utilized in public policy against the interests of Aboriginal people. Quoting especially inflammatory passages from Mc-Eachern's generally over-the-top prose—especially his infamous identification of pre-contact Gitksan and Wet·suwet·en life as "nasty, brutish and short" and his misspelling of Hobbes's name—became *de rigeur* in historical work on British Columbia, and the *Judgment* was routinely evoked as an ominous example of the real dangers of failing to adequately deconstruct or contextualize European views of Indigenous people and history.[57] Mc-Eachern's wedding of empire, history, and archive thus ironically provided historians with the motivation and opportunity to define themselves and their work as in opposition to imperialism, its knowledges, and its archival practices. This was a rejection of history's role as the explainer and interlocutor of empire that was unprecedented within the local context.

This scholarly response represented a necessary clarification of the relationship of historical and anthropological research and researchers to the fractious politics of possession and dispossession in British Columbia. Yet calling McEachern's ruling a "particularly heavy blow to both the First Nations and academic communities" presents scholars and Indigenous people as roughly equivalent subjects in this struggle, which is surely a dangerous act of scholarly solipsism.[58] In the rush to distance themselves from history's and anthropology's colonial past, observers risk valorizing contemporary scholarly practice, including that around archives. Fisher's argument that McEachern "appears to have no understanding of either the historical methodology or the conclusions of historians who have written about Native people in Canada" fails to acknowledge the extent to which historians' practice and knowledge-production can and has contributed to analyses like McEachern's.[59] We may wish that a positivist discipline rooted in an almost mystical reverence for the "primary document," assumed to be written and unpublished, was a thing of the past, but it remains very much with us, and a rigorous critique must acknowledge that as well as argue against it. Likewise, Robin Riddington's remark that " 'Primitive' is not part of an anthropological vocabulary" is not simply overly optimistic but a genuine denial of the continuing (if by now largely implicit) centrality of notions of primitivism and savagery to anthropological thought and practice.[60]

These dramatic gestures of distancing risk doing what Tennant and Furniss each warn against, and that is treating the McEachern judgment as a spectacular and singular example of racism and ignorance and failing to account for the extent to which the Justice spoke in the voice of mainstream settler British Columbia.[61] They also risk simplifying that settler voice. McEachern's panicky and hyperbolic defense of British Columbia as a European possession does not, I think, reflect a lack of understanding of the Indigenous past and its claim on the present and future, or at least not an uncomplicated one. Perhaps not unlike the Keith Windschuttle text analyzed by Curthoys, McEachern's *Judgment* is rooted in a profound if implicit recognition of Indigenous claims to settler lands and an utter inability to cope with the implications of this knowledge. However seemingly illogical and incongruous, outright denial of Aboriginal history and claims is one way that McEachern, like so many settlers before him, can continue to think of British Columbia as his own. But this is a denial that begins in knowledge of the Indigenousness of British Columbia, not its absence.

Historians' critiques also underestimate the extent to which McEachern's recapitulation of tired settler wisdom was enabled by available scholarly knowledge and practice. The yearning for a "total archive" and the belief that historians have or should have one that can genuinely substitute for the likes of McEachern's may begin with a critique of the colonial archive, but this is not sufficient to take us where that critique may and perhaps must lead us.[62] And that is to a postcolonial practice of history— one that acknowledges and utilizes the distinctive possibilities of all archives and embraces rather than denies the interpretive challenges posed to mainstream historical methodology by the Indigenous archive, alternative ways of reading the written one, and the simple admission that the ways we know the colonial past are not only multiple but necessarily and unevenly partial.

The Presence of the Past

McEachern's ruling is an unexpectedly ambivalent text, one that tells us much about how archives and historical scholarship operate within post-colonial settler societies. Jeff Sahadeo's analysis of Uzbekistan's archive demonstrates that state control over knowledge and history is rarely what it seems or claims to be. This is a fragility produced by the particularities of Uzbek poverty and instability, but it is not unique to it. In *Delgamuukw* the Justice made a sustained attempt to employ once hegemonic ideas of the past, the archive, and historical knowledge to render Gitksan and Wet·suwet·en peoples and claims to British Columbia's past and, by implication, its present illegitimate and indeed unreal. The lengthy ruling suggests that these notions have not only survived but retained a political purchase into the closing years of the twentieth century. We need not deny this point to acknowledge that it failed. McEachern knew well that his ruling would be appealed even as he wrote it, commenting that he could not "expect my judgment to be the last word on this case" (290). And, of course, it wasn't, even in narrowly judicial terms. In 1997 the Supreme Court of Canada reversed McEachern's judgment on appeal. That they did so on essentially archival grounds is worth noting. While they did not find explicit fault with British Columbia's Court legal decision, they did argue that McEachern had not paid sufficient attention to the oral archive. In doing so they both overturned the 1991 decision and made arguing Indigenous cases on the basis of oral evidence newly possible.

But the archive is an unstable ally in colonial politics in less obvious ways as well. Despite the seemingly glaring links between McEachern's conceptions of First Nations and colonial history and his findings in *Delgamuukw*, Furniss is correct to remark that the same hoary tropes—the empty land, the noble savage, settler benevolence—have also been used to justify legal decisions that are widely regarded as pro-Aboriginal.[63] It can also have unexpected effects. In *Delgamuukw*, McEachern's painstaking denial of an Aboriginal archive and an Aboriginal past had the ironic result of creating an entirely new sort of archive, one that spoke in a different voice and spoke different things. In *Delgamuukw*'s aftermath, Yagalahl (Dora Wilson) remarked:

> That's one of the things that we were criticized for. Our oral history. So now it is in black and white for everyone to read. Evidence that was given in the courtroom, thousands of documents, over thirty thousand documents, that were used as exhibits in this case. Maps. Everything you could think of. Genealogies. Letters that were written by our people in earlier days fighting this. All sorts of goodies in there are on record, and that is a real win for us as far as I am concerned. There is something positive there. Our history is on record.[64]

The *Judgment* thus produced the opposite of what it putatively used the power of the law to do. It brought into being a legal system willing to acknowledge the legitimacy of the Aboriginal oral archive, and it produced an Indigenous archive that even McEachern would acknowledge as such.

Putting the colonial archive on trial shows us how archives are not only about what they contain within their walls. They are also about absence, although the absences in the colonial archive are not neutral, voluntary, or strictly literal. They are, as Helena Pohlandt-McCormick argues elsewhere in this volume, silences borne of and perpetuated by violence and radical inequality. But these sorts of silences can speak very loudly, even when empires, courts, and states have least wanted them to. The Justice who listened to and read about the settler and Gitksan and Wet·suwet·en versions of the past tried almost desperately to use long-standing intellectual and legal assumptions about the stability and truth of the former and the unreliability of the latter to explain the desire that he shared with so many other settlers in British Columbia and elsewhere: to render Indigenous people and claims absent and proclaim settlers the true bearers of the territory and its history. But for all its apparent victory, this strategy was a failure. The Gitksan and Wet·suwet·en archive and the Gitksan and Wet·suwet·en people did not and would not go away. Like the scattered material found in the basement of a Seattle hotel that bears witness to the repressed history of the internment of Japanese Americans in World War II,[65] the words of Indigenous elders remain, as do the different possible readings of the written archive. And this, cumulatively, is an archive that puts colonialism on trial again and again.

Notes

1 On this, see Jean Friesen, "Magnificent Gifts: The Treaties of Canada with the Indians of the Northwest, 1869–76," *Transactions of the Royal Society of Canada* 5, 1 (1986): 41–51; Treaty 7 Elders and Tribal Council, with Walter Hilderbrandt, Sarah Carter, and Dorothy First Rider, *The True Sprit and Original Intent of Treaty 7* (Montreal-Kingston: McGill-Queen's, 1997); William C. Wicken, *Mi'kmaq Treaties on Trial: History, Land, and Donald Marshall Junior* (Toronto: University of Toronto Press, 2002).

2 See, on these points, Robert E. Cail, *Land, Man, and the Law: The Disposal of Crown Lands in British Columbia, 1871–1913* (Vancouver: University of British Columbia Press, 1974); Cole Harris, *Making Native Space: Colonialism, Resistance, and Reserves in British Columbia* (Vancouver: University of British Columbia Press, 2002); Paul Tennant, *Aboriginal Peoples and Politics: The Indian Land Question in British Columbia, 1849–1989* (Vancouver: University of British Columbia Press, 1990).

3 See, especially, the articles by Verne Harris and Brent Harris in Carolyn Hamilton, Verne Harris, Jane Taylor, Michele Pickover, Graeme Reid, and Razia Saleh, eds., *Refiguring the Archive* (Dordrecht: Kluwer Academic Publishers, 2002).

4 Carolyn Steedman, *Dust: The Archive and Cultural History* (New Brunswick, N.J.: Rutgers University Press, 2002), 164.

5 See Daniel W. Clayton, *Islands of Truth: The Imperial Fashioning of Vancouver Island* (Vancouver: University of British Columbia Press, 2000).

6 I borrow "proto-colonial" from Cole Harris, *The Resettlement of British Columbia: Essays on Colonialism and Geographical Change* (Vancouver:University of British Columbia Press, 1997).

7 See C. Harris, *Making Native Space*, 18–30. Also see Wilson Duff, "The Fort Victoria Treaties," *BC Studies* 3 (1969): 3–57.

8 The partial exception is that part of North-Central British Columbia covered by Treaty 8, negotiated in 1899. On this, see Arthur Ray, "Treaty 8: A British Columbia Anomaly," *BC Studies* 123 (1999): 5–58.

9 B. W. Pearse, B.C. Lands and Works Department, "Notes concerning Details of V.I. Branch of Land Office," 1869; transcript, British Columbia Archive, Add Mss C / A / B / 30.7m.

10 C. Harris, *Making Native Space*, chap. 3. On settler hegemonies in contemporary British Columbia, see Elizabeth Furniss, *The Burden of History: Colonialism and the Frontier Myth in a Rural Canadian Community* (Vancouver: University of British Columbia Press, 1999).

11 See Elizabeth Elbourne, "Land Right Claims and the Idea of Being 'Aboriginal': Networks in the Early-19th-Century White Settler Empire," paper presented to the "British World" Conference, University of Calgary, July 2004.

12 *Victoria Gazette*, April 13, 1860.

13 "Settlement of Indian Claims," *Colonist*, May 12, 1863.

14 *Papers Relating to the Commission Appointed to Enquire and the Condition of the Indians of the North-West Coast* (Victoria: Richard Wolfenden, 1888), 20.

15 The best analysis of this remains Tennant, *Aboriginal Peoples and Politics*.

16 Louise Mandell, "Address of the Gitksan and Wet·suwet·en Hereditary Chiefs to Chief Justice McEachern of the Supreme Court of British Columbia," *Canadian Native Law Reporter* 1 (1988): 17. This was also published as Gisday Wa and Delgam Uukw, *The Spirit in the Land: The Opening Statement of the Gitksan and Wet·suwet·en Hereditary Chiefs in the Supreme Court of British Columbia, May 11, 1987* (Gabriola Island, B.C.: Reflections, 1989).

17 Joel R. Fortune, "Constructing *Delgamuukw*: Legal Arguments, Historical Argumentation, and the Philosophy of History," *University of Toronto Faculty of Law Review* 51 (winter 1993): 89.

18 Mandell, "Address," 35.

19 This point is made in the published expert-opinion case of anthropologist Antonia Mills, *Eagle Down Is Our Law: Witsuwit'en Law, Feasts, and Land Claims* (Vancouver: University of British Columbia Press, 1994), 11. For an analysis of a contemporary case that relied largely on "expert" non-Aboriginal opinion, see Wicken, *Mi'kmaq Treaties*.

20 Delgam Uukw, "Delgam Uukw Speaks," in Gisday Wa and Delgam Uukw, *The Sprit in the Land*, 8. The incorrect spelling *Delgamuukw* has survived in the subsequent document and the literature that refers to it.

21 See Don Monet and Skanu'u (Ardythe Wilson), *Colonialism on Trial: Indigenous Land Rights and the Gitksan and Wet·suwet·en Sovereignty Case* (Philadelphia, Pa., and Gabriola Island, B. C.: New Society Publishers, 1992).

22 McEachern, C.J.S.C, *Delgamuukw v. British Columbia*, 1991, British Columbia Supreme Court, 12. Hereafter *Judgment*; quotations in text cited by page number.

23 See his preliminary ruling on evidence in McEachern, C.J.S.C, *Delgamuukw et al. v. The Queen in Right of British Columbia et al.*, *Dominion Law Reports*, 4th Series, vol. 40 (1988). Hereafter McEachern, *Evidence*.

24 Thomas Richards, *The Imperial Archive: Knowledge and the Fantasy of Empire* (London: Verso 1993).

25 See Joyce Appleby, Lynn Hunt, and Margaret Jacob, *Telling the Truth About History* (New York: W. W. Norton and Company, 1994).

26 Jorge Cañizares-Esguerra, *How to Write the History of the New World: Histories, Epistemologies, and Identities in the Eighteenth-Century Atlantic World* (Stanford, Calif.: Stanford University Press, 2001), especially chap. 2.

27 Anne McClintock, *Imperial Leather: Race, Gender, and Sexuality in the Colonial Conquest* (New York: Routledge, 1995).

28 Alexander Begg, *History of British Columbia from Its Earliest Discovery to the Present Time* (Toronto: McGraw-Hill Ryerson, 1972; orig. pub. 1894), preface.

29 See, here, Sally Merry Engle, *Colonizing Hawai'i: The Cultural Power of the*

Law (Princeton: Princeton University Press, 2000), and, locally, Elizabeth Furniss, "Indians, Odysseys and Vast, Empty Lands: The Myth of the Frontier in the Canadian Justice System," *Anthropologica* 41 (1999): 195–208.

30 McEachern, *Evidence*, 685, 689.

31 Brent Harris, "Archive, Public History, and the Essential Truth: The TRC Reading the Past," in Hamilton et al., eds., *Refiguring the Archive*, 177.

32 Bain Attwood and Fiona Magowan, "Introduction" in Attwood and Magowan, eds., *Telling Stories: Indigenous History and Memory in Australia and New Zealand* (Crowns Nest, Australia: Allen and Unwin, 2001); Gerald Torres and Kathryn Milun, "Translating *Yonnondio* by Precedent and Evidence: The Mashpee Indian Case," *Duke Law Journal* 4 (September 1990): 625–59.

33 Luise White, *Talking with Vampires: Rumor and History in East and Central Africa* (Berkeley: University of California Press, 2000).

34 Torres and Milun, "Translating *Yonnondio*," 629. Robert Paine argues that one of the failures of the case was the unwillingness of the plaintiffs' expert witnesses to interpret and explain this difference. My reading of the opening address—which clearly addresses questions of epistemological difference—suggests that this critique underestimates the complexity of the problem. See Paine, "In Chief Justice McEachern's Shoes: Anthropology's Ineffectiveness in Court," *PoLAR: Political and Legal Anthropology Review* 19, 2 (1996): 59–70.

35 Antoinette Burton, *Dwelling in the Archive: Women Writing House, Home, and History in Late Colonial India* (New York: Oxford, 2003), 21.

36 This is related by Gitksan and Wet·suwet·en counsel Leslie Hall Pinder's memoir of the trial, *The Carriers of No: After the Land Claims Trial* (Vancouver: Lazara, 1991), 5–7.

37 Dipesh Chakrabarty, *Provincializing Europe: Postcolonial Thought and Historical Difference* (Princeton: Princeton University Press, 2000).

38 Mary Louise Pratt, *Imperial Eyes: Travel Writing and Transculturation* (London: Routledge, 1992). Also see Fortune, "Constructing *Delgamuukw*."

39 Elizabeth Vibert, *Traders' Tales: Narratives of Cultural Encounters in the Columbia Plateau, 1807–1846* (Norman: University of Oklahoma Press, 1997), 85; and see Pratt, *Imperial Eyes*, 61–62.

40 McEachern, C.J.B.C., "Delgamuukw (Muldoe) et al. v. R. in Right of British Columbia and the Attorney General of Canada," in *British Columbia Law Reports*, Second Series, vol. 38 (1989), 166, 170. Hereafter McEachern, *Historical Documents and Learned Treatises*.

41 One source attributes this question to the Crown counsel, another to McEachern. See Dara Culhane, *The Pleasure of the Crown: Anthropology, Law, and First Nations* (Vancouver: Talon, 1998), 134–39, 125; Mills, *Eagle Down Is Our Law*, 20.

42 Julie Cruikshank, "Images of Society in Klondike Gold Rush Narratives: Skookum Jim and the Discovery of Gold," in Jennifer S. H. Brown and Elizabeth Vibert, eds., *Reading Beyond Words: Contexts for Native History* (Peterborough,

Ontario: Broadview, 1996) 452; Judith Binney, "Maori Oral Narratives, Pakeha Written Texts: Two Forms of Telling History," *New Zealand Journal of History*, 21, 1 (April 1987): 16. Cruikshank deals with these issues in *Delgamuukw* in her "Invention of Anthropology in British Columbia's Supreme Court: Oral Tradition as Evidence in *Delgamuukw v. BC*," *BC Studies* 95 (Autumn 1992): 25–42.

43 See Arthur J. Ray, "Creating the Image of the Savage in Defence of the Crown: The Ethnohistorian in Court," *Native Studies Review* 6, 2 (1990): 18.

44 Bruce Miller, "Introduction," *BC Studies* 95 (Autumn 1992) 4; this was a special issue on *Delgamuukw v. British Columbia*.

45 Paul Tennant, "The Place of *Delgamuukw* in British Columbia History and Politics—and Vice Versa," in Frank Cassidy, ed., *Aboriginal Title in British Columbia: Delgamuukw v. The Queen* (Victoria: Oolichan Books and the Institute for Research on Public Policy, 1992), 73; Furniss, "Indians, Odysseys and Vast, Empty Lands," 196.

46 Satsan (Herb George), "The Fire Within Us," in Cassidy, ed., *Aboriginal Title*, 56.

47 Dora Wilson-Kenni, "Time of Trial: The Gitksan and Wet-suwet'en in Court," *BC Studies* 95 (Autumn 1992) 10.

48 Medig'm Gyamk (Neil Serritt), "It Doesn't Matter What the Judge Said," in Cassidy, ed., *Aboriginal Title*, 303.

49 Miluulak (Alice Jeffrey), "Remove Not the Landmark," in Cassidy, ed., *Aboriginal Title*.

50 Elizabeth A. Povinelli, "Settler Modernity and the Quest for an Indigenous Tradition," *Public Culture* 11, 1 (1999): 19–48.

51 Noel Dyck and James B. Waldram, "Anthropology, Public Policy, and Native Peoples: An Introduction to the Issues," in Dyck and Waldram, eds., *Anthropology, Public Policy, and Native Peoples in Canada* (Montreal-Kingston: McGill-Queens, 1993).

52 See Bain and Magowan, "Introduction"; Ewan Morris, "History Never Repeats?: The Waitangi Tribunal and New Zealand History," *History Compass*, 2003, found at http://www.history-compass.com/Pilot.

53 On this see Frank Tough, "Introduction: Advocacy Research and Native Studies," *Native Studies Review* 6, 2 (1990): 1–12.

54 Ray, "Creating the Image of the Savage," 26. Also see Arthur J. Ray, "The Historical Geographer and the Gitskan-Wet·suwet·en Comprehensive Claim: The Role of the Expert Witness," in Garth Cant, John Overton, and Eric Pawson, eds., *Indigenous Land Rights in Commonwealth Countries: Dispossession, Negotiation and Community Action* (Christchurch, New Zealand: University of Canterbury, 1993).

55 Robin Fisher, "Judging History: Reflections on the Reasons for Judgement in *Delgamuukw v. B.C.*," *BC Studies* 95 (autumn 1992): 43–54.

56 Tennant, "The Place of *Delgamuukw*," 87.

57 See, for instance, Clayton, *Islands of Truth*, 61–62; Vibert, *Traders' Tales*, 261.

58   This is from Miller, "Introduction," 5.

59   Fisher, "Judging History," 44.

60   Robin Riddington, "Fieldwork in Courtroom 53: A Witness to *Delgamuukw v. B.C.*," *BC Studies* 95 (autumn 1992): 16.

61   See Paul Tennant, "The Place of British Columbia History and Politics in *Delgamuukw*—and Vice Versa," in Cassidy, ed., *Aboriginal Title*; Furniss, "Indians, Odysseys, and Empty Lands."

62   On this, see Burton, *Dwelling*, Epilogue.

63   Furniss, "Indians, Odysseys, and Vast, Empty Lands," 196.

64   Yagalahl (Dora Wilson), "It Will Always Be the Truth," in Cassidy, ed., *Aboriginal Title*, 204.

65   Kate Brown, "The Eclipse of History: Japanese America and a Treasure Chest of Forgetting," *Public Culture* 9, 1 (fall 1996); 69–92.

Ann Curthoys

The History of Killing

and the Killing of History

THE QUESTION "WHAT HAPPENED?" has become a source of public debate and anxiety in many societies in recent years, as differences between
historians about the past become the site for major political contestation
and debate. Sometimes these are debates over alleged wartime atrocities,
as in Japan (the Nanjing massacre) and the United States (the bombing of
Hiroshima).[1] In other cases, it is the very foundation of the nation that is in
question, as in Israel's divided historiography focusing on 1948.[2] Such debates are especially strong within the former British Empire, less in Britain
itself (where they remain academic rather than popular) than in its former
colonies of settlement—in countries like Australia, New Zealand, Canada,
and the United States—where they are prompted and prolonged by deep
psychic concerns about the morality of the nation itself. In such societies,
nationalist historians seek to justify and praise the nation through a particular version of its past, while revisionist historians aim to redeem and
enhance it through what they see as an honest coming to terms with its
darker history. Yet whatever the political motivation of the historians, it is
striking how in substance and detail (and these discussions have a tendency to become extraordinarily detailed) the debate always comes to rest
on the archive and its interpretation. As the battle over the national past
rages, curious and concerned national publics are treated to a quick course
in Historical Theory and Method I. In the process, historians learn that
they are even more divided than they knew on issues fundamental to their
discipline, such as whether documents can "speak for themselves," what
the relationship is between "fact" and "interpretation," and whether or
not one should "attempt to see the past in its own terms."

  In this essay I explore the ways in which the Australian "history wars" of
the early 2000s raise general questions of theory and method, forcing us to
reconsider what counts as reliable historical evidence, how archival mate-

rial should be read, and what the meaning and significance of divergent interpretations are. While the Australian history wars have been fought on a range of frontier conflicts, I focus here on the controversy over the settlement of just one Australian colony, Tasmania, and the large-scale (though, contrary to much international opinion, incomplete) destruction of the Indigenous population in its wake. For it is here that the "history wars" have to date been fought most bitterly.

The Australian History Wars Begin

The forerunner of the current disputes was a very protracted and open public debate over the nature and meaning of colonization in the wake of what is known as the *Mabo* decision by the Australian High Court in June 1992. This decision recognized for the first time in Australian law the prior occupation of the country by Aboriginal people, and in so doing also recognized the existence of Native Title, that is of indigenous rights in land that were not fully extinguished by the establishment of British settlement from 1788. The decision was truly historic, overturning two centuries of the legal fiction *terra nullius*, the doctrine whereby a colonizer's right to settlement was justified by the idea that since the Aboriginal people had no recognizable law or system of government, they could not be regarded as having prior rights over the land known as Australia. This legal fiction meant that Australia could be settled without treaties and the claims of Indigenous people denied.[3]

At the time, many welcomed the decision and the Native Title legislation which followed a year later as righting a long-standing wrong, providing a legal basis for the recognition of native title, and offering the beginning of a new deal for Aboriginal people. Many others, however, were horrified at the version of history on which the judgment rested: that Aboriginal people did have laws and government and that their lands had been seized from them without their consent. The judges were accused of being reforming or crusading judges who had swallowed the erroneous views of certain politically radical historians, most notably Henry Reynolds. Historians were not united either; Geoffrey Blainey, a respected conservative historian, thought the judgments rested on a misreading of Australian history.[4]

The question of history was again in public consciousness with the election of a Conservative government in 1996 and the formation of a minority populist party, One Nation, which was clearly opposed to recognition of distinctive and specific Aboriginal rights. In October 1996, Prime Minister John Howard said that he sympathized fundamentally with Australians who are insulted when they are told that they have a racist, bigoted past. In response to an outcry from historians, teachers, Aboriginal spokespeople, church leaders, the Human Rights Commission, and the Opposition, who said that Australia did have such a past and it was important to understand rather than deny it, the prime minister responded that "the balance sheet of Australian history presents a very positive view and he remains disturbed about the self-flagellation many indulge in about Australia's past."[5]

Public debate over Aboriginal history was further heightened in 1997, with the publication of the Australian Human Rights and Equal Opportunity Commission's *Bringing Them Home* report. The former Labor government had two years earlier asked the commission to conduct a national inquiry into the history and effects of Aboriginal child-removal policies and practices in the nineteenth and twentieth centuries. The completed report, which detailed the extensive practice and harmful effects of Aboriginal child removal, was now presented to a less than enthusiastic Conservative coalition government. One of the leading opponents of the report was a group associated with the conservative journal *Quadrant*, which sponsored a seminar on Aboriginal history over the weekend of September 9–10, 2000, at which a number of speakers defended Australia's record on child removal and condemned the report.

The debate soon broadened. At this same seminar there emerged a parallel debate on the extent of killing on the colonial frontiers, when Keith Windschuttle launched his attack on Henry Reynolds's estimate that approximately twenty thousand Aboriginal people were killed in the course of the European invasion and settlement of the continent. Windschuttle had, he says, been prompted to take up the question of frontier violence when asked to review a book by Rod Moran, *Massacre Myths*, published privately in 1994 and much discussed in Western Australia but little noticed in the rest of the country.[6] In his book Moran had systematically questioned the validity of reports of a massacre at Forrest Creek in northern Western Australia in 1926, through a study of the transcripts of the Royal Commission of investigation of 1927 and other materials and a challenging of the credibility of the main informant, the Reverend Ernest Gribble.

Historians have disagreed over Moran's argument, and the debate continues.[7] Windschuttle published three articles in *Quadrant* in late 2000, accusing historians—especially Henry Reynolds—of exaggerating the extent of frontier violence and killing.[8] A year later, in December 2001, at a symposium on frontier violence organized by the National Museum of Australia, he further criticized the work of a number of historians who, he said, were driven by a 1960s-style leftist agenda, openly seeing their history as assisting the political struggles of Indigenous peoples and conspiring to silence alternative voices like his own which sought to question that agenda. This essay appeared in a collection edited by Bain Attwood and Stephen Foster, *Frontier Conflict*, alongside many essays by historians critical of Windschuttle's arguments.[9]

Windschuttle's greatest media success came, however, with the publication of his 2002 book, *The Fabrication of Aboriginal History*, a detailed rebuttal of the widely accepted idea that Tasmania had witnessed a violent frontier. The work of nineteenth-century historians such as James Bonwick and his twentieth-century successors like Lyndall Ryan and Henry Reynolds had generally emphasized the violence of the Tasmanian frontier from the first British settlement in 1803 onward, and especially in the second half of the 1820s, though there were disagreements between them over how many died directly as a result of violent confrontations.[10] Historians had also emphasized the destructive effects on the Aboriginal population of the clearances conducted in 1830–31, when the remaining Aboriginal population was removed or enticed to Flinders Island, a small island off the Tasmanian coast, where many died.[11] The Tasmanian Aboriginal people today, Lyndall Ryan in particular pointed out, are largely the descendants of Aboriginal women who cohabited with European sealers and other settlers on the islands in eastern Bass Strait (between Tasmania and the Australian mainland), thus escaping the disastrous settlement on Flinders Island.[12]

Windschuttle now suggested that the rapid decline in the Indigenous population in Tasmania was the result, not of frontier violence (which, he argues, was minimal), but primarily the loss of reproductive capacity through venereal and other diseases and the selling of women by the men to whalers, sealers, and settlers. Not only, he argues, was there no policy of removal or destruction of the Tasmanians, but in fact governments tried to protect them. Where there was violence, the blame must be placed not with the colonizers, who were law-abiding good Christians defending their persons and property, but with the colonized, the Indigenous peoples themselves, who owed their survival through thousands of years of isolation "more to good fortune than good management." Their attacks on settlers were not motivated by resistance to the loss of land and food sources, their basic conditions of life; indeed they should not be seen as defending their country from invasion since they had no notion that the land was theirs. Rather, Aboriginal attacks on settlers should be seen as simply the products of mindless lawlessness and "senseless violence"; robbery and murder were "two customs they had come to relish." When settlers responded with force to such attacks, some Aboriginal people were killed; the number, however, was trifling, making Tasmania, and indeed the Australian continent generally, one of the least bloody of all colonial frontiers. "The British colonization of this continent," Windschuttle writes, "was the least violent of all Europe's encounters with the New World."[13] The book concludes with a list of "plausible killings," 118 in the first edition and 120 in the second.

One of the key issues raised by this book and the responses to it is that of how to read the documentary record. In *The Fabrication of Aboriginal History* and in various essays Windschuttle opposes historians giving Indigenous oral tradition serious attention. He treats oral evidence of both Aboriginal and white people as generally unreliable, being either politically motived or simply mistaken. Nor is he very interested in the evidence of archaeologists, anthropologists, and others; the case must stand or fall on the written evidence alone. His method is primarily to undertake research by tracking and checking the footnotes of those historians with whom he disagrees, and in some cases finding them inadequate to the point made in the text. His attack is sharpest against the main historian of the Aboriginal Tasmanians, Lyndall Ryan, whose book, *The Aboriginal Tasmanians*, first appeared in 1981 and was reprinted in 1996. In accusing her and others not only of making mistakes in their footnotes but of "fabricating" their claims, *Fabrication* went further than any other Australian historian has done. This charge placed the debate on a new footing.

Windschuttle's book was greeted with praise by right-wing commentators in both Australia and the United States, condemnation from Indigenous spokespeople and their supporters, and with a variety of conceptual criticisms from historians with expertise in Australian Indigenous history.[14] The furor was huge, with well over a hundred substantial articles including opinion-page pieces, book reviews, feature articles, and news stories appearing in the mainstream press, plus some coverage on television. While some Indigenous people, such as employees of the Indigenous affairs unit at a television station, expressed outrage through a public protest outside the book launch,[15] most have refrained from entering into the details of the debate. Indigenous people who write history usually focus on autobiography, biography, family history, and community history, telling a story of survival and achievement rather than one of violence, defeat, and loss. Many have seen the whole discussion as "white historians' business." As two doctoral history students at Melbourne University, Clare Land and Eve Vincent, wrote, "the Windschuttle debate has silenced Aboriginal respondents." They continue: "This is not an important historical debate. This is a political debate in which Windschuttle equips the right with a version of the national past that denies Aboriginal rights to land in the post-Mabo present."[16] Many non-Indigenous people have reacted similarly: this is a political and not a serious historical debate.

Many others, however, have thought that it *was* necessary to see this as a serious debate about history and to engage in the details. Unfortunately, the historians were slow to develop their responses, as historians often are, for it takes time to consult archives, reread voluminous material, and track down details. Moreover, the historian mainly under attack, Lyndall Ryan, had moved into a quite different research field, further inhibiting her ability to respond to such a detailed and extensive attack. Gradually, however, historians did develop detailed responses. Robert Manne edited a collection of responses under the title, *Whitewash: On Keith Windschuttle's "Fabrication of Aboriginal History,"* in which various historians took up different parts of the argument. Stuart Macintyre published *The History Wars*, which included some incisive discussion of Windschuttle's text.[17]

Clearly much more was involved than a historian's footnotes. At stake, many felt, was nothing less than Australians' sense of their own past, the moral basis of the nation; as the debate proceeded, it became one also concerned with the relationship between historians and public discourse at large. The debate has once again highlighted that oldest of questions for historians—should we judge the past from present vantage points? Many have been appalled by *Fabrication*'s unconcern at the loss of so many lives and the destruction of a whole society.[18] Helen Irving wrote that the debate has led us to ask, again, whose perspective should be conveyed. The answer, she says, is that we "should try to understand all, and condemn none. The historian's proper role is to step into the shoes of the past, to explain what people thought they were doing. . . . It is absurd to chastise the past for failing to live up to our standards."[19] Others, such as Alan Atkinson, have argued strongly that there is a place in historical work for the animating power of "moral disgust."[20] Windschuttle himself is entirely inconsistent on the question. At times he argues, in defense against the charge of heartlessness, that historians should be "dispassionate," should have no emotional attachments to the conflicts and people of the past. Yet the venom of his language and the savagery of his arguments, the clear allegiances he expresses both explicitly and implicitly with the colonizers and against the colonized belie this view; he is possibly the most passionate, the most clearly and unambiguously morally driven of all contemporary Australian historians.

Scrutinizing *The Fabrication of Aboriginal History*

Summarizing either Windschuttle's book or the many responses to it is very difficult, because of the sheer quantity of material involved and the opacity of much of the material to nonspecialist audiences. *Fabrication* is quite long (436 pages). On a first reading, it can seem very convincing because of the huge amount of detail, the many footnotes, the pursuing of many lines of inquiry down seemingly every possible track. When I first read it, it had a powerful effect. To begin with, there were personal as well as intellectual issues for me. I shared a house with Lyndall Ryan when we were both Ph.D. students and she was working in the archives, both in Tasmania and in Sydney. Later I had helped her proofread her thesis as she prepared it for submission in 1975. Keith Windschuttle and I had been friends since we both taught at the University of Technology, Sydney, in the early 1980s, though we had seen little of each other in recent years. I found *Fabrication* a fascinating and troubling read, leading to sleepless nights. I never believed in the charge of fabrication, but did Windschuttle's argument about the Tasmanian frontier nevertheless have some validity? *Was* the settlement of Tasmania in fact marked by relatively little bloodshed, as *Fabrication* claims, and the virtual disappearance of Indigenous Tasmanians the result of their initial small numbers (two thousand, as against the usual estimates of four thousand or more) and the effects of disease? *Had* my fellow historians made errors that undermined the validity of their arguments and interpretation? While *Fabrication*'s demeaning portrayal of Tasmanian Aborigines and its extremely sympathetic leanings towards the point of view of the settlers are immediately apparent, it is much harder to decide who is right about the details of particular events. It takes a very careful reading indeed to judge the accuracy and logic of Windschuttle's claims.

After a close reading of the book and the many responses to it, I have concluded that *The Fabrication of Aboriginal History* is an initially challenging but ultimately deeply flawed and inconsistent book, most of whose arguments do not stand up to scrutiny. This is not to say it is wrong on all counts, and debate over particular events seems bound to continue. The challenges Windschuttle poses have by no means all been met. Yet there are some major problems with his analysis. Some of these flaws concern the way it discusses the work of other historians, for example in treating them as authorities when it suits the argument and as fabricators when it does not. This is especially true in its discussion of that seminal text for this subject, James Bonwick's *The Last of the Tasmanians* (1870), as I discuss below. Further, it subjects to close inspection only those historians whose reputations it wishes to destroy and accepts without question the details supplied by those who can be used to support its case.[21] Its portrayal of an orthodox "school" elides the many differences between historians, as Stuart Macintyre and Bain Attwood both show.[22] Attwood in particular demonstrates there has been a much greater variety in argument and interpretation over frontier history than *Fabrication* suggests, with historians like Bob Reece and Richard Broome, in particular, questioning the emphasis on white violence and drawing attention both to Aboriginal-initiated violence and to the frequency of other responses to colonization, including accommodation and adaptation. Most unconscionable of all, *The Fabrication of Aboriginal History* equates mistakes in footnotes (real and alleged) and legitimate differences in interpretation from fragmentary or contradictory evidence with *fabrication*, with lying, with intent to deceive. This goes to matters of intent, where *Fabrication* has no evidence whatsoever to back its claims: a direct contradiction of Windschuttle's own position that all historical statements should be researched and sourced. Ryan's essay in reply, published in *Whitewash* in 2003, argues that some of the footnotes *Fabrication* queried were indeed correct, acknowledges that some were wrong but then provides the correct details, and in some cases suggests that what is involved is not "error" but matters of definition and interpretation.[23]

Yet it is not only a matter of poor scholarly protocol. The flaws in *Fabrication*'s own historical argument have been explored by a number of writers with detailed knowledge of Tasmanian Aboriginal history. Part of *Fabrication*'s argument rests on a low estimate of a population of only two thousand in Tasmania before British settlement.[24] As the archaeologists Tim Murray and Christine Williamson argue, this estimate is not well justified or convincing. Given insufficient archaeological studies which might lead to plausible predictions, we have no reason to prefer Windschuttle's low estimate to others: "the accuracy of estimation that Windschuttle rightly argues is central to his account of the consequences of European occupation of Tasmania is simply illusory."[25] Another element of the argument is that Aboriginal people died from disease, not direct killing. All historians agree on the importance of disease from 1832 onward, when the people were collected together on Flinders Island; the debate is over its earlier significance. *Fabrication* argues, contra Lyndall Ryan, that disease had a major impact from early in the century, but its evidence is inadequate indeed, with the earliest citation relating to 1829, and most of it later.[26] Contrary evidence indicating that disease had little effect before 1820 is ignored.[27] After reviewing the debates, James Boyce concludes judiciously and convincingly that "disease played only a limited role up to 1820, while between 1820 and 1830 the balance between violent deaths at the hands of whites and disease is not clear. Only from 1832 is the leading role of disease in the Aboriginal death rate conclusive."[28] There are other interpretative issues as well; for example, concerning the nature of Aboriginal attacks on settlers. *Fabrication* argues that Aboriginal Tasmanians had no concept of land ownership, and to support his case says there are no words for *land* in the wordlists collected by settlers.[29] Henry Reynolds demonstrates clearly that Tasmanian Aborigines did have a notion of country and of belonging to defined territory, as nineteenth-century colonists themselves recognized.[30]

But the main argument, and the main implication for what constitutes the historical archive and how it should be read, concerns the nature and extent of frontier violence. In concluding that it was minimal in Tasmania, *The Fabrication of Aboriginal History* suffers from exactly those defects with which it charges its opponents: selectivity driven by a political agenda. As many of the contributors to *Whitewash* demonstrate in some detail, again and again it accepts sources that minimize the intensity of conflict and the numbers of Aboriginal dead and rejects sources that do not.[31]

To illustrate this contention, that *Fabrication* consistently accepts evidence minimizing frontier violence and rejects evidence suggesting it may have been much higher, I review here its treatment of one particular event, the killing of Aboriginal Tasmanians at Risdon Cove on May 3, 1804. At issue here is a possible massacre for which the evidence is especially scant and conflicting, but which is important in that it is usually held to be the first instance of violent conflict, setting the pattern for later interactions, and living long in historical memory. It is still regularly cited as an example of a senseless massacre which soured Aboriginal-European relations forever and has functioned, as Marilyn Lake points out, "symbolically—like Eve's bite of the apple—as the originating transgression."[32] Yet what happened there is not well documented. What seems generally agreed is that on May 3,1804, at the seven months' old British settlement at Risdon on the eastern shore of the Derwent River, a party of around three hundred Aboriginal men, women, and children, apparently furious at the taking of animals on which they depended for survival, came to the tiny British settlement of around eighty people. Soldiers opened fire, and at least three Aboriginal people were killed, including a man and a woman whose child was left orphaned. No whites were killed.[33] So far, no dispute. What *is* disputed is who attacked first and whether considerably more than three Aboriginal people were killed. Given the importance of the episode, historically, historiographically, and in collective memory, we must do our best from highly selective and fragmentary evidence to work out what may have happened.

The story of the Risdon Cove killings is now two centuries old. It appears to have entered into local settler folklore, being frequently referred to as a reason for Tasmanian Aboriginal attacks on Europeans, as it is in what seems to be the earliest published reference, W. C. Wentworth's history of New South Wales and Van Diemen's Land in 1819.[34] Yet the archival record is sparse indeed. Few government documents for this period survive, and there is only one relevant diary, that of the colonial chaplain, the Reverend Knopwood, to whom two participants wrote at the time. The earliest government report, on which all historians in this field rely extensively, did not appear until twenty-six years later, in 1830, when the Risdon Cove events were reported in detail by an eyewitness, Edward White, and several others, including Knopwood, to a committee of investigation. The killings were described briefly in John West's *History of Tasmania* in 1852, which noted that "the accounts of this affair differ greatly."[35]

The first detailed historical account, however, appeared in 1870 in James Bonwick's influential and aforementioned book, *The Last of the Tasmanians*, and *Fabrication* goes to some lengths to reject its version of events.[36] To pursue the argument about what may have happened at Risdon Cove, this book and its author are worth a closer look.

An evangelical lay preacher and a schoolteacher, Bonwick had first become interested in the story of the Aboriginal Tasmanians after a visit in 1859 to Oyster Cove, whence the remaining Aboriginal population of forty-seven had been removed after the settlement at Flinders Island had proved a disaster.[37] Shocked by the desolation, poverty, and lack of religious instruction at the fast dwindling community, he decided to write a history of what had happened. Voyaging from Hobart to England in 1870, he actually sailed past Flinders Island, and in the book that he wrote on the ship, *The Last of the Tasmanians*, on the basis of research undertaken in Tasmania and Sydney during the 1860s, he notes: "As I gazed upon its storm-torn coast, and my eyes rested upon its bleak and fantastic hills, the whole story, in all its varied and stirring phases, came before me, and I felt quickened in my resolution to tell my countrymen the sorrows of the Tasmanians."[38] Bonwick, however, faced some serious difficulty when writing about the Risdon Cove killings. With no government records from the time surviving, he used the Reverend Knopwood's diary and the report of the Aborigines Committee of 1830. From these sources Bonwick concluded that the British soldiers had attacked first, and a massacre of some kind had happened, though its details and extent would remain unclear. He also recounts common folklore about these events, for example reporting that "a settler of 1804" had told him that the man who ordered the troops to fire on the Aboriginal people, Lieutenant William Moore, had been drunk at the time: he "saw double that morning from an overdose of rations' rum." Bonwick noted that Moore and his regiment had a reputation for hard drinking, which led some to believe "the whole was the effect of a half-drunken spree." Bonwick's account has formed the basis of most subsequent histories of these events.[39]

Windschuttle's *Fabrication* develops a long argument as to why the two informants who spoke at the time with Reverend Knopwood (one of whom was Lieutenant Moore) should be largely believed while Edward White, who was not involved and who witnessed what happened but gave his evidence twenty-six years later, should not.[40] Neither the poor reputations of the two witnesses he prefers nor the good reputation of Edward

White, whose evidence he rejects, are considered relevant.[41] He argues that White could not have seen the shootings he claimed; several scholars have demolished this by pointing to additional evidence indicating he could well have done so.[42] On balance, there seems to be no strong reason to conclude that White was not telling the truth or that local settler folklore about a massacre had no basis in actual events. It is, of course, a matter of judgment.

Yet there is more to come. Windschuttle discusses at length Bonwick's report of a settler having told him that Moore was under the influence of alcohol when he gave the order to fire and concludes that, since he, Windschuttle, cannot track down this "settler of 1804," this story and its details were "plainly Bonwick's inventions," a "fabricated tale."[43] While the missing settler is indeed something of a puzzle, there seem to be many possible solutions other than fabrication (for example, this may be less direct evidence than Bonwick remembered or understood it to be). Further, Windschuttle does not make it clear that Bonwick is reporting the common *belief* that "the whole was the effect of a half-drunken spree." Its veracity is in fact not essential to his main account of a gross military overreaction to an Aboriginal visit to the fledgling British settlement.

If Bonwick is indeed a fabricator, then we have lost one of the most valuable accounts of the destruction of Tasmanian society that we have. Yet Windschuttle does not, in fact, really think him a fabricator; indeed, his treatment of Bonwick is decidedly curious. He wants to portray him as totally unreliable, a fabricator, when it suits him to do so, yet also use him as an authority when *that* suits him. So, for example, in a discussion of the reasons for the rapid decline of the Aboriginal population in the 1830s and 1840s, he says: "On this issue, if few others, Bonwick was credible when he wrote: 'The absence of births even more than the frequency of deaths completed the destruction of the people.' "[44] Somewhat surprisingly in view of this remark ("if few others"), there are only four instances where *Fabrication* queries Bonwick's statements, and seven where he is cited as a reliable authority.[45] None of the four queries is serious (two relate to relaying unsourced oral information, something about which Bonwick is quite open and clear, one to an alleged selective reading of Select Committee evidence, and one to the exact date of the people's removal to Flinders Island, and the likely weather there at the time), and they are in any case very slight indeed when considered in the context of a long and detailed book. Bonwick was writing in a nineteenth-century context, when footnotes were very much slighter than they are today and historians were much more comfortable with literary imaginings of what historical actors might have felt than they are now. The impression of someone who cannot be trusted is belied by Windschuttle's own use of Bonwick as an authority.[46]

Creating Colonial Archives

It is particularly difficult to see Bonwick as a fabricator given his understanding of what constituted good historical practice and his own pivotal role in the use and creation of an Australian historical archive. Bonwick was, in fact, one of the earliest colonial historians to learn of the new "scientific" history emerging in Europe inspired by Ranke's declaration in 1824 that history should describe "what actually happened."[47]

For colonial historians like Bonwick inspired by Ranke's dictum, however, observing it was not always easy. The archive they had to work with was complex, frustratingly spare in some aspects, copious in others. On the one hand, there was usually careful record keeping by governors and other officials charged with reporting their actions in detail to the British colonial authorities. There were also many royal commissions and select committees reporting to legislatures in Great Britain and the colonies. Other colonial institutions also created extensive records; missionaries, for example, had to report to the London-based societies that funded them. Yet if the bureaucracy of colonialism led to plentiful record creation, there were also alternative tendencies leading to considerable record destruction or abandonment. In a situation where colonists were not following British government orders as faithfully as Britain hoped and understood (a common feature of colonial situations), records could easily vanish. When the first lieutenant governor of Van Diemen's Land died in 1810, many believed his papers had been burnt. As Bonwick reported, "The story goes that upon the sudden decease of the first governor, Captain Collins, found dead in his chair, two of the leading officers of the Government placed a marine outside the door, so that they might be undisturbed, and then proceeded to burn every document in the office!!!"[48] Whatever the fate of the documents, so great was the loss that a British inquiry looked into the matter in 1820; better record keeping began in 1824. In the quest for the missing documents, Collins's burial case was reopened in 1825, but no documents were found.[49] Even with improved record keeping, reporting on Aboriginal matters at first remained limited; as James Boyce points out, no governor "actively sought information in those areas they would rather not know about, let alone apprised a meddling London of the uncomfortable facts." It was only when Aboriginal attacks on settlers in Tasmania escalated in 1827, that Governor Arthur's record keeping and reporting to the colonial authorities on Aboriginal matters became intensive.[50]

The problems for colonial historians did not end with the fickle and political nature of government record keeping. There were in the 1870s no archival repositories like those in the United Kingdom, Canada, and South Africa; historians wishing to consult outdated government records had to gain special permission to do so.[51] Thus Bonwick had to gain access to early records from government officials; a few years later, another historian of the Aboriginal Tasmanians, J. E. Calder, consulted papers "deposited in the office of the Colonial Secretary, filling seventeen large volumes of manuscript papers."[52] Nor were government records the only problem. Other important documentary material, such as newspapers, pamphlets, and private records like journals and letters home were kept in a haphazard fashion, sometimes in public libraries, more commonly in private hands.[53]

For Bonwick, as an admirer and conscientious practitioner of the new "scientific history" confronted with these haphazard colonial archives, Tasmanian Aboriginal history provided an excellent example of "the difficulties of learning the truth of a story." In Europe, he remarks in *The Last of the Tasmanians*, nations are now learning as a result of this new history that their founding stories were myth rather than historical fact:

> We are gradually arriving at the belief that all, or nearly all, the early history of nations has no reference at all to actual events or persons, but to statements of a foreign nature, mythological or astronomical. A Niebuhr first robs us of our faith in Romulus, a Max Müller strips the Vedas of their romance and theology, and even our own Saxon heroes, Hengist and Horsa, have dissolved into thin air.

He muses that these problems do not exist only for the distant past; even in modern times there are great difficulties arising from the existence of conflicting accounts: "Such are the conflicting accounts, such the various ways of regarding the same object or circumstance, such the influences of personal character and interests involved in the narrative, that we are often puzzled with what might have been supposed the plainest facts of modern history." The problem exists for Risdon Cove in Tasmania as well: "The story of the first conflict of races in Tasmania is similarly involved in misty obscurity."[54] All the historian can do is reconstruct what may have happened from the scanty evidence available.

In addition to writing his own histories, Bonwick contributed to the development of a better colonial archive. He not only used the existing archive, but was also one of those who worked, as Antoinette Burton puts it in her introduction to this volume, "backstage." He was the first to address one of the major problems colonial historians faced, namely that many important early government records were held in Britain but not in the Australian colonies themselves. His chance to act came when the centenary of the initial British settlement at Sydney Cove began to loom in the early 1880s. As governments began to turn their minds to celebration, they for the first time regarded this lack of resident archives *as* a problem.[55] When Bonwick retired to England in 1882, he successfully suggested to several colonial governments that they follow the Canadian example and have the London-based archival materials transcribed.[56] He then spent the last fifteen years of his life in the Public Records Office in London, transcribing these documents for the parliamentary or public libraries of New South Wales, Queensland, South Australia, Victoria, and Tasmania.[57]

So, to return to Windschuttle, it is surprising indeed to see Bonwick, one of the originators of Australian colonial archives and a man keenly aware of the new scientific history, emerge as a fabricator. The charge is in fact purely rhetorical, a means of doing away with a particular story. There is another issue here, however. On the question of Moore's sobriety or drunkenness, Bonwick was relying, as he makes perfectly clear, on oral information, since most of the relevant records had been destroyed. He presents it simply as a story that may well have been true. In characterizing this practice as "fabrication," Windschuttle has taken an extreme position. There is nothing in the tradition of post-Rankean "scientific history"—let alone in classical figures like Herodotus and Thucydides, held to be its progenitors—that would disregard oral evidence in this absolutist way. On the contrary, these historians used oral evidence constantly; frequently it was all they had.

Interpreting Colonial Archives

Reading the colonial archive raises not only technical problems shared
with the historical enterprise generally; it has some interpretative problems of its own. Readings of colonial archives differ enormously according
to the stance of the historian in relation to the colonizers, the colonized,
and colonial processes more generally. The Australian History Wars in fact
follow an earlier skirmish over just these issues involving some of the same
players. Windschuttle is probably best known internationally for his earlier
book *The Killing of History* (1994), which argues against the influence of
post-structuralist or "postmodern" cultural theory on the discipline of
history, and especially against the generally accepted idea that historians
inevitably bring cultural and historically specific assumptions to their reading and interpretation of historical evidence.[58] *The Killing of History* is
sharply critical of historians who advance cultural explanations of human
affairs and seeks to defend narrative history against postmodern cultural
theorists like Paul Carter, who characterize all narrative history as "imperial history." Yet in the context of a critique of postmodernism and a
defense of narrative history, *The Killing of History* praised those Australian historians like Charles Rowley and Henry Reynolds who emphasised
the destructiveness of colonization for Aboriginal people. Reynolds was
praised for demonstrating that it was possible through European evidence
to allow "Aboriginal voices to tell the story," while Rowley was admired
for showing that the violence against Aborigines "formed a great unbroken arch of systematic brutality, dispossession and incarceration stretching
from the late eighteenth century to the twentieth." Rowley, said Windschuttle, had done nothing less than redefine "the great drama of Australia
history as the conflict between Europeans and Aborigines."[59]

Clearly, *The Fabrication of Aboriginal History* represents a marked departure from the earlier book. The target shifts from historians influenced by
postmodernism and cultural theory to conventional narrative historians,
not postmodernists at all, who emphasize the destructiveness of colonization for Aboriginal people; Henry Reynolds, in particular, has moved from
hero to villain. Yet there is also an important continuity between the two
books—both defend the colonizers and condemn the colonized. *The Killing of History* is a wide-ranging attack on cultural theorists and historians
who are more ready to criticize colonizing societies than the cultures of
the colonized, and it advocates a much more positive appraisal of Western

societies, as based on Enlightenment reason and scientific method, and a much more critical evaluation of traditional cultures. *Fabrication* applies this general argument specifically to the colonization of Australia in a way *The Killing of History* does not. The Tasmanians now become an example of Indigenous cultures and peoples that are backward and contemptible, necessarily overrun by a superior civilization.

In both books Windschuttle sees European colonization as an unstoppable by-product of human progress, and therefore morally justified, in much the way colonizers seeking to appropriate land did at the time. Most modern historians, in contrast, stand back a little from this triumphalist narrative and recognize the depth of the human tragedy that followed invasion and colonization. Yet as the debate has unfolded in the Australian public arena, the idea that modern Australia needs to come to terms with its colonial past has taken a severe beating. More people now think there is no morally questionable past to contend with: history as tragedy and pathos and as requiring searching self-examination and redress has been replaced by history as reassurance and evolutionary inevitability. Indeed the image in *Fabrication* of settlers in Tasmania having to defend themselves, that *they* rather than the people whose lands they took are the victims, reprises a long-standing trope in Australian consciousness of victimology. Many non-Indigenous Australians today have difficulty in seeing themselves as the beneficiaries of the colonization process because they see themselves not as oppressors but as victims—of the difficulties of colonization, the harshness of the land in fire, drought, and flood, and later, of British wartime commanders at Gallipoli. If they are victims, how can they ever see themselves as perpetrators? *Fabrication* has and will, I think, reinforce this traditional understanding of events and impede recognition of land-taking, dispossession, and the consequent destruction of whole societies and peoples.[60] The fact that shocks most who learn for the first time of what happened in Tasmania—that a whole people virtually disappeared within a few decades of British settlement—has again been negated and drained of its moral, legal, historical, and political importance.

Nevertheless, the question of history remains a lively one in Australian public life, as it does in postcolonial societies generally, as Adele Perry, Helena Pohlandt-McCormick, and Jeff Sahadeo all illustrate so dramatically in this volume. And none of the foregoing discussion is meant to, or indeed ever could, close the debate over what happened in Tasmania in the first four decades of the nineteenth century. How we view the colonial frontier is necessarily in a constant state of revision and reformulation. While there is much to question in *Fabrication*—its methods, assumptions, and argument, and especially its contemptuous account of the Indigenous peoples of Tasmania—it has in fact stimulated a good deal of new research and historiographical reflection, and it is clear that we still have a great deal of historical work to do.

This particular antipodean "archive story" also has some very large implications for historical practice. The debates now dubbed "the Australian History Wars" highlight how difficult it is to decide what constitutes reliable historical evidence and provide a stark reminder that the acceptance or rejection of evidence is closely related to the historian's overall approach to the subject. Though it sounds trite to say it yet again, we are reminded that in a situation of inadequate and conflicting evidence, our moral sympathies, political understanding, and cultural assumptions will all affect what is seen as likely to be true. This debate reminds us to recognize our own arguments and narratives for what they are, present attempts to understand what may have happened in the past, rather than a representation of the past itself. Yet again, it seems to me, we are confronted with the "doubleness" of history as a practice, its impossible but endlessly productive combination of narrative form, storytelling from a particular point of view, with scientific aspiration and method.[61]

Most of all, this debate is revealing of the relationship between historians and their audiences. Historians themselves, as Perry points out in her contribution to this volume, are still quite divided over questions of fact and interpretation, and positivist approaches are still very much with us. While many historians take divergent interpretation to be an essential part of the discipline, others (like Windschuttle) still proclaim their histories to be objectively true and deny the possibility of different legitimate interpretations of the same historical archive. In the introduction to this volume, Burton reminds us that even those historians who *do* recognize history as an interpretative act rarely recognize how this affects their own practice. And if historians themselves are divided on these issues, public audiences find the idea of historical disagreement even more difficult and unsettling. They ask us what really happened, and are frustrated and suspicious when we do not agree on the answer. Those who say there is only one correct answer are welcomed with relief, while those who insist that interpretations will differ are regarded as fence-sitting relativists and nasty postmodernists who believe that you can have any version of the past you like. The historians under attack in this particular dispute have learned the hard way that pointing to the inevitability of interpretative difference is an insufficient response when historical disagreements become matters of public interest and concern. Historians lose public trust if they do not *also* seek to explain, with clear reference to the historical archive, just how and why they reached their conclusions and present an argument for preferring their interpretation to that of their opponents.

One danger for historians of history "going public" is the temptation to react to these public demands for absolute historical truth by valorizing extremely empiricist theories of history which take no account whatsoever of the ways in which the present shapes the past, that is, of the historical and cultural specificity of historical knowledge itself. We have to insist that a keen recognition of the vagaries of the archive and a desire for self-reflexive narration can go comfortably hand in hand with quite traditional disciplinary practices such as extensive research, careful interpretation, clear argument, and intelligible writing. When versions of the past become embedded in current political debates, historians must continue to struggle to maintain their allegiance to a rigorous and independent scholarship while recognizing and accepting the political consequences and meaning of their work.

Notes

1 For debates over Nanjing, see Joshua A. Fogel, ed., *The Nanjing Massacre in History and Historiography* (Berkeley: University of California Press, 2000). For U.S. debates, see Edward T. Linenthal, "Anatomy of a Controversy," in Edward T. Linenthal and Tom Engelhardt, eds., *History Wars: The Enola Gay and Other Battles for the American Past* (New York: Metropolitan Books, 1996); and Robert Jay Lifton and Greg Mitchell, *Hiroshima in America: A Half Century of Denial* (New York: Avon, 1995).

2 For Israel debates, see Avi Shlaim and Eugene Rogan, eds., *The War for Palestine: Rewriting the History of 1948* (Cambridge: Cambridge University Press, 2001).

3 Note, however, Bain Attwood's recent challenge to this account of the importance of "terra nullius" in past Australian legal and historical thinking in "*The Law of the Land* or the Law of the Land?: History, Law and Narrative in a Settler Society," *History Compass* 2 (2004): 1–30.

4 G. Blainey, "Mabo Decision Looked Back through Modern Blinkers," *The Australian*, 10 November 1993, 9; Attwood, "Mabo, Australia and the End of

History," in Attwood, ed., *In the Age of Mabo: Aborigines, History and Australia* (Sydney: Allen and Unwin, 1996), 100–116.

5 *The Australian*, October 25, 26–27, 1996.

6 Rod Moran, *Massacre Myth: An Investigation into Allegations Concerning the Mass Murder of Aborigines to Forrest River, 1926* (Bassendean: Access Press, 1999; 1st ed.1994). For an account of its influence on Windschuttle, see *The Australian*, December 6, 2002, 12.

7 For a respected supporter of Moran's case, see Geoffrey Bolton's preface in Rod Moran, *Sex, Maiming and Murder: Seven Case Studies into the Reliability of Reverend E. R. Gribble, Superintendent, Forrest River Mission 1913–1928, as a Witness to the Truth* (Bassendean: Access Press, 2002). For continuing debate see Neville Green, "Ahab Wailing in the Wilderness," *Quadrant*, June 2003, 30–33, and "The Evidence for the Forrest River Massacre," *Quadrant*, July-August 2003, 39–43; Rod Moran, "Grasping at the Straws of 'Evidence,'" *Quadrant*, November 2003, 20–24.

8 Keith Windschuttle, "The Myths of Frontier Massacres in Australian History," *Quadrant*, October 2000, 8–21; November 2000, 17–24; December 2000, 6–20.

9 Keith Windschuttle, "Doctored Evidence and Invented Incidents in Aboriginal Historiography," in Bain Attwood and Stephen Foster, eds., *Frontier Conflict: The Australian Experience* (Canberra: National Museum of Australia, 2003), 99–112.

10 Lyndall Ryan, *The Aboriginal Tasmanians*, 2nd ed. (Sydney: Allen and Unwin, 1996; 1st ed., 1981); Henry Reynolds, *The Fate of a Free People* (Melbourne: Penguin, 1995).

11 See Reynolds, *Fate of a Free People*; Ryan, *The Aboriginal Tasmanians*, chaps. 12 and 13.

12 Ryan, *The Aboriginal Tasmanians*, chap. 15.

13 Keith Windschuttle, *The Fabrication of Aboriginal History* (Sydney: Macleay Press, 2002), 386, 129, 3.

14 Geoffrey Blainey, "Native Fiction," a review of Windschuttle in *The New Criterion* 21, 8 (April 2003), http://www.newcriterion.com/archive/21/apr03/blainey.htm.

15 Keith Windschuttle, *Sydney Morning Herald*, December 29, 2003, concerning the protest by Special Broadcasting Service Indigenous Affairs unit outside the book launch for *Fabrication* in December 2002.

16 Eve Vincent and Clare Land, "Silenced Voices," *Arena Magazine* 67 (October–November 2003): 19.

17 Robert Manne, ed., *Whitewash: On Keith Windschuttle's "Fabrication of Aboriginal History"* (Melbourne: Black Inc. Agenda, 2003); Stuart Macintyre with Anna Clark, *The History Wars* (Melbourne: Melbourne University Press, 2003), 161–70.

18 As Windschuttle himself summarizes, "Macintyre condemned the book's 'complete lack of compassion,' Manne its 'pitilessness,' Martin Krygier its 'denigrating moralism' and James Boyce its 'slander' of Aboriginal culture" (*The Australian*, December 29, 2003). He could have added Reynolds's comment that

"Sympathy, empathy—even understanding—are missing from Windschuttle's book" ("Terra Nullius Reborn," in Manne, *Whitewash*, 133), or the comment by Ron Brunton, a conservative scholar who finds "much to praise" in *Fabrication*, that he is devoid of compassion ("Fabrication fury but the rest is history," *The Courier Mail*, December 28, 2002, 24).

19 Helen Irving, *Sydney Morning Herald*, December 13, 2003.

20 Alan Atkinson, "Historians and Moral Disgust," in Attwood and Foster, *Frontier Conflict*, 113–19.

21 As Cassandra Pybus points out, *Fabrication* accepts uncritically the picture of Aboriginal society and of Robinson and Truganini drawn in Vivien Rae Ellis's *Black Robinson* (1988) while subjecting Lyndall Ryan, Henry Reynolds, and others to detailed and severe scrutiny ("Robinson and Robertson," in Manne, *Whitewash*, 258–76; this comment at 260). George Augustus Robinson was employed by the governor to conciliate with the remaining Aborigines and successfully persuaded them to remove to Flinders Island. Truganini is usually cited as the last Tasmanian of full descent; her death in Hobart in 1876 is seen as signifying "the last of her race."

22 Macintyre, *History Wars*, 164; Bain Attwood, "Historiography on the Australian Frontier," in Attwood and Foster, *Frontier Conflict*, 169–84.

23 For Windschuttle's response to Ryan's essay in *Whitewash*, see Keith Windschuttle, "*Whitewash* Confirms the Fabrication of Aboriginal History," *Quadrant*, October 2003, 14–15. While disputes over details continue and to my mind some issues remain unresolved, the charge of "fabrication" is merely reasserted but not argued.

24 Windschuttle's minimization of the Tasmanian population can be seen as an example of a very old practice within extinction discourse of severely underestimating initial numbers. See Patrick Brantlinger, *Dark Vanishings: Discourse on the Extinction of Primitive Races, 1800–1930* (Ithaca: Cornell University Press, 2003), 11.

25 Tim Murray and Christine Williamson, "Archaeology and History," in Manne, *Whitewash*, 315.

26 On disease, see *Fabrication*, 373–75. To support its argument that disease probably started with the sealers and whalers who encountered the Tasmanians even before British settlement was established in 1803, *Fabrication* (375) cites James Bonwick, *Daily Life and Origin of the Tasmanians* (London: Samson Low, Son, and Marston, 1870), p. 87. Bonwick was reporting the Flinders' Island Aboriginal people's accounts that "before the English ships arrived in Sullivan's cove [Hobart], a sudden and fearful mortality took place among the tribes." While sealers and whalers could indeed have introduced disease, this quotation hardly proves the point, and no other evidence is given (see next note). Significantly, there was no smallpox outbreak, unlike those on the mainland on at least two occasions, 1789 and 1829. The most detailed source for smallpox information is Judy Campbell, *Invisible Invaders: Smallpox and Other Diseases in Aboriginal Australia, 1780–1880* (Melbourne: Melbourne University Press, 2002), see esp. chap. 1.

27 James Boyce, "Fantasy Island," in Manne, *Whitewash*, 43. See also Boyce's excellent discussion in "Better to Be Mistaken than to Deceive: *The Fabrication of Aboriginal History* and the Van Diemonian Record," *Island* 96 (Autumn 2004): 9–37.

28 Boyce, "Fantasy Island," 44.

29 Windschuttle, *Fabrication*, 110–11.

30 Reynolds, "Terra Nullius Reborn," 109–38.

31 See the arguments presented by Boyce, Tardif, Hansen, Ryan, Pybus, and McFarlane in Manne, *Whitewash*.

32 Marilyn Lake, "History and the Nation," in Manne, *Whitewash*, 166.

33 Ryan, *The Aboriginal Tasmanians*, 75; Windschuttle, *Fabrication*, 16–19; Phillip Tardif, "Risdon Cove," in Manne, *Whitewash*, 218; Boyce, "Fantasy Island," 40; Lloyd Robson, *A History of Tasmania*, vol. 1 (Melbourne: Oxford University Press, 1983), 46.

34 W. C. Wentworth, *A Statistical, Historical and Political Description of New South Wales and Its Dependent Settlement in Van Diemen's Land* (London: Whitaker, 1919), 116–17, quoted in Windschuttle, *Fabrication*, 15.

35 John West, *The History of Tasmania*, vol. 2 (Launceston: Henry Dowling, 1852), 6.

36 A few years later another important account appeared: James Calder, *Some Account of the Wars, Extirpation, Habits, etc of the Native Tribes of Tasmania*, (Hobart: Henn and Co, 1875; facsimile edition, Hobart: Fullers Bookshop, 1972).

37 Ryan, *The Aboriginal Tasmanians*, 210.

38 James Bonwick, *The Last of the Tasmanians, or the Black War of Van Diemen's Land* (London: Samson Low, 1870), 271.

39 Ibid., 32–35; quotes at 35.

40 Windschuttle, *Fabrication*, 16–26.

41 Tardif, "Risdon Cove," 219.

42 Naomi Parry, "'Many deeds of terror': Windschuttle and Musquito," *Labour History* 85 (November 2003): 207–12, see esp. 207; Tardif, "Risdon Cove," 218–24.

43 Windschuttle, *Fabrication*, 25 and 41.

44 Ibid., 376.

45 The four queries are in *Fabrication*: pp. 20, 25–27, 41 (re whether Lieutenant Moore was drunk or not when ordering firing upon Aborigines); p. 43 (where Bonwick's story of a convict or settler cutting the flesh off live Aborigines to feed his dogs—Windschuttle gives no page reference—is discounted without argument); p. 149 (where he criticizes Bonwick for not mentioning that Gilbert Robertson's evidence to the 1830 committee concerning a massacre at Campbell Town in 1828 was disputed by two other witnesses); p. 229 (where he questions Bonwick's evocative account that it was raining the day the people were taken to Flinders Island). The argument about the likely weather when the Aboriginal people arrived at Flinders Island seems particularly silly, given especially that the passage in question on Bonwick's p. 247 seems to be evoking the weather gener-

ally, not the weather on the date of removal specifically. The seven instances where Bonwick is cited without criticism as an authority are pp. 54, 175, 228, 251, 281, 284, and especially pp. 375–76 re disease before 1829, discussed with my notes 26–28, above. Note that Windschuttle's references are all to Bonwick, *The Last of the Tasmanians*, except that on p. 375, which is to Bonwick, *Daily Life and Origin of the Tasmanians*.

46 *Fabrication* displays a similar ambivalence in using Calder, *Some Account of the Wars*, at times seeing it as making impossible comparisons between Tasmania and the Spanish conquest of the Americas or imputing to Aborigines motives and ideas they could not have had, and at other times using it as an authority on the state of conflict. This text is in my reading much more pro-settler in its sympathies than *Fabrication* indicates.

47 Leopold von Ranke, "Introduction," *History of the Latin and Teutonic Nations*, first published 1824, reprinted in Roger Wines, ed., *Leopold von Ranke: The Secret of World History. Selected Writings on the Art and Science of History* (New York: Fordham University Press, 1981), 58.

48 Bonwick, *The Last of the Tasmanians*, 39.

49 Boyce, "Fantasy Island," 27. Boyce takes his account from John Currey, *David Collins: A Colonial Life* (Melbourne: The Miegunyah Press, 2000), 307–8.

50 Boyce, "Fantasy Island," 27–29, quote at 27–28.

51 Brian Fletcher, *Australian History in New South Wales 1888–1938* (Sydney: University of New South Wales Press, 1993), 8.

52 Calder, *Some Account of the Wars*, 3; also cited in Boyce, "Fantasy Island," 27. In his preface Bonwick thanks "those government officials in New South Wales and Tasmania who had given him access to 'early records' " (iv).

53 Fletcher, *Australian History in New South Wales*, 8; Henry Reynolds, "The Written Record," in Attwood and Foster, *Frontier Conflict*, 90.

54 Bonwick, *The Last of the Tasmanians*, 32.

55 Fletcher, *Australian History in New South Wales*, 7–8.

56 Stuart Macintyre, "Bonwick," in Graeme Davison, John Hirst, and Stuart Macintyre, eds, *The Oxford Companion to Australian History* (Oxford: Oxford University Press, 1998), 80; Fletcher, *Australian History in New South Wales*, 16–17.

57 Macintyre, "Bonwick," 80. Others contributed, such as J. F. Watson and R. W. Giblin; see foreword by W. W. Giblin, in Ronald Worthy Giblin, *The Early History of Tasmania* (Melbourne: Melbourne University Press, 1939; 1st ed. 1928).

58 *The Killing of History* began as a self-published book (Macleay, 1994) but was then taken up by the U.S. publisher Encounter Books (San Francisco, 1996), and was widely sold and reviewed in the United States and elsewhere.

59 Windschuttle, *The Killing of History*, 117.

60 Ann Curthoys, "Constructing National Histories," in Attwood and Foster, *Frontier Conflict*, 185–200.

61 See Ann Curthoys and John Docker, *Is History Fiction?* (Sydney: University of New South Wales Press, 2005).

Select Bibliography

Aly, Götz, and Karl Heinz Roth. *Die restlose Erfassung: Volkszählen, Identififizieren, Aussondern in Nationalsocialismus*. Berlin: Rotbuch, 1984.

Appadurai, Arjun, ed. *The Social Life of Things: Commodities in Cultural Perspective*. Cambridge: Cambridge University Press, 1986.

Arondekar, Anjali. "Without a Trace: Sexuality and the Colonial Archive." *Journal of the History of Sexuality* 14, 1–2 (winter–spring 2005): 10–27.

Assmann, Aleida. *Erinnerungersäume: Formen und Wadlungen des Kulturellen Gedächtnisses*. Munich: C. H. Beck, 1999.

Ballantyne, Tony. "Archive, Discipline, State: Power and Knowledge in South Asian Historiography." *New Zealand Journal of Asian Studies* 3, 2 (June 2001): 87–105.

——. *Orientalism and Race: Aryanism in the British Empire*. London: Palgrave-Macmillan, 2001.

Bann, Stephen. *The Clothing of Clio*. Cambridge: Cambridge University Press, 1984.

Bass, Randy. "Story and Archive in the Twenty-First Century," Symposium: English 1999, *College English* 61, 6 (July 1999): 659–70.

BC Studies, special issue on *Delgamuukw v. British Columbia*, 95 (autumn 1992).

Booth, Marilyn. *May Her Likes Be Multiplied: Biography and Gender Politics in Egypt*. Berkeley: University of California Press, 2001.

Brown, Jennifer S. H., and Elizabeth Vibert, eds. *Reading Beyond Words: Contexts for Native History*. 2nd ed. Peterborough, Ontario: Broadview, 2003.

Brown, John Seely, and Paul Duguid. *The Social Life of Information*. Boston: Harvard Business School Press, 2000.

Broyles-González, Yolanda. *Lydia Mendoza's Life in Music / La Historia de Lydia Mendoza: Norteño Tejano Legacies*. New York: Oxford University Press, 2001.

Buder, Stanley. *Visionaries and Planners: The Garden City Movement and the Modern Community*. New York: Oxford University Press, 1990.

Burton, Antoinette. *Dwelling in the Archive: Women Writing House, Home, and History in Late Colonial India*. New York and Oxford: Oxford University Press, 2003.

Campt, Tina M. *Other Germans: Black Germans and the Politics of Race, Gender and Memory in the Third Reich*. Ann Arbor: University of Michigan Pres, 2004.

Cañizares-Esguerra, Jorge. *How to Write the History of the New World: Histories, Epistemologies, and Identities in the Eighteenth-Century Atlantic World*. Stanford, Calif.: Stanford University Press, 2001.

Cassidy, Frank, ed. *Aboriginal Title in British Columbia: Delgamuukw v. The Queen.* Victoria, B.C.: Oolichan Books and the Institute for Research on Public Policy, 1992.

Chandler, James. *England in 1819: The Politics of Literary Culture and the Case of Romantic Historicism.* Chicago: University of Chicago Press, 1998.

Chandler, James, Arnold I. Davidson, and Harry Harootunian, eds. *Questions of Evidence: Proof, Practice, and Persuasion Across the Disciplines.* Chicago: University of Chicago Press, 1994.

Cohn, Bernard. *Colonialism and Its Forms of Knowledge: The British in India.* Princeton: Princeton University Press, 1996.

Crawford, Margaret. *Building the Workingman's Paradise: The Design of American Company Towns.* London: Verso, 1995.

Creese, Walter. *The Search for Environment: The Garden City, Before and After.* New Haven: Yale University Press, 1966.

Crimp, Douglas. *Melancholia and Moralism: Essays on AIDS and Queer Politics.* Cambridge, Mass.: The MIT Press, 2002.

Culhane, Dara. *The Pleasure of the Crown: Anthropology, Law, and First Nations.* Vancouver, B.C.: Talon, 1998.

Deguilhem, Randi, and Manuela Marin, eds. *Writing the Feminine: Women in Arab Sources.* London: I. B. Tauris, 2002.

Derrida, Jacques. *Archive Fever: A Freudian Impression*, trans. E. Prenowitz. Chicago: University of Chicago Press, 1995.

Dirks, Nicholas B. "Annals of the Archive: Ethnographic Notes on the Sources of History." In Brian Keith Axel, ed., *From the Margins: Historical Anthropology and its Futures*, 47–65. Durham: Duke University Press, 2002.

——. *Castes of Mind: Colonialism and the Making of Modern India.* Princeton: Princeton University Press, 2001.

Ecchevarría, Roberto González. *Myth and Archive: A Theory of Latin American Narrative.* Durham: Duke University Press, 1998.

Ernst, Wolfgang. *Im Namen von Geschichte: Sammeln—Speichern—(Er)Zählen : infrastrukturelle Konfigurationen des deutschen Gedächtnisses.* Munich: Wilhelm Fink, 2003.

Fawwaz, Zaynab. *Riwayat Husn al-'awaqib aw Ghadat al-Zahira.* Cairo: Matba'at Hindiyya, 1899 [1316].

Featherstone, Mike. "Archiving Cultures." *British Journal of Sociology* 51, 1 (January-March 2000): 161–84.

Fitzpatrick, Sheila, and Lynne Viola. *A Researcher's Guide to Soviet Social History in the 1930s.* Armonk, N.Y.: M. E. Sharpe, 1990.

Flores, William V., and Rina Benmayor, eds. *Latino Cultural Citizenship: Claiming Identity, Space, and Rights.* Boston: Beacon Press, 1997.

Foucault, Michel. *The Archaeology of Knowledge and the Discourse on Language*, trans. A. M. Sheridan Smith. New York: Pantheon, 1972.

Fritzsche, Peter. *Stranded in the Present: Modern Time and the Melancholy of History.* Cambridge, Mass.: Harvard University Press, 2004.

Furniss, Elizabeth. *The Burden of History: Colonialism and the Frontier Myth in a Rural Canadian Community*. Vancouver: University of British Columbia Press, 1999.

Ghosh, Durba. "Decoding the Nameless: Gender, Subjectivity, and Historical Methodologies in Reading the Archives of Colonial India." In Kathleen Wilson, ed., *A New Imperial History: Culture, Identity, Modernity, 1660–1840*, 297–316. Cambridge: Cambridge University Press, 2004.

Gordon, Avery F. *Ghostly Matters: Haunting and the Sociological Imagination*. Minneapolis: University of Minnesota Press, 1997.

Gosden, Chris, and Yvonne Marshall. "The Cultural Biography of Objects." *World Archaeology* 31, 2 (October 1999): 169–78.

Hall, Peter. *Cities of Tomorrow: An Intellectual History of the Planning and Design of Cities in the Twentieth Century*. Oxford: Blackwell, 1988.

Hamilakis, Yannis. "Stories from Exile: Fragments from the Cultural Biography of the Parthenon (or 'Elgin') Marbles." *World Archaeology* 31, 2 (October 1999): 303–20.

Hamilton, Carolyn, Verne Harris, Jane Taylor, Michele Pickover, Graeme Reid, and Razia Saleh, eds. *Refiguring the Archive*. Cape Town: David Philip, 2002; Dordrecht: Kluwer Academic Publishers, 2002.

Hegemann, Werner. *Report on a City Plan for the Municipalities of Oakland and Berkeley*. Oakland and Berkeley, Calif.: The Municipal Governments of Oakland and Berkeley and Others, 1915.

Hegemann, Werner, and Elbert Peets. *The American Vitruvius: An Architect's Handbook of Civic Art*. New York: Princeton Architectural Press, 1988.

Hise, Greg, and William Deverell. *Eden by Design: The Olmsted-Bartholomew Plan for the Law Region*. Berkeley: University of California Press, 2000.

James, Wilmot, and Linda Van de Vijver, eds. *After the TRC: Reflections on Truth and Reconciliation in South Africa*. Cape Town: David Philip Publishers, 2000; Athens: Ohio University Press, 2001.

Joseph, Betty. *Reading the East India Company: Colonial Currencies of Gender*. Chicago: University of Chicago Press, 2004.

Kennedy, Elizabeth Lapovsky, and Madeline D. Davis. *Boots of Leather, Slippers of Gold: The History of a Lesbian Community*. New York: Routledge, 1993.

Khalid, Adeeb. *The Politics of Muslim Cultural Reform: Jadidism in Central Asia*. Berkeley: University of California Press, 1998.

Linenthal, Edward T., and Tom Engelhardt, eds. *History Wars: The Enola Gay and Other Battles for the American Past*. New York: Metropolitan Books, 1996.

Lowe, Lisa, and David Lloyd, eds. *The Politics of Culture in the Shadow of Capital*. Durham: Duke University Press, 1997.

Luong, Pauline Jones, ed. *The Transformation of Central Asia: States and Societies from Soviet Rule to Independence*. Ithaca: Cornell University Press, 2004.

Macintyre, Stuart, with Anna Clark, *The History Wars*. Melbourne: Melbourne University Press, 2003.

Manne, Robert. *Whitewash: On Keith Windschuttle's Fabrication of Aboriginal History*. Melbourne: Black Inc. Agenda, 2003.

Matsuda, Matt. *The Memory of the Modern*. New York: Oxford University Press, 1996.

Mbembe, Achille. "The Power of the Archive and Its Limits." In Hamilton et al., eds., *Refiguring the Archive*, 19–26.

Mills, Antonia. *Eagle Down Is Our Law: Witsuwit'en Law, Feasts, and Land Claims*. Vancouver: University of British Columbia Press, 1994.

Morris, Meaghan. *Too Soon Too Late: History in Popular Culture*. Bloomington: Indiana University Press, 1998.

Osborne, Thomas. "The Ordinariness of the Archive." *History of Human Sciences* 12, 2 (1999): 516–64.

Pratt, Mary Louise. *Imperial Eyes: Travel Writing and Transculturation*. London: Routledge, 1992.

Raleigh, Donald J. "Doing Soviet History: The Impact of the Archival Revolution." *Russian Review* 61, 1 (2002): 16–24.

Richards, Thomas. *The Imperial Archive: Knowledge and the Fantasy of Empire*. London: Verso, 1993.

Rosenzweig, Roy. "Scarcity or Abundance? Preserving the Past in a Digital Era." *American Historical Review* 108, 3 (June 2003): 735–62.

Sanker, Pamela. "State Power and Record-Keeping: The History of Individualized Surveillance in the United States, 1790–1935." Ph.D. diss., University of Pennsylvania, 1992.

Scott, Joan. "The Evidence of Experience." *Critical Inquiry* 17 (1991): 773–97.

Sekula, Allan. "The Body and the Archive." *October* 39, 3 (1986): 3–64.

Sentilles, Renée. *Performing Menken: Adah Isaacs Menken and the Birth of American Celebrity*. New York: Cambridge University Press, 2003.

Smith, Richard Cándida. "The Other Side of Meaning: George Kubler on the Object as Historical Source." *Intellectual History Newsletter* (2001): 85–95.

Spivak, Gayatri Chakravorty. "The Rani of Sirmur: An Essay in Reading the Archives." *History and Theory* 38 (1985): 247–72.

Starn, Randolph. "Truths in the Archives." *Common Knowledge* 8, 2 (2002): 387–401.

Steedman, Carolyn. *Dust: The Archive and Cultural History*. Manchester: Manchester University Press, 2001; New Brunswick, N.J.: Rutgers University Press, 2002.

Stoler, Ann Laura. *Carnal Knowledge and Imperial Power*. Berkeley: University of California Press, 2002.

——. "Colonial Archives and the Arts of Governance: On the Content in the Form." In Hamilton et al., eds., *Refiguring the Archive*, 83–100.

Tanselle, G. Thomas. "The World as Archive." *Common Knowledge* 8, 2 (2002): 402–6.

Taylor, Diana. *The Archive and the Repertoire: Performing Cultural Meaning in the Americas*. Durham: Duke University Press, 2003.

Tillett, Lowell. *The Great Friendship: Soviet Historians on the Non-Russian Nationalities*. Chapel Hill: University of North Carolina Press, 1969.

Walch, Timothy, ed. *Guardian of Heritage: Essays on the History of the National Archives*. Washington, D.C.: National Archives and Record Administration, 1985.

Windschuttle, Keith. "Doctored Evidence and Invented Incidents in Aboriginal Historiography." In Bain Attwood and Stephen Foster, eds., *Frontier Conflict: The Australian Experience*, 99–112. Canberra: National Museum of Australia, 2003.

———. *The Fabrication of Aboriginal History*. Volume 1, *Van Diemen's Land, 1803–1847*. Sydney: Macleay Press, 2002.

White, Hayden. *Metahistory: The Historical Imagination in Nineteenth-Century Europe*. Baltimore: Johns Hopkins University Press, 1973.

White, Luise. *Talking with Vampires: Rumor and History in East and Central Africa*. Berkeley: University of California Press, 2000.

Contributors

TONY BALLANTYNE is a senior lecturer in the History Department at the University of Otago in New Zealand. His research explores the connections between colonial knowledge production and community formation in the British Empire, with a particular emphasis on India and the Pacific. His publications include *Orientalism and Race: Aryanism in the British Empire* (Palgrave-Macmillan, 2002) and *Bodies in Contact: Rethinking Colonial Encounters in World History* (Duke University Press, 2005), which he co-edited with Antoinette Burton.

MARILYN BOOTH is an associate professor in the Program in Comparative and World Literature at the University of Illinois, Urbana-Champaign. She is author of *May Her Likes Be Multiplied: Biography and Gender Politics in Egypt* (University of California Press, 2001), *Bayram al-Tunisi's Egypt: Social Criticism and Narrative Strategies* (Middle East Centre, St. Antony's College, Oxford, by Ithaca Press, 1990), and numerous articles on intersections of literary discourse and gender politics in the Arab world, translation theory and practice, vernacular Arabic literature, and freedom of expression issues, as well as many translations of fiction and autobiography from the Arabic.

ANTOINETTE BURTON is professor of history and an affiliated faculty member of the Program in Gender and Women's Studies and the Unit for Criticism and Interpretive Theory at the University of Illinois, Urbana-Champaign. She is co-editor, with Ania Loomba, Suvir Kaul, Matti Bunzl, and Jed Esty, of *Postcolonial Studies and Beyond* (Duke University Press, 2005) and, with Tony Ballantyne, of *Bodies in Contact: Rethinking Colonial Encounters in World History* (Duke University Press, 2005). Her most recent monograph is *Dwelling in the Archive: Women Writing House, Home, and History in Late Colonial India* (Oxford University Press, 2003), and she is working on a study of the postcolonial careers of the travel writer Santha Rama Rau.

ANN CURTHOYS is Manning Clark Professor of History at the Australian National University. She writes about many aspects of Australian history, including Aboriginal-European relations, racially restrictive immigration policies, Chinese in colonial Australia, journalism, television, and "second wave" feminism, as well as more generally about the theory and practice of historical writing. Her most recent book is *Freedom Ride: A Freedomrider Remembers* (Allen and Unwin, 2002). She is currently working on several collaborative projects, including (with John Docker) a book entitled *Is History Fiction?* and (with Ann Genovese and Alex Reilly) a report on the ways historical expertise is used by the law in cases involving Indigenous litigants.

PETER FRITZSCHE is professor of history at the University of Illinois, Urbana-Champaign. A former Guggenheim fellow, he is the author of numerous books, including most recently *Stranded in the Present: Modern Time and the Melancholy of History* (Harvard University Press, 2004).

DURBA GHOSH is an assistant professor in the History Department at Cornell University. She has published articles in the *Historical Journal*, *Modern Asian Studies*, the *Journal of Imperial and Commonwealth History*, and several edited volumes. Her book on sexual relationships between British men and Indigenous women in early colonial India is forthcoming from Cambridge University Press.

LAURA MAYHALL is associate professor of history at the Catholic University of America in Washington, D.C. She is author of *The Militant Suffrage Movement: Citizenship and Resistance in Britain, 1860–1930* (Oxford University Press, 2003) and co-editor, with Ian Christopher Fletcher and Philippa Levine, of *Women's Suffrage in the British Empire: Citizenship, Nation, and Race* (Routledge, 2000). Her current work explores the relationship between citizenship and celebrity in late-nineteenth-century and early-twentieth-century Anglo-America.

JENNIFER S. MILLIGAN is a lecturer in history and literature at Harvard University and a cultural historian of modern France. Her most recent publication is "The Problem of Publicity in the Archives of the Second Empire," in *Archives, Documentation, and Institutions of Social Memory*, edited by Fran X. Blouin and William G. Rosenberg (University of Michigan Press, 2004). She is currently finishing a book manuscript, "Making a Modern Archives: The Archives Nationales in Nineteenth-Century France," and is working on a study of the political imaginary of utopian communities in French India.

KATHRYN J. OBERDECK is associate professor of history at the University of Illinois, Urbana-Champaign, where she teaches U.S. cultural and intellectual history. She is the author of *The Evangelist and the Impresario: Religion, Entertainment, and Cultural Politics in America, 1884–1914* (Johns Hopkins, 1999) and articles in *American Quarterly*, *Radical History Review*, and *Gender and History*. She is currently working on a history of the cultural politics of space and place in Kohler, Wisconsin, focusing on the intersecting visions of company officials, landscape architects, residents, workers, and vacation visitors.

ADELE PERRY teaches history at the University of Manitoba, where she is Canada Research Chair in Western Canadian Social History. Her research mainly deals with gender, colonialism, and migration over the long nineteenth century. This is her first foray into the law and its many meanings.

HELENA POHLANDT-MCCORMICK is currently an assistant professor at St. Olaf College in Northfield, Minnesota. She was born in Germany and grew up in Johannesburg, South Africa. She completed an M.A. in communications at the Ludwig Maximilians University in Munich in 1984 and an M.A. in journalism at the University of Michigan in 1986, where she worked as a journalist for the *Detroit News*. She completed her Ph.D. in 1999 at the University of Minnesota. Her research and teaching interests include South African cultural and social history; African women's history and comparative women's history; methodology (oral history, life histories, and autobiography); and memory and history. In 1993 she was awarded a John T. and Catherine D. MacArthur Foundation Research and Writing Grant to support her research on the Soweto Uprising. Her book *"I Saw a Nightmare . . ." Doing Violence to Memory: The Soweto Uprising, June 16, 1976* was published by Columbia University Press in 2004. Her new research focuses on the exile experience in South Africa (1960–90).

JOHN RANDOLPH is an assistant professor of Russian history at the University of Illinois, Urbana-Champaign. His current project, "The House in the Garden: The Bakunin Family and the Romance of Russian Idealism," examines how family life framed attempts to imagine social consciousness in eighteenth- and nineteenth-century Russia. He also has a box of letters that his grandfather wrote while fighting in the Philippines during World War II, but has only read the one his grandmother liked the most.

CRAIG ROBERTSON is an assistant professor of communication at Northeastern University. He is the co-editor, with Jeremy Packer, of *Thinking with James Carey: Essays on Communication, Transportation, History* (Peter Lang, 2005). He is currently completing a book on the emergence of the passport in the United States.

HORACIO N. ROQUE RAMÍREZ, a Salvadoran immigrant, is assistant professor in Chicana and Chicano studies at the University of California, Santa

Barbara, and teaches courses on interdisciplinary queer Latina / Latino community history, oral history, and Central American migrations. He earned his Ph.D.
in comparative ethnic studies at the University of California, Berkeley with a
designated emphasis on "Women, Gender, and Sexuality." He has contributed to
the *Journal of the History of Sexuality* and the anthology *Queer Migrations: Sexuality, U.S. Citizenship, and Border Crossings*, edited by Eithne Luibhéid and Lionel
Cantú, Jr. (University of Minnesota Press, 2005). He is completing a book entitled
*Communities of Desire: Memory and History from Queer Latinas and Latinos in the San
Francisco Bay Area, 1960s–1990s*.

JEFF SAHADEO is an assistant professor at the Institute of European and Russian
Studies and the Department of Political Science at Carleton University. He has
contributed articles on Russian colonial society in Uzbekistan to *Slavic Review*,
Canadian Slavonic Papers, and the *Canadian Review of Studies in Nationalism*. He is
completing his manuscript on late imperial and early Soviet Tashkent, and is now
examining Uzbek migration to Russia in the late Soviet period.

RENÉE M. SENTILLES is assistant professor of history and director of American
Studies at Case Western Reserve University in Cleveland, Ohio. She received her
Ph.D. in American Studies at the College of William and Mary in Williamsburg,
Virginia. Her first book, *Performing Menken: Adah Isaacs Menken and the Birth of
American Celebrity*, was published in 2003 by Cambridge University Press and
the American Antiquarian Society, where she held an Andrew W. Mellon post-
dissertation fellowship. She is currently working on "American Tomboys, 1830–
1920," which examines the emergence of the tomboy as an American archetype,
focusing particularly on girlhood history, politics, sexuality, popular culture, and
constructions of white identity.

Index

ANTOINETTE BURTON is professor of history at the University of Illinois, Urbana-Champaign, where she holds the Catherine C. and Bruce A. Bastian Chair in Global and Tansnational Studies. She is the author of *Dwelling in the Archive: Women Writing House, Home and History in Late Colonial India* (2003); *At the Heart of the Empire: Indians and the Colonial Encounter in Late-Victorian Britain* (1998); and *Burdens of History: British Feminists, Indian Women, and Material Culture, 1865–1915* (1994). She is also editor of *After the Imperial Turn: Thinking with and through the Nation* (Duke, 2003); *Family History: Majumdar/Janaki Agnes Penelope,* (2003); *Politics and Empire in Victorian Britain: A Reader* (2001); and *Gender, Sexuality, and Colonial Modernities* (1999).

Library of Congress Cataloging-in-Publication Data

Archive stories : facts, fictions, and the writing of history /
edited by Antoinette Burton.
p. cm.
Includes bibliographical references and index.
ISBN 0-8223-3677-4 (cloth : alk. paper)—ISBN 0-8223-3688-x (pbk. : alk. paper)
1. Archives—Social aspects. 2. History—Methodology.
I. Burton, Antoinette M., 1961–
CD971.A72 2005
027—dc22   2005026005